THE EU AND THE BALTIC SEA AREA

This book explores the role of the European Union (EU) in the cooperation and regulation of the Baltic Sea Region (BSR), from both an institutional and a substantive perspective. It particularly focuses on the role of the Union in advancing the broader marine governance framework in the region. Questions investigated include: in what way does the Union participate in, or otherwise influence, the activities of states, international organisations and other actors involved in BSR cooperation and regulation, and what is the importance and substantive outcome of the Union's specific role in this respect? How has the membership of eight out of nine Baltic Sea coastal states in the EU affected cooperation in the region, in terms of substance as well as procedure, and what is the influence of the BSR over the EU? These questions are discussed from different perspectives by leading experts in both the fields of EU law and the law of the BSR.

Volume 118 in the Series Modern Studies in European Law

Modern Studies in European Law

Recent titles in this series:

The Relative Authority of Judicial and Extra-Judicial Review: The EU Courts, the Boards of Appeal and the Ombudsman
Michal Krajewski

Responsive Human Rights: Vulnerability and the ECtHR
Corina Heri

The Architecture of Fundamental Rights in the European Union
Šejla Imamovic

The EU and its Member States' Joint Participation in International Agreements
Edited by Nicolas Levrat, Yuliya Kaspiarovich, Christine Kaddous and Ramses A Wessel

The UN Convention on the Rights of Persons with Disabilities and the European Union: The Impact on Law and Governance
Carmine Conte

EU Criminal Law, Second Edition
Valsamis Mitsilegas

The EU as a Global Digital Actor: Institutionalising Global Data Protection, Trade, and Cybersecurity
Elaine Fahey

Exporting the European Convention on Human Rights
Maria-Louiza Deftou

Judicial Authority in EU Internal Market Law: Implications for the Balance of Competences and Powers
Vilija Velyvyte

The Changing European Union: A Critical View on the Role of Law and the Courts
Edited by Tamara Capeta, Iris Goldner Lang and Tamara Perisin

The Structural Transformation of European Private Law: A Critique of Juridical Hermeneutic
Leone Niglia

The Future of EU Constitutionalism
Edited by Matej Avbelj

The Changing Role of Citizens in EU Democratic Governance
Edited by Davor Jancic

The EU and the Baltic Sea Area
Edited by Allan Rosas and Henrik Ringbom

For the complete list of titles in this series see www.bloomsbury.com/uk/series/modern-studies-in-european-law/

The EU and the Baltic Sea Area

Edited by
Allan Rosas
and
Henrik Ringbom

•HART•
OXFORD • LONDON • NEW YORK • NEW DELHI • SYDNEY

HART PUBLISHING

Bloomsbury Publishing Plc

Kemp House, Chawley Park, Cumnor Hill, Oxford, OX2 9PH, UK

1385 Broadway, New York, NY 10018, USA

29 Earlsfort Terrace, Dublin 2, Ireland

HART PUBLISHING, the Hart/Stag logo, BLOOMSBURY and the Diana logo are trademarks of Bloomsbury Publishing Plc

First published in Great Britain 2023

A catalogue record for this book is available from the British Library.

A catalogue record for this book is available from the Library of Congress.

ISBN: HB: 978-1-50995-624-1
ePDF: 978-1-50995-626-5
ePub: 978-1-50995-625-8

Typeset by Compuscript Ltd, Shannon

PREFACE

This book is the outcome of two workshops hosted at Åbo Akademi University in Turku/Åbo, Finland, in January and November 2021, in which all authors participated. The workshops sought to assess and analyse in some detail the role and impact of the European Union (EU) in the cooperation framework of the Baltic Sea Region (BSR). The perspective was interdisciplinary, covering both law and political sciences.

The initiative forms part of the Baltic Sea Area Legal Studies (BALEX) network (www.balex.fi), in which Åbo Akademi University, together with the University of Turku and other partners around the region, seek to analyse questions relating to the regulation and governance of the BSR.

On behalf of the organisers of the two events, we wish to extend our sincerest thanks to everybody who contributed, both with their own contributions and through insightful commenting on others' contributions. Particular thanks are also due to Hart Publishing for their help and support in securing the smooth publication of the book. Finally, thanks are owed to the Eugen Schauman Foundation for financially supporting the seminars and to LLM Saara Ilvessalo for her editorial assistance throughout the book project.

All website references in the book were verified on 20 August 2022.

Henrik Ringbom and Allan Rosas
Turku/Åbo, 10 November 2022

CONTENTS

LIST OF CONTRIBUTORS

Henrik Ringbom Professor of Marine Law, Åbo Akademi University, Turku/Åbo, Finland; Professor II, Scandinavian Institute of Maritime Law, University of Oslo, Norway.

Allan Rosas JD, JD hc multi, PD hc, Professor Emeritus, University of Turku and Åbo Akademi University; Chair of the EU Article 255 TFEU Panel and of the Independent Ethical Committee of the European Commission; former Principal Legal Adviser and Deputy Director-General of the European Commission; former Judge at the European Court of Justice.

Antti Belinskij Professor of Environmental Law, Department of Law, Center for Climate Change, Energy and Environmental Law (CCEEL), University of Eastern Finland, Joensuu; Research Professor, Freshwater Centre, Finnish Environment Institute SYKE, Helsinki, Finland.

Viljam Engström Adjunct Professor (Docent) in Public International Law; Senior Lecturer in Constitutional and International Law, Åbo Akademi University, Turku/Åbo Finland.

Stefan Gänzle Professor of Political Science, University of Agder, Kristiansand, Norway.

Sam Grönholm PhD, University Lecturer in Public Administration, Åbo Akademi University, Turku/Åbo Finland.

Kristine Kern Professor, Leibniz Institute for Research on Society and Space, Erkner, Germany and Åbo Akademi University, Turku/Åbo, Finland.

Mirka Kuisma Doctor of Laws; Legal Secretary (oikeussihteeri), Supreme Administrative Court of Finland.

David Langlet Professor of Environmental Law, Uppsala University, Sweden. Langlet has previously held positions as, inter alia, Professor of Ocean Governance Law at the University of Gothenburg and Research Fellow at Oxford University, UK.

Esa Paasivirta Adjunct Professor, University of Helsinki, Finland; formerly Legal Adviser, European Commission.

Suvi-Tuuli Puharinen Suvi-Tuuli Puharinen, doctoral researcher in EU Environmental Law, Department of Law, Center for Climate Change, Energy and Environmental Law (CCEEL), University of Eastern Finland, Joensuu.

Helena Tuuri Ambassador for Baltic Sea Affairs, Ministry for Foreign Affairs of Finland; served previously as Ambassador to the Czech Republic and Slovakia and as State Under-Secretary for EU Affairs, Prime Minister's Office.

Nina Tynkkynen Professor in Environmental Governance and Policy, Åbo Akademi University, Finland.

Teija Tiilikainen Director of the European Centre of Excellence for Countering Hybrid Threats, Helsinki, Finland; Professor (part-time) of Security Politics, European University Institute (School of Transnational Governance), Florence, Italy.

Petteri Vuorimäki Arctic Ambassador/Senior Arctic Official, Ministry for Foreign Affairs, Finland.

LIST OF FIGURES AND TABLES

1

Introduction

HENRIK RINGBOM AND ALLAN ROSAS

I. General

The European Union (EU) is in many ways an awkward player on the international scene. Its authority and power to enforce its policies upon its own Member States are not matched by its international status. And both its internal and external competence and powers vary greatly depending on the subject matter and pursuant to a complex set of rules which is often hard even for legal experts to grasp. In some areas, the Union possesses far-reaching competences and powers, including competences of an exclusive character. Internally, its status and importance are particularly conspicuous in areas such as the internal market with its four economic freedoms as well as competition and state aid law. On the international scene, the role of the EU is particularly visible and relevant when it comes to trade in goods, services and intellectual property rights and increasingly also in the investment field – while in other areas the world's largest trading bloc struggles to make an impact, or even to have a seat at the table.[1]

In areas such as economic, social and territorial cohesion, environment, transport, trans-European networks and justice and home affairs[2] the competence of the Union is in principle shared with its Member States. While in the external action area, the existence of EU legislation in these and other fields may cause the competence to become exclusive, the relevant legal rules are often open to different interpretations and even in situations where the law would clearly point to a Union exclusive competence, the reality on the ground may be different, with the Member States rather than the Union in the driving seat. The EU's potential to make an impact may then be reduced by its own internal political divergencies or by procedural difficulties of knowing whether the Union acts as a single body or as a gathering of 27 Member States. A further difficulty may stem from the fact that

[1] See, eg, A Rosas and L Armati, *EU Constitutional Law: An Introduction*, 3rd rev edn (Oxford, Hart Publishing, 2018) *passim*.

[2] The great bulk of justice and home affairs is regulated in part III, Title V of the Treaty on the Functioning of the European Union (TFEU) under the title Area of freedom, Security and Justice.

despite the existence of Union competences, whether exclusive or shared, the EU may not be a full member of an international organisation dealing with matters of direct interest for the EU. A telling example is the ambivalent observer status of the EU in the International Maritime Organization (IMO), which deals with matters affecting EU maritime policy and legislation.[3]

These and other problems and challenges are on full display with respect to the EU's involvement in Baltic Sea Region (BSR) governance and cooperation. As is demonstrated, inter alia, by the participation of the EU in the work of the Council of the Baltic Sea States (CBSS) and by the EU Strategy for the Baltic Sea Region (EUSBSR), adopted in 2009,[4] the EU is in many ways involved in BSR-related activities. Already the wide mandate of the CBSS and the broad range of subjects dealt with in the EUSBSR imply that the Union's involvement covers a very wide and diverse field. Most of the subject areas covered arguably belong to areas where competence is shared between the Union and its Member States, but high-sea fisheries belong to an area of Union exclusive competence[5] while some BSR-related subject matters may even belong to areas falling outside both exclusive and shared competence (so-called parallel and supplementary competences).[6] However, these legal classifications do not always match actual practice and institutional realities. The EU is very much present in BSR-related governance and cooperation but its status, role and real impact vary from one sector to another, and display a mismatch of institutional, regulatory and substantive solutions.

To the above must be added the radical geopolitical change which has taken place in the BSR during the last 30 or so years. When, as a result of the fall of the Berlin Wall in 1989 and the dissolution of the Soviet Union in 1991, the original CBSS was founded in 1992, it comprised only two EU Member States (Denmark and Germany) and eight non-EU Member States. The situation today is that eight Baltic Sea state members of the CBSS are EU members (Finland and Sweden since 1995 and Estonia, Latvia, Lithuania and Poland since 2004) and only three, of which two, namely Iceland and Norway, are closely associated with the EU by the Agreement on European Economic Area), are EU non-Member States. In political terms, this has made BSR cooperation very much an affair between the EU and its Member and associated states, one the one hand, and the Russian Federation (successor to the Soviet Union) on the other.

[3] In Case C-161/20 *Commission v Council* ECLI:EU:C:2022:260, paras 53–78, the European Court of Justice (ECJ) held that as neither the European Community nor its successor the EU had entered into an arrangement with the IMO, 'the European Union does not have any status within the IMO' (para 57). By contrast, the European Commission had in 1974 concluded an arrangement providing for the right of the Commission to participate as an observer in the work of the IMO. See also, Case C-45/07 *Commission v Greece* ECLI:EU:C:2009:81; and H Ringbom, *The EU Maritime Safety Policy and International Law* (Leiden, Martinus Nijhoff Publishers, 2008) *passim*.

[4] See, in particular, the chapters by Helena Tuuri (ch 4) and Allan Rosas and Petteri Vuorimäki (ch 8) in this volume.

[5] See Art 3(1)(d) and Art 4(2)(d) TFEU.

[6] Parallel competences include research, technological development and humanitarian aid (Art 4(3) and (4) TFEU) while economic policy is of a supplementary nature (Art 5 TFEU).

This political constellation can also be seen in the institutional frameworks in which the EU is participating. The membership of the CBSS consists of 11 Member States, among them Russia, and the EU as a Member with somewhat lesser status. The Baltic Marine Environment Protection Commission (HELCOM or Helsinki Commission) has 10 Contracting Parties, comprising the EU, eight EU Member States as well as Russia. The Northern Dimension Policy (which is not an international organisation proper) is characterised as a joint policy of four equal partners: the EU, Russia, Norway and Iceland. The EUSBSR is, of course, a macro-regional strategy for the EU, but the Strategy has cooperated in various ways with Russia and Belarus. On 10 March 2022, the Russian war of aggression against Ukraine led the National Coordinators Group of the EUSBSR to order the suspension of all cooperation with Russia and Belarus. Cooperation between Russia and the EU and its Member States in the work of the CBSS, HELCOM and the Northern Dimension will, of course, also be deeply affected by the war in Ukraine, but at the time of writing it is too early to make any definitive assessments in this regard.

In the existing literature relating to BSR cooperation, the role of the EU comes up in varying degrees, depending on which institutional or regulatory framework is at issue. There is, however, no comprehensive study focusing on the specific status and role of the EU, both in comparison with state and other actors and between different institutional and regulatory frameworks and subject matters. The purpose of this book is to fill this gap by analysing in some detail, but also against the backdrop of BSR cooperation in general, the specific role and contribution of the EU in shaping BSR governance and cooperation. The perspective is mainly institutional and regulatory, but a broader understanding of developments also calls for a political science-based approach. As to substantive focus, management of the marine environment (marine governance) takes pride of place. One of the questions put to the authors of individual chapters was to consider what the situation today might look like without any involvement from the EU. In other words, what can be surmised to have been the added impact (and hopefully added value) of the participation of the Union in various institutional and regulatory frameworks and in BSR cooperation in general? At the same time, it must be acknowledged that, as was pointed out above, the EU is a complex and somewhat strange animal which often makes it difficult to draw the line between genuine Union activities per se and more or less coordinated action by the EU Member States, perhaps with some input from the Union as well.

II. The Social Science Perspectives

The book kicks off with an analysis of the broader policy framework for regionalism within the EU. Teija Tiilikainen (chapter two) assesses how the Union relates to other forms of regional cooperation that takes place within its legal and institutional framework. She analyses the variety of regional groupings within Europe in terms of policy and institutional setting and highlights the difference between internal cooperation within the EU and regional cooperation that involves non-EU partners. Both categories feature within the BSR. While the EU's relationship to internal regionalism is described as 'relaxed', the latter form of cooperation is characterised as 'complicated'. Tiilikainen concludes that while the EU seems to be able to manage the regionalism within its own borders, regional organisations cutting across its borders have been more difficult, as they may even appear as competitors to the Union and its interests within the region in question.

In chapter three, Sam Grönholm studies the governance of the BSR more closely, from the particular perspective of multi-level governance. The BSR is characterised as a 'pioneer' of multi-level governance and a 'laboratory' for its innovative use. The chapter accordingly focuses on experimental use of multi-level governance, outside the sphere of law. Network-based governance of the BSR is considered to have the ability to augment the capacity of public policy-making and to pursue innovative policy solutions to solve concrete transboundary problems. Best practice and pilot studies sustain and proliferate experimental multi-level governance by serving as tools for replicating policy innovations in and across the BSR. Prominent EU project funding schemes, such as the BSR Interreg programmes, are applied to develop and influence policy development, implementation and evaluation and induce changes in the design of policy activities. Grönholm concludes that the influence of the EU in the BSR has increased and expanded, thus facilitating the formation of new BSR networks. However, structural challenges and path dependencies make it difficult to establish new cross-sectoral collaboration for innovative policy-learning. He proposes a three-step path for catalysing experimental multi-level governance in the BSR, based on further coordination through the EU's Strategy for the EUSBSR; increasing multi-layered knowledge; and enhancing the 'contextual intelligence' of the actors involved.

Helena Tuuri (chapter four) in part takes up this challenge, by assessing the EUSBSR in more detail, covering its background, ambitions, successes and failures from the point of view of an Ambassador for Baltic Sea Affairs. While Tuuri acknowledges that the close cooperation and collaboration network within the BSR generally has been a success, it is less certain whether the EUSBSR itself has had a role in this development. At process level, much has been achieved, but in terms of substantive achievements, the answer varies from one policy area to another. Like Grönholm, Tuuri considers that the governance framework of the strategy has been unsatisfactory to date. Despite this criticism, however, Tuuri considers that recent developments, not least the conclusion of a revised Action Plan in 2021, have removed certain obstacles and paved the way for a shift of the Strategy 'from an experimental phase to maturity', towards more result-oriented cooperation in the BSR.

Chapter five by Stefan Gänzle, Nina Tynkkynen and Kristin Kern analyses the development from a different perspective, from the point of view of non-EU organisations in the BSR. The authors assess how well certain key organisations in the BSR, the CBSS, HELCOM and the Union of Baltic Cities (UBC) have managed to deal with external change in the past three eventful decades, including the growing influence of the EU and the latest 'hypercritical juncture' following Russia's invasion of Ukraine in 2022. The authors conclude that the impact of geopolitical change varies significantly between the organisations, and that specific purpose organisations, such as HELCOM and the UBC's 'Sustainable Cities' Commission' appear to be better equipped to manage conflicts with other organisations and may thus also be more robust with respect to geopolitical changes.

III. The Legal-Institutional Perspectives

The legal aspects of the EU's external relations policy and the limitations and opportunities offered by law in enhancing the Union's presence in Baltic Sea governance is discussed by Mirka Kuisma in chapter six. The principles of EU external relations law become relevant when Member State external action falls into the substantive scope of EU law. In such situations, EU law may curb Member State independent action and hence impact the practical functioning and output of BSR organisations. Following a thorough assessment of the EU's external relations law, in particular in the field of shared competences, Kuisma analyses the practical consequences of the EU law principles for the activities of two BSR organisations: HELCOM and the CBSS. She concludes that problems may be caused both by the EU's dominance and by its passivity in these organisations. On the one hand, EU external relations law contributes to an ongoing intensification of the Union's role that may already be perceived as invasive by outsiders. On the other hand, passivity may occur where Member States might be barred from unilateral action by the rules of EU external relations law. Kuisma accordingly concludes that the EU may appear at the same time as a desired partner and a bogeyman overshadowing regional cooperation in the BSR, noting that recent case law could be taken as supporting a more active involvement of the Commission, in the BSR organisations and beyond.

On a closely related theme, Viljam Engström, in chapter seven, identifies the structures and functions of the interactions between the EU and three BSR institutions: HELCOM, the CBSS and the 'Visions and Strategies Around the Baltic Sea' (VASAB). Engström notes that EU law has been regionalised and BSR governance Europeanised, both phenomena emphasising the central role of the EU in the region. He also discusses ways in which the three rather different forms of interaction can generate normative effects. Each of the studied forms of interaction between the BSR institutions and the EU give rise to their own set of concerns, both from the perspective of EU law and for the BSR institutions concerned. Engström concludes that the variation in forms of interaction, expresses a functional approach to regional governance and that the functional approach enhances integration in the EU's macro-regions, and is likely to continue to do so, notwithstanding certain concerns of drawbacks linked to the EU's involvement.

A more detailed institutional case study is offered by Allan Rosas and Petteri Vuorimäki (chapter eight), who study the relationship between the EU and the CBSS in legal and more practical terms. Among other things, the authors study the implications that follow from status of the CBSS as a 'soft organisation' (established by a political declaration, rather than by a legally binding agreement) and the many turns relating to the EU's representation at the organisation over the years. Their chapter also analyses the role that the EU has played in the organisation in practice, including the reasons for maintaining a fairly low profile, the links to other Baltic Sea-related policy initiatives, such as the EUSBSR, and what EU-based participation in the activities of the CBSS tell about the Union's role in BSR cooperation more generally. The authors conclude that the participation of the EU in the CBSS has had certain advantages for both organisations: for the EU in terms of closer contacts with the BSR, including Russia; for the CBSS in terms of recognition of its concrete work in the field of BSR cooperation through its projects and networks, which – at least for the pre-2022 period – is described as 'reasonably successful'.

IV. The Legal-Maritime Perspectives

As an introduction to the section of the book that deals with substantive legal issues linked to the EU's maritime policies in the BSR, Esa Paasivirta (chapter nine) offers a review of the EU's law of the sea impact with a particular focus on the Baltic Sea. Through examples and relevant case law concerning the BSR, he illustrates how EU legislation, directly and indirectly, has come to affect maritime realities in the region. What is the EU's marine territory, what sort of EU rules apply in the coastal maritime zones and how should the competences between Member States and the Union be allocated in these areas? Paasivirta provides answers to such questions, both on the basis of the case law of EU courts that has clarified several open questions and through assessing EU legislation with a particular maritime profile. He also assesses the relationship between international law instruments, such as the Law of the Sea Convention (UNCLOS) and other multilateral environmental agreements, and the regional seas conventions, notably the Convention on the Protection of the Marine Environment of the Baltic Sea Area (the Helsinki Convention). Three case studies are explored in more detail, dealing with substantive issues as diverse as multinational gas pipelines (the *Nord Stream 2* case), oil spills by tankers (the *Bosphorus Queen* case) and peace and security in the BSR. Paasivirta concludes that EU legislation plays a dominant legal role in the Baltic Sea, and also in a law of the sea context. This has helped to ensure uniform rules, and a common institutional framework promoting efficient application and enforcement, which is considered to be more effective than the alternative, to develop new treaties in the region. In the field of peace and security, Paasivirta concludes that NATO is likely to have an increased role in the BSR in the future, through increased coordination with the EU, but that the missing link is Russia, whose belligerent actions lie in the way of fully resolving the legitimate maritime uses of the Baltic Sea.

In chapter ten, Suvi-Tuuli Puharinen and Antti Belinskij analyse the shift towards goal-based, or ecosystem-based, rules in regulating marine environmental protection in the region. The new type of marine environmental protection rules that have been introduced at EU-level since the turn of the millennium represent a new, goal-oriented and ecosystem-based, strategy to marine environmental protection, which is assessed here from the point of view of combatting eutrophication (ie, reducing the input of nutrients) in the Baltic Sea. This subject, too, involves intricate interrelationships between EU law secondary legislation and the Helsinki Convention framework. The authors conclude, among other things, that the EU marine directives, together with other sectoral EU legislation, establish a concrete framework for formulating and implementing measures to tackle nutrient inputs. Environmental status objectives for individual water bodies, as set out in the 'Water Framework Directive' appear to be a much more concrete spatial basis for legal obligations than targeting the entire Baltic Sea, as the 'Marine Strategy Framework Directive' does. More generally, too, the former instrument is considered to be a more successful example of how the EU may complement national and regional legal structures. In this field, too, subsequent case law from the Court of Justice of the European Union has significantly served to clarify and specify open-ended provisions in the directives concerned. Overall, the conclusion of chapter ten is that the post-millennial EU marine environment rules complement long-term international cooperation under the Helsinki Convention by providing the national and water body-specific scales for the objectives and measures needed to achieve them. The EU's contribution in this field is accordingly assessed positively, even if many challenges remain in this particular field.

The two last chapters address the two most obviously marine sectors that fall under marine governance. In chapter eleven, Henrik Ringbom addresses the EU's role in the regulation of shipping, which has traditionally been closely regulated and governed at global level, but in which the EU has assumed a gradually increasing role. Regulation of shipping offers interesting case studies of multi-level regulation, where different layers have assumed different substantive responsibilities, usually complementing each other in a constructive manner. Specific attention is given in the chapter to the most topical regulatory topic of today: the regulation of climate change from shipping, where both the EU and international maritime organisations are involved in negotiating key rules for the decades to come. It is concluded that the EU has made a substantive contribution to the regulation and governance of shipping in the past few decades, and that this policy is substantively different from that of its Member States acting cumulative in their national interests. In contrast to many Member State national shipping policies, the EU has generally sided with the interests of coastal States, the environment and passengers, at the expense of the concerns of flag states and shipowners, often as a consequence of specific shipping accidents occurring in European waters. The Baltic Sea States have normally not objected to the EU's increased role in shipping regulation, but it is more difficult to assess their impact in actually shaping the EU's shipping policy. Currently, the EU is particularly involved in influencing the regional and global standards relating to greenhouse gases from ships, but does not seem to be overly preoccupied with the concerns of a few Baltic Sea States relating to the challenges posed by ice and winter navigation conditions.

The final chapter (chapter twelve) concerns the oldest area of common EU maritime policies: fisheries management. David Langlet offers a comprehensive review of the background and key features and development of the EU's common fisheries policy. In the latter part of the chapter, he analyses the role of the EU in BSR fisheries in light of the pre-existing regime based on a regional fisheries convention and the extent to which the BSR has managed to make its own concerns heard within the EU's fisheries policy, inter alia, through several regional advisory councils and fisheries fora. He notes that despite the poor state of Baltic fisheries in recent years, which is due to many factors extending beyond management issues, the Baltic Sea has in some respects served as a role model for more proactive and regionally grounded fisheries management in the EU at large. Langlet observes that unsustainable fishing practices in the Baltic Sea predates the time when EU law became applicable to most of the BSR. Whether fisheries management would have been more successful without the involvement of the EU is hard to know, but in view of the specific natural and geographic conditions of the Baltic Sea it is hard to see how rational or sustainable fisheries can be achieved under such conditions without far-reaching cooperation and coordination among the states concerned. Langlet concludes that the EU at least offers a platform where policies for tackling the various challenges confronting the Baltic Sea can be developed and their coordination gradually improved, and that there are good reasons to believe that both coordination and enforcement can be more effective within the EU than through the traditional platforms for regional fisheries cooperation in the BSR.

V. Concluding Remarks

A common thread of the chapters in this book is their acknowledgment of the increasing role of the EU in the BSR, not only in a geographical sense, but also in substantive terms, over the past three decades. The variety of conclusions within the chapters also illustrate that the EU has many faces, in the sense that its role and responsibilities vary widely from one substantive field to another.

The general tendency is that the role and responsibility of the EU in the region has increased significantly in the past three decades and in particular since the fall of the Berlin Wall and the new security situation in the BSR for which this paved the way. Since the 2000s there appears to be a general willingness from the EU's side to leave certain key decision-making authority to regional decision-makers, hence increasing flexibility in the governance of the region.

Some institutions have tackled the EU's increasing dominance better than others, the institutions with a clearly focused – and practically oriented – mandate appear to be those best placed to tackle such changes.

Yet, all chapters also acknowledge that the increasing role of the EU is not exclusively positive and entails certain risks. For example, the EU's own external relations rules may constitute significant barriers for regional decision-making without its involvement in many key BSR policies. The increasing involvement of the EU, in other words, brings along a responsibility for the Union to follow up and to actively engage in regional marine governance matters. This responsibility has not always materialised.

Another common feature of the chapters circles around the complex interaction between rules, institutions and policies between the EU and BSR institutions. This appears in the form of the uncertain legal status of key documents, unclear powers and competences of key stakeholders, and uncertainties in the division of responsibilities between the parties involved. Such uncertainties have remained unsettled in some of the fields studied, while in others, legal institutions, notably EU courts, have taken an active role in clarifying the situation and in filling some of the gaps.

Nevertheless, the general verdict on the substantive impact of the EU appears that, on balance, the EU's increasing involvement has been a positive development for the region, albeit that it has introduced a number of new risks and complications. The EU is broadly regarded as a well-coordinated regulatory machinery bringing hope for effective enforcement of agreed policies in the region, which in itself may stimulate further coordination of policies. The EU's potential role as a financial contributor to implementing policies that are important for the BSR is highlighted in several chapters.

While the above holds true for the eight EU Member States in the region, the relationship with Russia has also changed significantly with the increased role of the EU. The EU–Russia relationship – in the BSR and elsewhere – was always difficult and the tensions between the EU and Russia have exacerbated in the past decade, reaching an all-time low in 2022 with the Russian war of aggression against Ukraine. The new situation, of which there is still a lot of uncertainty, will no doubt have profound effects on BSR collaboration, as well as on general security situation in the Baltic Sea.

2

The EU and Regional and Sub-Regional Cooperation

TEIJA TIILIKAINEN

I. Introduction

The EU (European Union) is an expression of very special regional cooperation. But how does the Union relate itself to other forms of regional cooperation taking place entirely or partly in its legal and institutional framework? Every now and then there have been efforts to institutionalise regionalism and the regional approach in the Union but these efforts have never led very far. In theory, such an approach might also be seen to nourish identities and interests which could turn out to be divisive in respect of EU unity and thus call for a critical approach from the Union.

Regionalism, in general, takes very different forms as a phenomenon linked with European integration. Various forms of regionalism can – to start with – be found within the EU in a more or less institutionalised shape. Other forms, in turn, cut across the Union's borders thus involving Member States of the Union as well as third countries. The Union's external policies further include regionalist approaches towards geopolitically important adjacent regions also incorporating other than state actors.

All in all, the EU seems to be supportive of regional and sub-regional cooperation as long as it remains compatible with the general principles and objectives of EU law. Taking into account the diversity of existing examples of regional cooperation within the EU, the Union can be considered to have found its modus operandi in accommodating the phenomenon within its own framework.

This chapter focuses on this modus operandi by analysing forms of regional cooperation in the EU from different perspectives. First, it studies the key normative framework and the key parts of EU law affecting the role of regional cooperation. As all internal cooperation in the EU taking place among a smaller group of Member States is not necessarily 'regional', a key normative framework to be carefully studied here is the one of 'differentiated integration'.

The second dimension of regional cooperation to be discussed concerns its political legitimacy as a part of European politics. How strong and legitimate is regionalism in the EU with respect to the identities or interests that it represents? This part of the chapter studies to what extent regional cooperation within the EU builds on a bottom-up approach, which is firmly anchored in the civil societies of the countries in question, including their political cultures and values.

All forms of regional cooperation involving a smaller number of EU Member States cannot, however, be considered internal to the Union as it also includes non-Member States. The EU has very different roles and forms of engagement in regional cooperation involving non-Member States, such as the Council of the Baltic Sea States (CBSS), the Arctic Council (AC) and the Nordic Council (NC). A brief discussion on these forms as examples of regionalism in the Union's context will take place at the end of this chapter.

II. Legal and Institutional Approaches to Regional Cooperation in the EU

Regional cooperation in its traditional form refers to intergovernmental cooperation, among a group of EU Member States, encompassing a certain level of institutionalisation. Benelux-cooperation as well as the V4 cooperation among the four Visegrad states belong to this form.[1] It is questionable whether the bilateral relationship between France and Germany – whose general goals are confirmed in the Elysée Treaty (1963) and further in the Aachen Treaty (2019) – can be characterised as regional cooperation even if it clearly also includes this dimension.

Nordic cooperation is of a *sui generis* type, as, apart from the Nordic EU Member States, it also covers Norway and Iceland which, despite being non-Member States of the EU, are closely attached to the Union through their membership of the European Economic Area Agreement (EEA). In the case of Norway, it also includes participation in parts of the EU's defence cooperation. Nordic cooperation in the EU reflects the firmly institutionalised cooperation among the Nordic countries taking place outside the EU in the realm of the NC and the Nordic Council of Ministers. The less institutionalised but regular Nordic–Baltic cooperation (NB8) belongs to the same category. The EU's relationship with the numerous regional organisations cutting across its borders takes very diverse forms.

[1] Benelux-cooperation was the only form of regional cooperation whose role was confirmed in the original treaties (Treaty establishing the European Economic Community and Related Instruments [11957E], (EEC Treaty), Art 233), which stipulated that 'The provisions of this Treaty shall not be an obstacle to the existence or completion of regional unions between Belgium and Luxembourg and between Belgium, Luxembourg and the Netherlands, in so far as the objectives of these regional unions are not achieved by application of this Treaty'. The provision can currently be found in TFEU, Art 350 (Consolidated version of the Treaty on the Functioning of the European Union [2016] OJ C202/47). See J Wouters and M Vidal, 'Towards A Rebirth of Benelux' (2008) Leuven Centre for Global Governance Studies Working Paper No 2, available at: www.kuleuven.be. V4 cooperation includes the Czech Republic, Hungary, Poland and Slovakia.

Regionalism in the EU can also revolve around historical regions cutting across state borders and also involving actors other than governments. The EU's current four macro-regional strategies encompass regions which are closely interconnected through economic, cultural and historical ties. These regions cover both EU Member States and non-Member States. For the time being, there are four examples of macro-regional strategies: the Baltic Sea Region, the Danube Region, the Adriatic and Ionian Region and the Alpine Region.[2] The macro-regional strategies are policy frameworks endorsed by the European Council based on Article 22 of the Treaty on European Union (TEU).[3] The strategies may be supported by EU funds, including the European Structural and Investment Funds. Their level of institutionalisation and governance vary with the European Commission, however, playing a key role in the coordination of the strategies' delivery.

There is still at least one form of institutionalised regionalism within the EU that, due to its different character, will not be covered in this chapter. It is the form of regionalism expressed by the Committee of the Regions that was established as its institutional embodiment in the Maastricht Treaty. It encompasses various regionalisms revolving around historical or administrative communities, within EU Member States, with different levels of autonomy or around local self-government. There was a general willingness to empower these regions in the 1990s as a part of the efforts to enhance the EU's political legitimacy. The Committee, the members of which are nominated by EU Member States, is an advisory body that has to be consulted in the Union's legislative processes on topics affecting local and regional interests. The Committee can also issue opinions on its own initiative.[4] As this form of regionalism aims to incorporate the perspectives of different regions to the Union's decision-making, rather than promote or manage regionalism and regional cooperation as such, it will not be further discussed in this chapter.

III. The Legal Framework for Regional Cooperation

The EU's legal framework provides both enablers and constraints for regional cooperation within the Union. When defining the enablers, the possibilities the Treaties provide for differentiated integration is the key.

[2] While the Baltic Sea Region covers only EU members the Danube Region also covers Bosnia-Herzegovina, Serbia, Montenegro, Ukraine and Moldova. In addition to four EU members the Adriatic and Ionian Region covers four accession countries: Bosnia and Herzegovina, Serbia, Albania, Montenegro and North Macedonia. The Alpine Region covers five EU members and Switzerland and Lichtenstein plus 48 regions from these countries.

[3] Consolidated version of the Treaty on the Functioning of the European Union [2016] OJ C202/47 (TFEU).

[4] See TFEU, Art 307.

The EU's system of flexibility – or differentiated integration – provides the main legal and institutional framework for regional cooperation in the EU, at least in its usual intergovernmental form. In his working paper on the legal perspective on differentiated integration, Bruno de Witte divides the main instruments for the framework into opt-outs, forms of enhanced cooperation as defined in the Treaties and intergovernmental agreements among a smaller group of Member States.[5] It is obvious that the two latter ones could be used for the purposes of regional cooperation as long as their key conditions are fulfilled. Apart from these general instruments, the Treaties establish a number of specific possibilities for small group cooperation. These include, for example, Permanent Structured Cooperation in Security and Defence Policy and a possibility to carry out crisis management operations by a smaller group of countries.[6] In the field of economic governance, the Treaties even allow the Eurozone countries – as a smaller group of countries – to adopt special legislation in a specific field of EU competence.[7]

Enhanced cooperation, as defined in Article 20 of the TEU, establishes criteria for small group cooperation within any field of the EU's non-exclusive competences. It enables a group of at least nine Member States to launch deepened cooperation on a particular issue provided that the Council decides on it on qualified majority. This instrument is mainly meant for cooperation of a limited form, such as a piece of new legislation or a policy. It is obvious that no single form of existing regional cooperation would fulfil the criteria, but could, however, take the lead in launching such a process to which some other EU Member States would join. A study of the four existing cases of enhanced cooperation does not, however, reflect a very strong regional approach in the respective memberships.[8] It is interesting to note that the group of countries taking part in them, since their inception, is the same in all the four cases: Austria, Belgium, France, Germany, Greece, Italy, Portugal and Slovenia. Instead of a regional driver, membership in the Eurozone seems to be the unifying factor.

The flexibility instrument consisting of intergovernmental agreements closely linked with the Union's policies and *acquis* forms the most flexible option for any internal small group cooperation. Examples of existing arrangements of this type cover agreements – such as the one on the European Stability Mechanism (ESM), the earlier Schengen Agreement or the Social Protocol – which later

[5] B de Witte, 'The Law as Tool and Constraint of Differentiated Integration' (2019) EUI Working Papers RSCAS 2019/47, 5.

[6] Consolidated version of the Treaty on the European Union [2016] OJ C202/13 (TEU), Art 42(7) and Art 22.

[7] TFEU, Art 136(1).

[8] The Rome III Regulation (Law applicable to divorce and legal separation) 2012; Unitary Patent (European Patent with unitary effect) 2012; Property Regime Rules for International Couples 2016; and European Public Prosecutor's Office 2017. See 'The Implementation of Enhanced Cooperation in the EU' (2018), Study requested by the AFCO Committee, The European Parliament, 28–33, available at: www.europarl.europa.eu.

have been incorporated into the Treaty framework. The difference between these agreements and those on existing regional cooperation, such as the one on V4 or Benelux-cooperation is, however, clear. While the first-mentioned agreements, although usually involving a large majority, do not cover all Member States – which is the reason for their content not being made a part of the EU Treaties – regional agreements cover just a limited group of regional neighbours. Intergovernmental agreements can also be divided on the basis of their relationship with the EU's competences. De Witte refers to the vast group of bilateral or multilateral agreements between EU members in areas where the Union does not have any law-making competence or has shared competence with the Member States.[9] The purpose of these agreements differs from agreements which are more closely related to the EU's competences and aim to deepen cooperation in this framework with a different mechanism. Many agreements in this group are planned to be incorporated into the EU Treaties at a later stage, in accordance with the example of the Schengen Agreement, the more recent ESM Agreement or the Fiscal Compact.[10]

When it comes to the existing constraints on regional cooperation within the EU, the unity and inviolability of the Union's legal and institutional framework seems to be their obvious goal. There are, consequently, also specific criteria for intergovernmental agreements within the EU – which formally are not a part of the EU's legal order – aiming to safeguard the unity of this legal order. Like national law, these agreements also have to comply with EU law, otherwise their rules will be declared void.[11] EU law thus creates a framework for what can be agreed by a smaller number of Member States. This is currently relevant in respect of agreements in relation to the Economic and Monetary Union (EMU), but naturally affects any plans for differentiated integration outside the treaty framework. There are plenty of court cases where the European Court of Justice (ECJ) has found intergovernmental agreements between EU members to be in conflict with EU law due to various reasons.[12] Some of these reasons relate to the integrity of EU law which agreements have been found to violate. There is also an interesting legal discussion about whether the enhanced cooperation mechanism should be prioritised as a flexibility instrument at the expense of intergovernmental

[9] de Witte (n 5) 7–8. He refers to these agreements as *inter se* agreements as they cover a group of EU members but not all, and aim to complement a larger treaty (EU Treaties).

[10] The intention to include the key rules of the Schengen Agreement into the Treaties was expressed in a declaration adopted by its parties while the Fiscal Compact (The Treaty on the Stability, Coordination and Governance in the Economic and Monetary Union of 2 March 2012) included a provision (Art 16) according to which, within five years after its entry into force, measures shall be taken to incorporate it into the EU Treaties. What comes to the ESM Agreement the Commission proposed in 2017 that it would be transformed into an EU body. See Commission, 'Proposal for a Council Regulation on the establishment of the European Monetary Fund' COM (2017) 827 final. This proposal was, however, not approved by the Eurozone members.

[11] de Witte (n 5) 12.

[12] ibid refers to cases such as Case C-503/03 *Commission v Spain* [2006] ECR I-01097 and Case C-284/16 *Slowakische Republik v Achmea* ECLI:EU:C:2018:158.

agreements.[13] While there seem to be some legal grounds for this view, political and practical reasons tend to support a more balanced view due to the greater flexibility provided by international agreements in respect of non-Member participants or access to national financial instruments for instance.

With the primacy of EU law in mind, there are some parts of the EU Treaties that seem to be of particular importance when it comes to differentiated integration outside the Treaties. This form of cooperation is not meant to help Member States escape from their Treaty obligations, which is crystallised in Article 4(3) of the TEU as follows: 'the Member States are obliged to ensure fulfilment of the obligations arising out of the treaties and refrain from any measure that would jeopardise the attainment of the Union's objectives'. Nor shall such cooperation violate the equality among Member States or citizens.[14] The implications that intergovernmental cooperation external to the Treaties may have for the EU's institutional framework have recently been brought to the fore in the context of the special agreements on economic and financial cooperation.[15]

All in all, the legal-institutional conditions should be favourable for active regional and sub-regional cooperation taking place in the context of European integration. As many of the EU's fields of competence seem to call for strong regional interests and perspectives, there is every reason to believe that different types of regionalisms would come to the fore in the Union's political system and that there would be serious efforts taken to use the existing legal and institutional possibilities. This is the next question to be addressed in this chapter.

IV. Regional Identities and Cooperation in the EU's Policymaking

How large is the willingness within the EU to use the possibilities mentioned above in regional cooperation? This question can be answered by looking at coalitions emerging at various levels of the Union's policymaking, and assessing the appetite for regionalism in this way. In general, it could be argued that regional alignment within the EU plays a smaller role than for instance alignment based on longer-term policy-lines or traditions in key policy fields, such as economic or security policy. There seems to be quite a lot of variation in alignment among Member States depending on whether the question is approached in terms of joint policy proposals, voting patterns in the Council or public opinion, as reflected in EU-wide opinion polls (Eurobarometer).[16]

[13] de Witte (n 5) summarises this legal discussion.

[14] TEU, Art 4(2) and Art 9.

[15] E Chiti and P Teixeira, 'The Constitutional Implications of European Responses to the Financial and Public Debt Crisis' (2013) 50 *Common Market Law Review* 683, 685.

[16] Eurobarometer is the polling instrument which has been used by the European Commission since 1974 to monitor public opinion in Europe. See: www.europa/eu/eurobarometer/screen/home.

As mentioned above, the formal mechanisms available for small group cooperation do not bring any particular trends towards regionalism to the fore. The existing examples of enhanced cooperation stress the importance of the Eurozone as a core group of like-minded countries, and the same trend is emphasised – due to more institutional reasons however – in many of the recent intergovernmental agreements concluded among a smaller group of Member States, such as those on the ESM or the Fiscal Compact.

When it comes to different types of informal policy proposals made (non-papers and the like) there seem to be very few stable coalitions among EU members cutting across different policy fields.[17] The Franco–German alliance appears to be almost the only stable coalition, both when it comes to the time perspective and the scope of cooperation across different policy fields, extending from economic and financial policy to border security, migration policy, security and defence policy.[18] The role of the other historic alliance within the EU, the Benelux countries, seems to vary over time and have less political impact.[19] The Benelux coalition has recently been significantly divided on issues dealing with the EU's economic and financial policy as well as the common migration policy.[20]

Other coalitions and groups of like-minded countries seem to have much more of an ad hoc character, with their composition being strongly linked with a particular policy field. The EU's Baltic Sea Member States or the Nordic–Baltic countries (NB8) do not seem to appear as a stable coalition in any policy field of the EU. The members of the latter do have similar interests in the Union's economic and financial policy as well as the development of the single market, but tend to promote these goals in coalitions larger than the NB8. The 'New Hanseatic League', established as an informal coalition, covered this group of countries together with Austria and the Netherlands.[21] The group had a more conservative view on proposals made in the context of the development of the EMU, where new fiscal instruments and enlargement of the Union's powers had systematically been proposed by Southern European Member States. Later on, when the Union's recovery package of 2020 was discussed, the group was split and the 'Frugal Four' including the Netherlands, Austria, Sweden and Denmark, adopted a stricter policy than the rest of the group. The group of NB8 is divided between net-payers and net-receivers which leads to differences in detailed questions on the EU's economic policy and budget.

[17] J Janning, C Zunneberg and C Klavehn (eds), *Exploring EU Coalitions* (London, European Council on Foreign Relations, 2017).

[18] For examples of broad Franco-German policy proposals, see U Krotz and J Schildt, *Shaping Europe: France, Germany and Embedded Bilateralism from the Elysée Treaty to Twenty-First Century Politics* (Oxford, Oxford University Press, 2012) chs 5–9.

[19] Wouters and Vidal (n 1) 24.

[20] The Netherlands has played a key role both in 'The Hanseatic League' and in the more recent 'Frugal Four' which both represented a counterforce to Southern European aspirations to enlarge the Union's competences in fiscal policy and, consequently, its common budget. See A Verdun, 'The Greatest of the Small? The Netherlands, the New Hanseatic League and the Frugal Four' (2021) 31 *German Politics* 302, available at: www.tandfonline.com.

[21] ibid, 302–03.

The group is equally divided with respect to its key security policy solutions, which affects approaches to the Union's security and defence policy.

A regional approach clearly plays a larger role in the EU's external relations,[22] where both the institutionalised forms of small group cooperation and more general regional approaches seem to affect state interests. Both Nordic countries and V4 countries have authored joint proposals on issues relating to the Union's external relations. As the EU's then new militarily non-aligned neighbours, Finland and Sweden took the initiative in the establishment of the Union's crisis management capacity – both military and civilian – in the 1990s, partly to steer attention away from more far-reaching military cooperation.[23] On this question, the policies in the Nordic region, however, have changed and it is questionable if a common Nordic – not to mention a Nordic–Baltic – approach towards the Union's security and defence policy still exists This does not, however, prevent the NB8 countries from cooperating in concrete projects, such as the EU's Battlegroups.[24]

No strong like-mindedness has ever prevailed among the group of Nordic or Nordic–Baltic EU countries concerning the Union's relations with Russia, as historical identities have rather diversified policies. One early example of this is the EU's Northern Dimension (ND) Policy which was profiled as a Finnish project rather than a joint Nordic (or later Nordic–Baltic) endeavour.[25] The early stages of the EU's current Baltic Sea Region Strategy appeared as a competing project with the ND Policy.

Also the four Visegrad-countries have clearly shared common interests in the Union's external policies concerning cooperation with Western Balkan countries and had their accession to the EU as a clear joint goal. The group of V4 countries is also an important proponent of the Union's Eastern Partnership Policy and the need to deepen the relationship of the Eastern Partnership countries with the EU.

Studies on voting patterns in the Council prove the diversity of foundations on which coalition-building in the EU is based.[26] The regional approach is just one of the foundations and, on the basis of the more recent studies, its impact seems to have been decreasing due to the increasing politisation of the Union's

[22] F Bicchi and L Aggestam, 'New Directions in EU Foreign Policy Governance: Cross-loading, Leadership and Informal Groupings' (2019) 57 *Journal of Common Market Studies* 515.

[23] T Tiilikainen, 'The Nordic Countries and the EU–NATO Relationship' in A Bailes, G Herolf and B Sundelius (eds), *The Nordic Countries and the European Security and Defence Policy* (Oxford, Oxford University Press, 2006) 57.

[24] JJ Anderson, 'If Not Now, When? The Nordic EU Battlegroup' (2015) *Issue Alert*. The European Union Institute for Security Studies, available at: www.iss.europa.eu.

[25] H Ojanen, 'The EU and its "Northern Dimension": An Actor in Search of a Policy, or a Policy in Search of an Actor?' (2000) 5 *European Foreign Affairs Review* 359.

[26] M Kaeding and T Selck, 'Mapping Out Political Europe: Coalition Patterns in EU Decision-Making' (2005) 26 *International Political Science Review* 271; M Hosli, M Mattila and M Uriot, 'Voting in the Council of the European Union after the 2004 Enlargement: A Comparison of Old and New Member States' (2009) 49 *Journal of Common Market Studies* 1249.

agenda in domestic contexts.[27] Regionalism in general seems to come to the fore as a general north–south dimension rather than in the form of more specific regional alignments. An earlier study, however, showed that the three Nordic EU Member States tend to vote in a similar way in the Council while no common pattern was found among the Benelux countries.[28] Left–right patterns or pro-less integrationist approaches can be found among the key factors significant for voting behaviour.

V. Do Regional Identities Matter?

Regional identities are among multiple identity factors, many of which operate at a deeper cultural level than regionalism, and seem to play only a minor role as factors determining regional cooperation and alignment in the EU. Regional identities appear to be strongest as geopolitical drivers, thus targeting the Union's external relations rather than its fields of internal policy. Earlier studies prove the impact of regional identities or political traditions – internal to the EU or cross-cutting its external borders – on the Union's external policies.[29]

When it comes to general approaches to European integration and the political legitimacy it enjoys, the key cultural and identity factors on the one hand originate in broader historical traditions and dividing lines than the more specific regional ones.[30] The role of these dividing lines will be discussed here briefly to assess their connections with regionalism in the EU's politics. The EU's legitimacy and approaches to European integration have, on the other hand, reflected both cultural background factors and perceptions of national benefits associated with membership (output legitimacy). Consequently, the convergence of political identities seems to take place in this context both in a broader and a more specific framework than the regional one.

To what extent can convergence of political identities be seen as a factor in support of regional cooperation in the EU?

Several studies show how political traditions building on historical religious doctrines affect EU Member State approaches to European integration.[31] The main dividing line goes between the Catholic and Protestant political cultures with the latter revolving around the notion of state sovereignty and, later on, an exclusive understanding of nationalism. This dividing line is still valid in the present Europe, where the Catholic heritage creates one important bond between the

[27] B Pircher and M Farjam, 'Oppositional voting in the Council of the EU between 2010 and 2019: Evidence for differentiated politicisation' (2021) 22 *European Union Politics* 472, 474.

[28] Kaeding and Selck (n 26) 280–81.

[29] Pircher and Farjam (n 27); Bicchi and Aggestam (n 22).

[30] B Nelsen and J Guth, *Religion and the Struggle for European Union* (Washington, DC, Georgetown University Press, 2015); S Hobolt and C de Vries, 'Public Support for European Integration' (2016) 19 *Annual Review of Political Science* 413.

[31] Nelsen and Guth (n 30); Hobolt and DeVries (n 30) 420–21.

group of original European Community (EC) Member States with a significant impact on their party systems. At a very general level, the EU Member States with a strong Catholic heritage are more favourable than their Protestant counterparts to the understanding of European integration as an ever-deepening process taking Europe towards a larger political unity. This dividing line is equally reflected in approaches towards European or national identity, as citizens of Southern European Member States tend to be more prepared for multiple political identities than people in Northern Europe.

The bonds of political culture create very strong ties among the original members of the EC even if the sense of unity has varied a lot in the course of time and depending on the context.[32] Most countries in this group are representatives of divided political cultures with an impact on their overall EU policy. Countries with a significant Catholic cultural impact that have joined the EC/EU later, such as Spain, Portugal, Ireland or Poland, could not accept this deep unity unproblematically due to the political effects of their more recent history.

The United Kingdom and the Nordic–Baltic countries are usually pointed out as the core group of the Protestant approach emphasising state sovereignty and the strength of national political identity. Strong scepticism towards enhanced forms of political integration or openly federalist solutions of policy or governance are characteristic of their EU policies. Countries affected by a Protestant heritage can hardly be seen to be aligned through their approach to the EU in the same way as their Catholic counterparts. Their overall EU policies seem to be significantly affected by other identity factors and factors of output legitimacy to the extent that creates decisive heterogeneity in the group.

The impact that the general cultural factors have on regionalism in the EU is easy to grasp. The Christian Democratic parties from the original EC Member States provide the most important political axis towards an EU with federalist structures, which in the current stage of the Union would imply changes in competences of the economic and financial policy as well as in external policies. The impact of the broader cultural factors can thus be seen in the strong political bonds existing among the original EC Member States and also reflecting themselves in the framework of Eurozone cooperation, where the group plays an important role. The historical factors can, however, also be found behind the north–south division of the EU going back to different understandings of the Union's political role and the mutual responsibilities it creates.

VI. The EU's Role in External Regional Cooperation

The final theme of this chapter deals with the Union's role in an institutionalised form of regional cooperation cutting across the Union's borders. Not even this

[32] Nelsen and Guth (n 30) 163–76.

form of cooperation is unitary, as its varies from the model represented by the Union of the Mediterranean where all the EU members are parties together with a large number of Middle East and North African countries, to the model of the ND where the EU is represented by the High Representative of the Union for Foreign Affairs and Security Policy and the External Action Service he leads. Also the legal character of regional bodies varies between a formal treaty-based international organisation and a political platform without any conferred powers or legal personality of its own.

As regionalism of the type where the whole EU is involved is not the focus of this chapter, attention will be paid to regional cooperation where only some EU members participate. The question to be addressed is, thus, how the EU's role and representation is constructed in legal-institutional terms in regional organisations, such as the AC, the Black Sea Economic Cooperation Organization or the CBSS. What do these forms of representation add to the Union's approach to regionalism in Europe? How does the EU see its role and objectives in regional cooperation cutting across its external borders and involving just a limited group of EU members and limiting itself to just a specific field of the Union's competences?

The EU's relationship with regional organisations cutting across its borders is not entirely unproblematic. First, there seems to be some tension between the Union's own internal policy and strategy for the region in question and the mandate of the regional organisation, which the EU cannot affect decisively. This tension is visible in the case of the CBSS and the Black Sea Economic Cooperation Organization but to some extent also in relation to the AC.[33] The EU's approach is furthermore affected by the fact that, due to institutional or political reasons, it cannot be granted full membership of these organisations with a role and rights equal to the organisations' Member States. For obvious reasons it is, thus, more difficult for the EU to manage this type of regionalism than the internal one with the result of an almost competitive relationship emerging between the EU and at least some of the regional organisations. This relationship is occasionally constrained by unrelated political or legal challenges complicating the generally uneasy situation.

The EU's legal-institutional relationships with the regional organisations in the Arctic, the AC and the Barents Euro-Arctic Council (BEAC), represent one model of regional cooperation, due to the similar characteristics and interrelated agendas of the two councils. Neither of the two councils is an international organisation with specific powers conferred on it by its Member States nor do they have a legal personality of their own.[34] The Arctic bodies are broad platforms of cooperation

[33] The European Union Strategy for the Baltic Sea Region was adopted in 2009 as the Union's first macro regional strategy and its Black Sea Synergy had already come into being two years earlier as the Union's policy initiative for the region. The latest Joint Communication (of the EU institutions) on the Arctic was adopted in 2021.

[34] Arctic Council, 'Declaration on the Establishment of the Arctic Council' (Ottawa, 19 September 1996).

focusing mainly on the particular environmental and societal vulnerabilities of Europe's northernmost regions, and also incorporating other than state actors. The founding Ottawa Declaration of 1996 defines the AC as a high-level forum to provide a means for promoting cooperation, interaction and coordination among the Arctic States with the involvement of the Arctic indigenous communities and other Arctic inhabitants on common Arctic issues. Apart from the membership and permanent participant categories for Arctic organisations and indigenous peoples, an observer status was established for non-Arctic states and international or inter-parliamentary organisations.

Due to an obvious connection existing with the EU's competences – and the increasing political role of the Arctic regions – the Union has tried to establish itself as an actor in both organisations, with its role in the AC becoming politicised and encountering difficulties. The BEAC, in turn, was established in 1993 as cooperation forum open for all states interested in its activities and has since emerged as an inclusive and less politicised forum.[35]

Since the publication of the EU's first Communication on the Arctic in 2008, the Union has pursued an observer status in the AC by referring to the significance of Arctic cooperation from the point of view of its policies and legislative competences.[36] The observer status was seen to enable the EU to provide its own input to the AC, where three of its Member States – Denmark, Finland and Sweden – are full members. The initial application was presented by the Commission 'representing the EU' but was blocked by Canada due to reasons of the EU's policy banning the trade of seal products. The next effort in 2012 was vetoed by Russia due to geopolitical reasons. These obstacles could not, however, prevent the EU – first the Commission and later also the European External Action Service and the Union's agencies – from taking part in the meetings of the AC, as well as its working groups and expert groups, on an informal ad hoc basis. Neither of the two councils takes any binding decisions but conduct their work by issuing political assessments or recommendations. The AC has also provided a platform for treaty negotiations.[37]

The EU's role in the CBSS has many similarities with its role in the bodies of Arctic cooperation. The CBSS is also a political platform for regional cooperation among Baltic Sea States, thus lacking the legal characteristics of an international

[35] The Kirkenes Declaration (1993) defines BEAC as follows: 'The Council will serve as a forum for considering bilateral and multilateral cooperation in the fields of economy, trade, science and technology, tourism, the environment, infrastructure, educational and cultural exchange, as well as projects particularly aimed at improving the situation of indigenous peoples in the North'. See Declaration: Cooperation in the Barents Euro-Arctic Region (Kirkenes, 11 January 1993).

[36] Commission, 'Communication from the European Commission to the European Parliament and the Council the European Union and the Arctic Region' COM (2008) 763 final.

[37] The three international agreements negotiated in its framework are the Agreement on Cooperation on Aeronautical and Maritime Search (2011); the Agreement on Oil Pollution preparedness and Response in the Arctic (2013); and the Agreement on Enhancing International Arctic Scientific Cooperation (2017).

organisation. The main fields of cooperation of this Council, which revolve around societal security, sustainable development and research and innovation, are also relevant from the point of view of the Union's competences. In the Terms of Reference adopted at the establishment of the CBSS, apart from the 11 Baltic Sea States, the European Commission was defined as a member. The Terms of Reference further specified how the Commission should be represented at the various levels of the CBSS.[38]

In addition to observations concerning the EU's political approach to the stated forms of regional cooperation cutting across the EU's borders, there are some interesting legal observations to be made concerning its form of representation. Erwan Lannon and Peter Van Elsuwege in their study on the EU's relationship with regional organisations refer to the seemingly vague legal ground on which the EU's initial representation in all of the three aforementioned regional councils builds.[39] That the Terms of Reference of both the CBSS and the BEAC refer to the European Commission and not to the European Community as a member of the organisation seems to result from the participant structure of their constitutive meetings. The Commission's local delegation enjoying at the time quite an independence and representing the European Commission in those meetings had consequences that, later on, were also viewed critically by the ECJ.[40] The Court states that even if the organisations did not have any binding powers within the field of EU competences, the Commission did not have the mandate to define the EU's position on them without a decision by the EU Council.

Likewise, the EU's Northern Dimension Framework is balancing between the EU's competences and those of its Member States. This cooperative framework between the EU and its northern neighbours, and Russia in particular, was established as an EU policy in the 1990s, but was turned into an intergovernmental policy framework in 2006 due to the challenges it had faced. Because of its broad scope, the policy framework goes beyond the EU's competences and involves the Member States, in this case mostly the northern ones, in policy implementation.[41] The Union is represented in the ND by the High Representative of the Union for Foreign Affairs and Security Policy.

The same collective form of representation was, however, also adopted in relation to the Black Sea Economic Cooperation Organization, which is an international organisation with a legal basis. The Commission was granted an observer

[38] According to the Terms of Reference (adopted in the CBSS's first ministerial meeting in March 1992), a member of the Commission should represent the institution in the CBSS Council meetings while the Head of the Commission should be the representative for the Baltic Sea State Summits.

[39] E Lannon and P Van Elsuwege, 'The EU and its Neighbourhood; A patchwork of regional strategies and institutions from the Mediterranean to the Arctic' in R Wessel and J Odermatt (eds), *Research Handbook on the European Union and International Organisations* (Cheltenham, Edward Elgar, 2019).

[40] Case C-233-02 *Commission v France* [2004] ECR I-02759, para 40; Case C-660/13 *Council v Commission* ECLI:EU:C:2016:616, paras 36–43.

[41] Lannon and Elsuwege (n 39) 561.

status in the organisation in 2007 based on a communication from the Commission of the previous year expressing this interest.[42]

The Union's relationship with the aforementioned regional organisations was formalised along with the changes the Lisbon Treaty brought about in its legal personality and external representation. Its representation is now more streamlined and in accordance with the general legal framework. The membership of the European Commission was turned into that of the EU.

All in all, the EU's policies towards regional organisations cutting across its external borders seem to be characterised by obvious ambiguities and lack of a standard model. The Union has actively pursued a role in some organisations while others have been of much less interest to it. The purely Nordic cooperation organisations, the parliamentary NC and the Nordic Council of Ministers, are examples of the latter as the EU doesn't have any role in them.

In 2021, the European Parliament established a formal relationship with the NC with an annual meeting as the key form of practice. The reason for the Union's lack of interest may deal with the membership of these organisations being limited to EU and EEA countries.

VII. Conclusions

This chapter has focused on the EU's approach to regional and sub-regional cooperation. The key question addressed was what the modus operandi is in relation to regional cooperation internal to the EU, on the one hand, and cooperation cutting across its external borders on the other. The conclusion must be different concerning these two forms.

Regionalism, in general, is a highly multifaceted phenomenon in the context of European integration. By abolishing internal borders and establishing a set of policies with a firmly regional focus, the EU, on the one hand, empowers historical regions and provides a platform for their mutual connections. But, on the other hand, the political and legal role of the EU grants the Union primacy in respect of any other forms of regional cooperation.

When it comes to internal forms of regional cooperation, this primacy seems also to be well anchored in attitudes and political practices, as there are hardly any examples of durable forms of regional cooperation that would systematically challenge the unity of the Union's legal or institutional system. On the contrary, there seems to be surprisingly little appetite to use the existing frameworks for flexible integration for the purposes of regional cooperation. In the EU's internal cooperation there are factors that affect state interests and identities and are both broader

[42] Commission, 'Communication from the Commission to the Council and the European Parliament on Strengthening of the European Neighbourhood Policy' COM(2006) 726 final.

and narrower than regional factors. Regional alignment, however, does play a role in relation to external policies where issues of a geopolitical character weigh more.

The EU's relationship to regional cooperation cutting across its borders cannot be characterised with similar relaxedness. First, the EU must define its relationship with these regional bodies case by case, depending on their role and mandate, from the point of view of the Union's competences and political interests. Considering the diversity of regional organisations, the EU can hardly adopt a very strategic or streamlined approach in relation to them. Second, the Union's adjustment to this form of regionalism is complicated by the fact that it can never achieve a position to equal that of the Member States of these organisations. This leads easily to quite a complicated situation, where the EU cannot use its full political and economic potential to promote its interests, but rather has to seek the support of those Member States that are parties in the particular organisations. There are also difficult issues of competence arising in relation to the Union's mandate in them.

While the EU seems to be able to manage the regionalism within its own borders, it can hardly be seen to show an equal ownership towards regional organisations cutting across its borders, as they might even appear as competitors in relation to the Union and its own interests with the region in question. The role of these bodies reminds the Union that it is not the only regional organisation in Europe and that there might even be regional entities predating the initial three European Communities coexisting with it and being politically significant.

3

The Impact of the EU on the Multilevel Governance of the Baltic Sea Region: Experimental Governing and Policy Practices

SAM GRÖNHOLM

I. Introduction

This chapter describes and analyses the governing and steering narrative of the Baltic Sea Region (BSR) with the help of the concept of Multi-Level Governance (MLG). MLG is used to describe, understand and explain governing and steering styles applied in the BSR, which have evolved through decades in a fragmented transnational setting.[1] This setting is shaped by multilayered societies, where actors operate through diverging interests and steering capacities. This disjointed setting, alongside the rising societal demands to govern the shared BSR problems, has made the area a pioneer in the application of new MLG modes.[2] The BSR is a laboratory for innovative MLG, as the demand of transformative governing is continuous. BSR MLG activities need endless reforms to adapt to the challenges of the Baltic Sea ecosystems.[3] The innovative mode stimulating the evolution of BSR MLG relates to the fact that the Baltic Sea ecosystem challenges are transboundary problems – ill defined, contested ecological, maritime and societal problems that transcend national borders.[4]

[1] M Gilek et al, 'Environmental Governance of the Baltic Sea: Identifying Key Challenges, Research Topics and Analytical Approaches' in M Gilek et al (eds), *Environmental Governance of the Baltic Sea* (Heidelberg, Springer, 2016).

[2] M Joas, D Jahn and K Kern (eds), *Governing a Common Sea: Environmental Policies in the Baltic Sea Region* (London, Earthscan, 2008).

[3] M Gilek and M Karlsson, 'Seeking Pathways Towards Improved Environmental Governance of the Baltic Sea' in M Gilek et al (eds), *Environmental Governance of the Baltic Sea* (Heidelberg, Springer, 2016).

[4] S Grönholm, *Governing the Baltic Sea: A Study of the Functionality of Contemporary Environmental Governance* (Turku, Åbo Akademi University, 2020).

The MLG of the BSR illustrates the complexity of modern governing and symbolises a steering narrative that relies on pluralistic and dispersed policymaking activity, where multiple actors at various political levels, from the supra-national to the sub-national, are engaged in solving transboundary problems. In MLG, no governing actor is superior to the other, underlining a mutual dependency through the intertwining of policymaking actions.[5] MLG represents an alternative to conventional governmental control, providing options to develop new modes of governing, which are joined in their attempts to design new policy solutions to transboundary problems.[6,7] This is the premise of the BSR MLG.

The MLG of the BSR denotes a transformation of traditional governing norms and practices.[8,9] Public actors operating on various MLG levels are dependent on non-hierarchical actions and multi-level processes to attain policy outcomes targeting transboundary problems. National governments do not assert hierarchical control of policy processes; instead, they are reliant on practices by actors outside public authority to augment policymaking capacity. The BSR MLG setting is defined by a regulatory realm that is faced with difficulties, where mandates enforced by law do not guarantee effectiveness vis-a-vis the governing of transboundary problems.[10] The position of governments is impaired and hierarchical principles are subverted to improve policymaking abilities. Formal governing, top-down steering, institutionalised structures, regulated processes for developing and implementing policies are interlinked with dispersed steering arrangements that are reliant on flexible and non-hierarchical processes driving the evaluation of MLG policy action.[11]

The MLG of the BSR is synonymous with autonomous network action that aspires to generate policy responses to the transboundary problems.[12] The MLG of the BSR transpires though designated networks.[13,14,15] These link and join the interest of public governing actors across the super-national, national, regional and local level with non-state actors. Network-based MLG of the BSR is viewed

[5] P Stephenson, 'Twenty years of multi-level governance: Where Does It Come From? What Is It? Where Is It Going?' (2013) 20 *Journal of European Public Policy* 817.

[6] G Marks et al, 'Competencies, cracks and conflicts: regional mobilization in the European Union' (1996) 29 *Comparative Political Studies* 164.

[7] S Piattoni (ed), *The Theory of Multi-Level Governance: Conceptual, Empirical and Normative Challenges* (Oxford, Oxford University Press, 2010).

[8] N Tynkkynen, 'The Challenge of Environmental Governance in the Network Society: The Case of the Baltic Sea' (2013) 23 *Environmental Policy and Governance* 395.

[9] Grönholm, *Governing the Baltic* Sea (n 4).

[10] H Ringbom and M Joas, 'Introduction: Multi-level regulation in the Baltic Sea region' (2018) 98 *Marine Policy* 187.

[11] Grönholm, *Governing the Baltic* Sea (n 4).

[12] ibid.

[13] S VanDeveer, 'Networked Baltic Environmental Cooperation' (2011) 42 *Journal of Baltic Studies* 37.

[14] S Grönholm, 'A tangled web: the Baltic Sea region governance through networks' (2018) 9 *Marine Policy* 201.

[15] ibid.

as having the ability to augment the capacity of public policymaking. At the core of augmenting BSR policymaking is a subset of interlinked MLG modes, namely adaptive, collaborative and experimental governance. These are used to pursue innovative policy solutions designed to solve the transboundary problems.[16] These distinctive subsets expand the innovative and transformative MLG modes in the BSR.

This chapter focuses on experimental MLG in the BSR. The governing options in a MLG setting are of a soft nature, as hard mandates enforced by regulation are not an option.[17] This facilitates and expands the use of experimentation without the threat of sanctions. Experimental MLG is motivated by the idea of improving BSR problem-solving capacities. MLG setting encourages experimentation to overcome governing deadlocks through exposure to ideas from outside that could transform policy understanding.[18] Experimental MLG emphasises deliberation, learning and alternative pathways to overcome the sectoral focus of hierarchical top-down policies.[19] The basis of experimental MLG in the BSR is knowledge exchange of innovative policy experiences by best practice and pilot studies.[20] These are tasked to support deliberation and expand policy learning by using the BSR horizontal and vertical steering arrangements, which enable policy collaboration between and across international, national and sub-national levels of authority. Best practice and pilot studies sustain and proliferate experimental MLG by serving as tools for replicating policy innovations in and across BSR MLG. This is the basic premise of experimental MLG in the BSR.

The aim of this chapter is to describe and analyse the governing challenges present in an experimental-based MLG of the BSR. The experimental MLG narrative is presented through a viewpoint that recognises the increasing influence of the European Union (EU) in the BSR. Experimental MLG is advocated by public entities, particularly by EU funding programmes, which serve as the largest funding bodies of BSR best practice studies.[21,22] These endorse policy innovation by making use of the flexible top-down and bottom-up MLG activities, which allow new cross-disciplinary and cross-sectoral policy interactions. EU funding bodies of best practice studies call for an explorative open-ended and innovative operative setting.[23] Key features of this setting are new forms of

[16] Grönholm, *Governing the Baltic* Sea (n 4).
[17] Stephenson (n 5).
[18] A Zito and A Schout, 'Learning theory reconsidered: EU integration theories and learning' (2009) 16 *Journal of European Public Policy* 1103.
[19] S Eckert and T Börzel, 'Experimentalist governance: an introduction' (2012) 6 *Regulation and Governance* 371.
[20] Grönholm, *Governing the Baltic* Sea (n 4).
[21] M Mazzucato, 'Missions: Mission-Oriented Research & Innovation in EU' (European Commission, 2018), available at: ec.europa.eu/info/sites/default/files/mazzucato_report_2018.pdf.
[22] European Commission, 'Missions in Horizon Europe' (2022), available at: ec.europa.eu/info/research-and-innovation/funding/funding-opportunities/funding-programmes-and-open-calls/horizon-europe/missions-horizon-europe_en.
[23] Mazzucato (n 21).

practices, processes and tools to share learning and inspiration from existing innovation activities.[24]

Initially, the chapter conceptualises and operationalises the innovation modes present in the BSR MLG. Then, the chapter describes from a BSR network perspective the governing norms and procedures, which constitute the operative basis for experimental MLG. This operative setting is subject to the influence of EU-endorsed policymaking norms. The analytical part of the chapter examines how experimental processes and action adheres with the premise of the BSR MLG. The analytical part is based on evaluating data compiled using a mix-methods approach. Data is aggregated by using sources upheld online by the most common EU funding programmes applicable in the BSR. The data offers an overview by which methods of experimental MLG are introduced, promoted and expanded into network-based BSR governing. The data also offers insights of these EU-based funding programmes, their governing norms, and provides a summary of funded best practice studies in the BSR during the last two decades. The data is used as a basis for analysing the challenges in an experimental network MLG of the BSR. The concluding part of the chapter reflects on the impact of EU-endorsed experimental governing and policy practices relative to improving BSR problem-solving capacities.

II. Innovative MLG Modes: Improving BSR Policymaking Capacities

Innovative MLG is linked to the demands to improve BSR policymaking capacities. Augmenting policymaking is viewed as improving the ability to govern BSR transboundary problems, such as eutrophication and overfishing in the Baltic Sea and combating climate change in the area. The proliferation of innovative MLG norms and processes is made evident by one of the strategic policy documents in the BSR: the Baltic Sea Action Plan (BSAP). The BSAP – which was adopted by the Helsinki Commission (HELCOM), a BSR network, in 2007 and updated in 2021 – aspires to reach 'Good Environmental Status for the Baltic Sea'.[25] The BSAP includes innovative MLG approaches and hitherto the plan has enabled a reduction in nutrient inputs in the Baltic Sea, improved the biodiversity and decreased maritime incidents and spills.[26]

The focus of the BSAP is to provide an efficient MLG of the ecosystems of the Baltic Sea. However, ecosystem processes and functions are complex and variable, and governing attempts are associated with uncertainty.[27] The BSAP is guided by

[24] European Commission, 'Missions in Horizon Europe' (n 22).
[25] HELCOM, 'Baltic Sea Action Plan' (2022), available at: helcom.fi/baltic-sea-action-plan/.
[26] ibid.
[27] UN, 'Food and Agriculture Organization of the United Nations. Basics of adaptive governance' (2022), available at: www.fao.org/3/y4810e/y4810e0f.htm.

the Ecosystem Approach to Management to achieve good environmental status of the Baltic Sea. The BSAP employs adaptive governance as a strategy to improve the status of the Baltic Sea, as it allows BSR actors to operate in the face of uncertainty.[28] Adaptive governance is designed to deal with the dynamic and non-linear nature of ecosystems and the absence of complete knowledge or understanding of their functioning.[29] Adaptive governance is embodied by a simple imperative: policies are experiments; learn from them.[30] Policies are viewed as experiments, which are subject to evaluation to improve ecosystem governing. Adaptive governance involves a learning process, which helps to adapt methodologies and practices to the ways in which these systems are being governed.[31] Adaptive governance underlines flexibility in policymaking and accentuates that policy development and implementation is subject to processes that aspire to improve policies and practices by learning from the outcomes of operational programmes.

The innovative BSR MLG modes, ie, adaptive, collaborative and experimental governance, emphasise policy learning as an element in bridging the knowledge gap associated with the governing of transboundary problems.[32,33,34,35] Policy learning and processes leading up to it are regarded as a suitable strategy to deal with complexity and uncertainty in the governing of ecosystems systems.[36,37] Experimental MLG encourages policy learning processes, where public actors engage with non-state actors to support policymaking, which is based on lessons drawn from experiences and from learning by doing.[38,39] Collaborative governance is vital for an experimental MLG of the BSR. Horizontal and vertical MLG collaboration is important in the design of experimental policy approaches.[40] Collaborative governance is regarded as increasing knowledge exchange to develop the understanding of BSR transboundary problems. It is viewed as offering holistic

[28] HELCOM, 'Original version of the Baltic Sea Action Plan' (2007), available at: www.helcom.fi/wp-content/uploads/2019/08/BSAP_Final.pdf.

[29] UN, 'Basics of adaptive governance' (n 27).

[30] KN Lee (ed), *Compass and Gyroscope: Integrating Science and Politics for the Environment* (Washington, DC, Island Press, 1993).

[31] UN, 'Basics of adaptive governance' (n 27).

[32] C Folke et al, 'Adaptive Governance of Social-ecological Systems' (2005) 30 *Annual Review of Environment and Resources* 441.

[33] R Brunner et al (eds), *Adaptive Governance: Integrating Science, Policy and Decision-Making* (New York, Colombia University Press, 2005).

[34] D Armitage, M Marschke and R Plummer, 'Adaptive Co-Management and the Paradox of Learning' (2008) 18 *Global Environmental Change* 86.

[35] D Wolfe, 'Experimental Governance: Conceptual approaches and practical cases. Background paper for an OECD/EC Workshop' within the workshop series *Broadening innovation policy: New insights for regions and cities* (2018), available at: www.oecd.org/cfe/regionaldevelopment/Wolfe(2018)ExperimentalGovernanceConceptualApproaches.pdf.

[36] C Pahl-Wostl et al, 'The importance of social learning and culture for sustainable water management' (2008) 64 *Ecological Economy* 484.

[37] M Reed, 'What is Social Learning?' (2010) 15 *Ecological Society* 1.

[38] C Ansell, 'Collaborative Governance' in D Levi-Faur (ed), *The Oxford Handbook of Governance* (Oxford, Oxford University Press, 2012).

[39] Wolfe (n 35).

[40] ibid.

policy solutions, which consider the fragmented BSR setting, by integrating public and non-public lay information in the design of policy.

The innovative MLG modes are also interlinked by the application of the same policy learning tools that drive and proliferate innovative actions. This is highlighted and made evident by the BSAP. BSAP action on BSR transboundary problems – such as to strengthen the resilience of the Baltic Sea to climate change, transition to circular economy and carbon neutrality – is developed and implemented by best practice studies.[41] These are envisioned as allowing and fostering exchange of knowledge on best available techniques, thereby enhancing mutual learning among BSR actors. Best practice studies function as hubs for learning and the transfer of policy practices across the BSR MLG, and are regarded as key to ensure suitable policy outcomes to target transboundary problems.[42]

III. The Increasing Relevance of the EU in the Network-Based MLG of the BSR

With a lack of institutionalised legislative entities with absolute authoritative power and exclusive enforcement competence over the various states in the region, public actors in the BSR have created space for a network-based MLG. The MLG of the BSR transpires though explicitly established networks. The first formal BSR network, the Nordic Council, was an inter-parliamentary network, established in 1952. During the 1970s the number of networks expanded and proliferated in the 1990s, as a reaction to the end of the Cold War. Currently over 20 networks constitute the basis for BSR MLG.[43] These link horizontally and vertically the super-national, national, regional and local level with civil society and the private sector. Examples include inter-parliamentary and intergovernmental networks of HELCOM, the Baltic Council of Ministers, the Council of the Baltic Sea States, the Nordic Council of Ministers and sub-national authority networks, such as the Union of the Baltic Cities and Baltic Sea States Sub-regional cooperation network.

A network-based MLG encapsulates the changing conditions of policymaking. Networks change the structural power division relative to the formation and design of policy. Networks erode the hierarchical basis and expand the scope of actors involved in policy processes, using multi-actor and multi-level cooperation processes and tools to generate policy outcomes. Network action is considered key in the production of efficient public governing, reflective of the current, fragmented and multilayered society.[44] Network action is viewed as providing adequate

[41] HELCOM, 'Baltic Sea Action Plan' (2022) (n 25).

[42] ibid.

[43] Grönholm, 'A tangled web' (n 14).

[44] E Sørensen and J Torfing, 'Network Governance and Post-Liberal Democracy' (2005) 27 *Administrative Theory & Praxis* 197.

responses to complex, conflict-ridden and ill-defined policy challenges.[45,46] Network-based MLG is not bound by hierarchical norms, but operates through a flexible approach.[47,48] In the MLG of the BSR, networks outline the norms for developing, implementing and evaluating policy.[49] BSR networks adhere to an institutionalised framework of rules, but are bound by the operating principles of networks, providing them with only soft, non-coercive tools to enforce said rules.[50]

Network-based MLG and the conditions that frame BSR policymaking have their origins in EU-shaped MLG. The formation of networks is encouraged by the EU, as networks are regarded as providing innovative MLG that enhances problem-solving capacity.[51] EU-formed MLG comprises multi-level, non-hierarchical and regulatory institutions interlinking a hybrid mix of state and non-state actors.[52,53] The EU's influence has gradually increased in the BSR. Since the mid-1990s, a Europeanisation of the BSR has taken place because of the expansion of the EU into the northern and eastern areas of Europe. This has shaped the BSR MLG and increased the EU's influence in setting the norms for policymaking in the area.[54,55,56] From a BSR MLG perspective, EU expansion has catalysed the formation of new BSR networks. The Northern Dimension Partnerships were created to extend the cooperation between EU and non-EU Member States. Also, existing formal BSR networks have pivoted towards the EU and have aligned their activities with EU policy documents. BSR networks established decades ago, based on different principles to pursue varied political and policy interests in the area, are now engaged in EU policy documents. In 2018, around half of the BSR networks were involved in policy action promoted by the EU 2030 Framework for Energy and Climate.[57]

[45] M Marcussen and J Torfing (eds), *Democratic Network Governance in Europe* (Basingstoke, Palgrave Macmillan, 2007).

[46] J Torfing and E Sørensen, 'The European debate on governance networks: Towards a new and viable paradigm?' (2014) 33 *Policy and Society* 329.

[47] Ö Bodin and BI Crona, 'The role of social networks in natural resource governance: What relational patterns make a difference?' (2009) 19 *Global Environmental Change* 366.

[48] J Newig, D Gunther and C Pahl-Wostl, 'Synapses in the Network: Learning in Governance Networks in the Context of Environmental Management' (2010) 15 *Ecology & Society* 24.

[49] Grönholm, *Governing the Baltic* Sea (n 4).

[50] Grönholm, 'A tangled web' (n 14).

[51] E Sørensen and J Torfing, 'Making governance networks effective and democratic through metagovernance' (2009) 8 *Public Administration* 23.

[52] S Hix, 'The study of the European Union II: the "new governance" agenda and its rival' (1998) 5 *Journal of European Public Policy* 38.

[53] T Börzel, 'Networks: Reified metaphor or governance panacea?' (2011) 89 *Public Administration* 49.

[54] Joas, Jahn and Kern (n 2).

[55] VanDeveer (n 13).

[56] S Grönholm and S Jetoo, 'The potential to foster governance learning in the Baltic Sea Region: Network governance of the European Union Strategy for the Baltic Sea Region' (2019) 29 *Environmental Policy and Governance* 435.

[57] Grönholm, 'A tangled web' (n 14).

The main incentive for networks to engage in EU policy action is resource dependency among BSR networks.[58] BSR networks rely on member contributions to maintain normal functions, but often use external funds to pursue policy development, implementation and evaluation to fulfil their aims of informing public policymaking. Simultaneously, the EU and the European Commission have made available best practice-based funding. The financial might of the European Regional Development Fund, the European Social Fund and the Cohesion Fund have become important revenue sources for many BSR networks to pursue activities within their mandated policy scope.

The BSR network resource dependency has allowed the EU to reshape the BSR operating structures, procedures and formats for developing, implementing and evaluating policy. Current BSR policy formation is modelled based on EU-endorsed policy beliefs and norms, proliferated with targeted EU funding programmes.[59] The funding principles of these programmes have changed BSR policymaking by altering the underlying structural and relational actor basis relative to the design of BSR network policymaking. The most important change is that the EU has reinforced an expansion of actors involved in the network-based MLG of the BSR. The EU has created new forms and pathways for public and non-public actors to engage in BSR MLG-based policy design, where processes and designs for developing, implementing and evaluating policy has traditionally been controlled by formal BSR networks and their members. EU best practice programme funding norms have expanded the formation of informal networks, operationalised and applied in the BSR setting as projects. Projects serve as tools for expanding policy innovation capacity. BSR projects are envisioned to offer platforms for cross-sectorial horizontal and vertical MLG cooperation, designed to enable and deliver policy learning.[60]

In a BSR MLG setting, projects are regarded as key in developing and implementing new policy solutions to BSR transboundary problems. The proliferation of BSR projects is enabled by EU funding programmes. The EU is the biggest project funder in the BSR. EU funding programmes advocate for projects to be used as hubs for testing and assessing the practical performance of different forms of experimentation for a limited time. This is in line with the basic principle of EU funding programmes, providing access to new policy knowledge, thereby facilitating innovative MLG.[61,62] Projects make it possible to draw new lessons regarding the replication of policy experiments. Replication of policy experiments refers to 'expanding, adapting and sustaining successful policies, programmes or projects in different places and over time to reach a greater number of people'.[63]

[58] ibid.

[59] Grönholm, *Governing the Baltic* Sea (n 4).

[60] ibid.

[61] A Marshall, 'Europeanization at the urban level: Local actors, institutions and the dynamics of multi-level interaction' (2005) 12 *Journal of European Public Policy* 668.

[62] Stephenson (n 5).

[63] K Kern, 'Cities as leaders in EU multilevel climate governance: Embedded upscaling of local experiments in Europe' (2019) 28 *Environmental Politics* 125.

Experiments are designed to be framed, targeted, measurable, time-bound and impact driven.[64] The ambition is to share, replicate and transfer policy innovation via best practice or pilot studies, which may be incorporated into EU policy programmes.[65]

IV. Central EU Programme Funds and their Relevance for the BSR

A. General

The EU is the key public actor promoting experimental MLG in the BSR. This is largely enabled by the governing norms and underlying aims of central EU programme funds. Most of these aspire to solve problems across national borders, such as transboundary problems. They advocate the use of shared actions and policy exchanges between national, regional and local actors from different EU Member States. EU programme funds are important policy tools. This is highlighted by the fact that 76 per cent of the EU budget is allocated to five central programme funds: the European Regional Development Fund (ERDF), the European Social Fund, the Cohesion Fund, the European Agricultural Fund for Rural Development and the European Maritime and Fisheries Fund.[66]

Among the EU programme funds, the European Territorial Cooperation (ETC) programmes, known as Interreg programmes, cater specifically to the MLG context of the BSR. ETC action is financially enabled by the ERDF. The Interreg programmes are not the only EU funding source in the BSR, but they are the most relevant in terms of size, and the programmes align with the geographical boundaries of the BSR MLG, as non-EU Member States are included as partner countries.[67] The BSR relevance of the ETC programmes is emphasised by the fact that they are particularly designed to solve transboundary problems. They function as a framework for developing and implementing shared policy action exchanges between national, regional and local actors from different EU Member States.[68]

The objective of the ETC programmes is to promote a harmonious economic, social and territorial development of the EU.[69] The ETC programmes are built around three types of cooperation: cross-border (Interreg A), transnational

[64] European Commission, 'Missions in Horizon Europe' (n 22).

[65] Marshall (n 61).

[66] European Union, 'Overview of the management of EU funds' (2021), available at: europa.eu/european-union/about-eu/funding-grants_en.

[67] European Commission, 'Historical overview of the INTERREG European territorial cooperation program' (2021), available at: ec.europa.eu/regional_policy/en/policy/cooperation/european-territorial/.

[68] ibid.

[69] ibid.

(Interreg B) and interregional (Interreg C). So far, five programme periods have succeeded each other.[70] Throughout the last three decades, Interreg has developed into a key instrument of the EU in supporting cooperation between actors across national borders of the EU Member States.[71] The foundation of Interreg cooperation is to tackle common problems together and find joint solutions by developing and sharing best practice studies among Member States in the same geographical area. The logic of Interreg cooperation extends to facilitate the exchange and transfer of successful policy experiences.[72]

Figure 1 The Evolution of Interreg 1990–2020

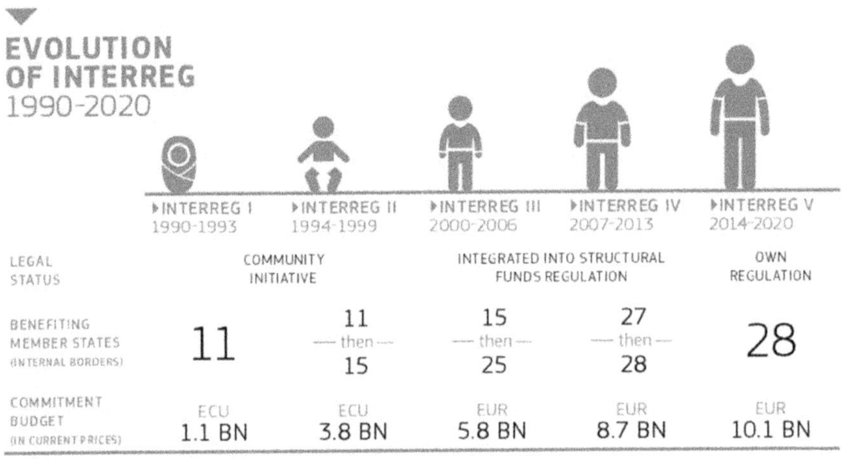

Source: 'Historical overview of the INTERREG European territorial cooperation program' (European Commission, 2021a), available at: ec.europa.eu/regional_policy/en/policy/cooperation/european-territorial/.

The programme period of 2014 to 2020 is based on 11 priorities agreed in the ERDF Regulation.[73] The priorities include research and innovation, information and communication technologies, competitiveness of small and middle-sized companies, low-carbon economy, climate change, environment and resource efficiency, sustainable transport, employment and mobility, social inclusion, better education and training and better public administration.[74] The ERDF Regulation is linked to Article 176 of the Treaty on the Functioning of the European Union, and aims to redress the regional imbalances in the EU.[75]

[70] Figure 1.
[71] European Commission, 'Historical overview' (n 67).
[72] ibid.
[73] European Commission, 'Legislative overview of EU policy funding programmes' (2021), available at: ec.europa.eu/regional_policy/en/information/legislation/regulations/.
[74] European Commission, 'Historical overview' (n 67).
[75] European Commission, 'Legislative overview' (n 73).

B. Overview of Interreg Programmes in the BSR

There are two types of Interreg programmes in the BSR: cross-border cooperation (Interreg A) and transnational cooperation (Interreg B). The Interreg programmes add a European element in developing responses to BSR transboundary problems. These responses are developed from analysis at European level and aim to provide an MLG response in tackling cross-border and transnational problems. The BSR Interreg programmes are developed to respond to different priorities, which are set for a period of six years. Interreg A and B are different in terms of BSR geographical scope, but are governed based on the same principles. The geographical scope of the Interreg A programmes in the BSR is defined based on their task in promoting cross-border cooperation. In the programme period from 2014 to 2020 there were 10 Interreg A programmes, each governed by their own Managing Authority or Joint Secretariat located in the eligible funding area.[76] The Joint Secretariat is made up of representatives of the EU Member States and non-EU Member States participating as partners in the Interreg programme. The Secretariat oversees the overall implementation and is responsible for the correct use of the funds.

Interreg B is not geographically restricted but covers all areas of the BSR. Interreg B cooperation covers 10 countries, the EU Member States in the BSR, including Iceland, and two neighbouring non-EU countries – Norway and Russia. Interreg B for 2014 to 2020 supported integrated territorial development and cooperation for an innovative, accessible and sustainable BSR.[77] Interreg B had four priorities for the programme period. The first, 'Capacity for innovation', was dedicated to actions strengthening the ability of the BSR to create and commercialise innovation, encouraging experimentation with new approaches and solutions to be practically tested through pilot actions. The aim was to increase the capacity of the public sector as an innovation driver.[78] The second priority, 'Efficient management of natural resources' aspired to enhance the capacity of public authorities and practitioners to ensure better environmental status of the BSR waters and to strengthen resource-efficient growth. This priority supported the development and testing of governing and funding models and technological solutions for production and distribution of renewable energy and for improved energy efficiency. The third priority 'Sustainable transport' covered capacity-building measures ensuring more sustainable BSR transport solutions. This priority aimed to improve accessibility in the BSR, as well as maritime safety and environmentally friendly shipping. The fourth and final priority was 'EU Strategy support' aimed at strengthening the implementation of the EU Strategy for the Baltic Sea Region (EUSBSR) by ensuring cooperation with all BSR countries; some of the cooperation in the aforementioned priority areas are linked to the implementation of the Action Plan of the EUSBSR.

[76] Table 1.
[77] Interreg Baltic Sea, 'Interreg B Programme, Homepage' (2021), available at: interreg-baltic.eu/.
[78] ibid.

Interreg B uses projects as tools to stimulate policy progress towards improving the problem-solving capacities in line with the priorities detailed above. Public authorities from national, regional and local levels; research and training institutions; sectoral agencies and associations; NGOs; and enterprises can take part in transnational Interreg B projects. As a rule, organisations of project partners and lead partners must be located in the programme area.[79] Interreg B requires the set-up of transnational partnerships among project partners, thereby bringing NGOs, representatives from the community and voluntary sectors, business leaders and other partners into the BSR MLG. A typical Interreg B project operates with a budget of between €1.5 million and €4.5 million for seven or more project partners that work together for two to three years.[80]

Figure 2 Interreg B governing structure

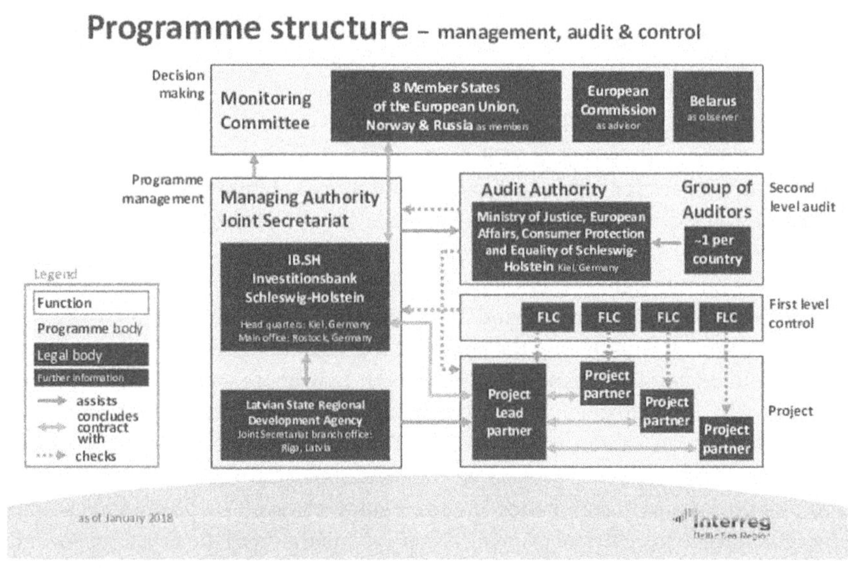

Source: Interreg B, Homepage (2021a).

The governing of the Interreg B programme is headed by a Monitoring Committee that includes representatives of all Baltic Sea States. It selects projects for funding, oversees the implementation and is responsible for the use of the funds.[81] The Investitionsbank Schleswig-Holstein acts as the Managing Authority or Joint Secretariat that is tasked with practical implementation. It is located in

[79] ibid.
[80] ibid.
[81] Figure 2.

Kiel and Rostock (Germany) and has a branch office in Riga (Latvia). The Audit Authority verifies the functioning of the management and control system of the programme.[82] It is hosted by the Ministry of Justice, European Affairs, Consumer Protection and Equality of the German Federal State of Schleswig-Holstein in Kiel, Germany. The Audit Authority is assisted by the Group of Auditors comprising representatives of the Baltic Sea States carrying out the second level audits. Besides these bodies, national sub-committees have a key role regarding the dissemination of programme-related information in the participating states.[83] Funding of the Interreg B programme originates from ERDF, national Norwegian sources and the European Neighbourhood Instrument. Around €279 million was allocated for the Interreg V programme period.

In the future, the Interreg B programme will be of continued significance for supporting innovative BSR policy action. The newly launched programme period covering the years from 2021 to 2027 has a focus on innovative societies.[84] The programme aims to contribute to increase BSR innovativeness and it has been allocated €250 million. The programme encourages experimentation to assist in the development of new water-smart and climate-neutral solutions in the BSR.[85] The planned Interreg B project financing will play a key role in supporting the implementation of strategic BSR policy documents. The updated BSAP has plans to use future Interreg B financing to support the implementation of the BSAP.[86]

C. Proliferating Experimental Governance with the Help of Interreg-Funded BSR Projects

Interreg funding has been instrumental in proliferating cross-sectorial-based BSR experimental MLG, by mainstreaming innovative policy action in the BSR. From 2014 to 2020, the Interreg A and Interreg B funding programmes financed 1,068 projects in the BSR, by allocating €953 million. Of this, Interreg A, implemented by 10 cross-border cooperation programmes, allocated €713 million and funded 964 projects, or circa 160 projects per year.[87] From 2014 to 2020, Interreg B financed 105 projects with €240 million.[88]

[82] ibid.
[83] ibid.
[84] Interreg Baltic Sea Region, 'New Baltic Sea Region Program for 2021–2027' (2022), available at: interreg-baltic.eu/get-funding/priorities-2021–2027/priority-1-innovative-societies/priority-1-innovative-societies-resilient/.
[85] ibid.
[86] HELCOM, 'Baltic Sea Action Plan' (2022) (n 25).
[87] Table 1.
[88] Table 2.

Table 1 Overview of Interreg A programmes in the BSR 2014–20

Funding programme	EU funding money (million)	Eligible funding areas	Funded projects
Interreg Central Baltic	€125	Finland – Estonia – Latvia – Sweden	137
Interreg South Baltic	€78	Poland – Denmark – Germany – Lithuania – Sweden	90
Interreg Oresund	€128	Sweden – Denmark – Norway	87
Interreg Botnia Atlantica	€34	Sweden – Finland – Norway	51
Interreg Nord	€75	Norway – Finland – Sweden	118
Interreg Sweden – Norway	€44	Sweden – Norway	94
Interreg Estonia – Latvia	€36	Estonia – Latvia	55
Interreg Latvia – Lithuania	€52	Latvia – Lithuania	134
Interreg Lithuania – Poland	€57	Lithuania – Poland	132
Interreg Germany – Denmark	€84	Germany – Denmark	66
Total	€713	N/A	964

Note: Table 1 is based on data available at keep.eu/countries-and-regions/. The data presented in table 1 is compiled from the Keep.eu portal (maintained by Interact) by the author. The author has summarised data by using a Baltic Sea region perspective to create an overview of Interreg A (Table 1) programmes. Keep.eu aggregates data regarding projects and beneficiaries of EU cross-border, transnational and interregional cooperation programmes among the Member States (MS), and between MS and neighbouring countries. The Interact Programme, with the support of the EC and the remaining Interreg, Interreg IPA cross-border, ENPI/ENI, and IPA-IPA cross-border programmes, built the database and maintains it. The database covers the 2000–06, 2007–13 and 2014–20 periods.

Interreg B has been an important funding source for supporting policy innovation in the BSR. Interreg B has for 20 years (2000–20) financed 331 projects, with a total budget of €680 million.[89] The number of projects and funding have been relatively stable during the decades. Interreg B projects are designed to tap into the innovation potential of the MLG setting. Interreg B projects are expected to contribute to the principal aim of building institutional innovation capacity.[90] The governing terms of the Interreg B funding programme require that projects must at a minimum involve at least three partners from three different states. The maximum number of project partners is 35.[91] The Interreg B project partnership model encourages applying a cross-sectorial, cross-cutting issue

[89] ibid.

[90] Interreg Baltic Sea Region, 'Program manual for Interreg B 2014–2020' (2022), available at: interregbaltic.eu/wpcontent/uploads/2021/08/2020.06.23_Programme_Manual_v._7.1_clean_cover.pdf.

[91] ibid.

and a multi-level approach. Thus, the design of the partnerships should involve representatives from relevant MLG sectors and areas, which have the mandate and policy knowledge to address the problems in question.[92] The partnerships should ensure a suitable mix of project collaboration between public and non-public actors. The project partnerships model is based on the idea of producing new solutions. Projects are envisioned to generate new knowledge with the help of project learning. Project learning represents a process where new transnational knowledge is acquired through joint testing, piloting or demonstration activities relating to developed, transferred or adapted services, products, structures or strategic documents.[93]

Table 2 Overview of Interreg B 2000–20

	2000–2006			**2007–2013**			**2014–2020**		
	Number of projects	**Number of partners**	**EU funding (million)**	**Number of projects**	**Number of partners**	**EU funding (million)**	**Number of projects**	**Number of partners**	**EU funding (million)**
Total	136	2583	217	90	1276	223	105	1409	240

Note: Table 2 is based on data available at keep.eu/countries-and-regions/. The data presented is compiled from the Keep.eu portal (maintained by Interact) by the author. The author has summarised data by using a Baltic Sea region perspective to create an overview of the Interreg B programme. Keep.eu aggregates data regarding projects and beneficiaries of EU cross-border, transnational and interregional cooperation programmes among the Member States (MS), and between MS and neighbouring countries. The Interact Programme, with the support of the EC and the remaining Interreg, Interreg IPA cross-border, ENPI/ENI, and IPA-IPA cross-border programmes, built the database and maintains it. The database covers the 2000–06, 2007–13 and 2014–20 periods.

The Interreg B project governing set-up has resulted in expanding the number of actors in pursuing policy experimentation in the BSR. During the last two decades the Interreg B project-based funding has brought together 5,268 project partners.[94] This is the result of each Interreg B project having had an average of 19 project partners from 2000 to 2006, 14 from 2007 to 2013 and from 2014 to 2020 projects convened an average of 13 transnational multi-level partners.[95] Collectively, Interreg B has facilitated and created an extensive number of transnational cooperation across the different BSR areas and sectors. This has increased not only the number of actors, but also the variety of actors involved and engaged in the pursuit of policy innovation in the MLG of the BSR.

Table 3 provides an overview of the project partners involved in Interreg B financed projects from 2014 to 2020. Interreg B has joined 1,409 project partners during a six-year period. There is a broad variability among the transnational

[92] ibid.
[93] ibid.
[94] Table 2.
[95] ibid.

project partners. The most common group involved in Interreg B projects is public actors, comprising 37 per cent of all Interreg B project partners.[96] These include national, regional, local authorities, infrastructure or public service providers and sectorial agencies. The first three public groups comprise 27 per cent of all project partners.[97] Higher education and research institutions in the BSR constitute the second largest group (29 per cent). Jointly, public actors and research institutions make up 66 per cent of all Interreg BSR project partners.

Public actors and research institutions are key to advancing experimental MLG in the BSR. Research institutions generate new knowledge in cross-sectorial and cross-cutting policy areas, whereas public actors are pivotal in terms of enhancing innovation capacity across BSR MLG levels. Other groups of actors in the Interreg BSR projects include interest groups or NGOs (12 per cent), business support organisations (10 per cent) and small and medium-sized businesses (8 per cent). These link business and societal perspectives in the generation of new knowledge that could help address the transboundary problems of the BSR.

From 2014 to 2020, the Interreg B programme financed 105 projects. The majority of these (58 per cent) aimed to improve the BSR MLG's 'Capacity for innovation'. Of this particular set of projects, most (62 per cent) had a technical approach to policy innovation.[98] In comparison, there were fewer projects pursuing a non-tech innovation approach focusing, for example, on new approaches to deal with the diverging societal interests vis-a-vis BSR transboundary problems, underpinned by the varied BSR socio-cultural dimensions.

Table 3 Overview of Interreg B project partners 2014–20

	First call in 2015	**Second call in 2017**	**Third call in 2018**	**Total**
Local public authority	37	68	56	161
Regional public authority	58	42	29	129
National public authority	34	35	22	91
Infrastructure or public service provider	32	20	13	65
Sectorial agency	21	39	13	73
Education and schools	5	4	3	12
Higher education and research institutions	146	151	120	417
Small and medium size enterprises	53	35	19	107

(continued)

[96] Table 3.
[97] ibid.
[98] Interreg Baltic Sea Region, 'Overview of Interreg B projects' (2021), available at: interreg-baltic.eu/ongoing-projects/programme-2014–2020.

Table 3 ***(Continued)***

	First call in 2015	Second call in 2017	Third call in 2018	Total
Large enterprises	9	16	4	29
Business support organisations	36	71	35	142
Interest groups, including NGOs	67	63	39	169
International organisations	8	4	2	14
Total	506	548	355	1409

Note: Table 3 is based on data available at: interreg-baltic.eu/ongoing-projects/programme-2014–2020/. The data presented in Table 3 is obtained from the webpage of Interreg Baltic EU by the author. The author has summarised data from the webpage to create an overview of the number of project partners for Interreg B for the period 2014–20.

V. Experimental MLG and BSR Problem-Solving Capacities

From a network-based MLG perspective the aim of the Interreg projects is to generate new knowledge for transforming policy understanding. BSR projects constitute tools to inform and augment policymaking capacity relative to the MLG of BSR transboundary problems. In a network-based MLG setting, Interreg projects are designed to constitute policy-learning platforms, generating new insights from issue-based horizontal and vertical MLG cooperation. This cooperation structure and the policy focus of these learning platforms are decided by the governing norms of the Interreg funding programmes.

The key to the Interreg projects' ability to improve BSR problem-solving capacities is the involvement of public actors as project partners. In the Interreg B programme period from 2014 to 2020 public actors constituted the largest group of all project partners.[99] The involvement of public actors is imperative in terms of the feasibility of the Interreg projects' innovation output.[100] Public actors offer improved conditions for transmitting and anchoring new knowledge to guide and orient public policies across the BSR MLG. Low participation of public actors in Interreg projects impedes the transfer of project outcomes into public policies.[101]

[99] Table 3.
[100] Interreg Baltic Sea Region, 'Mid-term evaluation of the impact of the Interreg B Program. Final report' (2018), available at: interreg-baltic.eu/wp content/uploads/2019/01/2018.12.20_FINAL_BSR_midtermevaluation_finalreport.pdf.
[101] ibid.

However, there are general challenges of disseminating project policy knowledge and learning through the horizontal and vertical MLG levels with the aim to expand BSR problem-solving capacities.[102] Interreg projects encounter obstacles in their attempts to enhance the transnational institutional knowledge and innovation capacity of public actors involved in the network-based MLG of the BSR. The main obstacle is the non-hierarchical feature of the network-based MLG setting. There are no formal or institutionalised structures for supporting and guiding policy knowledge transfer in the BSR. The BSR MLG setting is linked through a disjointed web that operates without a designated point of authority.[103] No formal coordination authority guides the overarching BSR policy development, policy implementation and policy evaluation. This makes a coherent diffusion of the policy learning outcomes of the Interreg projects across horizontal and vertical levels difficult. As an example, for the programme period from 2014 to 2020 Interreg A and Interreg B funding programmes financed, on an annual basis, 178 BSR projects.[104,105] Considering that projects funded by Interreg B had an average of 13 project partners would indicate that there were potentially upwards of 2,300 project actors involved each year in generating new policy knowledge in the MLG of the BSR. The non-hierarchical and flexible structures of the network-based MLG of the BSR are not designed to effectively transmit the learning outcomes of the vast annual number of projects within and across this setting.

A number of factors hamper the uptake of new policy knowledge from Interreg projects.[106] First, there is a short window of opportunity to disseminate the outcomes of projects. Usually, the target group is confined to a rather closed circle of public authorities, practitioners and researchers that are involved in transnational project work.[107] This makes anchoring project-based knowledge on a national and local level challenging. Disseminating knowledge in a transnational context needs to confront language barriers, different cultural and societal values and a fragmented BSR MLG knowledge and competence base.[108] EU financed projects also condense their outcomes by using a standardised measurable approach, without much consideration for transnational contextual and cultural variances.[109] This is especially relevant in projects that have a technical approach to policy innovation and is symbolised by the use of best practice studies.

[102] Grönholm, *Governing the Baltic* Sea (n 4).
[103] Grönholm, 'A tangled web' (n 14).
[104] Table 1.
[105] Table 2.
[106] Interreg Baltic Sea Region, 'Evaluation' (n 100).
[107] ibid.
[108] ibid.
[109] Grönholm and Jetoo (n 56).

Second, Interreg projects are carried out in policy areas that are of an inter-sectoral and complex policy character.[110] This highlights the need for institutional public competence and coherency across MLG levels, especially on national and local levels across the BSR. Yet, there is insufficient cross-sectoral cooperation on national levels, whilst on a local level there is lack of policy competence.[111] Furthermore, there is in-built temporality in the BSR MLG, which impedes the uptake of inter-sectoral and cross-sectoral project results. This refers to changes in public personnel, comprising civil servants and elected officials, at national, regional and local levels in the BSR. In addition, formal BSR networks operate through a system of rotation of network personnel.[112] Collectively, this inhibits the creation of an institutional BSR MLG memory that would support a continuous and coherent diffusion of innovative and experimental policy knowledge.

Third, almost a third of all Interreg B projects partners are research institutions or representatives of higher education.[113] Although, research institutions are important for allowing and enabling policy innovation, there is a concern that they are overrepresented regarding responses generated to BSR transboundary problems. Many projects are expert-driven and technical, which complicates the mainstreaming of policy knowledge exchange with other BSR actors.[114] Scientific knowledge is not easily absorbed and interpreted by public actors. Moreover, the sharing of Interreg B project-generated academic insights is not prioritised in the transfer of project outcomes to public actors.[115] This may be related to weak linkages between public actors and academia as well as a fragmented BSR knowledge and competence base.

Fourth, and final, from a BSR MLG perspective the massive project proliferation enabled by the BSR Interreg programmes[116,117] do not support the creation of favourable policy conditions for governing BSR transboundary problems.[118] The vast number of Interreg projects and project partners expands an MLG temporality. Projects are tools that have a relatively short time frame, with a predetermined clear start and end date. This does not ensure policy coherence and continuity across BSR MLG levels. Project proliferation via the diffusion of best practice studies expands a short-term policy dimension relative to policy development and innovation practices, and it distorts the policy time frames of operating BSR actors. Generated information in projects is short-lived and the impacts of it minimal due to lack of contextual ownership. The temporary nature of projects inhibits the sedimentation of new knowledge; when projects dissolve

[110] Interreg Baltic Sea Region, 'Overview' (n 98).
[111] Interreg Baltic Sea Region, 'Evaluation' (n 100).
[112] Grönholm, 'A tangled web' (n 14).
[113] Table 3.
[114] Interreg Baltic Sea Region, 'Evaluation' (n 100).
[115] ibid.
[116] Table 1.
[117] Table 2.
[118] Grönholm, *Governing the Baltic* Sea (n 4).

and project participants move on the created knowledge is likely to disperse.[119] The pool of new policy knowledge is not necessarily institutionalised in the public sphere and it does not generally reach central problem-solving actors operating at national level. The result is policy fragmentation, causing friction concerning the stability, coherency and longevity of innovative policy action. This weakens the viability of experimental MLG in the BSR. Collectively, project proliferation reduces transparency and complicates the BSR MLG of transboundary problems.

VI. Conclusions: The Impact of EU-Endorsed Experimental Governing and Policy Practices

Since the mid-1990s, the influence of the EU in the BSR has gradually increased and expanded. Initially, the EU facilitated the formation of new BSR networks. Throughout the decades, the EU has tacitly shaped the general MLG setting by altering the underlying structural and relational actor basis relative to the design of BSR policymaking.[120] This has occurred with the purpose of inducing policy innovation as a method to govern the transboundary problems of the area. The EU has particularly expedited a narrative of a broader transformative process that captures the expansion of an experimental MLG in the BSR.

Currently, BSR MLG is generally based on EU-endorsed governing and policy beliefs, proliferated with the help of best practice studies.[121] The targeted funding of EU project programmes in the BSR fosters these beliefs. The BSR MLG setting is sympathetic towards EU-advocated governing and policy norms, since the setting operates in the absence of clearly defined governing and policy procedures and rules. As a result, the EU implicitly steers the BSR MLG policy agenda, as neither individual Baltic Sea States nor formal networks have the capacity, or the interest, to steer and shape MLG and policy conditions in the area.

Prominent EU project funding schemes, such as the BSR Interreg programmes, are applied to develop and influence policy development, implementation and evaluation. The EU funds that finance the majority of all BSR projects induce changes in the design of policy activities. For example, the Interreg programmes add a European element in developing responses to BSR transboundary problems. These responses are developed from analysis at a European level to provide an MLG response in tackling cross-border and transnational problems. In addition, EU funds combat resource dependency among actors and formal networks in the BSR. The EU project funding schemes are financially important for BSR networks and may suggest that policy activity only occurs in policy areas, where there is available funding for project activities.[122] Consequently, the EU is in a position to

[119] Grönholm and Jetoo (n 56).
[120] Grönholm, *Governing the Baltic Sea* (n 4).
[121] ibid.
[122] Grönholm, 'A tangled web' (n 14).

act as a 'grand-tactician' for setting the BSR MLG policy agenda and for shaping the experimental MLG conditions in the BSR.

The EU is reliant on soft governing options in developing and implementing policy action targeting BSR transboundary problems. The EU underlines an innovative learning and knowledge-based MLG of the BSR.[123] However, there are challenges in applying an expansive implementation of an innovative MLG approach. Most of these challenges are of a structural nature, because of existing institutional arrangements and embedded path-dependencies in the network-based MLG of the BSR.[124] This makes it difficult to establish new cross-sectoral collaboration for innovative policy learning. For example, multi-sector cooperation and participatory and adaptive governance have been given limited attention in the environmental MLG of the BSR.[125] The inclusion of non-state actors into processes of policymaking with regard to eutrophication in the Baltic Sea is undeveloped.[126] Despite ambitions to increase actor participation in environmental MLG, supporting structures and processes enabling broader inclusion and policy deliberation are often missing. When participation in policy processes is enlarged, actor participation and interaction are framed institutionally.[127] The instrumental framing of actor participation is a result of insufficient flexibility and adaptability of the MLG in the Baltic Sea. This originates from non-adaptive BSR MLG structures, lock-in effects and path dependencies.[128] Institutional path-dependencies impede an EU-advocated innovative-based MLG of BSR transboundary problems. EU-devised innovative action is generally reduced to short-term, one-sided and disjointed approaches.

The EU has increased the extensive and continued use of projects to target BSR transboundary problems. The operative basis of projects does not align with the operative MLG BSR setting, especially in the attempt to improve policymaking capacities. The operating principles of the network-based MLG of the BSR is not designed to support and interact with the operating principles of projects. There is a mismatch between project actor and MLG actor time frames. The BSR MLG setting is unable to interact coherently with the BSR project proliferation in terms of policy coordination and output. This mismatch is accentuated by projects operating unilaterally across MLG levels alongside formal BSR networks, but not necessarily in conjunction with them. In some cases, projects are designed to support formal networks in augmenting policymaking capacities. However, in many cases projects are detached from formal BSR networks and project learning outcomes are communicated to EU funding programmes instead of public

[123] Gilek et al, 'Environmental governance' (n 1).
[124] ibid.
[125] A Jönsson et al, 'Risk Communication and the Role of the Public: Towards Inclusive Environmental Governance of the Baltic Sea?' in M Gilek et al (eds), *Environmental Governance of the Baltic Sea* (Heidelberg, Springer, 2016).
[126] ibid.
[127] Gilek and Karlsson (n 3).
[128] ibid.

policymakers.[129] Projects have limited exposure relative to public policymakers operating at the national and local level in the Baltic Sea States. The EU funding programmes set the governing principles of projects and the projects are not subject to any BSR jurisdiction. The success of the project is determined based on their capacity to encourage policy experimentation, without any threat of legal sanctions, considering the non-hierarchical operative features of the network-based MLG of the BSR.

Experimentation as an MLG mode needs to confront governing complexities. An MLG setting adds complexity by linking traditional forms of governing with new political spaces and policy tools.[130] Complexity stems from non-hierarchical linkages connecting interdependent actors on different governing levels. Complexity increases because of time-based policy tools, linking administrative levels, which operate with varying degrees of autonomy.[131] The network-based MLG of the BSR is not subordinated by hierarchical interventions. Experimental MLG emphasises the mediating role of governing institutions operating within and at different levels within this setting. Experimental MLG relies on creating horizontal and vertical policy adherence and coherence. In effect, experimental MLG calls for increased coordination among policymaking actors residing at different MLG levels to foster the conditions necessary to support innovative policy action.[132]

Partly with the view to centralise and coordinate the networked MLG of BSR policy activities, the EUSBSR was unveiled in 2009.[133] The EUSBSR was an initiative of the European Parliament, which had called for a strategy to address the environmental challenges of the Baltic Sea.[134] The EUSBSR fosters cooperation for reconciling the transboundary nature of problems with the mosaic of BSR networks that are driven by different agendas and overlapping interests. Operationally, the Strategy is tasked to coordinate activities and dialogue needed for the MLG of BSR transboundary problems. Thus, the EUSBSR is an important addition to the network-based MLG of the BSR. The EUSBSR is key to support an EU-endorsed experimental-based steering of the area. The Strategy encapsulates the promise of BSR MLG, namely to expand learning and dialogue for disseminating new policy understanding across and between the formal BSR networks. The Strategy captures the policy boundaries of the shared BSR transboundary problems, as it interlinks the majority of the distributed policy-capacities of the

[129] Grönholm, *Governing the Baltic* Sea (n 4).

[130] H Bulkeley and M Betsill 'Revisiting the urban politics of climate change' (2013) 22 *Environmental Policy* 136.

[131] R Kaiser and H Prange, 'Managing diversity in a system of multi-level governance: The open method of co-ordination in innovation policy' (2004) 11 *Journal of European Public Policy* 249.

[132] Wolfe (n 35).

[133] Grönholm and Jetoo (n 56).

[134] EUSBSR, 'History of the EU Strategy for the Baltic Sea region' (2022), available at: www.balticsea-region-strategy.eu/history.

area. It is the principal knowledge and coordination broker for innovative MLG of the BSR.

However, as a coordinator of policy initiatives, development and implementation, serving to expand the BSR system capacity for improving policy coherency and continuity, the EUSBSR is bound by its limited steering ability.[135] It is an extension of the operating principles of network-based MLG, lacking regulatory and hierarchical methods to coordinate policy initiatives and activities. A first step towards assisting the EUSBSR to improve BSR experimental MLG practices is to strengthen its coordination capacity. This would constitute a logical response towards fulfilling the policy coordination void in the BSR MLG. Policy coordination of MLG action is complex with associated challenges. Policy coordination of governmental bodies, regulatory frameworks at the EU, Baltic Sea and national levels is a problem in the BSR context.[136] For the EUSBSR to become a BSR policy coordinator, institutional embeddedness and acknowledgement is required, particularly from public actors comprising the BSR MLG.

As a second step, experimental governing and policy practices in the BSR demand from the EUSBSR an institutionalised and structured exchange of new policy information stemming from BSR projects. Moreover, the design of experimental MLG commands the integration of dissimilar actors in advancing and in implementing policy. Currently, the MLG experimental policy design relies generally on technical improvements in relation to BSR transboundary problems.[137] These are generated with best practice studies. Technical improvements are easy to quantify and display to a larger audience, ie, EU project funding schemes. However, what is required to advance experimental MLG in the BSR is tacit multilayered knowledge, achieved by joining expert, lay and indigenous actor knowledge into the development of policy design. This would enhance the socio-cultural conditions for an informed experimental MLG approach of BSR transboundary problems.

Third and finally, a key component for catalysing an experimental MLG of the BSR is the contextual capacity of operative actors in the EUSBSR.[138] EUSBSR actors need to have contextual policy intelligence in order to make use of the amassed new policy knowledge enabled by BSR project proliferation. Contextual intelligence is obtained via a broad presence of actors with varied knowledge bases that would allow making full use of the amassed knowledge of projects. Currently, BSR and EUSBSR policy engagement is limited to institutional horizontal arrangement and interaction, enhancing policy actor similarity.[139]

[135] Grönholm and Jetoo (n 56).

[136] M Karlsson, M Gilek and C Lundberg, 'Eutrophication and the Ecosystem Approach to Management: A Case Study of Baltic Sea Environmental Governance' in M Gilek et al (eds), *Environmental Governance of the Baltic Sea* (Heidelberg, Springer, 2016).

[137] Grönholm, *Governing the Baltic* Sea (n 4).

[138] Grönholm and Jetoo (n 56).

[139] Grönholm, *Governing the Baltic* Sea (n 4).

This narrows the potential heterogeneity of new policy knowledge, as decision-making and policymaking capacity is confined to a restricted group of actors with similar types of institutional backgrounds. Yet, there is wide heterogeneity in the factors that define BSR transboundary problems. These problems are framed and reframed in different ways and from different perspectives. The socio-ecological problems of the BSR are contested and a shared view of the true nature of these problems does not exist.

4

The EU Strategy for the Baltic Sea Region: An Experiment Entering Maturity

HELENA TUURI

I. Introduction

The Strategy for the Baltic Sea Region (Strategy, or EUSBSR) is the eldest of the European Union's macro-regional strategies, launched in 2009. The European Union Strategy for the Danube Region was adopted in 2010, the Strategy for the Adriatic and Ionian Region in 2014 and the Strategy for the Alpine Region in 2015.

Time has come for the EUSBSR to develop from an experimental phase to maturity, towards a result-oriented cooperation platform. The chapter aims to demonstrate how the EUSBSR came about, how it developed – and how it could work more effectively.

II. Descriptions of the EUSBSR

A. Political Framework Supplemented by Action Plan

The EUSBSR is not a legal entity, but a political framework, supplemented by a technical policy document called the Action Plan. The political framework was launched by a Commission Communication, which was later adopted by the Council and endorsed by the European Council in 2009. In 2012, the objectives were modified. The Action Plan has been updated and revised several times.

In 2013, the Commission wanted to place the Strategy into the EU legal framework by including a definition of a macro-regional strategy in the Common

Provisions Regulation for 2014–2020.[1] The Council, however, responded that the EU macro-regional strategies were not limited to the cohesion policy domain but concern a wide range of policy areas.[2] It is disputable whether and to what extent the Common Provisions Regulation was in fact considered as the general legal basis for the EU macro-regional strategies.

The policy areas covered by the Strategy vary. The Strategy's direct achievements are of a soft law nature: networks, platforms, projects and processes, bringing people together. However, the EUSBSR can bring about legislative changes too. One of the reasons behind creating a macro-regional strategy for the Baltic Sea region was that the integrated approach characterising such a strategy might eventually give input to new policy initiatives nationally, in the Baltic Sea region, and at EU level.

The EUSBSR is based upon the EU principle of subsidiarity.[3] It is also based on the principle of partnership of cohesion policy, although it is not limited to the cohesion policy domain.

B. Development of Descriptions in the EU Documents

The EUSBSR was launched as a political and governance experiment. In the beginning there was only a rather general description of both a macro-region and a macro-regional strategy.[4]

In its resolution in 2006, the European Parliament[5] wanted to support the Northern Dimension (ND), which in its view formed a wide framework covering all the northern regions – the Baltic Sea and Barents regions and the Arctic – and all policy areas, both external and internal. It urged the Commission to come up with a proposal for an EU Baltic Sea Strategy in order to reinforce the internal pillar of the ND, cover horizontally different aspects of regional cooperation, promote synergies and avoid overlaps between different regional bodies and organisations. In 2007, the European Council invited the Commission to present

[1] Regulation (EU) No 1303/2013 of the European Parliament and of the Council of 17 December 2013 laying down common provisions on the European Regional Development Fund, the European Social Fund, the Cohesion Fund, the European Agricultural Fund for Rural Development and the European Maritime and Fisheries Fund and laying down general provisions on the European Regional Development Fund, the European Social Fund, the Cohesion Fund and the European Maritime and Fisheries Fund and repealing Council Regulation (EC) No 1083/2006 [2013] OJ L347/320.

[2] 'Council conclusions on the governance of macro-regional strategies' (21 October 2014).

[3] See Art 5 of the Treaty on European Union (TEU) and Protocol No 2 on the application of the principles of subsidiarity and proportionality annexed to the TEU and to the Treaty on the Functioning of the European Union (TFEU).

[4] Commission, 'Study on Macro-regional Strategies and their Links with Cohesion Policy' (Final Report, November 2017).

[5] European Parliament, 'European Parliament resolution on a Baltic Region Strategy for the Northern Dimension, 2006/2171(INI)' (Strasbourg, 16 November 2006).

an EU Strategy for the Baltic Sea region, underlining that the ND provided the basis for its external aspects.[6]

The first description of a macro-region in the broader context of EU policies was drafted in the Commission Communication in 2009. According to the Commission, the Baltic Sea region is a good example of a *macro region* – an area covering a number of administrative regions but with sufficient issues in common to justify a single strategic approach.[7]

In the same Communication and in the Action Plan annexed thereto, the Commission also presented the first description of a *macro-regional strategy*. According to it, the challenges and opportunities of the Baltic Sea region would be best addressed by an integrated and multi-sectoral regional strategy. According to the Action Plan, the EUSBSR would be an integrated framework to address the challenges and opportunities of the Baltic Sea region. It would allow the European Union (EU) and its Member States to identify needs and match them to the available resources through coordination of appropriate policies, thus enabling the Baltic Sea region to enjoy a sustainable environment and optimal economic and social development.

The European Council in 2009 shortened the description to read as follows:

> The strategy constitutes an integrated framework to address common challenges, ie, the urgent environmental challenges related to the Baltic Sea, and to contribute to the economic success of the region and to its social and territorial cohesion, as well as to the competitiveness of the European Union.[8]

The Commission and other EU institutions have later described the EUSBSR – as well as the other macro-regional strategies – in different ways, adding and reducing features. The changes have been due in part to developments of the strategies themselves and of the expectations placed on them. Some of these changes will be mentioned here.

The Commission Communication of 2012[9] included a useful description regarding the *functioning level* of the strategy: the macro-regional approach was created to offer an integrated framework for challenges that were too broad for the national level but too specific for an EU of 27 Member States. Furthermore, according to the Strategy, the EUSBSR – by practical steps to take into account the region's geographical characteristics and macro-regional dynamics – strengthens

[6] Council of the European Union, 'Brussels European Council 14 December 2007 Presidency Conclusions' (Brussels, 14 February 2008).

[7] Commission, 'Communication from the Commission to the European Parliament, the Council, the European Economic and Social Committee and the Committee of the Regions concerning the European Union Strategy for the Baltic Sea Region' COM(2009) 248 final.

[8] Council of the European Union, 'Brussels European Council 29/30 October 2009 Presidency Conclusions' (Brussels, 1 December 2009).

[9] Commission, 'Communication from the Commission to the European Parliament, the Council, the European Economic and Social Committee and the Committee of the Regions, concerning the European Union Strategy for the Baltic Sea Region' COM(2012) 128 final.

the use of available European and national resources, seeking to translate political commitments into commitment to action at every point.

The following year the Commission introduced the concept of a *macro-regional strategy*. According to this concept, the bases for macro-regional cooperation are a regional sense of identity, a wish for common strategic planning and a willingness to pool resources. The concept also incorporated the principles of integration, coordination, cooperation, multi-level governance and partnership.[10]

Furthermore, the Commission advised that initial definitions of a macro-regional strategy were being consolidated in the future Common Provisions Regulation for 2014–2020.[11] In its report the Commission defined a macro-regional strategy as follows: (i) it is an integrated framework relating to Member States and third countries in the same geographical areas; (ii) it addresses common challenges and opportunities; and (iii) it benefits from strengthened cooperation for economic, social and territorial cohesion. A macro-regional strategy should be endorsed by the European Parliament and the Council. The Council welcomed the Commission's clarifications of a macro-regional strategy in 2013 and referred to it again in 2014.[12]

Over time, new descriptions have emerged, including additions underlining continuity, long-term strategic objectives and efficiency in coordinating and effectively implementing and bringing added value to EU policies. For instance, in its report on the functioning of the EU macro-regional strategies from 2019, the Commission described the EU macro-regional strategies as policy frameworks initiated by EU and non-EU countries located in a defined geographical area to jointly address challenges and opportunities they have in common through setting shared, long-term objectives.[13]

In its report from 2020, which was written towards the end of the year, when the Covid-19 pandemic had already severely impacted European societies, the Commission described in detail how the macro-regional strategies can and will be of assistance. The macro-regional strategies provide, in the view of the Commission, an available and operational cooperation framework to ensure better coordination of actions, investments and projects within their territories. They are cross-sectoral, stakeholder inclusive and involve different governance levels. All these features can be of key importance in delivering EU priorities such as the

[10] Commission, 'Report from the Commission to the European Parliament, the Council, the European Economic and Social Committee and the Committee of the Regions concerning the added value of macro-regional strategies' COM(2013) 468 final.

[11] Regulation (EU) No 1303/2013 (n 1).

[12] Commission, 'Council conclusions on added value of macro-regional strategies' (22 October 2013); and Commission, 'Council conclusions on the governance of macro-regional strategies' (n 2).

[13] Commission, 'Report from the Commission to the European Parliament, the Council, the European Economic and Social Committee and the Committee of the Regions, concerning the implementation of the macro-regional strategies' COM(2019) 21 final.

European Green Deal, the European Digital Strategy, 'An economy that works for people' and a 'Stronger Europe in the world'.[14]

C. Other Descriptions and Definitions

There is a myriad of definitions of an EU macro-regional strategy, only a few of which will be mentioned here. Some researchers have been focusing on multi-country *coordination structures*. According to the Centre for European Policy Studies comparative study, the EU macro-regional strategies present a level of coordination that was missing before, a kind of cross-border national and regional bottom-up and top-down setting that institutionalises and encourages collaboration within existing policies. The strategies link the supranational EU level with the national and regional, not as a separate process, but as part of the existing architecture. They create groupings of countries and regions to identify common interests, an aspect that was missing in earlier EU policy approaches.[15]

The European territorial cooperation programme INTERACT claims that the *format* itself as a platform can sometimes bring inherent added value. According to this view, one of the main sources of such added value has been the integrated, cross-sectoral approach, transnational dimension and improved multi-level governance which the strategies bring by providing a platform for bringing together various actors, policies and financial resources.[16]

Another, very useful definition regards the EUSBSR as a kind of agreement between the EU Member States concerned and the European Commission. It is not, then, to be seen as a Commission instrument as such, but as a cooperative platform between the Commission and the Baltic Sea region's EU Member States, with the latter playing a key role in substantiating and implementing the Strategy.[17] Yet, while capturing the basic nature of the EUSBSR, this definition fails to provide a full picture of the Strategy, as it overlooks stakeholders other than the Commission and the EU Member States.

D. The EUSBSR in a Nutshell

The EUSBSR as well as the other EU macro-regional strategies are complex structures, difficult to define concisely in a simple and meaningful way. Therefore, it is

[14] Commission, 'Report from the Commission to the European Parliament, the Council, the European Economic and Social Committee and the Committee of the Regions on the implementation of the macro-regional strategies' SWD(2020) 186 final.

[15] JN Ferrer, M Catuti, C Stroia and J Bryhn, 'Comparative study on the governance structure and energy policies in EU macro-regional strategies' (Centre for European Policy Studies Research Report No 2019/02, July 2019).

[16] Interact, 'Added value of macro-regional strategies – programme and project perspective' (Final report of the study, February 2017).

[17] J Zaucha et al, 'EU macro-regional strategies for the Baltic Sea Region after 2020. A nutshell of beauty and possibilities' (2020) 38 *IGiPZ PAN* 51.

only logical that the definitions are either very general or very long and complicated. None of them has an official or established status. Hence, I would rather propose a practical description of the current EUSBSR, including its most essential features – the EUSBR in a nutshell.

The EUSBSR is a platform for collaboration and coordination between its eight EU Member States – Denmark, Estonia, Finland, Germany, Latvia, Lithuania, Poland and Sweden. Cooperation with the neighbouring non-EU countries in the region has been favoured across the activities within the Strategy, where relevant and appropriate. However, as a reaction to Russia's military attack and aggression against Ukraine in 2022, cooperation with the Russian Federation and the Republic of Belarus was suspended.

The Strategy focuses on challenges and opportunities that are more efficiently addressed in a coordinated manner within the Baltic Sea region. Those challenges and opportunities are often too broad for the national level, but too specific for the EU as a whole. The basis of the cooperation is the Member States' and other stakeholders' desire for common strategic planning and willingness to pool resources.

The Strategy consists of a political framework, complemented by a more technical policy document called an Action Plan. The Strategy has three overall objectives: Save the Sea, Connect the Region and Increase Prosperity. Each of them covers a wide range of policies and impacts on the other objectives. They are, in other words, interlinked and interdependent.

The Action Plan divides the work thematically into 14 Policy Areas. Each Policy Area has defined between two and four Actions, which are the basis of the implementation of the EUSBSR.

The governance of the EUSBSR is organised on three levels. The first level consists of the Member States and the Commission at a political level, providing political commitment and strategic orientation. The second level is the National Coordinators Group, consisting of representatives of all eight EUSBSR Member States. It meets regularly and is the core decision-making body within the EUSBSR. A representative of the Commission participates regularly in the meetings of the group. The third level is the Policy Areas, where the practical implementation of the Strategy and the Action Plan takes place. The Policy Areas represent the expertise in their areas of activity. They are managed by Policy Area Coordinators and supported by their respective Steering Groups. Each Policy Area develops Actions that contribute to achieving EUSBSR objectives. The format of activities implemented under each Action is decided by the Policy Area which best suits the needs of the Action. They can be – but are not limited to – projects, processes, networks and platforms.

The European Commission has to some extent withdrawn from the dominating governance role it had in the early days of the EUSBSR. However, it continues to play a key role by providing strategic coordination, advice, guidance, facilitation and reporting.

The EUSBSR Annual Forums are important discussion and networking platforms. The newly created Baltic Sea Strategy Point (BSP), discussed in more detail in section V.C below, provides administrative and technical support, institutional memory and communication, and coordinates capacity building within the Strategy.

III. What was to be Achieved by Launching the EUSBSR – And How Did it Develop?

A. Background

The ideas for an EU macro-regional strategy for the Baltic Sea region had their background in the regionalisation, which took place after the end of the Cold War. While the Baltic Sea region was a heterogeneous area, especially in economic and environmental terms, there was an enormous willingness to open up and cooperate again within this historical trading region, which had by force been divided for more than 40 years. Over time a very dense network of all kinds of international cooperation formats developed within the region. These were of multiple types, levels and sectors and often very different from each other. Some examples may be mentioned:

- *Governmental*: Nordic Council of Ministers; Helsinki Commission (HELCOM); Council of the Baltic Sea States (CBSS); Barents Euro-Arctic Council
- *Mixed*: Northern Dimension (ND)
- *Parliamentary*: Nordic Council; Baltic Sea Parliamentary Conference
- *Regional and local*: Baltic Sea States Subregional Co-operation; Conference of Peripheral Maritime Regions Baltic Sea Commission; Union of Baltic Cities
- *Universities, NGOs and private businesses* have their own pan-Baltic organisations.

After the three Baltic states and Poland became EU members in 2004, the idea of an EU strategy covering the region began to appear in the discussion agendas of regional policymakers. Some saw it as a possibility to help the numerous regional cooperation formats to fulfil their tasks or to help organise some division of labour between them.

In 2009, the Commission drafted a proposal for a Strategy as an answer to the requests from the European Parliament, the Council and the European Council. In the beginning, the Commission seemed to consider the Strategy solely as a Member State initiative, fulfilling their specific national and regional interests. This attitude changed when the Commission discovered that macro-regional strategies can also serve as essential tools to tailor EU policies and programmes to best suit the various macro-regions, and thereby make their implementation more efficient. The strategies can also help to foster cohesion and competitiveness across the macro-regions and make the EU more visible and closer to citizens.

B. Objectives, Sub-Objectives and Priority or Policy Areas

From the very beginning, the core objective of the Baltic Sea cooperation has been to improve the vulnerable state of the sea, the need to protect it and its marine environment. This is still true today, although the EUSBSR as a whole is much wider and covers multiple other important cooperation objectives as well. The scope of the Strategy has been a long-standing topic of discussion, for which it has been difficult to find a commonly agreed solution.

The European Parliament resolution of 2006[18] urged the Commission to come up with a proposal for a Baltic Sea Strategy, in order to help to improve the ecological state of the Baltic Sea. The European Council conclusions of 2007 also focused the scope of the Strategy on addressing the urgent environmental challenges of the Baltic Sea.[19]

Most of the Strategy's substance was initiated during the intensive consultation process, which the Commission arranged in 2008 among the EU Member States and stakeholders, such as regions, municipalities, NGOs, universities, national and pan-Baltic organisations. Based on the results, the Commission presented the first draft of the EUSBSR, accompanied by an Action Plan in 2009.[20] The Strategy, endorsed by the Council and adopted by the European Council,[21] included four main objectives:

- To enable a sustainable environment
- To enhance the region's prosperity
- To increase accessibility and attractiveness
- To ensure safety and security in the region

The Action Plan was divided into four thematic pillars, along those objectives. It included 15 Priority Areas and a Horizontal Section. These were foreseen to be implemented through detailed actions. Some actions were *strategic* for the Baltic Sea region as they were designed to address specific and important issues

[18] European Parliament, 'Northern Dimension' (n 5).

[19] Council of the European Union, 'Presidency Conclusions' (2008) (n 6).

[20] Commission, 'Baltic Sea Region' (n 7); and SEC(2009) 712 accompanying the Communication.

[21] Council of the European Union, 'Communication from the Commission to the European Parliament, the Council, the European Economic and Social Committee and the Committee of the Regions concerning the European Union Strategy for the Baltic Sea Region – Council Conclusions' (Brussels, 27 October 2009); and Council of the European Union, 'Presidency Conclusions' (2009) (n 8).

for the region, its citizens or enterprises. Others were *cooperative*, meaning they focused on the benefits in improving cooperation. All actions were to be understood without prejudice to the existing exclusive Community competences. In addition, the Action Plan presented examples of flagship projects, ie, projects of high significance.

The first progress report had been presented in 2011 and concluded that there was a need to revise the Strategy. One of the main findings was the need for better alignment of policies. Policy responses should better reflect the territorial nature of the region's challenges and opportunities, and policy initiatives should be more coherent and promote synergies.[22]

The aim of the revised Strategy presented in 2012 was to define the objectives more clearly.[23] The number of overall objectives was reduced to three, in order to get more focus and direction: to save the sea, to connect the region and to increase prosperity. These three main objectives are still in force.

The Action Plan was revised accordingly in 2013. The revised Action Plan divided the objectives into sub-objectives, in order to define the targets under each objective:

Save the sea

- Clear water in the sea
- Rich and healthy wildlife
- Clean and safe shipping
- Better cooperation

Connect the region

- Good transport conditions
- Reliable energy markets
- Connecting people in the region
- Better cooperation in fighting cross-border crime

Increase prosperity

- EUSBSR as a frontrunner for deepening and fulfilling the single market
- EUSBSR contributing to the implementation of Europe 2020 Strategy
- Improve global competitiveness of the Baltic Sea region
- Climate change adaptation, risk prevention and management

[22] Commission, 'Report from the Commission to the European Parliament, the Council, the European Economic and Social Committee and the Committee of the Regions on the Implementation of the EU Strategy for the Baltic Sea Region (EUSBSR)' COM(2011) 381 final. The Council agreed with these findings in its Conclusions on 15 November 2011.

[23] Commission, 'Baltic Sea Region' (n 9); European Council, 'Council conclusions on the completion of the review of the European Union Strategy for the Baltic Sea Region' (Luxembourg, 26 June 2012); and European Council, 'European Council 13–14 December 2012 Conclusions' (Brussels, 14 December 2012).

The Action Plan comprised 17 priority areas and five horizontal areas. The priority areas were: PA Agri, PA Bio, PA Crime, PA Culture, PA Education, PA Energy, PA Hazards, PA Health, PA Innovation, PA Internal Market, PA Nutri, PA Safe, PA Secure, PA Ship, PA SME, PA Tourism and PA Transport. The horizontal actions were: HA Involve, HA Neighbours, HA Promo, HA Spatial Planning and HA Sustainable development and Bio-economy.

The Action Plan was revised again in 2015 and updated in 2017. Both these versions kept the sub-objectives essentially intact. In the 2015 version of the Action Plan, the Priority Areas were renamed as Policy Areas and their number was reduced to 13 by merging some of them. The Policy Areas were PA Bioeconomy, PA Culture, PA Education, PA Energy, PA Hazards, PA Health, PA Innovation, PA Nutri, PA Safe, PA Secure, PA Ship, PA Tourism and PA Transport. The horizontal actions were HA Capacity, HA Climate, HA Neighbours and HA Spatial Planning.

The 2017 Action Plan version kept the same Policy Areas and Horizontal Actions.

During the negotiations that resulted in the adoption of the current version of the EUSBSR Action Plan (from 2021),[24] there was a lengthy discussion about whether the sub-objectives should be amended or removed. On the one hand, the sub-objectives were considered to be incompatible with many of the Policy Areas. Some of them were also outdated. On the other hand, they served to help in understanding the objectives of the Strategy. Finally, it was decided to include a list of the non-obsolete sub-objectives in the revised Action Plan.

The 2021 Action Plan includes the same 13 Policy Areas, but each of them includes fewer actions than in the past. All Horizontal Actions were discontinued. HA Spatial Planning became the fourteenth Policy Area. HA Climate change adaptation and mitigation and HA Cooperation with neighbouring non-EU countries were mainstreamed as essential elements into all the 14 Policy Areas. HA Capacity's tasks were included in the tasks of the new BSP.

C. Neighbouring Non-EU Countries

Unlike the other EU macro-regional strategies, the EUSBSR has only EU countries as members. The official EU documents do not include much information to explain why the EUSBSR should be limited to an EU internal strategy. All the essential preparation documents were based on this assumption.

However, from the very beginning the neighbouring non-EU countries of this macro-region were welcome to cooperate in EUSBSR projects and initiatives – not as members but as partners. This was already the message in the European

[24] Commission, 'Commission Staff Working Document EU Strategy for the Baltic Sea Region Action Plan [COM(2009) 248 final]' SWD(2021) 24 final.

Parliament's resolution in 2006 and in the European Council's conclusions of 2007.[25]

The Commission took the same view in its Communication in 2009,[26] where the importance of cooperating with the neighbours was well articulated. According to the Commission, the effectiveness of some of the proposed actions would be enhanced by continuing constructive cooperation with interested third countries in the region. The Commission also kept the neighbouring non-EU countries informed about the process from the beginning. The Council endorsed the Strategy in 2009, acknowledged its internal EU scope and noted that constructive cooperation with interested non-EU countries was most welcome.[27]

These positions were not changed in the later stages of the Strategy. They were repeated, even more strongly worded, in all Commission communications and reports, Council conclusions and other EU statements and documents.

During the launching phase of the Strategy, the idea was that the non-EU neighbouring countries would participate in its implementation through an existing *cooperation format*. According to the European Parliament's resolution in 2006, the Strategy would have been an internal part of the ND.[28] The European Council stated in 2007 that the ND framework provided the basis for the external aspects of cooperation in the Baltic Sea region.[29] Two years later, both the Commission and the Council were more flexible, stating that cooperation with non-EU neighbours could take place through existing well-functioning structures, notably but not exclusively within the ND.

By 2011, the list of suitable cooperation formats was longer. The Commission's first report on the implementation of the EUSBSR in 2011 stated that although the Strategy does not commit non-Member States, the three neighbouring non-EU countries most concerned – Russia, Norway and Belarus – had all indicated their support.[30] Cooperation with Russia had been pursued at several levels, including through the ND and existing regional bodies such as the CBSS and HELCOM. In its response to the report, the Council encouraged searching for the most relevant instruments and formats. Specifically, the ND, the CBSS, the Nordic Council of Ministers and HELCOM should serve as cooperation platforms, involving relevant partners, in particular the Russian Federation.[31]

[25] European Parliament, 'Northern Dimension' (n 5); and Council of the European Union, 'Presidency Conclusions' (2008) (n 6).

[26] Commission, 'Baltic Sea Region' (n 7); and SEC(2009) 712 accompanying the Communication (n 20).

[27] Council of the European Union, 'Council Conclusions' (2009) (n 21).

[28] European Parliament, 'Northern Dimension' (n 5).

[29] Council of the European Union, 'Presidency Conclusions' (2008) (n 6).

[30] Commission, 'Report from the Commission to the European Parliament, the Council, the European Economic and Social Committee and the Committee of the Regions' (22 June 2011).

[31] Council of the European Union, 'Council conclusions on the review of the European Union Strategy for the Baltic Sea Region' (Brussels, 15 November 2011).

The above list was not considered exhaustive. However, over time it became obvious that some of the neighbouring non-EU countries no longer considered it sufficient to participate through the ND, CBSS etc. Their citizens and organisations participated in EUSBSR projects, processes and in other initiatives and were willing to participate in the more strategic discussions too. As the Action Plan did not stipulate anything about the Steering Groups before 2021, some Policy Areas agreed to include representatives of non-EU neighbouring countries in them, as members or observers.

The Action Plan of 2021 also covers the Steering Groups, providing that a Steering Group may invite representatives of non-EU neighbouring countries or organisations to join the group as members or observers.

In its Communication of 2009, the Commission described the *geographical coverage* of the Strategy as follows: the Strategy covers the macro-region around the Baltic Sea. The specific scope depends on the topic. For example on economic issues it would involve all the countries in the region, on water quality issues it would involve the whole catchment area, etc. Overall, it would concern the eight EU Member States bordering the Baltic Sea. Close cooperation between the EU and Russia would also be necessary in order to tackle jointly many of the regional challenges. The same need for constructive cooperation applies also to Norway and Belarus.

However, the above list of non-EU cooperating neighbouring countries was not exhaustive either. Over time Iceland has been included in EUSBSR cooperation. It would also seem to allow the inclusion of Ukraine.

It was very clear from the very beginning that cooperation with the biggest non-EU neighbouring country Russia was especially important. This message was included in all the documents throughout the years.

The illegal occupation of Crimea by Russia in 2014 had only an indirect effect on the implementation of the EUSBSR through some stakeholders. For instance, the CBSS political level meetings – prime ministers and foreign ministers – were frozen.[32] The 2015 and 2017 EUSBSR Action Plans stipulated that although the EUSBSR is a strategy of the EU, it is clear that many of the issues can only be addressed by constructive cooperation with our external partners in the region, in particular Russia. As regards cooperation with Russia, developments in EU–Russia developments will be taken into account in accordance with the relevant Council and European Council conclusions.

In February 2022 when Russia invaded Ukraine there was an imminent reaction within the EUSBSR. Referring to the European Council conclusions of 24 February, 2022, the National Coordinators group decided to immediately suspend cooperation with the Russian Federation and the Republic of Belarus within the framework of the EUSBSR. According to the decision made on 9 March 2022, the National Coordinators Group will not support any actions

[32] See ch 8 by Allan Rosas and Petteri Vuorimäki in this volume.

of the Policy Areas of the EUSBSR that would include the Russian Federation and/or the Republic of Belarus as observers/partners/members of the Steering Groups of the Policy Areas and in any other capacity. The Policy Areas of the EUSBSR will also make sure that the cooperation to date be suspended with immediate effect and new partnerships with these countries will not be created. The National Coordinators Group will ensure the proper adjustment of the functioning of the EUSBSR in the changed circumstances.[33]

D. 'Three NOs Principle'

The governance of the EUSBSR is based on the so-called 'three NOs principle'. It means that there is no new EU funding, no new EU institutions and no new EU legislation. Thus, the implementation is supposed to be carried out within the existing EU legal framework, by the existing EU institutions and by utilising existing financial instruments and other resources.

This was not the idea of the European Parliament in 2006, which proposed that the Strategy would have its own budget line. The three NOs principle goes back to the Commission's consultations, when preparing its Communication of 2009. The conclusion drawn from the consultations was that numerous stakeholders were of the opinion that the Baltic Sea region already had enough cooperation structures and that one should avoid creating new ones that could impose added administrative overhead without contributing to effective action. Hence, the three NOs principle was included in the Commission's Communication in 2009, supported by the Council and endorsed by the European Council. Subsequently, the Council in particular has very strongly underlined this principle.

The principle has over the years led to misinterpretations. In the early days, even the Strategy's whole value and meaning could be called into question if and when it was perceived as just a new theoretical approach that had no significance in practice as it lacked everything normally expected from an efficient programme: a stable organisation, dedicated funding and a proper legal basis. Subsequently, the principle of the three NOs has rather had the opposite result: in other words it has led to an overly strict, literal interpretation of the principle.

For a long time, there was a damaging misinterpretation, according to which the EUSBSR could not have a secretariat. This argument was not valid, as a small, project-based secretariat or strategy point does not constitute a new *EU institution*. The other EU macro-regional strategies recognised this simple fact much earlier than the EUSBSR. The EU Strategy for the Danube Region (EUSDR) paved the way when the Danube Strategy Point was created in 2015.

[33] See: www.balticsea-region-strategy.eu/news-room/news/591323-statement-by-the-national-coordinators-group-of-the-eu-strategy-for-the-baltic-sea-region-concerning-the-suspension-of-cooperation-with-r.

Funding has always been one of the biggest challenges in the implementation of the EUSBSR. As the EUSBSR does not have specifically allocated financial resources, funding for operations under the Strategy has to come from existing financial instruments. The Interreg Baltic Sea Region Transnational Programme (Interreg BSR) has supported, and continues to support, the implementation of the Strategy, but its rather limited programme budget cannot cover all the needs of the Strategy. Furthermore, Interreg BSR has its own funding priorities. Although all its priorities are based on the Strategy's current Action Plan, they do not cover all of its Actions.

It is self-evident that the Strategy stakeholders need to mobilise additional funding sources. However, competition for project funding is fierce and the fact that all funding sources have their own eligibility rules and selection criteria does not help.

The funding problems have been known almost since the creation of the Strategy but, so far, no philosopher's stone has been found to solve them. Both the Commission and the Council have, time and again, underlined the importance of aligning the Strategy's priorities with relevant funding instruments.

A promising step forward was taken during the preparation of the EU long-term budget for the period 2021 to 2027, when funding for the EU macro-regional strategies was included in the mainstream European Structural and Investment Funds and in the EUSBSR Member State national programmes for implementing EU regional policy instruments. Unfortunately, the embedding process to facilitate the alignment of the Strategy priorities with the funding rules suffered from coordination and legitimacy problems within the EUSBSR governance. Assisting EUSBSR stakeholders in identifying relevant funding opportunities will be one of the main tasks of the new BSP.

Russia's military attack against Ukraine changed the situation suddenly regarding Interreg BSR and cross-border cooperation funding. Payments to Russian and Belarussian partners under ongoing programmes were immediately suspended, and Russian and Belarussian partners are no longer eligible for proposals for the 2021 to 2027 programming period.

E. Governance

The Commission Communication of 2009, as well as the accompanying Action Plan, did not pay much attention to governance and included only the most elementary aspects. However, quite soon after the launching of the EUSBSR, the Commission realised that the Strategy could not function well without a clear division of labour and firm leadership. Therefore, the Commission began to urge the EUSBSR Members States to take more responsibility and to lead the governance together with the Commission. The Members States' initial reaction was that they acknowledged the lack of leadership, but wanted to keep the Strategy governance anchored at the EU level as much as possible.

Finally, in 2014 the Commission and the Council agreed that the EUSBSR governance should be based on three levels and that the National Coordinators Group had to be strengthened to ensure appropriate leadership. However, this key element of the EUSBSR structure was not included in the Action Plan until 2021.

This chapter aims to describe more in detail how the EUSBSR governance developed.

According to the Commission Communication of 2009, the EUSBSR Member States would take care of the implementation of the Strategy, but the general strategic decisions would take place within the EU structures. The Commission would be responsible for coordinating, monitoring, reporting and facilitating implementation.

The Council endorsed the governance as part of the Strategy but asked the Commission to set up a high-level group with representation from all EU Member States, in order to assist the Commission in facilitating implementation. The group should be consulted about amendments to the Strategy and the Action Plan.[34] The High Level Group, an EU level body consisting of senior representatives from all EU Member States, was established accordingly.

In 2012, the Commission raised the problems caused by the non-existent *division of tasks* between the numerous EUSBSR stakeholders.[35] It also urged the National Coordinators to support the coordination and implementation of the Strategy not only in their respective home countries, but also at the overall level. The High Level Group would continue to ensure the EU-wide anchorage of the Strategy. The Council took note of the Roles and Responsibilities document, drafted by a working group with representatives of the Commission and EUSBSR Member States.[36] This document, which was included in the 2013 version of the Action Plan, did not solve the main problems – actually quite the contrary: it was complicated and unclear, especially regarding the leadership of the Strategy.

The Commission also highlighted the EUSBSR's governance problems in its report in 2013 on the added value of the macro-regional strategies.[37] In its view, the key to the future would be stronger leadership, reinforcing ownership in the regions concerned, delivering clear decision-making and greater visibility. The Commission would continue to play a key role. The choices must take into account issues of legitimacy, accountability and continuity. The Council underlined the responsibility and ownership of the Members States concerned and invited the Commission and the Member States to consider how to strengthen the role of the High Level Group using this forum for relevant policy-level discussion.[38]

[34] Council of the European Union, 'Council Conclusions' (2009) (n 21).
[35] Commission, 'Baltic Sea Region' (n 9).
[36] European Council, 'Council conclusions' (n 23).
[37] Commission, 'Report from the Commission' COM(2013) 468 final (n 10).
[38] European Council, 'Council Conclusions on the added value of macro-regional strategies' (Luxembourg, 22 October 2013).

In its report of 2014 concerning the governance of the macro-regional strategies,[39] the Commission continued in its efforts to persuade the Council to accept that the EUSBSR Member States would have to become more active. It proposed that the National Coordinators group would take on a leadership role in the EUSBSR, together with the Commission. It also described the cooperation within a macro-regional strategy as follows:

> Member States' and Commission's high political level, providing political commitment and strategic orientation; national coordinators, from each country, high level officials coordinating work at senior administrative level; experts, responsible for thematic priority areas, from each country, normally forming also a steering group.

The Council acknowledged that an improved governance required stronger political leadership and decision-making as well as greater clarity in the organisation of the work.[40] It also acknowledged the three governance levels: (i) political leadership and ownership; (ii) coordination; and (iii) implementation. These levels should be strengthened in order to ensure that the implementation of the strategies brings clear impacts and better results. The Council invited the Commission and the Member States to strengthen policy-level discussions by reinforcing the strategic roles of the High Level Group, and the National Coordinators to ensure strong leadership and ownership.

The Council also asked the Commission to refrain from setting up additional formal EU structures and encouraged the Commission and the Member States to better exploit and enhance the existing ones. This rather peculiar request was most probably a reflection of the Member States' strong desire to avoid adding to the administrative burden.

In 2014, the EUSBSR National Coordinators installed a rotating chairmanship, but the other elements of these Council conclusions were not implemented within the EUSBSR. The description of the roles and responsibilities of various actors remained essentially unchanged in the Action Plan versions of 2015 and 2017. The three levels of governance proposed by the Commission and acknowledged by the Council were not taken on board.

The Commission kept raising the problems of EUSBSR governance and the EUSBSR stakeholders kept complaining about weak governance and leadership, but no essential changes were made to the governance structures until the current Action Plan came into force in 2021.

[39] Commission, 'Report from the Commission to the European Parliament, the Council, the European Economic and Social Committee and the Committee of the Regions, concerning the governance of macro-regional strategies' COM(2014) 284 final.

[40] Council of the European Union, 'Council conclusions on the governance of macro-regional strategies' (Brussels, 28 November 2014).

F. Why the Achievements Have Not Met the Expectations

The complex cooperation and collaboration network within the Baltic Sea region has generally been a success story. It has achieved many, even most of its objectives. First and foremost, it has removed the barriers that kept the region apart before the 1990s. However, it is not easy to determine what the EUSBSR's contribution has been in this development.

The EUSBSR was a newcomer in the Baltic Sea regional cooperation architecture when it was launched in 2009. The main idea was not to compete with the existing cooperation formats, but rather to help these by offering a common platform, to avoid overlaps and to foster further cooperation and collaboration. Some of the older cooperation structures even hoped that the EUSBSR would help them in agreeing on a sensible division of tasks.

The Strategy was based on open and transparent participation. The EUSBSR's wide thematic coverage and the multi-level and cross-sectoral cooperation model provided opportunities for a wide range of stakeholders. Hence, the Strategy was successful in creating fairly quickly a common platform and engaging a wide range of stakeholders. With the EU's resources and soft power, the Strategy soon became a dominant cooperation platform in the region.

The assessment of the EUSBSR's success depends on what kind of achievements we have in mind. One can for instance make a distinction between process and general achievements, on the one hand, and more concrete and substantive achievements on the other.[41]

There is a wide consensus among EUSBSR stakeholders that the Strategy has been successful and that its *general achievements* have been outstanding. They have been visible even in the early years, but the Strategy has also continued to improve its performance over time. The outcomes relating to these activities mostly concern a strengthened exchange of experience and improved contacts between the region's stakeholders. The key value added has been to bring together new actors across different sectors and countries, especially by increasing the cross-sectoral cooperation and supporting multi-level governance. The engagement of regions and municipalities is appreciated, as is also the increased interaction with Commission services. From a more general perspective, the Strategy has contributed to making the EU more visible and closer to its citizens in this part of the Union.

All in all, a positive evaluation of the EUSBSR's general and process outcomes is also prevalent in academic circles. However, there are also critical opinions, concerning, inter alia, the maturity of the Strategy and the capacity of its stakeholders.

[41] In the Commission, 'Study on Macro-regional Strategies' (n 4), these are called process achievements and content achievements.

The assessments of the Strategy's *substantive achievements* vary. Quite a few of them are less favourable than those regarding general achievements. The overall assessment is that there are some very successful Policy Areas and that all Policy Areas have made at least some progress and achieved some results. However, the governance framework of the Strategy has been poor and has hindered the work of the Policy Areas. Therefore, the Strategy's substantive achievements do not quite match the expectations.

In its 2020 biannual report on the implementation of EU macro-regional strategies, the Commission expressed satisfaction with the EUSBSR's achievements but urged a reform of the Strategy's governance structures. According to the report, the Strategy has brought significant results in such diverse areas as innovation, safety and pollution prevention of maritime transport, preparedness for maritime emergencies and a reduction in plastic and air pollution. The Strategy has also contributed to shaping and developing policies on energy, navigation, environment and climate change. Furthermore, the Commission expressed confidence that all the EU macro-regional strategies could and would be of help in combating the severe impacts caused by the Covid-19 pandemic.[42]

The problem of weak governance hindering the achievement of substantive results, measuring these and communicating about them has been a feature of the EUSBSR for a long time. This was well described in a 2017 study commissioned by the Commission Directorate General for Regional and Urban Policy (DG REGIO), covering all the EU macro-regional strategies.[43] While the study presented quite a positive assessment of the EUSBSR's achievements, it strongly criticised the Strategy's poor governance.

The Strategy's achievements were said to be numerous, but difficult to accumulate and synthesise. For instance, when comparing the achievements with the EUSBSR's objectives, all Policy Areas show progress. However, when comparing the performance of the Policy Areas against the specific EUSBSR targets, only some Policy Areas have reached the targets set in the Action Plan. Many targets are broadly formulated, with limited monitoring and no milestones defined. Moreover, external factors have a significant influence and it is not clear that there is a direct link between the activities of the Policy Areas and the selected indicators.

The study also gave an additional explanation to the rather limited number of substantive achievements of the Strategy. It proposed a model to describe how a macro-regional strategy, like any other governance arrangement, undergoes successive phases of development: Phase I relates to the capacity of the internal strategy actors. In Phase II there is development of institutional capacity and performance of the internal strategy actors managing the strategy, as well as capacity of the external stakeholders to respond to the strategy. In Phase III the internal

[42] Commission, 'Report from the Commission to the European Parliament, the Council, the European Economic and Social Committee and the Committee of the Regions on the implementation of EU macro-regional strategies' COM(2020) 578 final.

[43] Commission, 'Study on Macro-regional Strategies' (n 4).

and external stakeholders and the whole region are implementing relevant actions to the macro-regional strategy, and their contribution becomes visible through the achievements of the respective objectives.

According to this model, it is generally only in Phase III that Policy Areas can produce tangible results which are visible to outsiders as well. The study argued that most of the EUSBSR's Policy Areas have not yet reached Phase III and that they therefore have not been able to achieve the tangible results expected of them. Therefore, the Strategy's monitoring and reporting mechanism should recognise the existence of these phases and adjust the indicators and milestones accordingly.

The lack of maturity of the Strategy has also drawn the attention of researchers. For instance, Zauha et al draw a distinction between, on the one hand, issues which require macro-regional cooperation, consisting of duties typically handled by public authorities that must be performed at a supranational level and, on the other, transaction costs, whose coverage might trigger private sector actions and self-reinforcing processes of development.[44] The latter is a much more subtle type of intervention involving the steering of private interactions across national borders. Unfortunately, the EUSBSR is still – after more than 10 years in existence – at an initial stage of delivery of public benefits. The private sector actions remain a pending challenge.

Towards the end of the EU financing period of 2014 to 2020, it became even more obvious than ever that the implementation of the EUSBSR did not function as anticipated. Most of the criticism – although not all – was aimed at the weak governance of the Strategy. The challenges mentioned most often by stakeholders and researchers, were the following:

- Too broad substantive scope
- Lack of focus and results-orientation
- Fading political support
- Lack of strategic leadership and approach
- Insufficient ownership of some key players
- Not enough visibility for the Strategy
- Complicated governance structure
- Unclear roles and responsibilities of stakeholders
- No administrative help and no institutional memory
- No proper monitoring, reporting and evaluation framework
- Ad hoc approach with regard to collection and maintenance of project results
- Unhelpful flagship definition, with this label offering no guarantee of quality

[44] Zaucha et al (n 17).

- Capacity building not tailored to the needs of stakeholders
- Lack of funding, especially long-term funding
- Lack of human resources
- Too limited private sector participation

IV. Addressing Challenges in the Revised EUSBSR Action Plan of 2021

A. Background

Following the updating of the Action Plan in 2017, there was consensus among the stakeholders that a new, more profound revision was required. The broad substantive scope of the Strategy had been addressed in 2015, but the number of priorities still remained very high. The governance structure needed urgent attention, and the EU's new strategic frameworks as well as the orientations of the forthcoming 2021–2027 Multiannual Financial Framework had to be taken into account. Furthermore, the Action Plan needed to be amended to cover the UN Sustainable Development Goals and to take into account emerging global challenges, such as climate change, pandemics, demographic changes and migration.

The Commission's DG REGIO started the revision process by making an analysis of the future needs of the Strategy. New Actions were defined by the Policy Area Coordinators (PACs), in cooperation with their respective Steering Groups, expert networks and the Commission services. The National Coordinators Group, including the Commission representative, planned and lead the revision process and drafted the general and governance parts of the revised Action Plan.

The Action Plan was thoroughly reformed, to address the above-mentioned long-standing challenges. The most profound changes were made to the governance part of the Action Plan. The whole text was drafted to be as concise and clear as possible, to be easy to use. The number of pages was reduced from 176 to 77.

B. More Focus and Reinforced Results-Orientation

The revised Action Plan adopted in 2021 is more focused than the previous ones. There was no appetite to merge two or more Policy Areas because some of the former mergers had not been successful. Poor indicators and poor substance reporting also did not provide the basis for an objective comparison and a possible discontinuation of some Policy Areas based on their achievements.

Therefore, the solution was to keep all the Policy Areas but reduce the number of Actions per Policy Area. As a result, the total number of Actions was reduced from 73 to 44.

Given the well-established need for realistic, measurable and informative indicators and a well-functioning monitoring and evaluation framework, indicators were defined for all Actions and activities in the Action Plan. Indicators had been included in earlier versions of the EUSBSR Action Plan (as from 2013). However, this time more efforts were spent on this task, and the PACs and their respective Steering Groups were offered support by a consultant in this work.

Under the revised Action Plan the achievements of the Policy Areas will be monitored and evaluated more thoroughly than before, and the results of this evaluation will have effects on the future prospects of the Policy Areas. The Commission will continue its biannual reports on progress made in implementation of all EU macro-regional strategies. In addition, there will be a new overall monitoring and evaluation framework within the EUSBSR. The PACs prepare and their Steering Committees endorse work plans and annual substance reports. The substance reports are expected to provide more factual evidence of the Policy Areas' actual achievements and value added than what has been available in the past.

C. Baltic Sea Strategy Point

As mentioned above, the governance and implementation of the Strategy has been hampered by the weak management capacity and a lack of institutional memory. Therefore, one of the most essential novelties introduced in the Action Plan of 2021 is the creation of the long-desired secretariat for the Strategy: the project-based Baltic Sea Strategy Point (BSP). It was created in order to enhance the Strategy's governance, leadership, implementation and results-orientation. It should provide administrative and technical support, institutional memory and communication and coordinate capacity building measures.

The BSP's main tasks are set out in the Action Plan. The Strategy Point is guided by and accountable to the National Coordinators Group, which decides on its priorities and detailed tasks. Its day-to-day work is conducted in close contact with the presidency of the National Coordinators Group.

The role and set-up of the BSP are largely based on the model of the Strategy Point of the EUSDR. The development of the EUSDR Strategy Point experienced several challenges that required adjusting the role of this function. In light of this experience, the EUSDR Strategy Point recommended that it should be made very clear that the EUSBSR Strategy Point is a supporting body, not another autonomous actor within the EUSBSR governance structure. This recommendation formed the basis for an important assessment criterion for the EUSBSR's National Coordinators Group in the selection process of the BSP implementation organisation.

D. Clear Roles and Responsibilities, Effective Leadership and Decision-Making

It is inevitable that a governance structure of such a multifaceted strategy is somewhat complicated. However, the structure can still be reasonably easy to comprehend if its main components and rules are clear, logical and transparent.

In the EUSBSR the three governance levels have been clear and logical since 2014, but they were not reflected properly in the versions of the EUSBSR Action Plan produced before 2021. This has led to misunderstandings and inefficiencies, especially regarding the division of tasks and the leadership of the Strategy. The current Action Plan aims at providing clear roles and responsibilities of the various actors and enabling effective leadership, decision-making and implementation.

The three levels of governance, acknowledged by the Council as early as 2014, form the basis of the revised Action Plan.

The *first* of them consists of the Member States and Commission at the political level, providing political commitment and strategic orientation. As the EUSBSR Members State ministers do not convene separately to discuss the Strategy, the political level commitment and strategic orientations are most often included in the Council conclusions. This method is also used to decide on amendments to the Strategy.[45] Another platform where politicians – ministers, commissioners, parliamentarians etc – show their commitment is the EUSBSR Annual Forum, but it is not a decision-making body.

The *second* level is the National Coordinators Group, consisting of senior representatives of all the EUSBSR Member States. This is the core decision-making body within the governance structure of the EUSBSR, acting as its executive board. It works closely with the Commission (DG REGIO), whose representative also participates in its meetings.

The group's tasks include general leadership, coordination and development of the Strategy. It establishes priorities and represents the Strategy in its overall relations. It ensures the development of the modes of operation. It also ensures that the implementation rules in force, including the operational framework and detailed guidance about the modes of operation, are published on the EUSBSR website.[46] The current guidance on modes of operation was approved by the National Coordinators Group on 11 May 2021.

Before the publication of the 2021 Action Plan, some expected the core decision-making body on the second governance level (government officials) to be the High Level Group. This misunderstanding is understandable, as this was indeed an idea discussed in the early days of the Strategy.

[45] Amendments to the Strategy need to be adopted by the Council. The Council does not adopt or endorse Action Plans, although it has sometimes taken note of them.

[46] See: www.balticsea-region-strategy.eu.

However, the High Level Group is an EU-level body, consisting of senior officials of all EU Member States and the non-EU countries that are members of one or more EU macro-regional strategies. Most of the representatives in the group are their respective countries' National Coordinators.

The High Level Group convenes normally only once a year and is therefore not flexible and quick enough to serve as a hands-on governing body of the EUSBSR. In particular, after the launch of the other three macro-regional strategies, the High-Level Group has concentrated on common questions of interest to all the EU macro-regional strategies. It advises the Commission on the coordination and monitoring of these. It is also a forum where the approaches and practices of the strategies are compared, in order to encourage mutual learning and to maximise the leverage and impact of the strategies. However, the High Level Group can also provide overall strategic guidance for individual strategies such as the EUSBSR. The group is also consulted on modifications of the Action Plans.

The *third* governance level consists of the experts implementing the Strategy within the thematic Policy Areas. Their governance consists of PACs and their respective Steering Groups. It is at this level we also find all the stakeholders and participants of the Policy Areas' numerous unofficial groups, networks, platforms, projects and processes.

The PACs are key actors in terms of the functioning and success of the Strategy. Their basic roles have not changed in the revised Action Plan, but they will now be expected to cooperate more closely with their Steering Groups. The most essential new elements in their tasks are the work plans and annual substantial reports, which constitute key parts of the new monitoring and reporting framework.

Even in the past, most of the Policy Areas had a Steering Group, but the tasks of these groups were not properly described or harmonised. The groups were also chaired by the PACs and could therefore not provide independent assessments of the performance of PACs. The current Action Plan made Steering Groups obligatory and gave them two main tasks: supporting the respective PACs in fulfilling their tasks, and monitoring and evaluating the Policy Area, including endorsing the work plans and annual substantial reports.

A Steering Group member also performs the tasks of a *focal point* in his or her home country, regarding the respective Policy Area(s). The separate focal point tasks were discontinued to simplify the governance structure.

A large number – maybe even most – of the stakeholders at the third governance level come from backgrounds other than national governments. They are local and regional officials or working for national, international, or pan-Baltic organisations, universities, civil society organisations etc. Stakeholders from neighbouring non-EU countries can also participate in the cooperation.

The *Commission* continues to play a key role within the Strategy although it does not participate in its day-to-day governance as much as before. The change in the Commission's DG REGIO's role had begun some years before the latest revision of the Action Plan started. The Commission still provides strategic coordination and advice to the National Coordinators Group regarding the management and development of the Strategy. DG REGIO, as well as other Directorates General, also provide guidance and facilitation to EUSBSR stakeholders within the Policy Areas.

The role of the *Annual Forums* did not change in the current Action Plan. The Forum is not a decision-making body. Its purpose is to communicate achievements, to stimulate policy discussions, to disseminate results and to provide stakeholders with a major networking occasion and to enhance the visibility of this form of macro-regional cooperation.

E. Empowering Stakeholders and Increasing their Ownership

The aim of the Action Plan is to empower all actors to take over and fully implement their roles and responsibilities. A clear division of labour and more concretely formulated Actions create the necessary basis for productive work. Another way of empowerment is to give stakeholders more flexibility in implementation with fewer and less detailed rules.

The Policy Areas are free to choose the format of the activities implemented under each Action to best suit the needs of the Action, in accordance with the operational framework and guidance published on the EUSBSR website.

This freedom differs very much from previous thinking, where the aim was to limit the actions and activities to a precisely described mode of operation, called 'flagships'. The designation process of flagships was complicated and slow. A flagship needed to be recommended by the respective Commission Directorate General and endorsed by the National Coordinators Group. And still, in practice, a flagship designation was not always a guarantee of quality and therefore over time lost much of its credibility and ability to mobilise funding.

The term 'flagship project' had already been included in the first Action Plan of 2009, which presented examples of flagship projects, described as projects with high significance. At that time there were no rules regarding their modes of operation. These were developed later.

According to the current Action Plan, a Policy Area can continue to use the flagship concept. The National Coordinators Group's guidance, published on the Strategy's website, stipulates only that a flagship must be aimed at implementing particularly essential parts of one or several Actions of one or several Policy Areas. The decision on using the designation of flagship is taken by the Policy Area's Steering Group. The Policy Area is advised to notify the Commission, but the National Coordinators Group's endorsement is no longer required.

Furthermore, one of the key challenges of the EUSBSR has been the lack of ownership of the Strategy on the part of the EUSBSR Member State line ministries. This has been a serious problem as the line ministries are vital in implementing the Strategy. The current Action Plan aims at increasing their ownership by strengthening the role of the Steering Groups and the line ministries' role within the Steering Groups.

In the revised Action Plan, each Policy Area has a Steering Group, consisting of representatives of the national or regional governments of the EUSBSR Member States. These should come from key ministries or authorities in the relevant field and have sufficient capability, mandate and resources to fulfil their tasks. The objective is that all Steering Groups include members from all EUSBSR Member States. However, a Member State can choose not to participate in a specific Steering Group. A Steering Group should convene at least twice a year and its presidency should rotate among its members, normally on an annual basis.

The Steering Group members have two kinds of task. On the one hand, they represent their governments in their respective Steering Groups. On the other hand, they perform their tasks as focal points at the national level. The aim is an efficient flow of information in both directions allowing the Member States' views to be taken into account within Policy Areas and the Policy Areas' needs and achievement to be taken into account in the Member States' national policies.

F. Multi-Level Governance

The Strategy has been of interest throughout its existence because of its experimental governance model. The interest has grown over time. Some even seem to think that multi-level governance as such is the most essential part of the EUSBSR.

It is true that multi-level governance has been a strength for the EUSBSR, in more ways than one. Its strategic approach helps to achieve more and better results by pooling existing resources. It has been proved to function and achieve results. The Strategy also has effects at a more general level. The fact that it engages with a wide range of stakeholders to network, collaborate and cooperate makes the EU more visible and closer to its citizens.

In 2009, the Strategy's multi-level governance was new and experimental. Now it has matured and its governance and implementation modalities have developed. One clear trend is that the opportunities for various stakeholders to participate in the implementation and development of the Strategy have increased.

As an internal EU strategy, the EUSBSR has always limited decision-making at the first two governance levels solely to the EUSBSR or EU Member States and the Commission. The fact that previous versions of the EUSBSR Action Plan did not properly reflect this limitation has caused some misunderstandings.

According to the current Action Plan, representatives of other countries, organisations and cooperation formats can be invited by the presidency to participate in the National Coordinators Group meetings on an ad hoc basis, but they cannot participate in the decision-making. The group can of course also invite experts.

Hence, most of the other stakeholders' participation takes place at the third governance level, in the Policy Areas with their projects, processes, platforms and other networks. It is also possible for stakeholders to become a PAC or member of the Steering Committee. Over the years, the situation has changed so that PAC tasks are increasingly handled by actors other than ministries, such as regional governments, municipalities, pan-Baltic or NGOs.

As explained above, the Steering Groups consist of representatives of the national or regional governments of the EUSBSR Member States. The composition was designed in order to increase the ownership of the line ministries and to ensure the flow of information between the EUSBSR Member States and the Strategy stakeholders. The Steering Groups endorse by consensus their respective Policy Area's work plans and annual reports.

However, the composition of Steering Groups was not designed to exclude other stakeholders. A Steering Group may invite representatives of non-EU neighbouring countries and organisations to join the group as members or observers, upon a decision taken by consensus by the EUSBSR Member State representatives in the group and endorsed by the National Coordinators Group. They cannot block the decisions of the EUSBSR Member States, but they may choose to opt out of specific decisions.

Furthermore, the above applies to the official Steering Group meetings, which convene to endorse work plans and annual reports. If there are interested stakeholders within the Policy Area, a Steering Group can hold informal meetings with a broader composition. The PACs can also initiate other kinds of expert groups and networks.

The Annual Forums are of course excellent platforms for all stakeholders and other interested parties to obtain and share information and to network.

G. Legitimacy and Accountability

As explained before, the EUSBSR is not a legal entity but a rather loose political framework. Its governance has until recently been weak and complicated. This has led to misunderstandings, especially regarding leadership and the division of roles and tasks. Some stakeholders have even disputed the division of the Strategy into three governance levels and the authority of the bodies representing the Member States, such as the National Coordinators Group and the High Level Group.

The weak governance may also have led some to think that normal requirements, such as the obligation to comply with the Strategy or with legal principles of legitimacy and accountability, may not apply. This is of course not true: they do apply at all times. The importance of the EUSBSR governance to be based on legitimacy and accountability has been underlined by both the Commission and the Council.[47]

[47] Commission, 'Report from the Commission' COM(2013) 468 final (n 10); and European Council, 'Council Conclusions' (n 38).

The current Action Plan was drafted to be as clear, transparent and understandable as possible, in order to help all actors to apply the Strategy and the legal principles of legitimacy and accountability.

H. Political Support

One of the biggest challenges of the Strategy is its fading political support. In the beginning, during the initiation and launching phase, the Strategy received a lot of high-level political attention in the EUSBSR Member States. However, quite soon the political interest was directed elsewhere, to new initiatives and challenges.

Both the Commission and the Council recognised this challenge and several times urged the EUSBSR Member States to maintain their political commitment in the longer term and to translate it into institutional and administrative support, with sufficient staffing and continuity of personnel. They also recommended ministerial and other political level meetings to take place, for instance to be included in the respective Council agendas or arranged separately or in the margins of some other assemblies.[48]

In recent years, EUSBSR Member State politicians have most often been directly involved with the Strategy when addressing the Annual Forums. The stakeholders appreciate their participation very much. Most of them would like the EUSBSR to follow the example of the EUSDR by arranging ministerial meetings back-to-back with the Annual Forums. This would be easier to achieve if the Annual Forums were organised in the country holding the EUSBSR presidency.

There may be several reasons why political ownership and support have faded. The revised Action Plan may help tackle one of these. Politicians expect results – concrete measurable results and not only networking, no matter how useful that might be. To date, there have been too few tangible results, which would have been easy to demonstrate and understand.

We all know that the Strategy has achieved results. It has brought, and keeps bringing, people together and closer to the EU. It makes the EU more visible to citizens. There are also some concrete substantive results, but most of these are technical or otherwise difficult to describe to non-experts. And – first and foremost – there is a multitude of results we do not know about because the Strategy's monitoring and reporting framework has not been what it should have been.

This is a kind of vicious circle. If the Strategy cannot report reasonable results, it risks losing political ownership and support. After having lost them, the Strategy will not get the resources to try harder.

The current Action Plan's answers to this problem are more focus and more result-orientation. The new monitoring and evaluating framework with measurable indicators should help to show results. This will be important in order

[48] Council of the European Union, 'Council conclusions' (n 31); European Council, 'Council conclusions' (n 23); and European Council, 'Council Conclusions' (n 38).

to safeguard and sustain the political support required to continue this macro-regional cooperation framework into the next EU long-term budget period.

V. Conclusion

My conclusion is the old cliché: nothing is as permanent as constant change. Based on the documents relating to the birth and development of the EUSBSR, it seems safe to conclude that at the beginning nobody really knew what kind of platform the Strategy was going to become. In the early days, it was in search of itself, and, in terms of substance, it found a purpose, at least to some extent. Unfortunately, for too long weak governance prevented the Strategy from achieving more concrete results.

It is impossible to say much about the future. The only certainty we have is that it will include surprises. Regarding the Strategy, it is now time to leave the governance debate for a while and concentrate on implementation. The Policy Areas and stakeholders now have a few years to achieve results.

Competition for resources will most probably become fiercer. The future of the Strategy may be at stake when preparations for the next EU multiannual financing period start in 2025/26. This may also trigger an even stronger focus with fewer Policy Areas. The Strategy must be able to persuade the relevant decision-makers that it is worth keeping. It needs to show real, measurable results.

In any case, the Strategy has to prepare for the next financing period, which begins in 2028. That process needs to begin well beforehand. The Action Plan needs to be updated or revised. It may be a good idea to consider whether the Strategy itself needs some updating too.

5

Baltic Sea Cooperation after the Cold War: How Sub-Regional Organisations Deal with Critical Junctures*

STEFAN GÄNZLE, NINA TYNKKYNEN AND KRISTINE KERN

I. Introduction

How international organisations adapt to external challenges is one of the core questions posed by scholars of both international relations and public administration. Historical institutionalism, for example, seeks to grasp the dynamics unleashed by fundamental ruptures and during 'windows of opportunity'. External challenges in the guise of 'critical junctures'[1] often create the starting point for new path-dependent processes. Junctures are precisely '"critical" because they place institutional arrangements on paths or trajectories, which are then very difficult to alter'.[2] More recent research has gauged the extent to which organisations become more robust vis-à-vis external challenges and stress, with the aim of (self-)protecting the internal organisational integrity.[3] Public administration scholarship has joined this debate by considering how transnational and international public organisations face turbulence, situations 'where events, demands and support interact and change in highly variable, inconsistent, unexpected or

* This chapter is an updated version of Stefan Gänzle, Kristine Kern & Nina Tynkkynen (2022): 'Governing the Baltic Sea Region at critical junctures (1991–2021): How do transnational and intergovernmental organizations cope with external regional change?', *Journal of Baltic Studies*, DOI: 10.1080/01629778.2022.2140356. *Thanks to Taylor & Francis.*

[1] G Capoccia and R Kelemen, 'The Study of Critical Junctures: Theory, Narrative, and Counterfactuals in Historical Institutionalism' (2007) 59 *World Politics* 341.

[2] P Pierson, *Politics in Time: History, Institutions, and Social Analysis* (Princeton, NJ, Princeton University Press, 2004) 135.

[3] On 'resilience' in the EU, see eg, J Joseph, *Varieties of Resilience, Studies on Governmentality* (Cambridge, Cambridge University Press, 2018).

unpredictable ways'.[4] To understand the internal coping mechanisms, it is necessary to 'unbox' organisations in their efforts to cope with turbulence.

This chapter contributes to this unboxing by exploring intergovernmental and transnational network organisations in the Baltic Sea Region (BSR). We ask how three prominent regional organisations – the intergovernmental Council of the Baltic Sea States (CBSS) and two transnational network organisations, the Helsinki Commission for the Protection of the Marine Environment of the Baltic Sea (HELCOM) and the Union of Baltic Cities (UBC, particularly its Sustainable Cities Commission UBC SCC) – have responded to significant critical junctures affecting the region ranging from the demise of the Soviet Union 1991–92, to Russia's invasion of Ukraine in 2022.

As the fault line between the West and the East, the BSR has experienced several (geo)political changes over time, which have impacted the transnational space and organisations.[5] 'Europeanisation', in other words, the expansion of EU-centred political transformation in Europe,[6] increased since Sweden and Finland, and the three Baltic states and Poland, became European Union (EU) members in 1995 and 2004, respectively. Strategies and policies aimed at facilitating regional collaboration – including the Northern Dimension (ND) Initiative in 1997, which morphed into a common policy in the EU, Iceland, Norway, and Russia in 2006, and the launch of the EU Strategy for the Baltic Sea Region (EUSBSR) in 2009 – presented yet another important step towards Europeanisation, with an effort to also engage the Russian Federation closer into regional cooperation. Then again, the region has been affected by the changing foundations of the EU–Russia relationship after the so-called Ukraine crisis that started in 2014 and escalated into a full-scale war on 24 February 2022.[7] This has led to the subsequent endorsement of mutual sanction regimes and a *zeitenwende* in several countries such as Germany, Finland and Sweden,[8] following Russia's war in Ukraine in 2022. Because of this unilateral aggression, the country's membership in all regional organisations under scrutiny has been affected in very different ways.[9] Whereas Russian membership in the UBC has been in decline for many years (with the last remaining cities deprived of membership in the aftermath of the Russian invasion), Russia is still formally part of the HELCOM organisation

[4] C Ansell and J Trondal, 'Governing Turbulence: An Organizational Institutional Agenda' (2018) 1 *Perspectives on Public Management and Governance* 43, 43.

[5] See, eg, J Metzger and P Schmitt, 'When Soft Spaces Harden the EU Strategy for the BSR' (2012) 44 *Environment and Planning A* 263.

[6] JP Olsen, 'The Many Faces of Europeanization' (2002) 40 *Journal of Common Market Studies* 921.

[7] The chapter was mainly written before Russia's invasion of Ukraine (February 2022); it was revised May–June 2022. The focus is therefore on the pre-war situation with some remarks on the current situation.

[8] Part of the puzzle is the impact of NATO expansion in the region, first to include Poland in 1999 and then the three Baltic states in 2004 which occurred in sync with the EU enlargement. Currently, the situation is further exacerbated by the imminent bid of Finland and Sweden for NATO membership because of Russia's war in Ukraine.

[9] See T Etzold, 'Auf Eis gelegt: Die regionale Zusammenarbeit in Nordeuropa distanziert sich von Russland' (*Vifanord*, 4 April 2022), available at: portal.vifanord.de/blog/auf-eis-gelegt-die-regionale-zusammenarbeit-in-nordeuropa-distanziert-sich-von-russland/.

in legal terms; the CBSS, in turn, was among the first international organisations to suspend Russian membership in early March 2022 which eventually triggered Russia's formal withdrawal from the organisation in May 2022 (see further below).

For the purpose of our chapter, we consider the following junctures as critical and of paramount importance: the end of the East–West conflict 1989–91; the EU's enlargement of 1995 and 2004, flanked by conciliatory policy attempts vis-à-vis Russia; and the geopolitical implications of the Ukraine crisis since 2014. One could argue that the end of the Soviet Union provided ample opportunities for expanding interdependence among the various actors of the BSR, whereas the fallout of the war in Ukraine seemed to reduce the conditions for 'positive interdependence'.[10] Although these processes often overlap and continue in parallel, we use them as empirical yardsticks to indicate a major change in the overall geopolitical context. We introduce organisational perspectives in a systematic and comparative way, focus on key features of the three organisations, and examine how they have been impacted externally and over different scales of transnational governance.

The chapter leans on document analysis of various reports, meeting minutes and memorandums of the organisations. The empirical data include a dozen interviews with current or former representatives of the organisations conducted from 2014 to 2020. The semi-structured interviews have primarily been used as supplementary material to validate our assessments of institutional developments along core organisational characteristics, such as membership and policy scope. While we have primarily relied on primary and secondary sources, we were particularly interested in distilling evidence from our material on how these actors have adjusted to these periods of critical junctures.

II. A Historical Institutionalist Approach: Intergovernmental and Transnational Network Organisations and Exogenous Change

The transnational sphere today includes states, intergovernmental organisations, non-governmental organisations (NGOs) and transnational network organisations (TNOs). Consequently, governance in transnational spaces 'is not exclusively the product of the bureaucratic action of state and local governments … It is also undertaken by international organisations, corporate actors, NGOs, and other network actors that coalesce into transnational policy communities'.[11]

[10] See the various contributions on the concept in K Raik and A Rácz, *Post-Crimea shift in EU–Russia Relations: From Fostering Interdependence to Managing Vulnerabilities* (Tallinn, International Centre for Defence and Security, 2019).

[11] D Stone and K Moloney, 'The Rise of Global Policy and Transnational Administration' in D Stone and K Moloney (eds), *The Oxford Handbook of Global Policy and Transnational Administration* (Oxford, Oxford University Press, 2019) 4.

Whereas HELCOM and the UBC clearly qualify as TNOs, we conceive of the CBSS as an intergovernmental organisation with still strong anchorage in the (neo)realist order with states as the main actors. Although the CBSS has undergone significant institutional change in the highly transnational environment of the BSR, its treatment as an intergovernmental organisation is fully in line with its perception as an intergovernmental platform for the region. TNOs, in contrast, link autonomous and independent actors and form a larger entity based on mechanisms for cooperation and coordination of their members beyond the nation states. Both transnational network organisations as well intergovernmental organisations can be either general-purpose or specific-purpose, and they may focus on a broad range of issues or be task-specific on exclusive issues, such as environmental protection.

We depart from a historical institutionalist analysis of which the theoretical perspective of critical junctures is 'an essential building block'.[12] The concept seeks to explain how geopolitical change can become a catalyst for positive and negative institutional developments.[13] Critical junctures have been defined 'as *relatively* short periods of time during which there is a *substantially* heightened probability that agents' choices will affect the outcome of interest'.[14] Some scholars conceive critical junctures as episodes of political and institutional challenge during which the agency decides to set an institution on a new developmental path.[15] Contrary to crisis, but like research on 'turbulence',[16] the emphasis here is on transformation.

The institutional adjustments made during turbulent times often have long-lasting effects. Therefore, critical junctures deviations from the established institutional path typically are triggered by some sort of major political, economic, social, or security disruption. A simple typology of sources of change within international organisations, be they intergovernmental, non-governmental, or transnational network organisations, distinguishes between exogenous and endogenous sources of change.[17] To eventually explain organisational change, we are interested in changes in the transnational space in which the organisations are embedded. In general, these kinds of changes in the external environment affect international organisations in somewhat contradictory ways. Key characteristics of the regional organisation in question – its goals and instruments, governance

[12] Capoccia and Kelemen (n 1) 341.

[13] K Calder and M Ye, 'Regionalism and Critical Junctures: Explaining the "Organization Gap"' (2004) 4 *Journal of East Asian Studies* 191.

[14] Capoccia and Kelemen (n 1) 348.

[15] G Capoccia, 'Critical Junctures and Institutional Change' in J Mahoney and K Thelen (eds), *Advances in Comparative Historical Analysis in the Social Sciences* (Cambridge, Cambridge University Press, 2015).

[16] Ansell and Trondal (n 4).

[17] D Kapur, 'Processes of Change in International Organizations' in D Nayyar (ed), *Governing Globalization: Issues and Institutions* (Oxford, Oxford University Press, 2002).

and financial structure – shape the specific trajectory of change consequent to exogenous changes together with the 'precipitating factors driving change'.[18] Although we identify three junctures as critical in the context of our study to which it provides structural background, our analysis focuses on a historical institutionalist account rather than engaging with critical junctures theory – and its emphasis on the importance of counterfactuals.[19] Our core question is: what kinds of changes have occurred in terms of the subsequent organisational development that can be attributed to critical junctures? We assume that organisational factors, such as the overall character as an intergovernmental or TNO and its aims as a specific-purpose or general-purpose organisation, play a significant role.

We focus on the evolution of the key organisational characteristics: legal status, organisational structure, objectives, main issue areas, leadership and funding schemes, and how these aspects evolved over time amidst the exogenous changes that have taken place in the BSR since the early 1990s. We have selected three major regional organisations active in the BSR, which ultimately represent four cases (see Table 1): (1) the CBSS as a general-purpose intergovernmental organisation of regional nation-states including Iceland, Norway and Russia, as well as the EU Member States of the region; (2) HELCOM as a specific-purpose organisation focusing on protecting the Baltic Sea marine environment with the same types of members, ie, nation states in the BSR, including Russia and the EU; (3) the UBC as a general-purpose organisation with cities as members, including many coastal cities around the Baltic Sea; and (4) the UBC SCC as a specific-purpose organisation working with UBC member cities as well as cities that are not (or no longer) members of the UBC. For reasons of space constraints and lack of research data commensurate to that accumulated in the three other instances, we could not include the case of the Baltic Sea States Subregional Co-operation network (BSSSC) or some other organisation which, as noted, are many in the case of the BSR. Perhaps our approach inspires other scholars to address this desideratum in terms of future research.

Table 1 Organisational scale and scope of the studied TNOs

	Organisational scope	
Organisational scale	**General-purpose**	**Specific-purpose**
Nation states	Council of Baltic Sea States (CBSS)	Helsinki Commission (HELCOM)
Subnational authorities	Union of the Baltic Cities (UBC)	UBC Sustainable Cities Commission (SCC)

Source: Own compilation.

[18] ibid.
[19] Capoccia and Kelemen (n 1).

The organisations were selected as they represent important instances of regional cooperation at different levels and are often mentioned as indicators of network governance in the BSR.[20,21,22,23] Regarding membership, the studied organisations concentrate on national and sub-national governance in the region, including Iceland and Norway in the case of the CBSS. Norway does not border the Baltic Sea, but it was a founding member of the CBSS, and Norwegian cities (Bergen, Kristiansand) became founding members of the UBC.

III. Legal Status, Objectives and Issue Areas: CBSS, HELCOM and the UBC (SCC)

In March 1992, the Russian Federation, Estonia, Latvia, Lithuania, Poland, Germany, Denmark, Norway, Sweden and Finland agreed to form the Council of Baltic Sea States (CBSS) as an intergovernmental organisation. The founding vision of this 'regional undertaking [was] to promote new ideas for cooperation while maintaining close relations with other States and international organizations'.[24] The founding declaration has been neither formally signed nor put into a legally binding international agreement. The legal status of the CBSS has been characterised by institutional and cooperative flexibility and, consequently, has been referred to as an instrument of 'soft law'.[25] Over time, this flexible governance architecture has allowed members to programmatically move ahead without the risk of slowing cooperation through national procedures, which would be triggered by default via an international treaty. Yet, such a procedural approach embodies the risk that cooperation will not be fully embraced by domestic actors.

The declaration did not formulate specific objectives but agreed on six areas of cooperation:[26] (1) assistance for new democratic institutions; (2) economic and technological assistance and cooperation; (3) humanitarian matters and health; (4) protection of the environment and energy; (5) cooperation in the fields of culture, education, tourism and information; and (6) transport and communication. Thus, the CBSS clearly qualifies as a general-purpose organisation. However, its activities have changed over time. Prior to the EU's Eastern enlargement

[20] S Grönholm, *Governing the Baltic Sea: A Study of the Functionality of Contemporary Environmental Governance* (Turku, Åbo Akademi University, 2020).

[21] T Koivurova and A Rosas, 'The CBSS as a vehicle for institutionalised governance in the Baltic Sea Area, in comparison with its two sister organizations in the north' (2018) 98 *Marine Policy* 211.

[22] S VanDeveer, 'Networked Baltic Environmental Cooperation' (2011) 42 *Journal of Baltic Studies* 37.

[23] N Tynkkynen, 'The Challenge of Environmental Governance in the Network Society: The Case of The Baltic Sea' (2013) 23 *Environmental Policy and Governance* 395.

[24] CBSS, '1st Ministerial Session – Copenhagen Declaration Conference of Foreign Ministers of the Baltic Sea States (Copenhagen, 5–6 March 1992).

[25] Koivurova and Rosas (n 21) 212.

[26] CBSS, '1st Ministerial Session' (n 24).

of 2004, the CBSS covered a wide range of issues, including youth and intercultural dialogue, entrepreneurial and creative industry collaboration, labour markets, research, innovation and science, climate change mitigation and adaptation policy coordination, spatial planning, law enforcement cooperation, critical infrastructure protection and emergency preparedness, child protection and human trafficking. Over several years, the CBSS also supported the EuroFaculty in the Baltic states, Kaliningrad and Pskov. Addressing several potential common 'soft security' threats, the CBSS has meticulously avoided engaging in military matters or 'hard security'.[27]

Following the EU enlargements at a time when the EU reformed its previously 'external policies' for the region, including the ND, the future of the CBSS moved into the spotlight. The Lithuanian Foreign Minister Vygaudas Ušackas (2009)[28] recommended upholding the CBSS's political dimension:

Its broad membership, comprising all Baltic Sea countries, is the CBSS's biggest advantage, providing it with a strong position in the region's political landscape. The CBSS is still able to create an environment for a better understanding among participating countries and could provide a natural platform for EU relations with Iceland, Norway and Russia.

Russia itself called for the independence of the CBSS vis-à-vis the EU.[29] To foster reform, the CBSS refocused its core objectives and in 2008 subscribed to five long-term goals: (1) environment; (2) economic development; (3) energy; (4) education and culture; and (5) civil security and the human dimension.[30] Only six years later, in 2014, the priority objectives were reduced to three: (1) regional identity; (2) a sustainable and prosperous region; and (3) a safe and secure region. This can be seen as a collective effort to ensure the future relevance of the body by gauging its activities towards a core of objectives that somewhat stress its unique selling points as the core intergovernmental organisation of the region bridging a growing divide which emerged between its EU Member States and Russia in the aftermath of the Ukraine crisis. Thus, we can see that the critical juncture of EU enlargement ultimately excluded other institutional trajectories of the CBSS and eventually restricted it to being primarily a body where EU Member States and Russia could, by and large, engage in functional cooperation along a set of comprehensive and narrowly defined objectives outside the context of the EU.

Currently, the CBSS is focusing on its long-term strategy to contribute to the implementation of the United Nations Sustainable Development Agenda 2030.

[27] H Hubel and S Gänzle, 'The Soft Security Agenda at the Sub-Regional Level: Policy Responses of the Council of the Baltic Sea States (CBSS)' in H Moroff (ed), *European Soft Security Risks: The Northern Dimension* (Berlin, Institut für Europäische Politik, 2002).

[28] V Ušackas, 'Together we are Stronger' Interview with the Lithuanian Minister for Foreign Affairs (Autumn 2009) *Balticness* 1–4.

[29] See A Makarychev, 'Russia – EU: Competing Logics of Region Building' in E Sandschneider (ed), *DGAPanalyse* (Berlin, Forschungsinstitut der Deutschen Gesellschaft für Auswärtige Politik e.V. 2012) 9.

[30] Declaration on the Reform of the Council of the Baltic Sea States CBSS Ministers (Riga, 3 June 2008) 2.

In 2018, a report of experts was submitted containing further recommendations on areas for future cooperation,[31,32] also reflecting the impact of the Ukraine crisis. On 3 March 2022, the Norwegian presidency of the CBSS declared an intention 'to suspend Russia from further participation in the Council's activities in response to the unprovoked and illegal war now being waged by Russia against Ukraine, the Ukrainian people and the country's authorities',[33] and in May Russia eventually withdrew its membership from the CBSS.

HELCOM was established to govern the Convention on the Protection of the Marine Environment of the Baltic Sea Area.[34] The Convention entered into force in 1980, marking the starting date of HELCOM as a regional organisation. In 1992, the new Convention, which was expanded to cover the entire catchment area including inland waters, was born as a result of the dissolution of the Soviet Union.[35]

The Helsinki Convention is a binding agreement of international law, but its provisions are vague.[36] It is amended when deemed necessary, thus following, for example, the developments in international environmental and maritime laws.[37] The main obligation is that 'the Contracting Parties shall … take all appropriate legislative, administrative or other relevant measures to prevent and eliminate pollution'. The Convention leaves a lot of discretion to the parties regarding implementation. The Baltic Sea Action Plan (BSAP), which currently serves as the main instrument under the Convention, has an unclear legal status.[38] All the HELCOM parties have given specified statements to HELCOM on their acceptance and intention to abide by the BSAP.

The main tasks of HELCOM include fostering international collaboration in the sphere of the environment, environmental monitoring and promoting new knowledge about the marine environment.[39] HELCOM's role in maintaining good diplomatic relations in the BSR is also acknowledged.[40] HELCOM prepares pollution load compilations, periodic assessments and holistic assessments about the state of the Baltic Sea. Non-binding recommendations are issued on measures

[31] Koivurova and Rosas (n 21) 216.

[32] Council of the Baltic Sea States (CBSS), 'Vision for the Baltic Sea Region Beyond 2020: Report by the Council of Baltic Sea States Vision Group' (2018), available at: www.eeas.org.

[33] 'Russia suspended from the Council of the Baltic Sea States' (Norwegian Ministry of Foreign Affairs, 2022), available at: www.regjeringen.no/en/aktuelt/russland-suspenderes-fra-ostersjoradet/id2903009/.

[34] Convention on the Protection of the Marine Environment of the Baltic Sea Area (Helsinki Convention) (Helsinki, 22 March 1974).

[35] M Valman, *Three Faces of HELCOM: Institution, Organization, Policy Producer* (Stockholm, Department of Political Science, Stockholm University, 2014) 15.

[36] B Bohman, 'Regulating Eutrophication – Flexible Legal Approaches and Environmental Governance in the Baltic Sea Area' in H Ringbom (ed), *Regulatory Gaps in Baltic Sea Governance: Selected Issues* (Berlin, Springer, 2018) 51.

[37] HELCOM, 'About us' (2019), available at: www.helcom.fi/about-us.

[38] Bohman (n 36) 51.

[39] Valman (n 35) 16.

[40] See, eg, HELCOM, *30 Years of Protecting the Baltic Sea HELCOM 1974–2004* (Helsinki, Helsinki Commission, 2004) 24.

which the Contracting Parties should implement through their national legislation. Since the beginning of the 1980s, some 260 recommendations have been adopted.[41] External changes have not had a major impact on the legal status of HELCOM.

Since the early 1990s, various programmes and plans have formed the backbone for action within HELCOM. The first programme, the Joint Comprehensive Environmental Action Programme (JCP) adopted in 1992, was a 20-year programme to address pollution hot spots and strengthen the formal institutions in the region. After the JCP, the BSAP was signed in 2007.[42] HELCOM has been strongly affected by the first of our three critical junctures: the dissolution of the Soviet Union. This landmark event was critical in terms of launching a new convention which would subsequently expand the functional tasks and activities of the body, as well as in terms of the eagerness of newly independent ex-Soviet countries (including Russia) to engage actively in the organisation throughout the 1990s. On 4 March 2022, members of HELCOM declared that they 'unanimously agree that they cannot currently engage in business as usual with the Russian Federation in the context of HELCOM'[43] – and eventually suspended all meetings to the end of June 2022.[44]

Cooperation between cities in the BSR can be traced back long in history and go back to the days of the medieval Hanseatic League. City cooperation, particularly the twinning relationships between these cities (such as the one between Turku and Leningrad of 1953), even endured during the Cold War period. Thus, it is no surprise that the UBC developed relatively spontaneously soon after the fall of the Berlin Wall, based on the initiative of the mayors of Gdansk (Poland) and Kalmar (Sweden).[45,46] The UBC was founded in Gdansk in September 1991 by 32 cities from 10 countries around the Baltic Sea; it grew quickly and soon had more than 100 members.[47]

The UBC and its seven commissions, including the Environment Commission, were established in 1991. The UBC's objectives are stated in its Statute, including: (1) to promote, develop and strengthen cooperation and exchange of experience among the cities in the BSR; (2) to advocate for common interests of the local authorities

[41] HELCOM, 'Recommendations' (2020), available at: helcom.fi/helcom-at-work/recommendations/.

[42] HELCOM, 'Baltic Sea Action Plan' (Krakow, 15 November 2007), available at: helcom.fi/media/documents/BSAP_Final.pdf.

[43] Statement by the German Chairmanship of HELCOM on behalf of the European Union and the Contracting Parties to HELCOM that are Member States of the European Union (Dessau, 4 March 2022), available at: helcom.fi/wp-content/uploads/2022/03/german-chairmanship-statement-on-ukraine.pdf.

[44] This was the situation at the time of writing. Cooperation may well be frozen way beyond that date.

[45] K Kern, 'Transnationale Städtenetzwerke in Europa' in E Schröter (ed), *Empirische Policy- und Verwaltungsforschung. Lokale, nationale und internationale Perspektiven* (Opladen, Leske and Budrich, 2001).

[46] Union of the Baltic Cities (UBC), *UBC 10th Anniversary, 1991–2001, Past, Present, Future* (Gdansk, Union of the Baltic Cities, 2001).

[47] See, eg, K Kern and T Löffelsend, 'Governance Beyond the Nation State: Transnationalization and Europeanization of the Baltic Sea Region' in J Detlef, M Joas and K Kern (eds), *Governing a Common Sea: Environmental Policies in the Baltic Sea Region* (London, Earthscan, 2008).

in the region; (3) to act on behalf of the cities and local authorities in common matters towards regional, national, European and international bodies; (4) to strive to achieve sustainable development and optimal economic and social development in the BSR with full respect for the European principles of local and regional self-governance and subsidiarity; and (5) to contribute to joint Baltic identity, cohesion and common understanding in the region.[48]

During the 2010s, the UBC developed several strategies, most recently the UBC Strategic Framework 2016–21 (at 3 ff), with the following priorities: (1) implementing the UBC Sustainability Action Programme 2016–21 ('Stairway towards Sustainable Baltic Cities'); (2) the EU Strategy for the Baltic Sea Region (EUSBSR) and Blue Growth strategies; (3) the EU Urban Agenda; (4) promoting smart growth and digitalisation; and (5) making the UBC stronger, more proactive, goal-oriented, and member-driven.[49] This list of priorities clearly documents the increasing Europeanisation of the UBC.

Thus, it is primarily EU enlargement that accounts for a significant critical juncture in the subsequent development of the UBC after the transnational city alliance was incepted as a consequence of the demise of communism in its member countries off the south-eastern coastline. Regarding Russian members, the ongoing war in Ukraine is the most critical juncture. In May 2022, the UBC terminated the membership of its two remaining Russian members – St Petersburg and Gatchina. While St Petersburg was a founding member of the UBC, Gatchina only joined in January 2021.

IV. Analysing Intra-Organisational and Inter-Organisational Change: A Comparison of the CBSS, HELCOM and the UBC (SCC)

A. Membership

The CBSS consists of 11 countries – Denmark, Germany, Estonia, Finland, Latvia, Lithuania, Norway, Poland, and the Russian Federation, Sweden and Iceland (since 1995) – and the EU represented by the European Commission or External Action Service (since 2010). The admission of the European Commission was symbolic of a common future for the region inside the EU.

The CBSS has been significantly affected by Finland and Sweden (1995) and Estonia, Latvia, Lithuania and Poland (2004) joining the EU, underlining 'the unique position of Russia as the only non-EU Member'[50] together with Iceland

[48] UBC, 'Statute of the Union of the Baltic Cities' (1992) Art 1.

[49] UBC, 'UBC Strategic Framework 2016–2021' (2021), available at: archive.ubc.net/download/2015_12/8871.pdf.

[50] Koivurova and Rosas (n 21) 214.

and Norway; the latter have been closely tied to the EU via the Economic Area Agreement (EEA). The CBSS presently has 11 countries designated with observer status: Belarus (2009), France (1999), Hungary (2016), Italy (2000), the Netherlands (2001), Romania (2009), Slovakia (2001), Spain (2009), Ukraine (1999), the United Kingdom (1999) and the United States (1999).

Originally, the Helsinki Convention Contracting Parties included seven countries: Denmark, Poland, Sweden, Finland, the USSR, the GDR and the FRG. Since 1992, the Contracting Parties are all the coastal countries – Finland, Sweden, Denmark, Germany, Poland, Lithuania, Latvia, Estonia and Russia – and the European Community. Changes in membership resulted from the dissolution of the USSR and the reunification of Germany. In the 1992 Convention, the European Community also became a contracting party, even if only two of the HELCOM countries were EU members at that time. Since then, there have been no changes in membership. HELCOM has a long list of observers, including the governments of Belarus and Ukraine.

Shortly after its foundation in 1991, the UBC grew quickly; small towns as well as the largest cities in the BSR joined. Cities from EU Member and Transition States were evenly attracted and represented in the Union as the UBC started as an initiative by the mayors of Gdansk and Kalmar. The mayor of Kalmar became the first UBC President, and the Secretariat has been located and funded by the city of Gdansk from the outset.[51] In the early 2000s, the UBC had over 100 members, with almost 90 per cent of the founding members still participating. Joining and staying in the UBC was mainly motivated not by specific characteristics of the municipalities, but by their sense of belonging to the BSR.[52] As the UBC sees itself in the tradition of the Hanseatic League, it was particularly attractive to many former Hanseatic cities. Today, the 72 member cities still range in size from 5,000 (Mielno) to 5,000,000 (St Petersburg) inhabitants, but the composition of member cities has changed considerably (see Table 2). Membership is relatively stable or growing in Finland, Poland, Latvia, Lithuania and Norway, but has dropped in Sweden, Denmark, Germany, Estonia and Russia. Important cities in the region have left the UBC, including Stockholm, Uppsala, Gothenburg, Copenhagen, Aalborg, Lübeck and Vilnius. Membership losses in Sweden can be explained by the election of a new generation of council members and mayors, which became interested and involved in politics only long after the fall of the Berlin Wall. They are more locally and nationally oriented and set different priorities for local politics. Russia is particularly striking because six of its seven member cities (including Kaliningrad) left the UBC. In 2020, the only remaining city from Russia was St Petersburg, due to its size and importance as the second largest Russian city and its long-lasting relationships with many sister cities in the region (Aarhus, Gdansk, Gothenburg, Hamburg, Kaunas, Riga, Tallinn, Turku, Vilnius).

[51] Kern (n 45).
[52] ibid.

For example, Turku in Finland was the first city in the world to establish official city relations with the Russian metropolis of St Petersburg back in 1953. Turku has maintained an office in St Petersburg to coordinate and improve existing ties. This cooperation helped the idea of sustainable city development to reach the national political agenda in the Russian Federation.[53]

Table 2 Membership of the Union of the Baltic Cities

	2002	**2020**	**change**	**%**
Denmark	10	4	−6	−60.0
Estonia	15	8	−7	−46.7
Finland	10	11	+1	+10.0
Germany	7	4	−3	−42.8
Latvia	8	7	−1	−12.5
Lithuania	6	8	+2	+33.3
Norway	3	3	0	0.0
Poland	12	12	0	0.0
Russia	7	1	−6	−85.7
Sweden	24	14	−10	−41.7
All cities	**102**	**72**	**−30**	**−29.4**

Source: Own compilation.

B. Organisational Structure

Politically, the organisational set-up of the CBSS is determined by the Council of Foreign Ministers of Member States and a member of the European Commission meeting annually under the CBSS presidency.[54] Whereas other ministers meet on an ad hoc basis, the CBSS foreign ministers convened annually until 2003 and have convened biannually since then. The annual presidency rotates between the members (except for the Commission/European External Action Service) in a troika format, thus linking the previous, current and incumbent presidency.[55] Since 1996, the ministerial meetings have been complemented by meetings of heads of state and government, the so-called Baltic Sea Summits taking place

[53] Interview 1 with a UBC representative (2020).

[54] After entry into force, the European Commission representative was replaced by a member of the European External Action Service (together with a member of GD Regio). Instead of the European Community (and its representative, the Commission), it is now the European Union which is a member of the Council of the Baltic Sea States.

[55] T Etzold, 'Live and Let Die. Adaptability and Endurance of Regional Organisations in Northern Europe' (unpublished PhD thesis, Manchester Metropolitan University, 2010) 91.

biannually. However, the later format has been suspended as a consequence of the EU's sanction regime in the aftermath of the Ukraine crisis; however some ministerial meetings have been held. As put forth by a CBSS official:

> While crafting consensus is difficult sometimes, it remains a powerful tool of the CBSS Ministerials …, [a] unique strength, that only the CBSS holds in the region. And even if formal Ministerial Councils were not organised, meetings on a political level took place nearly every year.[56]

At the administrative level, the Committee of Senior Officials (CSO), which consists of officials of Foreign Ministries and the European Commission, is the workhorse of the CBSS. At the time of the CBSS's inception, the CSO was supported by three working groups focusing on nuclear safety, democratic institutions and economic cooperation. Whereas the latter two were discontinued in 2009, nuclear safety has become part of an expert group for nuclear and radiation safety. The expert group is a professional and policymaking body aiming to improve cooperation among national regulatory authorities.[57] Today, the following specialised units are the Baltic 2030 unit (Expert Group on Sustainable Development, Baltic 2030 Network, B2030); Children at Risk unit (Expert Group on Children at Risk, CAR); and the Task Force against Trafficking on Human-Beings (TF-THB). In the words of a CBSS official: 'Expert Groups are good examples of CBSS activities having both political (policy-shaping and collaboration building) and practical (initiating projects) impact'.[58]

Political controversies could not be avoided given the mandate of some of the CBSS institutions. In 1994, the post of CBSS Commissioner on Democratic Institutions and Human Rights was created to provide a focal point for observing the development of human rights and minorities in the Member States of the CBSS, some of which exhibited a number of challenges, for example, with regard to Russian-speaking minorities. The position was abolished in 2003. As expressed by one CBSS official, what is important today is that the CSO aims for the following: '[to] give more support to the work with line ministries because the substance of the work is not that high a political dialogue; it lies on a plain with practical cooperation'.[59]

Since 1998, the CBSS has been operated by a small Secretariat based in Stockholm. The Secretariat employs around one dozen officials on limited-term appointments (which rose to 27 in 2020, excluding trainee assistants), several of which also perform tasks for other bodies of Baltic Sea cooperation, such as Children at Risk, the Baltic Sea Region Energy Cooperation, or the EUSBSR. The Northern Dimension Partnership for Public Health and Social Well-being shares the office in Stockholm ensuring space for mutual exchange. Currently, there are a

[56] Written correspondence with a CBSS official (2021).
[57] Etzold, 'Live and Let Die' (n 55) 92.
[58] Written correspondence with a CBSS official (2021).
[59] Interview 4 with a CBSS official (2020).

Director General, a Deputy Director and six senior advisers in the top leadership of the Secretariat. Their role has developed somewhat from the original path:

> [Their role] was mostly to go to conferences, to represent CBSS, to provide speeches, and to make notes. Nowadays, senior advisors are responsible for everything: they make fundraising, implement long-term priorities which the senior advisor is responsible for, and they meet a lot of people and networks in the Baltic Sea region.[60]

These CBSS bodies and institutions dispose of their own decision-making procedures and budget but make use of the Secretariat's technical infrastructure and institutional memory as one of the hubs of intergovernmental cooperation in the region. While maintaining its own agenda, the CBSS Secretariat has become closely involved in the governance architecture of the EUSBSR, providing ample evidence for increased Europeanisation. One might argue that the critical juncture of EU accession has, on the one hand, contributed to defining the Council's own role and contribution to Baltic Sea cooperation as a link between Russia and the EEA/EU Member States that it represents. In terms of it organisational structure, CBSS staff have become more project-oriented and managerial than one would perhaps expect from other examples of classical intergovernmental organisations. Yet, in the aftermath of the Ukraine crisis, diplomacy as the CBSS key organisational role has been put forward again.

HELCOM meets annually, with the Heads of Delegation representing the contracting parties.[61] A ministerial meeting every few years brings together the responsible ministers, usually ministers of the environment and the EU Commissioner for the Environment. The meetings result in the adoption of political declarations that complement the Convention.[62] The Commission adopts recommendations for the protection of the marine environment, decides on the budget and makes other key decisions. Decisions are made by consensus; each contracting party has one vote. In addition, ministerial-level meetings are held every few years. The HELCOM chairmanship rotates between the parties every two years, starting on 1 July, according to their alphabetical order in English. The chairman for 2018–20 is Finland. Russia has held the presidency once, from 2008 to 2010. HELCOM has a permanent Secretariat based in Helsinki, Finland.

In the early years, HELCOM worked through expert committees, such as the Scientific Technological Committee, the Maritime Committee and the Environmental Committee.[63] The Programme Implementation Task Force assisted by the JCP's implementation. Nowadays, the expert working groups (WG) implement strategies and propose issues for discussion at the meetings of the Heads of Delegations, where decisions are made. The five permanent groups have addressed

[60] ibid.

[61] HELCOM, 'Organisation' (2019), available at: www.helcom.fi/about-us/organisation.

[62] See HELCOM, 'Ministerial meetings' (2020), available at: helcom.fi/helcom-at-work/ministerial-meetings/.

[63] Interview 3 with a HELCOM official (2020).

different aspects of HELCOM's work since 2014: WG Gear, WG Maritime, WG Pressure and WG State and Conservation. There are also time-limited groups and several other expert groups with more specific tasks.[64]

In the EUSBSR Action Plan, some of the BSAP implementation projects were taken as flagship projects,[65] thus channelling some financing for the implementation of the BSAP. This enabled the establishment of some new working groups, such as the HELCOM–VASAB Maritime Spatial Planning Working Group in 2010.[66] Overall, the groups were streamlined in 2014 with the key aim of achieving 'a more efficient and flexible HELCOM'.[67] In sum, HELCOM's organisational structure has been rather stable; no major changes have taken place except for the working groups, which were somewhat affected by the EUSBSR.

The organisational differentiation of the UBC is well developed. The Union's most important organs are: (1) the General Conference of the delegates of the member cities; (2) the President; (3) the Presidium, consisting of the President and four Vice Presidents; (4) the Executive Board; (5) the Secretariat; (6) the Commissions of the Union; and (7) the Board of Audit.[68] The Executive Board, which is elected by the General Conference for a two-year period and chaired by the President, is the Union's highest authority between the General Conferences. It consists of one member-city representative from each country where the UBC has member cities plus the President and the Vice Presidents. The Executive Board has the right to formulate and adopt internal regulations and approve the budget. Its main responsibilities include approving new member cities, ensuring the implementation of the UBC Strategy, and guiding the work of the Secretariat and the UBC Commissions. From 2017 to 2019, Executive Board meetings took place in Elva (Estonia), Gdynia (Poland), Kristiansand (Norway), Lahti (Finland), Liepäja (Latvia), Næstved (Denmark), Rostock (Germany), St Petersburg (Russia), Touragé (Lithuania), Växjö (Sweden) and Gdansk (Poland). Between Board meetings, the Presidium is authorised to make decisions for the proper management of the Union.

In 1999, the UBC had commissions covering the whole range of (transnational) urban policy: (1) business cooperation; (2) culture; (3) education; (4) environment; (5) health and social affairs; (6) sport; (7) tourism; (8) transportation; and (9) urban planning. Several networks with cross-sectional functions were established, for example, the Local Agenda 21 Network, the Women's Network and the Youth Network. A number of reorganisations have taken place during the last

[64] HELCOM, 'Groups' (2020), available at: www.helcom.fi/helcom-at-work/groups.

[65] Commission, 'Commission Staff Working Document EU Strategy for the Baltic Sea Region Action Plan [COM(2009) 248 final]' SWD(2021) 24 final.

[66] Interview 4 with a HELCOM representative (2020).

[67] HELCOM, 'The new HELCOM. Key results from the streamlining process in 2013–2014' (2019), available at: www.helcom.fi/Documents/About%20us/Organisation/Streamlining%20HELCOM_Summary.pdf.

[68] UBC, 'Statute' (n 48) Art 4.

20 years; in 2020, the UBC had seven commissions: (1) Cultural Cities; (2) Inclusive and Healthy Cities; (3) Planning Cities; (4) Safe Cities; (5) Smart and Prospering Cities; (6) Sustainable Cities; and (7) Youthful Cities.

Environmental policies have been on the UBC agenda from the outset, and the Environment Commission has been one of the most active UBC Commissions. The UBC Agenda 21 Action Programme was launched in 1999 and updated in 2001 and 2003.[69] An exchange of best practices was high on the agenda and promoted via workshops, seminars and twinning and by developing European Common Indicators for Urban Sustainable Development as benchmarking tools. Some projects aimed to establish temporary twinning agreements for mutual learning in environmental policy. In addition, an award scheme (Best Environmental Practice in the Baltic Cities Award) was set up to complement this approach.

The Environmental Commission was renamed, and today, the Sustainable Cities Commission (SCC) is still the central body for the implementation of the goals associated with sustainable development at the local level. The SCC is administered through a Secretariat in Turku, Finland. The SCC coordinates the UBC Sustainability Action Programme – Stairway towards Sustainable Baltic Cities for the period from 2016 to 2021. This programme, which is closely linked to the EUSBSR, guides the Union's work in sustainable development. For the next five years, the programme will focus on green urban economies, climate-smart cities, sustainable urban ecosystems and natural resources.

C. Leadership

Leadership, in principle, occurs at two levels: political and administrative. At the political level, leadership can be assumed by members with a strong interest in the BSR. Most members held medium interest only, with Sweden and Russia more positive about the CBSS in the late 1990s – according to a specialist of the CBSS.[70] The EU as a collective actor has shown considerably less interest. Direct influence and leadership can be exercised at the Baltic Sea Summit, presumably the highest political authority of Baltic Sea cooperation, as well as during a country's presidency of the CBSS. The diplomatic rank of a country's CSO, ambassadorial or not, can often be interpreted as a proxy of how much reputation the CBSS has in a given country. Indirect leadership can be exercised in alternative diplomatic arenas such as the EU. In this regard, both Finland and Sweden have made instrumental use of their EU membership by advocating for the ND and for the so-called Eastern Partnership within the European Neighbourhood (Sweden and Poland's initiative in 2008). Further, the EUSBSR was promulgated under the Swedish EU Council Presidency in 2009. In all these initiatives, the CBSS was identified as one

[69] UBC, UBC 10th Anniversary (n 46) 7.
[70] Etzold, 'Live and Let Die' (n 55) 118.

of the core institutional hubs for Baltic Sea cooperation. Leadership can also be prompted at the administrative level: here, it is the CBSS Secretariat which assumes a key role, particularly the leader of the administration, ie, the Director General. Leadership contains an element of both personality and opportunity. Director General Jan Lundin (2010–16), a Swedish career diplomat, was acknowledged as a personality who pushed the Secretariat towards stronger project orientation and integration into the EUSBSR governance architecture set up by the EU following a CBSS decision.

Similarly, in HELCOM, leadership takes place at two interconnected levels. At the political level, ministerial meetings every few years bring together the responsible ministers and the EU Commissioner for the Environment. These meetings are 'important forums for shared discussions and agreements on a high level', and they result in a political declaration.[71] Rotating chairmanship is crucial from a commitment viewpoint. For instance, when the BSAP was being negotiated, Poland had the chairmanship, and thus it was easier to commit the country to it.[72] Moreover, Sweden held the EU presidency (latter half of 2009) and started its HELCOM chairmanship (2010–12) right after, which motivated it to negotiate funding synergies between EU instruments such as the EUSBSR and HELCOM.[73] Russia also demonstrated leadership during and right after its chairmanship, 2008–10. At that point, Russian actors heavily emphasised HELCOM's role in balancing the EU's dominance in the BSR which, according to their view, emerged after its enlargement in 2004 and the launch of the EUSBSR in 2009.[74]

At the administrative level, all decisions are made in the Commission meetings of the Heads of Delegation unanimously and in accordance with the Convention. The HELCOM Secretariat, including the Executive Secretary, has relatively significant powers. According to HELCOM's rules, '[It] shall have the power of initiative, ie, to prepare and present to the Heads of Delegation proposals on strategies, policies, Commission Recommendations and decisions and any other actions on administration, budget, etc'.[75]

UBC political leadership is exercised primarily by the Union President and the four Vice Presidents, who perform statutory functions and are members of the Executive Board chaired by the Union President. From 1991 to 2019, the UBC had only two Presidents. The first President of the Union, Anders Engström, served for 10 years, from the UBC's foundation in 1991 until 2001. As Mayor of Kalmar (Sweden), he was one of the initiators of the UBC and was considered a charismatic and visionary leader. In 2001, Per Bødker Andersen, the Mayor of

[71] HELCOM, 'Ministerial meetings' (2020) (n 62).

[72] Interview 4 with a HELCOM representative (2020).

[73] ibid.

[74] A Korppoo, N Tynkkynen and G Hønneland, *Russia and the Politics of International Environmental Regimes: Environmental Encounters or Foreign Policy?* (Cheltenham, Edward Elgar, 2015) 70–71.

[75] HELCOM, 'Rules of Procedure of the Helsinki Commission – Baltic Marine Environment Protection Commission' (Minutes of HELCOM HOD 41/2013, Annex 5, 2013) 9.4, available at: helcom.fi/media/documents/Rules-of-Procedure-2013.pdf.

Kolding (Denmark), was elected UBC President and held this position until the autumn of 2019, ie, a period of 18 years. While he managed to stabilise the UBC in the 2000s, more and more cities left the Union during the last couple of years. At the General Conference in Kaunas (Lithuania) in October 2019, Mantas Jurgutis, Deputy Mayor of Kaunas, was elected as President for a two-year period. The four Vice Presidents elected in 2019 come from Turku, Gdansk, St Petersburg and Kristiansand.

The UBC Secretariat in Gdansk coordinates the UBC's daily work, is responsible for the communication, administration and organisation of UBC events, and helps Commissions and other UBC bodies. The Secretary General is elected for a four-year period by the Executive Board. Similar to political leadership, administrative leadership has not changed for a long time, and Secretary General Paweł Żaboklicki is still in office.

D. Funding and Budget

In the early 1990s, the CBSS was dependent on the EU for financial support for its Commissioner on Democratic institutions and minority rights. It was praised for the EuroFaculty project, which promotes educational cooperation and cultural exchange financed through the EU's Tempus/Phare and Tempus/Tacis programmes.

To date, the CBSS does not dispose of an operative budget in its own right.[76] For the financial year 2006, for example, the budget amounted to approximately €868,000 and relied on financial contributions from its Member States. The three Baltic states and Iceland each contribute 4 per cent to the overall budget; the remaining countries pay 12 per cent each.[77] Member State contributions have increased over the years and made up €3.65 million in 2019. This also includes 'additional project funds received from Germany, Norway, Sweden, European Commission, Interreg Baltic Sea Region Program 2014–2020, European Social Fund, European Erasmus + program and Swedish Institute'.

Since 2012, the CBSS has a Project Support Facility, with the main objective of co-financing the development and implementation of cooperation projects. The three priorities are to develop regional identity and a sustainable, prosperous and secure region. The total amount of the CBSS Project Support Facility for three years is €1 million with one call per year. The projects initiated by a legal entity of CBSS Member States need to be transnational in character and should aim to have a sustainable outcome.

[76] T Etzold, 'Reorganization Processes in Small International Organizations. The Nordic Councils and the Council of the Baltic Sea States' in MW Bauer and C Knill (eds), *Management Reform in International Organizations* (Baden-Baden, Nomos, 2007) 156.

[77] ibid.

The CBSS was granted money from the European Investment and Structural Funds and the European Social Fund (ESIF). The CBSS can compete for and partake in project implementation primarily through active participation in EU funding schemes provided through cohesion policy, ESIF and transnational cooperation (Baltic Sea Transnational Cooperation).[78] The establishment of a dedicated fund for Baltic Sea cooperation under the auspices of the CBSS has been contemplated for quite some time, and the CBSS Vision Group has suggested 'the creation of a Baltic Sea Cooperation Fund, based on voluntary contributions from interested Member States'.[79] Yet, it seems that for the time being, as a consequence of the deteriorating relations between the EU and Russia, there seem to be limits for such innovative solutions which potentially could also strengthen the visibility and autonomy of the CBSS.

As for HELCOM, financial provisions for the Commission are established in the Convention and state that 'the total amount of the budget, including any supplementary budget adopted by the Commission, shall be contributed by the Contracting Parties in equal parts, unless the Commission unanimously decides otherwise'.[80] The European Economic Community contributes, at most, 2.5 per cent of the administrative costs.

The annual budget has remained around €2 million for the last 15 years.[81] The contributions from the three Baltic States and Russia were lagging significantly behind, which caused discussion among the contracting parties, and there were several requests to increase their shares to an equal level.[82] For example, in the 2012/13 budget, the national contribution shares were 6 per cent for Latvia, 5.5 per cent for Lithuania, 11.11 per cent for Russia and Estonia, and 14.3 per cent for Denmark, Finland, Germany, Poland and Sweden. Since then, contributions have become almost equal, with Latvia and Lithuania lagging slightly behind in the budget for 2019/20.[83] Russia's contribution has remained rather stable throughout the years, with constant incremental increases and following the request by the Commission for an equal share of contributions.

The total funding of HELCOM activities comes from various sources and is thus difficult to assess. To finance the implementation of the BSAP, national budgets and EU structural funds are used. A BSAP Fund was established by the Nordic Investment Bank and the Nordic Environmental Finance Corporation in 2009 to support grants, for instance, for technical assistance.[84] The Fund capital

[78] Interview 2 with a CBSS official (2017).

[79] CBSS, 'Vision' (n 32) 10.

[80] HELCOM, 'Convention on the Protection of the Marine Environment of the Baltic Sea Area, 1974 (Helsinki Convention)' (Helsinki, 1993) Art 15.

[81] See: portal.helcom.fi.

[82] See, eg, HELCOM, 'Rules of Procedure of the Helsinki Commission' (n 75).

[83] HELCOM, 'Background document and a proposal for a way forward for HELCOM budget including budget estimate for 2020–2021' (2019), available at: portal.helcom.fi. See a long-term budget comparison on p 3.

[84] See, eg, M Pyhälä, 'HELCOM Baltic Sea Action Plan: An Ecosystem Approach to the Management of Human Activities' in M Reckermann, K Brander, BR MacKenzie and A Omstedt (eds), *Climate Impacts on the Baltic Sea: From Science to Policy* (Berlin, Springer, 2012).

stood at €11 million.[85] In addition, various international financial institutions finance projects to meet HELCOM recommendations. For example, the European Investment Bank has allocated significant sums to support Russian projects, contributing significantly to upgrading water quality in the Baltic Sea and thus benefiting all neighbouring Baltic Sea countries.[86]

Sources of financing UBC activities primarily include membership fees, but intergovernmental organisations, funding agencies and individual cities also contribute, and donations and legacies are given by private persons. Based on a proposal by the Executive Board, the General Conference decides on the fees the member cities have to contribute to cover the Union activities and expenses.[87]

Although the UBC SCC receives some funding from the UBC, it is marginal compared with the expenses of the Commission with its more than 20 employees. Funding is also provided by the city of Turku (eg, expenses for the premises), but most funding is external for projects, particularly EU-funded projects. Due to the successful attraction of third-party funding, the SSC is better equipped than all other UBC Commissions and even the UBC Secretariat in Gdansk. This Europeanisation of SCC funding means that the Commission not only depends on EU funding, but also that it cooperates with many European cities that are not UBC members.

E. Inter-Organisational Relations

The EU's approaches to the BSR already identified the CBSS as 'an important complement to the Union's bilateral relations in the region and serves important political and economic purposes for all participating countries'.[88] Subsequently, the CBSS came to occupy a central role in the EU's ND. As part of the EUSBSR governance architecture, the CBSS began co-coordinating several priorities, such as those in civilian security and climate change, which was considered 'a smart move by the EU by recognising that they really need the existing institutions'.[89] The CBSS did not occupy a central role at the launch of the EUSBSR in 2009 but was gradually recognised as an important player in the revised Action Plans of February 2013 and June 2015 when it started managing several macro-regional projects. Since then, the CBSS has also co-coordinated an EUSBSR Policy Area focusing on civil contingencies and two Horizontal Actions: Neighbours and Sustainability.

[85] Nordic Environmental Finance Corporation (NEFCO), 'The BSAP Fund' (2015), available at: www.nefco.int/wp-content/uploads/2019/04/nefco_bsap_brochure_2015_EN.pdf.

[86] HELCOM, 'The Helsinki Commission' (EIB (European Investment Bank) 2020), available at: www.eib.org/en/projects/regions/eastern-neighbours/framework/helsinki_commission.htm.

[87] For 2020–21, membership fees range from €500 for municipalities with less than 10,000 inhabitants to €7,250 for cities with more than 500,000 inhabitants. This equals around €231,000 in membership fees.

[88] Commission, 'Communication from the Commission to the Council Orientations for a Union Approach Towards the Baltic Sea Region' SEC(94) 1747 final.

[89] Interview 1 with a CBSS official (2014).

Since 2001, the CBSS has maintained relations with 17 strategic partners in order to further enhance regional cooperation on specific sectors. Strategic partners include, for example, HELCOM, the UBC and the International Organisation of Migration, among others. Within the framework of strategic partnership, the CBSS is also collaborating with, for example, the Union for the Mediterranean on climate change issues and with the Central European Initiative on questions concerning migration.[90] Compared with the Arctic Council and the Barents Euro-Arctic Council, the CBSS has engaged in more varied tasks but also 'more demanding fields of activity, such as cooperation on border control, civil protection, nuclear and radiation safety, trafficking human beings or organized crime'.[91] Most importantly, however, two of the three current main priorities are identical to the EU's core objective for the BSR as part of the EUSBSR. Thus, one may argue that the CBSS has drawn increasingly closer to the EU as one of the main cornerstones – together with Russia – of political order in the BSR.

Other organisations lean on HELCOM for environmental issues but also 'come to its field', which sometimes causes duplication.[92] Although there are examples of some institutional interactions, for example between HELCOM and the International Maritime Organization, there are noticeable and potential institutional gaps in the interaction and coordination between HELCOM and other marine and sectoral institutions.[93]

HELCOM cooperates with several organisations, institutions and frameworks, which often have observer status. The BONUS programme (scientific cooperation between the BSR countries), the EU Marine Strategy Framework Directive (MSFD), the EUSBSR, the International Council for the Exploration of the Sea, the OSPAR Commission,[94] and the UN Environment Programme are in different HELCOM websites mentioned as key partners.[95] This list demonstrates the strong effort of HELCOM to emphasise its scientific character: HELCOM often hides behind the scientific mandate and underplays political aspects. The observer list also has international NGOs, including the World Wildlife Fund for Nature and the UBC.

In particular during the 1990s and early 2000s, international financial institutions (IFIs) financed HELCOM-related activities. For instance, the European Bank for Reconstruction and Development and the Nordic Investment Bank contributed a lot to projects addressing HELCOM hot spots, particularly in Russia and

[90] Interview 2 with a CBSS official (2017).

[91] Koivurova and Rosas (n 21) 218.

[92] Interview 3 with a HELCOM representative (2020).

[93] J Raakjær, J van Leeuwen, J van Tatenhove and M Hadjimichael, 'Ecosystem-based Marine Management in European Regional Seas Calls for Nested Governance Structures and Coordination – a Policy Brief' (2014) 50 *Marine Policy* 373.

[94] OSPAR is the mechanism by which 15 governments of the western coasts and catchments of Europe, together with the EU, cooperate to protect the marine environment of the Northeast Atlantic.

[95] HELCOM, 'About us' (2022), available at: helcom.fi/about-us.

other former Soviet countries. IFIs have significantly decreased their engagement in recent years, partly due to sanctions but also to policy change.[96]

The EU was rather invisible in HELCOM in the early years. After Finland and Sweden joined the EU in 1995, the Commission took a bigger role.[97] HELCOM was identified by the EU as the main instrument in advocating for related EU policies, including the environmental parts of the EUSBSR and directives in the field of marine protection, such as the MSFD.[98] The launch of the HELCOM BSAP coincided with the introduction of a set of EU legislation including the Water Framework Directive in 2000 and the MSFD in 2008. Article 6 of the MSFD states that 'Member States shall, where practical and appropriate, use existing regional institutional cooperation structures, including those under Regional Sea Conventions, covering that marine region or subregion'. The BSAP was seen as such a structure; moreover, one of the most important tasks of HELCOM WG Gear is to implement the MSFD.[99] Here, the impact of Europeanisation is clearly visible, but contrary to the CBSS, the EU uses HELCOM as a venue for implementing and coordinating its policies in the region rather than limiting HELCOM's work as such.

EU structural funds are used to finance, for example, the implementation of the HELCOM BSAP. Sometimes, issues that fall under the mandate of HELCOM in principle are handled bilaterally between various EU institutions and Russia, which has caused discussion regarding the share of responsibilities.[100] Critical voices have also questioned the purpose and future of HELCOM, whether it is merely duplicating the EU regulations on the one hand or implementing them on the other.[101] Arguments for HELCOM state that it is important to engage Russia, the only non-EU Baltic Sea coastal country.

The UBC combines transnational relations at the local level with the cooperation of other organisations in the region and an active outreach towards European and international levels. The origins of the UBC show that the various forms of city-to-city cooperation are interdependent: the basis was provided by a long-standing relationship between Gdansk and Kalmar, seeking to win the support of their respective twin cities for this institutional innovation.

UBC cooperation with other regional organisations started with project-based cooperation and involvement in the Baltic 21 process launched by the CBSS and its role as an observer in HELCOM. The UBC even became involved in developmental aid. It collaborated with the Lake Victoria Regional Local Authorities Co-operation, which started with a project financed by the Swedish International Development Agency and concentrated on environmental management, urban

[96] Interview 3 with a HELCOM representative (2020).
[97] ibid.
[98] ibid.
[99] Interview 4 with HELCOM representative (2020).
[100] Interview 3 with a HELCOM representative (2020).
[101] ibid.

planning, budgeting, human resources policy, equality policy and cooperation between local authorities.

The UBC Strategic Framework 2016–21 states that the UBC actively seeks partners and works closely with key stakeholders in the region: national governments, local authority organisations and organisations such as the CBSS, HELCOM, the BSSSC, the Baltic Sea Parliamentary Conference, the Baltic Development Forum, the Baltic Sea Region NGO Network, the Baltic Sea Region University Network and the Euroregion Baltic.[102] Additionally, the UBC tries to offer its member cities an opportunity to enter the European political arena and develop into European players. The UBC's work priorities for 2016 to 2021 show that cooperation with EU institutions is of strategic importance for the organisation. The UBC Strategic Framework explicitly refers to the EUSBSR (including Blue Growth strategies) and the EU Urban Agenda. Together with the Baltic Sea NGO Network and the Swedish Institute, the UBC coordinates the Horizontal Action 'Capacity', aiming to increase the project capacity, skills and competence of all stakeholders involved in the strategy through training programmes.

V. Discussion and Conclusion

Our analysis dissects the implications of geopolitical changes on important features gauging the organisational development of our three cases. We find that the impact varies quite significantly from one organisation to another. We have seen that the first major change occurred after the dissolution of the Soviet Union, resulting in a change in HELCOM membership as the newly independent states and the EEC joined its organisation, in the establishment of the CBSS, and in the institutionalisation of cooperation between cities (UBC). It also impacted HELCOM so that its activities became project-based with extensive funding from the IFIs and other funding bodies. The new openness in the former Soviet space also revealed pollution sources so that environmental hot spots could be identified and tackled.

Furthermore, we identified both EU enlargement and the launch of the EUSBSR as other major critical changes in terms of the region's overall exposure to Europeanisation and some dominance of the EU. The main drivers of Europeanisation were various pieces of EU legislation (eg, the WFD and MSFD), pertaining policies and strategies which needed to be implemented by all Member States, and the EUSBSR, which became the EU's first macro-regional strategy. Our analysis shows that, as a result of these processes, Europeanisation affected the organisations in various ways. The EU became a founding member of the CBSS, and even before 2004, it received a lot of attention from states located in the BSR. In recent years, the CBSS has witnessed a significant concentration of

[102] UBC, 'UBC Strategic Framework 2016–2021' (n 49) 3.

its focus to ensure its overall relevance in the region. Until early 2022, it was the only political body bringing both EU Member States and Russia together at the sub-regional level, despite a row of mutual sanctions in place between both actors at the global level. One may argue that the CBSS has reacted in a flexible way since 2014 – 'while political dialogue became problematic, the Council engaged in projects, which have important influence on defining key issues in region and building capacity to deal with them'.[103]

As a result of Europeanisation, the UBC oriented itself gradually toward 'Brussels', too; most projects of the UBC SCC are funded by the EU Commission today. HELCOM, in turn, has contributed to the implementation of EU legislation. HELCOM's approach changed in the late 2000s from a sectoral-based to an ecosystem-based approach to management as an impact of the EU directives that were based on an approach similar to the MSFD.

Increasing EU integration on the one hand, and the changing relationship between the EU and Russia on the other appear to be parallel but mutually reinforcing processes.[104] Europeanisation has had a disintegrating flipside due to Russia's special role as the only non-Member State in the BSR. Yet, in the late 2000s, Russia used its stake in the regional organisations to balance against Europeanisation – for example, when it held the HELCOM chairmanship, showcasing regional activity through the respective organisation[105] – at some distance from the EU.

Finally, the so-called Ukraine crisis and the subsequent war in Ukraine have had a deteriorating impact on Russia's role as well as on the relationship between Russia and other countries in the BSR, thus affecting the organisations in various ways regarding membership, participation in meetings and altered funding schemes. As noted, the UBC terminated the membership of its remaining Russian members (St Petersburg and Gatchina) in May 2022. Until February 2022, Russia gradually became less active in HELCOM, but was still engaged. After February 2022 Russian participation has – like other bodies of cooperation in the BSR and adjacent regions, like the Arctic – been suspended for the time being.[106] It is, at the time of writing (May 2022), difficult to imagine how collaborative efforts and processes may reassume any time soon. It seems fair to assume that the 'hyper-critical juncture' inflicted onto the region by Russia's President Putin is comparable in its scope and size to the end of the Soviet Union more than 30 years ago – the first historical juncture discerned in our chapter. The situation is further exacerbated by the imminent bid of Finland and Sweden for NATO membership.

[103] Written correspondence with a CBSS official (2021).

[104] A Makarychev and A Sergunin, 'Russia's Role in Regional Cooperation and the EU Strategy for the Baltic Sea Region (EUSBSR)' (2017) 48 *Journal of Baltic Studies* 465.

[105] For the CBSS, see also, I Oldberg, *Soft Security in Baltic Sea Region. Russian Interests in the Council of the Baltic Sea States* (Stockholm, Swedish Institute of International Affairs, 2012).

[106] Etzold, 'Auf Eis gelegt' (n 9).

In conclusion, as noted by Kapur,[107] external changes can be identified as 'critical junctures' that create distinctively new conditions and pressures for institutional evolution – with the most recent one as some kind of 'hyper-critical juncture'. Our comparison of the three organisations indicates that HELCOM, as an organisation, has been least affected by the changes in the BSR in relative terms. This is partly rooted in the fact that HELCOM has the longest history and an institutional path dependency that makes it slow before changes, but it is simultaneously more perseverant. Its robustness also has to do with its specific-purpose scope: HELCOM focuses exclusively on the environment, which is traditionally considered a relatively easy and non-political scientific field of cooperation.[108] Yet, its workings has been stalled as a consequence of the Russia war in Ukraine which may eventually trigger some long-term consequences. Still, HELCOM has also been heavily impacted by Europeanisation, which may ultimately question its existence in the future if its role and function are limited to the implementation of the EU regulations only.

Finally, the development of the organisations, as well as the comparison between general-purpose organisations (CBSS, UBC) and specific-purpose organisations (HELCOM, UBC SCC) suggest that specific-purpose organisations are rather well equipped to manage conflicts with other organisations and might also be more robust with respect to geopolitical changes compared with general-purpose organisations. From that angle, we expect technical cooperation with the Russian Federation to reassume more promptly in HELCOM than in the CBSS. Naturally, there are also other, contextual factors that play a role, and it is very likely that the CBSS will continue as an intergovernmental forum for EU/EEA Member States of the BSR for the time being – and perhaps more coherent an actor given its exclusive EU/EEA membership.

[107] Kapur (n 17) 342.

[108] R Darst, *Smokestack Diplomacy. Cooperation and Conflict in East–West Environmental Politics* (Cambridge, MA, MIT Press, 2001).

6

Cooperation in the Baltic Sea Region and EU External Relations Law

MIRKA KUISMA

I. Introduction

According to an adage of EU (European Union) constitutional law, the founding Treaties of the EU, unlike ordinary international treaties, established a new legal order with its own institutions, for the benefit of which the EU Member States limited their sovereign rights.[1] In external affairs, the extent of those limitations is determined by the doctrines of EU external relations law. From the internal vantage point of EU law, said doctrines determine whether and to what extent the EU and/or its Member States may act in international fora, and circumscribe their policy discretion. As the rules of EU external relations law do not, as such, bind third parties with whom the Union and/or its Member States cooperate, they could be seen as having little importance from such parties' vantage point. Yet, the binding effect of these rules on the EU and its Member States has a practical effect on the policy choices that the Union and its Member States can make as well as the modes of action that they may assume, thus affecting international cooperation beyond the internal vantage point of EU law.

This chapter contextualises and analyses the division of labour between the EU and its Member States in Baltic Sea Region (BSR) cooperation from the vantage point of EU external relations law. Of particular importance in this context is the question of mixity, ie, the possibility that both the Union and (some of) its Members States participate in international agreements or organisations, instead of the Union or the Member States acting alone vis-a-vis third parties.

This chapter shows, first, how the principles of EU external relations law affect task-sharing between the Union and its Member States in international fora. It is suggested that because of the environmental focus and soft-law nature of much

[1] Opinion 1/09 *(Accord sur la création d'un système unifié de règlement des litiges en matière de brevets)* [2011] ECR I-01137, ECLI:EU:C:2011:123, para 65.

of BSR cooperation, the Member States retain discretion to act in their own right. However, there is an important possibility that cooperation could trigger the exclusivity of EU competences or that the principles of EU external relations law could otherwise limit the Member States' leeway. Second, this chapter discusses the practical effect that the rules of EU external relations law could have on the internal functioning of BSR bodies. Using an example drawn from the context of HELCOM,[2] this chapter notes how Member State activities in said body are tightly bound to the Union's internal policy setting, and how the Union takes an active role in the field. Contrary to the narrative commonly assumed in the EU external relations *acquis*, this may not only lead to effectiveness, but also irritations with non-EU partners in the region. By contrast, in other contexts of BSR cooperation, such as that of the Council of the Baltic Sea States (CBSS),[3] the European Commission appears reluctant to assume a policy leadership role. Although cooperation is left to the Baltic Sea States, the question arises whether EU external relations law could have an unintended freezing effect even where the Union would welcome the Member State-led progress gained through regional cooperation.

The discussion proceeds as follows. The first section discusses the existence of EU competence and its effect on task-sharing between the Union and its Member States. The second section explores the rules and practices of mixity in general and in the BSR context in particular. In the third section, the implications of the duty of cooperation are introduced. After that, building on observations made in previous research on BSR cooperation, the fourth section discusses the effects of the principles of EU external relations law on the practical functioning of BSR bodies. In conclusion, it is suggested that because of the rules of EU external relations law, BSR cooperation that produces more robust regulative action is likely to require the Union's (more active) involvement.

II. Existence and Effect of Union Competence

The impact of EU law on its Member States' external action hinges, in part, on the existence and nature of the Union's competence. This section introduces the rules

[2] HELCOM is a platform for environmental policymaking in the BSR established in 1974 under the Convention on the Protection of the Marine Environment of the Baltic Sea Area (the Helsinki Convention). It is composed of the Contracting Parties of the Helsinki Convention which include the EU, its Baltic Member States and Russia. See ch 10 by Suvi-Tuuli Puharinen and Antti Belinskij in this volume.

[3] The CBSS is a regional platform for tackling global and regional problems ranging, inter alia, from climate change and sustainable development to the fight against human trafficking and the protection of the rights of the child. It consists of the EU, eight of its Member States, two EEA Member States and Russia. Its establishment in 1992 took place through a Ministerial Declaration commonly perceived as a non-binding soft law instrument; see CBSS, '1st Ministerial Session – Copenhagen Declaration Conference of Foreign Ministers of the Baltic Sea States (Copenhagen, 5–6 March 1992). In literature, see eg, T Koivurova and A Rosas, 'The CBSS as a vehicle for institutionalised governance in the Baltic

on Union competence and explains how, despite their superficial clarity, the external task-sharing between the EU and its Member States requires an important amount of case-by-case evaluation – even in the BSR context.

For the Union to act (externally), it must enjoy competence to do so. This is due to the 'principle of conferred powers', according to which the Union may only act where it has been given powers through the founding Treaties.[4] The competences that have not been expressly conferred to the Union remain with the Member States.[5]

At the same time, it is inherent in the canon of EU constitutional law that the Treaties should be interpreted in a manner that secures their *effet utile*. This entails that the Union's powers must be effective. In the field of external relations law, this has historically led the European Court of Justice (the EU Court) to conclude that in addition to the powers explicitly laid down in the Treaties, the Union has been conferred such implied competences which are necessary for it to fully utilise its express powers.[6] Thus, even though the Treaties were originally largely silent on any general Union competence to act externally,[7] the Union was held to enjoy competence to act externally where the use of its internal powers so required.[8] These powers have since been codified with the entry into force of the Lisbon Treaty.[9]

As a rule, the Member States are pre-empted from using their powers in ways that would obstruct or undermine the Union's use of its conferred competences. The severity of the limiting effect is determined by the nature of the Union's competence. The Treaties mention three different types of competence: shared; exclusive; and supportive, coordinating and supplementing.

According to Article 4 of the Treaty on the Functioning of the European Union (TFEU), the Union's competence is, as a rule, shared with the Member States in fields upon which the Treaties do not entail any provisions to the contrary. A non-exhaustive list in the same Article mentions many fields that are directly relevant to BSR cooperation: agriculture and fisheries; environment; transport; energy; as well as the area of freedom, security and justice. In fields of shared competence, the Member States may continue to use their powers to the extent that the Union has chosen not to make use of its competence (the so-called rule of

Sea Area, in comparison with its two sister organisations in the north' (2018) 98 *Marine Policy* 211, 212. See also ch 8 by Allan Rosas and Petteri Vuorimäki in this volume.

[4] Consolidated version of the Treaty on the European Union [2016] OJ C202/13, Art 5(1) (TEU).

[5] TEU, Arts 4(1) and 5(2).

[6] See, eg, G de Baere, *Constitutional Principles of EU External Relations* (Oxford, Oxford University Press, 2008) 16–29.

[7] Express external powers have, however, historically been granted in the Treaties, eg, with regard to the common commercial policy and association agreements.

[8] Case 22/70 *Commission v Council (ERTA)* [1971] ECR-0263, ECLI:EU:C:1971:32; Joined Cases 3, 4 and 6/76 *Kramer* [1976] ECR-1279, ECLI:EU:C:1976:114; and Opinion 1/76 *(Laying-up Fund for Inland Waterway Vessels)* [1977] ECR-0741, ECLI:EU:C:1977:63.

[9] Consolidated version of the Treaty on the Functioning of the European Union [2016] OJ C202/47, Art 216 (TFEU).

pre-emption).[10] In addition, in the fields of research, technological development and space, the Union has been granted a competence, the use of which does not prevent the Member States' use of theirs.[11]

Where the Union's competence is exclusive in nature, Member State action is pre-empted by default. This may result from sectoral competence conferral under Article 3(1) of the TFEU, encompassing, for example, the conservation of marine biological resources under the common fisheries policy (ie, the regulation of fishing).[12] In addition, the exclusivity rules relating to the conclusion of international agreements in Article 3(2) of the TFEU are of central importance for external task-sharing. In the latter case, the establishment of exclusivity hinges on a purposive evaluation attaching to the objectives of the Union's use of its powers. In particular, the ERTA doctrine[13] codified in the second leg of Article 3(2) of the TFEU may prove decisive for determining the modes of action available for the Member States in the BSR. Because of its centrality to the discussion in this chapter, the premises of the doctrine will be discussed next in some detail.

According to the ERTA doctrine, the Union's competence to conclude international agreements is exclusive where the envisaged commitments may affect common rules, ie, legislation passed under the EU Treaties, or may alter their scope.[14] Despite the narrow formulation referring to the conclusion of international agreements, the doctrine is applied to a broader range of stance-taking in international bodies: according to the EU Court, to preserve the practical effect of Article 3(2) of the TFEU, the rule also applies 'at an earlier stage, when such an agreement is being negotiated and, at a later stage, when a body established by the agreement is called upon to adopt measures implementing it'.[15]

The criterion of common rules being affected has been elaborated upon in the case law of the EU Court.[16] In short, the international commitment must touch upon an area where the Union has previously taken legislative action.[17] In this analysis, of importance is not only the current Union law, but even the foreseeable development of it.[18] There need not be any discrepancy between the international

[10] TFEU, Art 2(2).

[11] TFEU, Art 4(3).

[12] See ch 12 by David Langlet in this volume.

[13] *ERTA* (n 8).

[14] As other grounds for exclusivity, Art 3(2) of the TFEU mentions situations where the conclusion of an international agreement is provided for in a legislative act of the Union or is necessary to enable it to exercise its internal competence.

[15] Joined Cases C-626/15 and C-659/16 *Commission v Council (Antarctic MPAs)* ECLI:EU:C:2018:925, para 112.

[16] In addition to *ERTA* (n 8) see Opinion 2/91 *(ILO Convention)* [1993] ECR I-01061, ECLI:EU:C:1993:106; Opinion 1/94 *(WTO Agreements)* [1994] ECR I-05267, ECLI:EU:C:1994:384; the so-called 'Open Skies' cases, eg, Case C-467/98 *Commission v Denmark (Open Skies)* [2002] ECR I-09519, ECLI:EU:C:2002:625; Opinion 1/03 *(Lugano Convention)* [2006] I-01145, ECLI:EU:C:2006:81.

[17] Opinion 1/94 (n 16) para 77.

[18] Opinion 1/03 (n 16) para 126.

commitments and Union rules; instead, what is required is a material coincidence between the objects of regulation.[19] The ERTA test thus hinges upon whether 'the discretion enjoyed by the Union legislature is reduced where commitments are entered into vis-a-vis third countries'.[20]

For the ERTA effect to arise, at stake must be an international commitment that produces legal effects. This may prove crucial for task-sharing between the Members States and the EU in the BSR context, as the output of many of the BSR bodies takes the form of recommendations, which are not formally legally binding decisions.[21] However, according to established case law, common rules can sometimes even be affected by 'non-binding measures' adopted by or discussed in an international body. This is exemplified by *Commission v Greece (IMO)*, where the Greek Republic was found to have acted in breach of exclusive Union competence and the duty of cooperation when it submitted a proposal to an International Maritime Organization (IMO) Committee inviting it to examine the creation of tools for monitoring ships' and port facilities' compliance with the International Convention for the Safety of Life at Sea (SOLAS Convention).[22] The Court held that the ERTA effect was triggered, as the Member State had 'submitted to that committee a proposal which initiates a procedure which could lead to the adoption by the IMO of new rules'.[23] More recently in *Commission v Council (IMO)*, in a dispute relating to a submission to the IMO on the introduction of guidelines on the reduction of greenhouse gas emissions from ships, the European Commission has argued that 'the submission of *proposals or information papers* to the IMO' by the Member States instead of the EU could breach exclusive Union competence.[24]

There are established rules even relating to the kinds of Union rules that may be 'affected'. Exclusivity usually does not arise where the Union's powers (eg, in the field of research) are of such a kind that Member State action does not take away from the Union's action.[25] In this regard, of particular importance for marine environmental protection in the BSR context may be the so-called 'minimum harmonisation' rule. In Opinion 2/91 *(ILO Convention)*, it was established that where both pre-existing Union rules on chemical safety at work and

[19] Opinion 2/91 (n 16) para 25; *Commission v Denmark (Open Skies)* (n 16) paras 88–92 and 101.

[20] Opinion of AG Kokott in Case C-137/12 *Commission v Council (Conditional access services)* ECLI:EU:C:2013:441, para 101.

[21] Koivurova and Rosas (n 3) 213.

[22] Case C-45/07 *Commission v Greece (IMO)* [2009] ECR I-00701, ECLI:EU:C:2009:81, para 10.

[23] ibid, paras 20–23.

[24] Case C-161/20 *Commission v Council (IMO)* ECLI:EU:C:2022:260, para 20. At para 71, the Commission's action was rejected on the grounds that the Union was not itself a member of the IMO and that, as a result, only the Member States were able under the IMO rules to present the submission to said body (emphasis added); see discussion in section V below.

[25] J Heliskoski, *Mixed Agreements As a Technique for Organizing the International Relations of the European Community and its Member States* (The Hague, Kluwer Law International, 2001) 39–40; A Rosas, 'Exclusive, Shared and National Competence in the Context of EU External Relations: Do Such Distinctions Matter?' in I Govaere et al (eds), *The European Union in the World: Essays in Honour of Professor Marc Maresceau* (Leiden, Brill/Nijhoff, 2014) 19.

the provisions of an ILO Convention in the same field amounted to minimum harmonisation, Member State action was not barred by the ERTA rule as neither Union law nor the Convention prevented the adoption of stricter standards.[26] In a similar vein, Union rules on environmental protection are, as a rule, adopted in the form of minimum harmonisation, which enables the Member States to opt for more ambitious protection measures.[27] Where, for example, the binding standards adopted by HELCOM as annexes to the Helsinki Convention exceed EU regulation in ambition but do not compel the Member States, it may be possible to construe that the rules of EU external relations law do not prevent the Member States from acting in the context of HELCOM where such standards are discussed, and from opting for the HELCOM standard over the level of EU regulation. However, the Opinion delivered by the EU Court on the *Marrakesh Agreement*[28] provides a cautionary tale: where the international commitments require the Member States to choose a certain regulatory approach that is voluntary under Union law, Union rules can be seen to be affected to such an extent that ERTA-based exclusivity is triggered.[29] It is also noteworthy that the European Commission has been known to oppose such unilateral Member State action in the context of mixed agreements in the field of environmental protection that could affect EU environmental regulation adopted in the form of minimum harmonisation.[30] If such a view is accepted by the EU Court, this means that the Member States cannot unilaterally agree to such terms on the international plane without breaching their obligations under Union law.

The EU Court has taken a systemic approach to the application of the ERTA test: instead of comparing Union rules and international acts word by word, it assesses whether the envisaged act might affect the 'unified and coherent system of rules' created in Union law.[31] This approach finds its roots in the doctrine according to which Union rules may not only be affected where the areas covered by the international commitments and those covered by the Union rules coincide fully, but also where an area is already covered to a large extent by Union rules.[32] As an result, in Opinion 1/03 *(Lugano Convention)*, it was held that ERTA-based exclusivity is triggered even where the Union has only exercised its legislative powers in parts covered by 'the main provisions' of an international agreement.[33] A similar approach was adopted for instance towards the Convention on the civil

[26] Opinion 2/91 (n 16) paras 13–18; see M Kuisma, '*ERTA*, Mixity and the Duty of Co-operation in the Conclusion of International Agreements: *Opinion 2/91*' in G Butler and R Wessel (eds), *EU External Relations Law: The Cases in Context* (Oxford, Hart Publishing, 2022).

[27] TFEU, Art 193.

[28] Opinion 3/15 *(Marrakesh Treaty)* ECLI:EU:C:2017:114.

[29] ibid, paras 126–29.

[30] Case C-246/07 *Commission v Sweden (PFOS)* [2010] ECR I-03317, ECLI:EU:C:2010:203, para 58. On mixity in the field of environmental protection, see below.

[31] Opinion 1/03 (n 16) paras 151, 162–63 and 172.

[32] Opinion 2/91 (n 16) paras 25–26.

[33] Opinion 1/03 (n 16) paras 159–60.

aspects of international child abduction in Opinion 1/13 *(Hague Convention)*,[34] the subject matter of which coincides with some of the endeavours of the CBSS in the BSR. The approach can be attributed to pragmatic concerns informed by the reality of international cooperation: the Court has implied that 'an international agreement normally forms a whole, where everything may have an impact on everything, and … splitting this whole up into small parts would be foreign to the reality of international treaty negotiations'.[35] Systemic is not, however, equal to holistic:[36] as there needs to be a link to previous or ongoing use of Union competence, the expansion of exclusive external competence is ultimately limited by the principle of conferred powers.

Finally, irrespective of which type of EU competence discussed above is at hand, it has been assumed as a premise of Union legislation that Union acts should have as few legal bases as possible. In situations where an act touches upon more than one field, the so-called 'centre of gravity test' is used to identify the dominant field which shall determine the competence basis to be used.[37] In addition, a doctrine concerning the so-called 'ancillary provisions of international agreements' has been developed in case law, according to which aspects of international agreements that are merely ancillary in nature may be subsumed under the main competence basis governing the international commitment at stake.[38] These seemingly technical rules have important repercussions for the task-sharing between the EU and its Member States. It has been accepted in case law that the centre of gravity test also becomes applicable in so-called 'vertical relations', where the choice is between competence heads involving the Union or the Member States.[39] By virtue of the principal aim of the rules at hand, the Union has, for example, been found competent to adopt rules incorporating international standards on the prevention of ship-source pollution into Union law, as well as to establish criminal penalties for infringement of those rules on the basis of its competence in the field of common transport policy, although regulation of criminal matters was, prior to the Lisbon Treaty, in principle left to the Member States.[40] This practically entails that the Union may, in its external action, gain competence on issues which, if judged individually, would belong to the Member States.

[34] Opinion 1/13 *(Accession of Third States to the Hague Convention)* ECLI:C:2014:2303, para 83.

[35] A Rosas, 'EU External Relations: Exclusive Competence Revisited' (2015) 38 *Fordham International Law Journal* 1073, 1089.

[36] See Opinion of AG Hogan in Opinion 1/19 *(Istanbul Convention)* ECLI:EU:C:2021:198, para 95.

[37] See, eg, Case C-263/14 *Parliament v Council (Pirate Transfer Agreements)* ECLI:EU:C:2016:435, paras 43–44 with references.

[38] Opinion 2/15 *(EUSFTA)* ECLI:EU:C:2017:376, para 276 with references; Case C-25/94 *Commission v Council (FAO)* [1996] ECR I-01469, ECLI:EU:C:1996:114, para 47.

[39] See L Prete 'The constitutional limits to the choice of mixity after *EUSFTA*, *COTIF I*, *MPA Antarctic* and *COTIF II*: towards a more constructive discourse?' (2020) 45 *European Law Review* 113, 117–19.

[40] Case C-440/05 *Commission v Council (Maritime Pollution)* [2007] ECR I-09097, ECLI:EU:C:2007:625, paras 61–66.

The preceding discussion has emphasised the need for case-by-case determination inbuilt in the rules on the EU's external competence. This means that the delimitation between different heads of competence may prove difficult. Disagreements have often arisen between the European Commission and the Council and/or the Member States, for example, on how projects that primarily aim at environmental protection goals but also affect other policy interests should be characterised in relation to the Union's powers. These difficulties partly relate to the general role of environmental protection in the Union's policies. Environmental protection was originally introduced in the EU in the 1970s as a flanking policy to the single market.[41] In this tradition, the Treaties still necessitate environmental protection requirements to be integrated in all Union policies and activities,[42] including, for example, actions falling within the field of the Union's exclusive competence on the conservation of marine biological resources under the common fisheries policy. In addition, environmental protection also features as a separate competence head of a shared nature.[43] Where an action falls into the field of this shared competence, the Member States retain their principled ability to act in their own name, provided that the Union has not decided to use its competence. However, if the project is seen to affect pre-existing Union rules (even in another policy field) or if its centre of gravity falls into a field where the Union enjoys an exclusive competence, the Union assumes responsibility for external action.

The identification of the centre of gravity of a project in which marine environmental protection interests were entangled with fisheries regulation proved to be a key issue in *Antarctic MPAs*,[44] in which the European Commission and Member States clashed over the nature of the Union's competence with regard to the establishment of marine protected areas (MPAs) in the Antarctic waters under the auspices of the executive organ of the Convention for the Conservation of Antarctic Marine Living Resources (CCAMLR). The Council and the Member State governments involved held that the question fell within the field of environmental protection. The Commission, by contrast, construed the question as pertaining to the conservation of marine biological resources under the common fisheries policy; and, by way of a secondary argument, sought to rely on ERTA-based exclusivity established

[41] Statement of the Heads of State or Government from the Paris European Summit (19–21 October 1972) (Bulletin of the European Communities, October 1972, No 10, Office for official publications of the European Communities 1972) 14–26; and Declaration of the Council of the European Communities and of the representatives of the Governments of the Member States meeting in the Council of 22 November 1973 on the programme of action of the European Communities on the environment [1973] OJ L112/1. For a historical overview see, eg, K Kulovesi and M Cremona, 'The evolution of EU competences in the field of external relations and its impact on environmental governance policies' in C Bakker and F Francioni (eds), *The EU, the US and Global Climate Governance* (Abingdon, Routledge, 2016).

[42] TFEU, Art 11.

[43] Now TFEU, Art 4(2)(e).

[44] Antarctic MPAs (n 15).

by Union regulation of fishing activities. The EU Court eventually found that the initiative fell within the field of environmental protection, and that ERTA-based exclusivity had not been established as the Commission had failed to show that the CCAMLR activities could affect the 'meaning, scope and effectiveness' of common rules on fisheries.[45] As will be seen below, similar delimitation issues have been encountered in the sphere of BSR cooperation as well.

III. Mixity

Where an international commitment falls within the scope of non-exclusive Union competence, a window opens for 'mixity', ie, action by both the Union and its Member States side by side.[46] As has been emphasised by the EU Court, mixity does not mean that either actor, the Union or the Member States, would assume and utilise each other's powers: rather, both act within the sphere of their own.[47] In the case of shared Union competence, for instance, it may be decided that the Union will exercise its competence with regard to certain aspects of an international agreement, leaving other aspects untouched and, thus, free for the Member States to act upon in their own name.

It is noteworthy that the window of opportunity does not automatically lead to mixity, as mixity in the field of shared Union competence is often 'facultative', meaning that the Union institutions have discretion to decide that the Union alone shall act and thus pre-empt Member State action.[48] Mixity is thus contingent on the EU's political choice, and remains in the Member States' own discretion only where their action is deemed to be of such a character that it does not obstruct or undermine the Union's use of its powers.[49] However, where the international commitment concerns issues upon which the Member States have retained their powers and the Union thus lacks competence altogether, mixity becomes obligatory. Only the Member States are competent to conclude such parts of an international commitment that remain in their sole competence. As the membership of BSR organisations attests, mixity can even be incomplete; not all EU Member States need necessarily be parties to a mixed agreement.[50]

The practice usually followed in the field of environmental protection is that the Union participates in international agreements alongside the Member States.[51]

[45] ibid, paras 113–24.

[46] Generally on mixity, see Heliskoski, *Mixed Agreements* (n 25).

[47] Opinion 1/19 *(Istanbul Convention)* ECLI:EU:C:2021:832, paras 258–59.

[48] Confirmed, eg, in *Antarctic MPAs* (n 15) para 126.

[49] See examples of such situations in section II.

[50] In case law see, eg, Opinion 1/76 (n 8) paras 6–7; and more recently, Opinion 1/19 (n 47) para 260. On the geographical justification for incomplete mixity, see J Heliskoski and G Kübek, 'A Typology of EU Mixed Agreements Revisited' in N Levrat et al (eds), *The EU and its Member States' Joint Participation in International Agreements* (Oxford, Hart Publishing, 2022) 35–39.

[51] See Kulovesi and Cremona (n 41) 91.

The BSR is no exception in this regard: from the vantage point of EU external relations law, the Helsinki Convention is a mixed agreement. The history of the Union's accession to the Convention shows how the existence of a window for mixity often divides opinions.

The Helsinki Convention was originally signed by seven coastal Baltic Sea States in 1974. The Union's accession was originally initiated by EU Council authorisation in 1977; however, the accession was initially blocked by the opposition of 'one Contracting Party to the Convention, not a [EU] Member State'.[52] The Union's interest in the developments within HELCOM was nonetheless evident: the European Commission has participated as an observer in HELCOM meetings since 1991.[53] When the process resumed in 1993, the Union's accession was justified by the Commission with reference to the fact that the Convention covered the same fields as the then European Community's 'abundance of legislation' on water matters. The Commission thus argued that 'in accordance with the [EU Court's] findings in [ERTA], the Community has the power to conclude such a Convention'; '[b]esides', according to the Commission, the participating EU Member States 'alone are not able to meet all the obligations deriving from the Convention'.[54] It is unclear whether these statements were merely meant to justify the existence of a Union competence to act, or whether in the Commission's view, the Union's competence vis-a-vis the Helsinki Convention was exclusive in nature. Mixity appears to have been seen as obligatory by some; it was held by one of the Union's preparatory organs that the areas of application of the Helsinki Convention fell 'partly within the Community's jurisdiction and partly within the jurisdictions of the individual Member States'.[55] Ultimately, the EU Council Decisions on the accession as well as on the conclusion of the revised Helsinki Convention of 1992 on behalf of the Union were based on the Treaty provisions on the environment, that is a shared competence basis.[56] Article 130r(4) of the EC Treaty (now Article 191(4) of the TFEU) conferred on the Union a power to conclude international agreements in the field that was without prejudice to Member State competence to negotiate in international bodies and to conclude international agreements. This has been taken to 'essentially [mean] that both

[52] Commission, 'Proposal for a Council Decision on the Accession of the Community to the Convention on the Protection of the Marine Environment of the Baltic Sea Area (Helsinki Convention – 1974)' COM(93) 284 final, 2.

[53] ibid, 4.

[54] ibid, 2.

[55] ECOSOC, Opinion on the proposal for a Council Decision on the accession of the Community to the Convention on the Protection of the Marine Environment of the Baltic Sea Area (Helsinki Convention – 1974) [1994] OJ C34/6.

[56] Council Decision 94/156/EC on the accession of the Community to the Convention on the Protection of the Marine Environment of the Baltic Sea Area 1974 (Helsinki Convention) [1994] OJ L73/1; and Council Decision 94/157/EC on the conclusion, on behalf of the Community, of the Convention on the Protection of the Marine Environment of the Baltic Sea Area (Helsinki Convention as revised in 1992) [1994] OJ L73/19.

the EU and its twenty-seven Member States will negotiate multi-lateral environmental agreements'.[57]

It is noteworthy that mixity may even be conditioned by the rules of the international organisation at hand. It has been held by the EU Court that the Union's powers must be exercised in observance of international law.[58] Thus, the EU rules on mixity and the applicable institutional rules must be observed in tandem. This is illustrated by the previously discussed *Antarctic MPAs* case, in which the EU Court found that the establishment of MPAs fell into the scope of a Union competence of a shared nature. Observed from the vantage point of Union law alone, this would mean that the Union could choose to act alone, thus pre-empting the Member States' right to participate in the work of the CCAMLR.[59] However, the EU Court found that exclusive Union action was barred because of the institutional rules of the Antarctic Treaty which did not confer the Union a fully autonomous position in the CCAMLR, and that the Member States' involvement was therefore required.[60]

A similar interaction between Union rules and regional institutional rules can be found in the context of HELCOM. Although EU law could allow joint action by the Union and its Member States in environmental matters dealt with in HELCOM, the voting rules in Article 23(2) of the Helsinki Convention practically rule out mixity in HELCOM decision-making. The Article lays down the premised rule according to which either the Union or its Member States shall exercise their right to vote in HELCOM. This means, practically, that it is up to the Union and its Member States, observing the limits deriving from the division of competences under the EU Treaties, to agree among themselves which party, the Union or the Member States, will exercise the voting right.

An agreement to the benefit of the latter does not, however, necessarily entail that the Member States are free to decide how to cast their vote. It has been emphasised, with regard to similar decision-making mechanisms in other international treaties, that unilateral Member State action could lead to a breach of the 'duty of co-operation'.[61] This principle is discussed next.

IV. Duty of Cooperation

Member State obligations under EU law are only applicable within the scope of application of Union law. It bears emphasising that the scope of EU law does not

[57] H Vedder, 'The formalities and substance of EU external environmental competence: stuck between climate change and competitiveness' in E Morgera (ed), *The External Environmental Policy of the European Union* (Cambridge, Cambridge University Press, 2012) 19.
[58] *Antarctic MPAs* (n 15) para 127.
[59] ibid, para 126.
[60] ibid, paras 128–33.
[61] *PFOS* (n 30) paras 92–94.

necessarily coincide with the ambit of the EU's competences. Crucially, within the scope of Union law, the Member States may derive obligations from the general principles of EU law even where they are competent to act on their own.[62]

A key principle applicable in the scope of EU law is the principle of sincere cooperation laid down in Article 4(3) of the Treaty on European Union (TEU). It requires the Union and the Member States to assist each other in carrying out tasks which flow from the Treaties, and the latter to facilitate the achievement of the Union's tasks and to refrain from any measure which could jeopardise the attainment of its objectives. In the context of external relations, this foundational principle provides the basis for the so-called 'duty of cooperation'.[63]

Justified by the EU Court with reference to a 'requirement of unity in the international representation' of the Union,[64] the duty of cooperation requires 'close cooperation between the Member States and the [Union] institutions, both in the process of negotiation and conclusion and in the fulfilment of the commitments entered into'.[65] It requires the Member States to refrain from any action that would contradict the Union's aims where the international commitment falls within the scope of Union law.[66] The principle is even referred to as the basis for the Member States' duty to 'act jointly in the Union's interest' in such international bodies from which the Union is barred due to the rules of the institution at hand.[67] The duty of cooperation thus determines the leeway that the Union institutions and the Member States have in their external policy-setting and action from the vantage point of EU law.[68] Similar to the rules on Union competence, the duty of cooperation may be triggered by international action that is, as such, non-binding; preparatory acts that have been found to trigger it include a proposal of the addition of a substance to an Annex of the Stockholm Convention on Persistent Organic Pollutants from which the Union was able to opt out,[69] as well as the submission of a reflection paper on a future proposal for the establishment of an MPA in Antarctic waters.[70]

[62] J Heliskoski, 'Adoption of Positions under Mixed Agreements (Implementation)' in C Hillion and P Koutrakos (eds), *Mixed Agreements Revisited: The EU and its Member States in the World* (Oxford, Hart Publishing, 2010) 140–41.

[63] See, eg, C Hillion, 'Mixity and Coherence in EU External Relations: The Significance of the "Duty of Cooperation"' in C Hillion and P Koutrakos (eds), *Mixed Agreements Revisited: The EU and its Member States in the World* (Oxford, Hart Publishing, 2010).

[64] Opinion 2/91 (n 16) para 36.

[65] *PFOS* (n 30) para 73.

[66] See, eg Opinion 2/91 (n 16) para 38; Opinion 1/94 (n 16) paras 106–10; *FAO* (n 38) paras 48–50; Case C-459/03 *Commission v Ireland (MOX Plant)* [2006] ECR I-04635, ECLI:EU:C:2006:345 paras 174–75; *Commission v Greece (IMO)* (n 22) para 25; *PFOS* (n 30) paras 104–05; Case C-620/16 *Germany v Commission (COTIF II)* ECLI:EU:C:2019:256, para 94.

[67] Opinion 2/91 (n 16) paras 5 and 37.

[68] See, eg, C Eckes, 'Disciplining Member States: EU Loyalty in External Relations' (2020) 22 *Cambridge Yearbook of European Legal Studies* 1.

[69] *PFOS* (n 30) para 56.

[70] *Antarctic MPAs* (n 15) para 1.

The limits posed by the duty of cooperation on Member State discretion are even reflected by the rules of some BSR organisations. For instance, the interlinkage between HELCOM commitments and EU environmental law is recognised in HELCOM's Baltic Sea Action Plan (BSAP). The Preamble to the BSAP explicitly mentions that the agreement is 'without prejudice to international agreements and legislation of the European Community'. The recommendations attached to the BSAP expressly 'acknowledge' previous EU rules and policies, for example, in the field of maritime spatial planning, thus reducing the room for conflict between HELCOM and EU rules.[71] Certain BSAP obligations of EU Member States even reach further than the standard agreed upon by Russia in order to fulfil the Union's policy goals.[72] The BSAP also takes care to note where obligations incorporated in the BSAP have already previously existed in EU law and thus continue to bind the Member States as EU law obligations.[73] Although such precautions taken in the drafting of international commitments cannot generally remove a conflict with EU external relations law,[74] these details can be seen as symptomatic of the recognition in the HELCOM context that the EU Member States must respect their obligations as EU Member States.

A concrete example of the coordination required by the duty of cooperation is the adoption of and adherence to Union positions for meetings of bodies established under (mixed) international agreements.[75] Under Article 218(9) of the TFEU, the European Commission proposes, and the EU Council adopts, decisions establishing the positions to be adopted on the Union's behalf in a body set up by an agreement, when that body is called upon to adopt acts having legal effects. The positions may target a specific meeting or even span several years of work in the context of a particular international body.[76] They may be adopted as Union, common, or coordinated positions.[77]

[71] HELCOM, 'HELCOM Recommendation 28E/9' (Adopted 15 November 2007); HELCOM, 'HELCOM Baltic Sea Action Plan' (HELCOM Ministerial Meeting, Krakow, Poland, 15 November 2007) 57–58 (BSAP).

[72] See, eg, a stricter framework for the reduction of nitrogen emissions in order to strengthen the emission targets for nitrogen under Directive 2001/81/EC of the European Parliament and of the Council on national emission ceilings for certain atmospheric pollutants (National Emissions Ceilings Directive) [2001] OJ L209/22; BSAP (2007) 11.

[73] See, eg, with regard to the obligations stemming from the International Convention on the Control of Harmful Anti-fouling Systems on Ships (AFS Convention, London, 5 October 2001); BSAP (n 72) 24.

[74] According to established case law, an initiative seeking to avoid contradictions between EU law and the international commitment 'does not remove the obligation to determine, prior to the conclusion of the agreement, whether it is capable of affecting' Union rules; Opinion 1/03 (n 16) para 129.

[75] See Heliskoski, 'Adoption of Positions under Mixed Agreements (Implementation)' (n 62).

[76] See, eg, the description of the five-year positions for Union participation in the CCAMLR in *Antarctic MPAs* (n 15) paras 16–18 and 27.

[77] See M Chamon and M Cremona, 'The Representation of the EU and its Member States in Multilateral Fora: The *AMP Antarctique* Effect' in N Levrat et al (eds), *The EU and its Member States' Joint Participation in International Agreements* (Oxford, Hart Publishing, 2022) 99. For a third-party perspective, see P Olson, 'Mixity from the Outside: The Perspective of a Treaty Partner' in C Hillion and P Koutrakos (eds), *Mixed Agreements Revisited: The EU and its Member States in the World* (Oxford, Hart Publishing, 2010) 339.

Similar to the conclusion of international agreements, the preparation of positions may give rise to disagreements over the nature of the Union's competence, or over whether the Union should exercise its competence at all. Even in the context of Article 218(9) of the TFEU, the concept of 'acts having legal effects' has been interpreted broadly.[78] For instance, it has been found by the EU Court that the Union could establish a position to be adopted on its behalf regarding the adoption of recommendations in the International Organisation of Vine and Wine (OIV) – an organisation to which the Union was not itself party – aiming to help the OIV to achieve its objectives relating, inter alia, to standardisation activities. It proved decisive that the EU legislature incorporated the OIV recommendations in EU rules within the framework of the common organisation of the wine markets; as a result, the recommendations were found by the EU Court to have legal effects, which meant that a Union position could be adopted.[79]

Examples of similar disagreements are even found in the context of BSR cooperation. In the preparation, in 2013, of a HELCOM meeting anticipated to decide on the submission of an application to the IMO on the designation of the Baltic Sea as a Nitrogen Oxide Emission Control Area (NECA), the European Commission had proposed the adoption of a Council Decision establishing a position to be taken on the matter in HELCOM, according to which the EU Member States should support the proposed designation of the Baltic Sea as a NECA.[80] This suggestion practically meant that the Union would use its shared competence. However, the Council disagreed. As it emerges from the minutes of the Committee of Permanent Representatives meeting, 'a large majority of delegations had considered that the Union had not exercised its competence on the particular area of NOx emissions from international shipping and that it would not be opportune to do so'.[81] The outcome was that no Union position was adopted. According to the Council, this meant that the HELCOM Member States could voluntarily coordinate their positions with the Commission prior to the meeting.[82]

The failure to formally adopt a Union position does not, however, necessarily mean that the position is without any effect. This finds support in older case law pertaining to the adoption of common rules on the conservation of marine resources. In *Commission v the United Kingdom*, the European Commission had suggested a series of conservation measures, the adoption of which had been blocked by the Member States in the EU Council. The EU Court held that despite

[78] See the immediately preceding discussion; and, in the context of the existence of Union competence, section II above.

[79] Case C-399/12 *Germany v Council (OIV)* ECLI:EU:C:2014:2258, paras 57–64.

[80] Commission, 'Proposal for a Council Decision establishing the position to be taken in HELCOM and IMO concerning the designation on the Baltic Sea as Nitrogen Oxide Emissions Control Area (NECA)' COM(2013) 300 final.

[81] Council of the European Union, '2465th meeting of the Permanent Representatives Committee held in Brussels on 11 September 2013' (13605/13) 12–13.

[82] ibid.

their lack of formal adoption, the Commission proposals 'represent the point of departure' for concerted Union action in the field, and that the principle of sincere cooperation 'imposes on Member States special duties of action and abstention'.[83] Where a proposed position under Article 218(9) of the TFEU is similarly tied to ongoing policy development within the EU, it could be held to indicate the existence of a Union objective whose attainment the Member States are bound to support under their duty of cooperation.

V. The Practical Effect of EU External Relations Law on BSR Cooperation

A. General

The questions of mixity and duty of cooperation explored above mostly pertain to intra-EU task-sharing. Yet, they are by no means without implication for non-EU partners in the BSR.[84] As is clear from the preceding discussion, these doctrines factually condition the action of the EU and its Member States in international fora.[85] In what follows, it will be suggested that as a result, EU external relations law may impact the practical functioning and output of BSR organisations.

As a premise, it can be noted that BSR cooperation has various touching points with the Union's internal objectives and rules. The Union's objectives in the BSR are found in the European Union Strategy for the Baltic Sea Region (EUSBSR),[86] a macro-regional strategy guiding the cooperation between the Baltic coastal EU Member States[87] and neighbouring countries.[88] The most recent Action Plan[89] accompanying the EUSBSR recognises 14 different policy areas in which the BSR Member States are to act, including, inter alia, environmental protection, shipping, energy, security, tourism, culture, innovation, health, and education. The EUSBSR

[83] Case 804/79 *Commission v the United Kingdom* [1981] ECR-01045, ECLI:EU:C:1981:93, para 28.

[84] Portraying mixed agreements as a source of 'tremendous challenges for the EU's treaty partners', see Olson (n 77) 331.

[85] Accordingly, the decision on the legal bases of EU external action is viewed in the EU Court's case law as entailing 'indications to the other parties to that agreement' as regards the division of power between the Union and its Member States. See Opinion 1/19 (n 47) para 262.

[86] Commission, 'Communication from the Commission to the European Parliament, the Council, the European Economic and Social Committee and the Committee of the Regions concerning the European Union Strategy for the Baltic Sea Region' COM(2009) 248 final; adopted by the Council on 29 October 2009, see Council of the European Union, 'Presidency Conclusions', Brussels European Council 29/30 October 2009, 15265/1/09 (EUSBSR). See ch 4 by Helena Tuuri in this volume.

[87] Sweden, Denmark, Estonia, Finland, Germany, Latvia, Lithuania and Poland.

[88] Belarus, Iceland, Norway and Russia.

[89] Commission, 'Commission Staff Working Document EU Strategy for the Baltic Sea Region: Action Plan [COM(2009) 248 final]' SWD(2021) 24 final (EUSBSR Action Plan).

notes, inter alia, the Union's cohesion policy, integrated maritime policy, common fisheries policy, common agricultural policy, single market policies, the European Research Area, trans-European energy networks as well as EU Arctic policy as relevant for BSR cooperation. Given the broad substantive range of EU involvement in the area, EU external relations law has important potential for affecting practical BSR cooperation.

Building upon the findings of previous research on BSR cooperation, this section discusses two examples drawn from the region. First, previous research suggests that the intensity of the Union's involvement in HELCOM has caused irritation and affected cooperation in its sphere. As is explained below, the principles of EU external relations law contribute to the intensification of the Union's presence and may thus aggravate the situation, contrary to the common adage that EU external relations law produces efficiency in international cooperation. Second, previous research has identified a stakeholder wish for the European Commission's deeper involvement as a policy leader in the CBSS, an invitation which it has largely declined. Considering the effect of EU external relations law on the task-sharing between the EU and its Member States, it is tentatively suggested that in such a situation, EU external relations law might hamper Member State-led progress in regional cooperation, even if that progress would in principle be welcomed by the EU. These views are discussed in turn next.

B. The EU in HELCOM: A Challenge to the Orthodoxy of EU External Relations Law as a Source of Effectiveness?

The relationship between the EU and international organisations has been characterised as 'a "two-way flow of influence", entailing both an instrumental use by the EU of international organisations and an influence of international organisations on EU policies and policy making'.[90] This dynamic is also visible in the context of HELCOM and appears to affect the functioning of said body.

The policy areas and interests of the EUSBSR and HELCOM overlap to an important extent. HELCOM's areas of action span from agriculture and fisheries to environmental protection, maritime spatial planning, and shipping. Many of the material areas encompassed by its work thus fall within the field of shared competence under the EU Treaties, and its adoption of even non-binding recommendations may have an indirect bearing on the EU's discretion in adopting internal rules on same issues.[91] It is therefore no surprise that EU regulation of

[90] RA Wessel and J Odermatt, 'The European Union's engagement with other international institutions: Emerging questions of EU and international law' in RA Wessel and J Odermatt (eds), *Research Handbook on the European Union and International Organizations* (Cheltenham, Edward Elgar Publishing, 2019) 18.

[91] See the discussion on *Germany v Council (OIV)* (n 79).

marine environmental protection in the BSR is closely intertwined with HELCOM policymaking. Several factors contributing to this entanglement can be identified.

First, the Union's accession to the Helsinki Convention entails that the Convention is considered part of EU law, and as such binding on the Union as well as its Member States not only through their international commitment, but also under the EU Treaties. The implications are illustrated by the *Etang de Berre* cases, which dealt with another regional sea convention, the Barcelona Convention regulating the Mediterranean Sea. The cases arose from a local fishermen's syndicate's attempt to ban discharges into the Etang de Berre saltwater marsh by way of relying on a Protocol to the Barcelona Convention yet to be implemented by the French state, which required all discharges to be subjected to authorisation,[92] and from European Commission action against France for failure of implementation concerning the same provisions.[93] In the first-mentioned case, the EU Court found that the relevant provisions of the Protocol, as an instrument of EU law, prohibited any discharges where no authorisation had been issued by the national competent authorities, irrespective of the fact that no such national authorisation scheme yet existed in France.[94] In the latter case, the EU Court confirmed that insofar as the provisions of a regional environmental convention concluded by the Union and its Member States as a mixed agreement fall within the scope of Union competence, ensuring compliance with the commitments flowing from such a convention constitutes a Member State obligation towards the EU.[95] Thus, from the internal vantage point of EU law, EU accession in the Helsinki Convention has created a Member State obligation to implement any measures required to fulfil international commitments derived from the Convention, and may even entail that its provisions can be invoked before national courts irrespective of whether the Member State at stake has adopted the requisite national implementation measures.

Second, the Union has opted to utilise HELCOM as a policy platform in the field of the Union's integrated maritime policy. The Marine Strategy Framework Directive requires the EU Member States to use regional cooperation structures to coordinate among themselves and with third countries in the same region when developing their marine strategies.[96] HELCOM is used as such a regional cooperation structure in the field of marine environmental protection in the Baltic Sea area.[97] Consequently, HELCOM has been described as 'increasingly

[92] Case C-213/03 *Syndicat professionnel coordination des pêcheurs de l'étang de Berre et de la région v Électricité de France (EDF)* [2004] ECR I-07357, ECLI:EU:C:2004:464.

[93] Case C-239/03 *Commission v France (Étang de Berre)* [2004] ECR I-09325, ECLI:EU:C:2004:598.

[94] *Pêcheurs de l'étang de Berre* (n 92) paras 39, 45–47, and 52.

[95] *Étang de Berre* (n 93) paras 25–26.

[96] Directive 2008/56/EC of the European Parliament and of the Council establishing a framework for community action in the field of marine environmental policy [2008] OJ L164/19. For an overview, see D Langlet and S Mahmoudi, *EU Environmental Law and Policy* (Oxford, Oxford University Press, 2016) 237–45.

[97] HELCOM, 'HELCOM Ministerial Declaration on the Implementation of the HELCOM Baltic Sea Action Plan' (Moscow, 20 May 2010) 5.

focused on implementing European law and policy rather than developing their own international obligations to be implemented by their respective parties and the EU'.[98]

Third, there is a possibility that HELCOM's (non-binding) recommendations may become marine environmental standards binding upon the Member States as internal rules of EU law, if the Union legislator is inspired by HELCOM's work. This appears to be welcomed by HELCOM. The HELCOM BSAP expressly requires the HELCOM Members that are also EU Member States to incorporate various HELCOM measures into existing EU measures, thus making them doubly relevant for such Member States.[99] The BSAP further requires the EU and its Member States to influence the Union's internal policy-setting by providing input that is consistent with HELCOM objectives, inter alia, in the review of the EU common fisheries policy or in updating the lists of hazardous substances under the EU Water Framework Directive and the Registration, Evaluation, Authorisation and Restriction of Chemicals (REACH) Regulation.[100]

Based on the preceding discussion, it can be seen how the rules of EU external relations law are bound to intensify the internalisation effect already put to work by the above-mentioned HELCOM rules and EU regulation in the marine environmental sector. For, where HELCOM rules are transformed into binding rules of Union law or where the output of HELCOM otherwise tangents with existing EU rules, it results from the ERTA principle that the Union gains exclusive competence vis-a-vis such future HELCOM action that might affect said EU rules.[101] Even where the Union's competence is shared in nature, the EU's interest in the development of HELCOM's output might lead to the decision that the Union should act alone in HELCOM and pre-empt the Member States under Article 2(2) of the TFEU from using their own voice.

From the vantage point of the Union, this trajectory might be welcomed. The history of the Union's accession to HELCOM recounted above suggests that the EU's interest in contributing to Baltic Sea coastal states' efforts to protect the Baltic environment is partly invoked by its wish to protect its internal rulemaking, and partly by its perception that the Union's involvement is necessary for its Member

[98] B Bohman and D Langlet, 'Float or Sinker for Europe's Seas? The Role of Law in Marine Governance' in K Kern and M Gilek (eds), *Governing Europe's Marine Environment: Europeanization of Regional Seas or Regionalization of EU Policies?* (Farnham, Ashgate, 2015) 61.

[99] See, eg, inclusion of HELCOM measures aiming to reduce discharges and emissions of nutrients and hazardous substances to the programmes adopted under Directive 2000/60/EC of the European Parliament and of the Council establishing a framework for Community action in the field of water policy (EU Water Framework Directive) [2000] OJ L327/1; BSAP (n 72) paras 9 and 15.

[100] Regulation (EC) No 1907/2006 of the European Parliament and of the Council concerning the Registration, Evaluation, Authorisation and Restriction of Chemicals (REACH), establishing a European Chemicals Agency, amending Directive 1999/45/EC and repealing Council Regulation (EEC) No 793/93 and Commission Regulation (EC) No 1488/94 as well as Council Directive 76/769/EEC and Commission Directives 91/155/EEC, 93/67/EEC, 93/105/EC and 2000/21/EC [2006] OJ L396/1; BSAP (n 72) paras 16 and 21.

[101] On the EU Court's case law relating to the condition that common rules are affected, see section II.

States' success in the BSR. This corresponds to a broader tendency in the EU external relations discourse to view the streamlining effect of EU external relations law as a key ingredient of the Union's quest for a more effective attainment of the Union's objectives.[102] The exclusivity of the Union's competence is often seen as a guarantee for the expediency of EU external action.[103] This could be expected to be the case in HELCOM and the broader context of BSR cooperation as well: by the sheer weight of numbers, a unitary position advanced by the Union and its Member States represents the majority view and their joining of forces could be expected to lead to more effective decision-making in the BSR.

This vantage point can, however, be juxtaposed with the somewhat conflicting findings of research on the organisational dynamics inside HELCOM. Söderström and Kern have suggested that HELCOM negotiations have, in fact, been stifled by the knowledge that the recommendations adopted may turn into binding rules for all HELCOM Members but Russia. Furthermore, Russia has reportedly been put off by the increasing dominance of EU compliance control mechanisms[104] that ensues when HELCOM rules are turned into EU rules.[105] The phenomenon does not seem to be limited to HELCOM or the BSR alone.[106] Considering these findings, the internalisation effect to which EU external relations law contributes may in fact burden decision-making in HELCOM.

As the Union's interest in the developments within HELCOM is ultimately linked to its internal policymaking, it would appear at the first glance that EU external relations law cannot alone be relied on to remove the potential tensions. For the connection between the EU's internal policy-setting and enforcement and HELCOM recommendations is not lessened depending on which party, the Union or its Member States, acts in HELCOM. However, it cannot be ruled out that the identity of the party sitting at the table could have some bearing on the

[102] Noting the different variations of this construction emphasising the effectiveness of EU external action (a view favoured by the EU Commission) or the autonomy and primacy of EU law (a view subscribed to by the Court) see, eg, P Koutrakos, *EU International Relations Law* (Oxford, Hart Publishing, 2006) 125.

[103] By way of an example, the 'political complexity' attaching to the use of mixity has been highlighted recently in the context of the conclusion of trade agreements between the EU and third countries. See C Eckes and P Leino-Sandberg, 'The EU–UK Trade and Cooperation Agreement – Exceptional Circumstances or a New Paradigm for EU External Relations?' (2022) 85 *Modern Law Review* 164, 176.

[104] For an overview, see Langlet and Mahmoudi (n 96) 131–47. Noting that 'EU law stands a better chance of being effectively enforced than purely international agreements do', see Bohman and Langlet (n 98) 57–59.

[105] S Söderström and K Kern, 'The Ecosystem Approach to Management in Marine Environmental Governance: Institutional interplay in the Baltic Sea Region' (2017) 27 *Environmental Policy and Governance* 619. See also, N Tynkkynen, 'The Baltic Sea environment and the European Union: Analysis of governance barriers' (2017) 81 *Marine Policy* 124, 128.

[106] Noting a 'resistance to EU participation' and a need for the EU to 'be sensitive to the political climate of international institutions', see J Odermatt and RA Wessel, 'The challenges of engaging with international institutions: The EU and multilateralism under strain' in RA Wessel and J Odermatt (eds), *Research Handbook on the European Union and International Organizations* (Cheltenham, Edward Elgar Publishing, 2019) 671.

practical functioning of HELCOM decision-making. This question of optics is contingent on the politics of interpretation and application of the rules of EU external relations law, and it could be worth considering when the EU and its Member States prepare for action in HELCOM[107] and other international fora where the Union is actively involved.

C. The EU in the CBSS: A Desired Partner and Bogeyman at Once?

The premised view of the EU appears to be that the BSR belongs first and foremost to the Member States. The EUSBSR assigns BSR cooperation to the Member States and other BSR actors, and limits the European Commission's role to 'co-ordination, monitoring, reporting, facilitation of the implementation and follow-up' of the EUSBSR.[108] Yet, a wish for added EU involvement in the BSR emerges in the consultations conducted by the Commission in preparing the EUSBSR. The answers reveal a fatigue of sorts created by the numerosity of different institutional actors in the BSR. A call was repeated for the Commission to 'fulfil the need for an independent, multi-sector body that can guarantee the necessary co-ordination, monitoring and follow-up of the action plan'.[109]

Besides these general signals, calls have been made for the Commission to become more active in the CBSS more specifically.[110] The CBSS's stated aim has been to become 'a forum for all multilateral intergovernmental cooperation and dialogue in the Baltic Sea Region'.[111] However, the output of the CBSS has at times been perceived as modest[112] and it has been held to lack the capacity to 'clean up

[107] Note, however, that the meetings of HELCOM bodies with Russian involvement have at the time of writing been suspended: see HELCOM, 'Statement by the German Chairmanship of HELCOM on behalf of the European Union and the Contracting Parties to HELCOM that are Member States of the European Union' (4 March 2022).

[108] EUSBSR (above n 86) 10.

[109] ibid.

[110] Koivurova and Rosas (n 3) 218. On the role assumed by the EU in the CBSS, see ch 8 by Rosas and Vuorimäki in this volume.

[111] CBSS, 'Warsaw Declaration: Regional Responses to Global Challenges' (Meeting of Deputy Foreign Ministers of the Council of the Baltic Sea States, Warsaw, 8 June 2016). The ongoing EUSBSR actions of the CBSS, at the time of writing, aim at implementing the Union's climate change adaptation strategy, fostering cooperation in the fields of cultural heritage conservation and the labour market, preventing early school leaving, increasing research and innovation, protecting children and counteracting human trafficking, building networks of leaders in the field of civil security as well as improving fire and rescue capability development processes. See descriptions of the BSR Integrated Heritage Management project; Baltic Sea Labour Forum – BSLF (network); School to Work – S2W (network); Baltic Science Network (BSN); TRACE – Trafficking as a Criminal Enterprise; Baltic Leadership Programme in Civil Protection; Comprehensive and sustainable child protection; STROM II; FIRE-IN – First Responders Research and Innovation Network; as well as BSR Climate Change Dialogue Platform in the EUSBSR Action Plan (n 89).

[112] See discussion in ch 8 by Rosas and Vuorimäki in this volume.

the mess' of the overlapping multi-level forms of governance in the BSR.[113] Actors involved with the CBSS seem to value its existence and wish that it could live up to its full potential, yet despair over its lack of resources and ability to foster the development of concrete changes in legislation or practice.[114]

It is argued here that the regret over the Union's passivity suggests a mismatch in intra-EU expectations over the EU's role in the BSR. Fully establishing reasons for the calls for the Union to become more involved falls beyond the scope of the present contribution. However, it is suggested here that issues relating to the role-sharing between the Union and the Member States in external action may call for the Union's added presence in BSR cooperation. Namely, from the vantage point of EU external relations law, whether the EU chooses to be actively involved or not, its potential role casts a shadow on all Member State activity in the BSR. The EU and its Commission may thus be perceived as a desired partner and a bogeyman at once.

As a preliminary remark, it should be noted that in the CBSS Terms of Reference of 1992, last revised by the CBSS Ministers in 2020, it is the European Commission and not the EU that is recorded as a Member of the CBSS.[115] The implications of this arrangement can be analysed in light of the recent ruling in *Commission v Council (IMO)*, where the EU Court found that the conclusion of a Cooperation Arrangement between the IMO and the Commission did not entail that the EU would have entered into an arrangement with the IMO. As the IMO Convention was only open for state participation, the EU did not therefore have 'any status within the IMO' nor 'any basis on which it might itself be able to participate in the work of the institutions and committees of that organisation', unlike the Commission.[116] Accordingly, in the CBSS context, it can be concluded that only the Commission is a formal member of the CBSS. This may affect the ability of the EU as a body to participate in its proceedings. However, it does not remove the effects that may arise from the rules of EU external relations law, should actions taken in the CBSS fall into the field of EU law and/or the Union's competences. For where the EU is barred by the rules of an international body from participating itself in the proceedings, its competence may be exercised 'by the Member States acting jointly, under the duty of sincere cooperation referred to in Article 4(3) TEU, in the interest of the European Union'.[117]

A need for EU engagement might arise from several circumstances. First, the rules of the BSR institutions might require the Union's (or its Commission's) active contribution. This is particularly so in the context of BSR institutions like the CBSS

[113] Koivurova and Rosas (n 3) 218. For a view from within the CBSS Secretariat echoing these challenges, see A Krohn, 'The Council of the Baltic Sea States (CBSS): Fostering Cooperation in the Baltic Sea Region' (2000) 43 *German Yearbook of International Law* 65, 76.

[114] See references to interviews with CBSS actors in Koivurova and Rosas (n 3).

[115] CBSS, 'Council of the Baltic Sea States Terms of Reference' (1st CBSS Ministerial Session, March 1992, as revised by the CBSS Ministerial meeting, 19 May 2020).

[116] *Commission v Council (IMO)* (n 24) paras 54–60.

[117] ibid, para 69.

that take their decisions by consensus. This means that the Commission must be engaged for initiatives to get passed.

Second, the need for EU involvement is likewise clear where BSR bodies have undertaken to fulfil the EU's regulative aims. For example, the CBSS has been assigned as the Policy Area Coordinator for Policy Area Secure in the EUSBSR Action Plan.[118] Among the actions of the Policy Area is the aim of strengthening mechanisms for joint strategic and operational actions protecting human beings and societies from criminal threats, which translates, inter alia, into the facilitation and development of cooperation agreements on law enforcement and cross-border assistance in the field of human trafficking. The EUSBSR Action Plan identifies a host of EU policies and legislative measures which are touched by the Policy Area.[119] It seems clear that eventual progress on such international agreements in the CBSS will trigger the evaluation of whether the EU enjoys such (exclusive) competence in the field that pre-empts Member States from freely advancing these projects in the CBSS.

But in addition, a risk of non-compliance with EU external relations law looms even where the typically non-regulative 'indigenous' activities of BSR cooperation bodies are at stake. As was noted, the principles of EU external relations law affect initiative-taking in the context of international cooperation: the pre-emption rule relating to exclusive EU competence under Article 3(2) of the TFEU as well as the duty of cooperation have been held to be triggered even by preparatory acts.[120] This warrants caution towards unilateral initiative-taking in the context of regional action that tangents with Union policies.

Such a potential (and likely unintended) freezing effect of EU external relations law could be accentuated by the level of case-by-case evaluation and policy-discretion inherent in the rules of the EU external relations *acquis*. In addition, a political element can be identified in the enforcement of EU external relations

[118] EUSBSR Action Plan (n 89) 52 ff. Other EUSBSR projects that the CBSS has thus far been involved in include the development of information sharing and 'coast guard-like' services in the maritime domain; a project book developing regional risk scenarios and identifying gaps in order to anticipate disasters; enhanced cooperation and coordination among the municipalities of the BSA states to prevent human trafficking; exchange of knowledge and good practices on energy and resource efficiency in city management; as well as the establishment of youth camps and university seminars. See descriptions of the Baltic Sea Maritime Functionalities, Macro-Regional Risks Scenarios and Gaps Identification, STROM, BSR Dialogue Forum on Energy and Resource Efficiency – EFFECT, Council of the Baltic Sea States (CBSS) summer youth camp and Council of the Baltic Sea States (CBSS) Summer University actions in the EUSBSR Action Plan (n 89).

[119] According to the EUSBSR Action Plan (n 89), the most important include the UN Sendai Framework for Disaster Risk Reduction, see UNDRR, 'Sendai Framework for Disaster Risk Reduction 2015–2030' (2015); Decision No 1313/2013/EU of the European Parliament and of the Council on a Union Civil Protection Mechanism [2013] OJ L347/924; Directive 2011/36/EU of the European Parliament and of the Council on preventing and combating trafficking in human beings and protecting its victims, and replacing Council Framework Decision 2002/629/JHA [2011] OJ L101/1; and the UN Convention on the Rights of the Child (New York, 20 November 1989).

[120] See A Ott, 'Informalization of EU Bilateral Instruments: Categorization, Contestation, and Challenges' (2020) 39 *Yearbook of European Law* 569, 593–94.

law, adding to the unpredictability. It is noteworthy that the rules of EU external relations law do not automatically generate sanctions. Challenges to the Member States' (or the Union institutions') actions need to be brought before the EU Court by a party with a right of action – centrally the European Commission. Where Member State action in the BSR is deemed politically beneficial, some leeway might thus be gained through discretion in the enforcement of EU external relations rules. Prior examples can be cited. Originally in *ERTA*, the Court allowed the Member State-led negotiations of the road transport treaty at the heart of the dispute to be concluded despite having found that external competence rested exclusively with the Union, as this was seen beneficial 'with a view to ensuring most effectively the defence of the interests of the Community'.[121] In a similar vein, the Council has been known to adopt measures enabling Member States to maintain their international commitments in force after the EU Court had found those commitments to breach the Union's exclusive competence.[122] More recently, political salience seems to have played a role in the evaluation of international cooperation aimed at controlling the streams of migrants towards Europe; the Member States have been tacitly allowed to undertake such bilateral commitments with third countries that would seem prima facie contrary to the pre-emption rules laid down in primary Union law.[123]

It is not unimaginable that such politically sensitive cooperation between the EU Member States and, for example, Russia could develop in the BSR which the EU would deem beneficial and allow to take place bilaterally.[124] However, previous experience cautions that in less politically charged areas, the protection of the 'purity' of the EU external relations doctrine might be emphasised by the European Commission.[125] Disagreements concerning the role-sharing between the EU and Member States in HELCOM suggest that the rules of EU external relations law are enforced even in the BSR context.[126]

Where the Commission's message seems to be that the Member States own BSR cooperation and regional questions are thus virtually delegated to regional players, it would seem counterintuitive to sanction the Baltic Sea States for the

[121] *ERTA* (n 8) paras 86–87.

[122] M Cremona, 'EU External Relations Law: Unity and Conferral of Powers' in L Azoulai (ed), *The Question of Competence in the European Union* (Oxford, Oxford University Press, 2014) 74–77. For a recent example of a request that the EU Court should maintain the effects of an act later found to have breached the rules on exclusive external competence, see *Commission v Council (IMO)* (n 24) para 26.

[123] See Ott (n 120) 598.

[124] Note, however, that Russia's participation in the CBSS has been suspended at the time of writing: see Declaration by the Ministers of Foreign Affairs of Denmark, Estonia, Finland, Germany, Iceland, Latvia, Lithuania, Norway, Poland and Sweden and the High Representative of the European Union for Foreign Affairs and Security Policy on the participation by the Russian Federation and Belarus in the work of the Council of the Baltic Sea States (3 March 2022).

[125] See the case law in sections II, III and IV. eg, in *PFOS* (n 30) para 55, the crux of the EU Commission's opposition was that unilateral Member State action 'resulted in splitting the international representation of the [Union]'.

[126] See section IV.

progress made. Yet, it cannot be ruled out that the mere risk of enforcement action could factually affect BSR cooperation and thus, in part, explain the EU Member States' wish to involve the Commission more closely in the region.

VI. Conclusions

This chapter has sought to contextualise cooperation between the Union and its Member States in the BSR in the framework of EU external relations law. As was explained, the principles of EU external relations law become relevant whenever the Member States' external action falls into the substantive scope of EU law. In such situations, the Treaties may curb the Member States' independent action. If, moreover, the action may have legal effects and touches upon issues on which the EU has been granted competence to act in its founding Treaties, the Member States may be precluded from acting altogether and it is the Union that should exercise its competence in international fora. Given the large variety of issues encompassed by BSR cooperation that coincide with the Union's interests and powers, the evaluation of which player may act and whether mixity remains an option are part and parcel of the EU's and its Member States' activities in the BSR.

The preceding discussion has identified factors that may be relevant for determining the nature of the Union's competence and the consequent pre-emption of unilateral Member State action in the BSR context. It was noted how the prevalent environmental focus of BSR cooperation may bring about delimitation issues between different heads of Union competence, and how the minimum harmonisation approach to environmental regulation may also affect the evaluation of who gets to act. As exclusivity only applies where international cooperation could produce legal effects, it was also noted that the predominantly soft-law nature of the output of BSR bodies may entail that the issue does not arise. Yet, in EU external relations law, the question whether an international commitment produces legal effects and thus triggers the application of the various rules on competence division and sincere cooperation is interpreted broadly, and the evaluation takes place on a case-by-case basis. The Member States are bound by a duty of cooperation which requires them to be cautious so as not to interfere with the Union's prerogatives.

Discussing the impact that EU external relations law may have on the practical functioning of the BSR organisations, it was noted that in HELCOM, EU external relations law contributes to an ongoing intensification of the Union's role that may already be perceived as invasive by third actors. The experience gained with non-EU partners in the BSR thus somewhat contradicts the orthodoxy which portrays the streamlining effect of EU external relations law as a source of effectiveness. Although at the root of the Union's involvement are likely interests that pertain to its internal policy-setting, the rules of EU external relations law relating to participation could be relied upon to create more favourable optics to aid decision-making in HELCOM.

It was also noted that whereas EU dominance may cause problems, so may its passivity. Situations may occur in BSR cooperation where at least a doubt arises that the Member States are barred from unilateral action by the rules of EU external relations law. Without the Union's engagement, progress may thus remain unattainable. The rules of EU external relations law that aim at protecting the Union's policymaking autonomy and enhancing the fulfilment of the Union's external objectives might thus hinder progress in BSR cooperation. This is so even if the European Commission did not, as such, oppose the action at hand. It was therefore suggested that that the EU may appear at the same time as a desired partner and a bogeyman overshadowing regional cooperation.

Some support could be drawn from EU external relations law for the call on the Commission to adopt a more actively supportive role in the BSR. For the duty of cooperation, a cornerstone of EU external relations law, requires both the Member States and the Union. It has already been found by the EU Court in *Commission v Greece (IMO)* that the duty of cooperation obliged the Commission to allow the Greek proposal on new IMO rules to be discussed in the IMO Committee which it chaired.[127] The principle could thus be relied upon in support of more active involvement of the Commission in the BSR. After all, if BSR cooperation is expected to produce more robust regulative action, the rules of EU external relations law likely require that the Union should be on board.[128]

[127] *Commission v Greece (IMO)* (n 22) paras 25–26.

[128] This coincides with observations made regarding BSR cooperation more broadly. See H Ringbom and M Joas, 'The changing regulatory landscape of the Baltic Sea – An analysis' (2018) 98 *Marine Policy* 317, 318.

7

The EU's Interaction with Institutions in the Baltic Sea Region

VILJAM ENGSTRÖM

I. Introduction

Out of the Baltic Sea Region (BSR) coastal states, all but Russia are European Union (EU) members. The activities of these states in the region are governed by EU law and policies. At the same time, there is a vast number of other institutions active in the BSR. A 'Europeanisation' of the BSR is complemented by activities of a complex mix of actors with both substantively and normatively diverse approaches to governance of the BSR.[1] The EU has a formalised relationship with some of these actors, whereas with many there is none. In between, there is a range of institutions with different connections to the EU.

The aim of the present chapter is to illustrate modes of normative interaction between the EU and BSR institutions.[2] The chapter does this by looking at three BSR institutions in particular: the Baltic Marine Environment Protection Commission (HELCOM); the Council of the Baltic Sea States (CBSS); and Visions and Strategies Around the Baltic Sea (VASAB). The choice of these institutions is by no means random. First, they are pan-Baltic institutions. Second, they are implicated in the EU Strategy for the Baltic Sea Region (EUSBSR) and its Action Plan.[3] At the same time, all three illustrate different aspects of normative interaction with the EU.

[1] For an overview, see V Engström, 'Regulating the Baltic Sea – A Showcase of Normative Pluralism' (2018) 61 *German Yearbook of International Law* 347.

[2] 'Normative' in this context being used synonymously with 'regulatory'.

[3] Commission, 'Communication from the Commission to the European Parliament, the Council, the European Economic and Social Committee and the Committee of the Regions concerning the European Union Strategy for the Baltic Sea Region' COM(2009) 248 final; Commission, 'Commission Staff Working Document EU Strategy for the Baltic Sea Region Action Plan [COM(2009) 248 final] Revised Action Plan replacing the Action Plan of 17 March 2017 – SWD(2017) 118 final' SWD(2021) 24 final.

HELCOM is the monitoring body of the Helsinki Convention for the Protection of the Marine Environment of the Baltic Sea Area (Helsinki Convention).[4] The EU is a party to the Helsinki Convention, which brings the Convention into the realm of EU law. What also makes the interaction between EU and HELCOM of interest is the fact that the activities of the EU and HELCOM overlap in multiple ways. Whereas the Helsinki Convention and HELCOM are focused on the marine environment, the CBSS has a substantively broader purpose. At the time of its establishment, the CBSS was identified by the European Commission as the main regional actor for the coordination of EU activities in the BSR.[5] VASAB is a cooperation platform in spatial planning and development of BSR countries. Although VASAB may be the least prominent out of the three BSR institutions in terms of institutionalisation, its activities do, nevertheless, bring it within the realm of EU law and governance.

Although it is unclear whether the three institutions qualify as intergovernmental organisations in a strict sense of the term, the boundary between formal intergovernmental organisations and other institutional forms of cooperation is not decisive as far as regulatory impact is concerned. The present chapter identifies forms and functions of the interaction between the EU and the three BSR institutions and discusses ways in which this interaction can generate normative effects. The chapter begins with outlining the regionalisation of EU law and the Europeanisation of BSR governance. Both of these phenomena explain the central role of the EU in the region, and help to understand the impact of the EU's governance approach to regions. The chapter will then exemplify and discuss three normative features of EU engagement with BSR institutions: being a party to a treaty or a member of an institution; regulatory interdependence; and interaction through implementation. The chapter concludes by making some remarks on the pros and cons of EU interaction with other BSR institutions.

II. The Regionalisation of the EU and Europeanisation of the Region

The EU has evolved into the main regulatory actor in the BSR, exercising various degrees of competence in different policy areas.[6] As regulatory Europeanisation

[4] Convention on the Protection of the Marine Environment of the Baltic Sea Area (Helsinki Convention) 22 March 1974, 1507 UNTS 166; revised Convention on the Protection of the Marine Environment of the Baltic Sea, 1992 (with annexes, Helsinki Convention) 9 April 1992, 2099 UNTS 197.

[5] Commission, 'Communication from the Commission to the Council Orientations for a Union Approach Towards the Baltic Sea Region' SEC(94) 1747 final.

[6] In respect of shared competence, when EU law only sets minimum standards, members are free to adopt more strict obligations as long as they are compatible with secondary EU law, are proportional and not arbitrarily discriminatory in their effects on trade between the Member States. See, eg, G de Baere, 'EU External Action' in C Barnard and S Peers (eds), *European Union Law* (Oxford, Oxford University Press, 2014).

has become a feature of BSR cooperation, EU membership creates a de facto regulatory hierarchy for Baltic Sea States. In addition, policymaking in the BSR also becomes characterised by the governance approach of the EU. In this respect, a 'turn to governance' is a development particularly notable in the EU's approach to regions.[7] One expression of this is the adoption and ongoing development of macro-regional strategies. The Treaty of Lisbon elevated 'territorial cohesion' to one of the main aims of the EU.[8] European territorial cooperation is one of the goals of cohesion policy and provides a framework for the implementation of joint actions and policy exchanges between national, regional and local actors from different Member States. Macro-regional strategies are a means for the structuring and development of territorial cooperation.[9] The EUSBSR constitutes the overarching governance paradigm for the BSR, with the accompanying revised Action Plan identifying 14 Policy Areas (PAs) around which to cooperate in the region.[10]

EU legislation, as a point of departure, is of general applicability.[11] The Treaty on European Union (TEU) states that '[t]he Union shall respect the equality of Member States before the Treaties'.[12] This means that all provisions of EU law are to have the same meaning and are to be applied in the same fashion throughout the EU. As this is the case, the tailoring of EU law to regions requires intermediary mechanisms, such as the EUSBSR and its Action Plan. The EUSBSR sets priorities, highlights actors and cooperation patterns, and gives the Commission a notable role in governing EU BSR policies. As a device for regional implementation of EU legislation, it is both an example and generator of multi-level governance.[13] A distinguishing feature of macro-regional strategies is the rule of the 'three NOs'. This rule states that no new legislation can be introduced for developing and implementing macro-regional strategies, there is no own budget, and that instead of creating new institutions, the macro-regional strategies are to be supported by a multi-level and multi-actor governance approach. It hereby lies at the very heart of EU macro-regional strategies to think 'more strategically and imaginatively about the available means'.[14]

[7] For a general account, see PJ Cardwell, '"Governance" as the Meeting Place of EU Law and Politics' in PJ Cardwell and M-P Granger (eds), *Research Handbook on the Politics of EU Law* (Cheltenham, Edward Elgar Publishing, 2020); on this 'turn' and regionalisation, see, eg, S Gänzle and K Kern (eds), *A Macro-regional Europe in the Making: Theoretical Approaches and Empirical Evidence* (Basingstoke, Palgrave Macmillan, 2016).

[8] Treaty on European Union [2012] OJ C326/13 Art 3 (TEU).

[9] B Cristino et al, *New Role of Macro-regions in European Territorial Cooperation* (European Parliament, 2016) para 3; Commission, 'Commission Staff Working Document Accompanying the Document Report from the Commission to the European Parliament, the Council, the European Economic and Social Committee and the Committee of the Regions concerning the Added Value of Macro-regional Strategies [COM(2013) 468 final]' SWD(2013) 233 final.

[10] Commission, 'EU Strategy for the Baltic Sea Region Action Plan' (2021).

[11] Treaty on the Functioning of the European Union [2012] OJ C326/47, Art 288 (TFEU).

[12] TEU, Art 4(2).

[13] COM(2009) 248 final.

[14] Commission, 'Report from the Commission to the European Parliament, the Council, the European Economic and Social Committee and the Committee of the Regions concerning the added value of macro-regional strategies [SWD(2013) 233 final]' COM(2013) 468 final, 2.

The concrete impact of the EUSBSR is policy area specific.[15] However, the explicit aim of the Strategy is to reinforce the implementation of EU Directives.[16] As to its function, the EUSBSR Action Plan sets forth a list of concrete actions to be pursued. The characterisation of the EUSBSR as normatively 'soft', in other words, downplays its regulatory significance.[17] As with soft or guiding instruments more generally, macro-regional strategies also influence the implementation of EU policies and legislation.[18] When strategies highlight interconnections between actors and identify some as central for the cooperation, they also set priorities. Most importantly for present purposes, the PAs have an institutional presence, institutionalising cooperation with and among BSR actors. While cooperation with HELCOM is pinpointed as particularly important for the implementation of the EUSBSR, the Action Plan also acknowledges other institutions, including the CBSS and VASAB. In the Action Plan, the CBSS is granted the role as joint coordinator of PA Secure, while VASAB is designated together with HELCOM the role as coordinator of PA Spatial Planning.[19]

III. Characteristics of the Three Institutions

As the monitoring body of the Helsinki Convention, HELCOM consists of representatives of all Contracting Parties to the Convention, including the EU. Its tasks comprise monitoring the implementation of the Convention, making recommendations, setting objectives and promoting cooperation with other bodies.[20] Through state reporting and assessments, HELCOM follows up on the compliance by state parties with the Helsinki Convention and HELCOM recommendations. Reporting also serves the purpose of data production, and of displaying gaps in the framework. The HELCOM Monitoring and Assessment Strategy states as one of its purposes the production of assessment products for region-specific management purposes by also making use of data and

[15] Commission, 'Report from the Commission to the European Parliament, the Council, the European Economic and Social Committee and the Committee of the Regions on the Implementation of the EU Strategy for the Baltic Sea Region (EUSBSR)' COM(2011) 381 final, 8; K Böhme, 'Added Value of Macro Regional Strategies: A Governance Perspective Commission' in Commission, 'Commission Staff Working Document Accompanying the document Report from the Commission to the European Parliament, the Council, the European Economic and Social Committee and the Committee of the Regions concerning the added value of macro-regional strategies' SWD(2013) 233 final.

[16] Commission, COM(2009) 248 final, 10 (n 3).

[17] On the function of soft law in EU law, see, eg, L Senden, *Soft Law in European Community Law* (Oxford, Hart Publishing, 2004); and M Eliantonio, E Korkea-aho and O Ştefan (eds), *EU Soft Law in the Member States: Theoretical Findings and Empirical Evidence* (Oxford, Hart Publishing, 2021).

[18] See M Hartlapp and A Hofmann, 'The Use of EU Soft Law by National Courts and Bureaucrats: How Relation to Hard Law and Policy Maturity Matter' (2021) 44 *West European Politics* 134; F Terpan, 'Soft Law in the European Union – The Changing Nature of EU Law' (2015) 21 *European Law Journal* 68.

[19] Commission, SWD(2021) 24 final (n 3).

[20] Helsinki Convention, Art 20.

information produced for other fora, such as EU directives and various international institutions.[21] Through the Europeanisation of BSR governance, a claim has been made that HELCOM has been replaced by the EU as the most important actor in the region.[22] While this may be true as far as the capacity to issue normatively binding decisions is concerned, as will be explained below, EU legislative activity is closely intertwined with HELCOM work.

While the Helsinki Convention and HELCOM are focused on the marine environment, the CBSS has a substantively broader purpose. The members of the CBSS are all Baltic Sea States (plus Norway and Iceland) as well as the EU. The CBSS started as a loose framework in 1992, but established a permanent secretariat in 1998. By gradually widening its scope of action, the CBSS now covers almost every field of governmental activity.[23] At the time of its establishment, the CBSS was identified by the European Commission as the main regional actor for the coordination of EU activities in the BSR. For this reason, the Commission envisaged 'a permanent and active presence in this forum with a view to enhancing an efficient co-ordination of Union activities and programmes with those of other Baltic Sea States'.[24]

Like HELCOM, the CBSS displays many features of an intergovernmental organisation. The CBSS was established by the region's Foreign Ministers in 1992 through the adoption of a declaration. Even if the institutional structures of the CBSS are quite loose, it does have a permanent secretariat with legal personality, the capacity to contract, the right to acquire and possess property, and to participate in legal proceedings. The CBSS itself addresses its participants as 'Member States'.[25] The CBSS Council communiques and Heads of State Summit declarations or statements are in legal terms best characterised as recommendations (ie, political commitments). The CBSS has also refrained from sponsoring legal instruments. Whereas HELCOM recommendations, although formally non-binding, are subject to reporting and monitoring procedures, no such oversight mechanisms exist in the CBSS. There is also a notable difference in the substantive outcomes of the two institutions, with CBSS documents being more programmatic, whereas HELCOM recommendations define explicit thresholds for states to reach. This also means that the normative impact of CBSS acts is more difficult to quantify. While direct regulatory impact is absent,

[21] HELCOM, 'HELCOM Monitoring and Assessment Strategy' (HELCOM Ministerial Meeting, Copenhagen, 3 October 2013) para 2.3–2.5.

[22] N Tynkkynen et al, 'The Governance of the Mitigation of the Baltic Sea Eutrophication: Exploring the Challenges of the Formal Governing System' (2014) 43 *AMBIO* 105.

[23] See, eg, CBSS, 7th Baltic Sea States Summit, 'Chairman's Conclusions' (Riga, Latvia, 4 June 2008).

[24] SEC(94) 1747 final.

[25] Terms of Reference of the Secretariat of the Council of the Baltic Sea States (21 June 2004, revised in April 2009), available at: www.cbss.org/wp-content/uploads/2012/09/CBSS-Secretariat-Terms-of-Reference-2009.pdf. The Council of the Baltic Sea States (CBSS) has also been granted privileges and immunities in its host State (Sweden) through the Host Country Agreement. See M Cogen, *An Introduction to European Intergovernmental Organizations* (London, Routledge, 2016) 184–86.

the CBSS might nevertheless perform tasks that at least indirectly affect BSR cooperation.[26]

The third institution of interest for present purposes, VASAB, is a cooperation platform in spatial planning and development. Similar to HELCOM and the CBSS, VASAB includes all Baltic Sea States. VASAB is essentially intergovernmental as far as declarations are adopted by its Ministerial Conference. However, out of the three institutions of interest here, it displays the lowest degree of institutionalisation. VASAB has a secretariat to support its functions, but although decisions at the highest level are made by ministers responsible for spatial planning, VASAB has been characterised as something of a cooperation platform for those ministers. Importantly, however, there is an element of 'publicness' to VASAB acts.[27] As will be explained below, institutional interaction with the EU also brings VASAB into the realm of EU governance processes.

IV. Modes of Interaction

A. Interaction Through Treaty or Membership

The revised Helsinki Convention entered into force on 17 January 2000 and constitutes one out of four European Regional Seas Conventions. The EU, along with all Baltic Sea coastal states, is a party to the Helsinki Convention (ratified by the European Community in 1994). The Helsinki Convention covers the entire Baltic Sea, including internal waters, and is binding upon its parties.[28] The purpose of the Convention is two-fold. First, state parties undertake obligations that are to be implemented nationally. Article 3 establishes that states are to implement the Convention through relevant legislative, administrative and other measures. Second, it creates a legal basis for cooperation. Parties undertake to prevent and eliminate pollution caused by harmful substances from all sources.[29] The Convention incorporates several environmental law principles, but also contains more technical Annexes, which for example ban the discharge of a number of substances.[30] The Annexes are, according to Article 28, an integral part of the Convention. The Convention requires state parties to report regularly to HELCOM on legal and other measures taken.[31] HELCOM is also the forum

[26] T Koivurova and A Rosas, 'The CBSS as a vehicle for institutionalised governance in the Baltic Sea Area, in comparison with its two sister organisations in the north' (2018) 98 *Marine Policy* 211.

[27] A feature central to identifying actors with potential regulatory effects. See B Kingsbury, 'The Concept of "Law" in Global Administrative Law' (2009) 20 *European Journal of International Law* 23.

[28] Helsinki Convention, Art 32.

[29] ibid, Arts 5–15.

[30] ibid, Annex I, Part 2.

[31] ibid, Art 16.

within which environmental standards not set in the Convention or its Annexes are negotiated.

International agreements to which the EU is a party in principle prevail over EU secondary legislation.[32] As to agreements to which the EU is a party in addition to its Member States (like the Helsinki Convention), an obligation parallel to that of the Member States is created for the EU to implement the agreements, and to thereby transform the international obligations into EU law. There is, consequently, a large body of EU legislation that implements international obligations. This is particularly the case with respect to environmental agreements.[33]

In all areas of shared competence, there is a possibility of concluding mixed agreements that have both EU Member States and the EU as parties. Mixed agreements are concluded when EU competences do not cover the agreement in its entirety, as is the case of the Helsinki Convention.[34] Provisions falling under the Union's shared competence are a source of EU law obligation for the Member States, whereas implementation becomes a matter for Member States.[35] The Helsinki Convention constitutes a special case in being a so-called incomplete mixed agreement.[36] In such agreements only part of the EU Member States participate, which potentially gives rise to a set of concerns.[37] Nevertheless, the Court of Justice of the EU (CJEU) in *l'étang de Berre* concerning the Convention for the Protection of the Marine Environment and the Coastal Region of the Mediterranean, illustrates that regional mixed agreements can have direct effect. This means that both individuals and the Commission of the European Union can invoke those agreements before courts (domestic and CJEU).[38] By analogy, the same could apply to the Helsinki Convention.

For Contracting Parties to the Helsinki Convention recommendations adopted by HELCOM also become a part of the treaty regime. Following the sources of law doctrine, HELCOM recommendations do not, as a point of departure, create legal obligations. However, amendments to the Helsinki Convention Annexes

[32] Case C-344/04 *International Air Transport Association and European Low Fares Airline Association v Department for Transport* [2006] ECR I-403, ECLI:EU:C:2006:10.

[33] M Mendez, *The Legal Effects of EU Agreements: Maximalist Treaty Enforcement and Judicial Avoidance Techniques* (Oxford, Oxford University Press, 2013) xviii.

[34] P Eeckhout, *EU External Relations Law* (Oxford, Oxford University Press, 2011) 212.

[35] E Neframi, 'Mixed Agreements as a Source of European Union Law' in E Cannizzaro (ed), *International Law as Law of the European Union* (Leiden, Martinus Nijhoff, 2011) 348–49.

[36] H Ringbom, *The EU Maritime Safety Policy and International Law* (Leiden, Martinus Nijhoff Publishers, 2008) 88–91.

[37] See Joined Cases 3, 4 and 6/76 *Kramer* [1976] ECR-1279, ECLI:EU:C:1976:114; A Rosas, 'Mixity Past, Present and Future: Some Observations' in M Chamon and I Govaere (eds), *EU External Relations Post-Lisbon: The Law and Practice of Facultative Mixity* (Leiden, Brill/Nijhoff, 2020).

[38] Case C-213/03 *Syndicat professionnel coordination des pecheurs de l'étang de Berre and de la region v Electricite de France (EDF)* [2004] ECR I-07357, ECLI:EU:C:2004:464; TFEU, Art 358; V Frank, *The European Community and Marine Environmental Protection in the International Law of the Sea: Implementing Global Obligations at the Regional Level* (Leiden, Martinus Nijhoff Publishers, 2007) 143; Ringbom (n 36) 120–21.

(which in themselves are binding) can be made through recommendations.[39] This places HELCOM recommendations normatively in two different categories. Notably, the CJEU has held that legally binding decisions taken by bodies established by an international agreement to which the EU is a party, can have the same legal status as the agreement itself.[40] Annexes and amending recommendations would consequently fall under this category of acts.

Whereas the fact that the EU is a party to the Helsinki Convention introduces the possibility of enforcing it in EU law, the question of legal effect and relationship to EU law of the obligations of the Helsinki Convention can also concern HELCOM non-binding recommendations. This follows from the Treaty on the Functioning of the European Union (TFEU), which states that EU exclusive competence can also arise when international non-binding measures affect common rules or alter their scope. This rule, then, would also apply when a treaty body takes measures for implementing an agreement or commitment. Consequently, non-binding measures affecting EU law would preclude Member States from acting in an organisation.[41] As an instance of institutional interaction, as Mirka Kuisma discusses in her contribution to this book, EU membership may hereby under certain circumstances impose restraints on HELCOM and condition state action therein, with the consequent effect of hampering its functionality.[42]

Apart from the question of formal legal effect, the CJEU has recognised the value of, and directly relied upon, scientific information produced by committees, the decisions of which per se are not legally binding.[43] As to HELCOM acts in particular, the CJEU has explicitly noted the status of the EU as party to the Helsinki Convention, and through that status, indicated that the (non-binding) Baltic Sea Action Plan (BSAP), which constitutes the cornerstone of HELCOM activities,[44] sets the standard for determining whether nitrogen discharges from the inland and coastal waters of Finland and Sweden into the Bothnian Bay contribute to eutrophication of the Baltic Sea.[45] While this testifies to the scientific status of HELCOM data, it also demonstrates how HELCOM acts can have an impact beyond the compliance regime of the Helsinki Convention itself.[46]

[39] Helsinki Convention, Art 32.

[40] Case 30/88 *Hellenic Republic v Commission of the European Communities* [1989] ECR-03711, ECLI:EU:C:1989:422, paras 12–13.

[41] TFEU Art 3(2); Joined Cases C-626/15 and C-659/16 *Commission v Council (Antarctic MPAs)* ECLI:EU:C:2018:925; Case C-45/07 *Commission v Greece Republic (IMO)* [2009] ECR I-00701, ECLI:EU:C:2009:81, paras 21–22.

[42] See ch 6 by Mirka Kuisma in this volume.

[43] See, eg, Case C-344/03 *Commission of the European Communities v Republic of Finland* [2005] ECR I-11033, ECLI:EU:C:2005:770.

[44] For an overview, see eg, H Backer et al, 'HELCOM Baltic Sea Action Plan – A Regional Programme of Measures for the Marine Environment Based on the Ecosystem Approach' (2010) 60 *Marine Pollution Bulletin* 642.

[45] Case C-335/07 *Commission of the European Communities v Republic of Finland* [2009] ECR I-09459, ECLI:EU:C:2009:612; and Case C-438/07 *Commission of the European Communities v Kingdom of Sweden* [2009] ECR-09517, ECLI:EU:C:2009:613.

[46] For another example of HELCOM/EU interplay, see M Karlsson and M Gilek, 'Governance of Chemicals in the Baltic Sea Region: A Study of Three Generations of Hazardous Substances' in M Gilek et al (eds), *Environmental Governance of the Baltic Sea* (Heidelberg, Springer, 2016) 107–08.

As a matter of EU law, such reference is not equivalent to the HELCOM BSAP itself being reviewable before the Court. In order to be reviewable, a measure needs to be authored by an EU institution as well as be intended to produce legal effects.[47] As to the authorship criteria in *Deutsche Shell*, the CJEU concluded that 'measures emanating from bodies which have been established by an international agreement …, and which have been entrusted with responsibility for its implementation, are directly linked to the agreement which they implement, they form part of the Community legal order'.[48] The most important concern in respect of the second requirement is a mismatch between the effects of soft law and the readiness of the CJEU to acknowledge them. In other words, justiciability depends on the extent to which the CJEU is willing to give legal weight to the effects of such instruments in practice.[49] Recent studies note that soft law is mostly used as interpretative tools by Advocates General, whereas the CJEU does not, as yet, clearly acknowledge a legal effect of soft law acts.[50]

Out of the institutions discussed in this chapter, the EU also has a formalised relationship with the CBSS. Although there does not seem to have been an original intention to provide the CBSS with the status of an intergovernmental organisation, as noted above, its institutionalisation has consequently evolved through the establishment of a permanent secretariat, with legal personality as well as privileges and immunities. The CBSS refers to itself as an intergovernmental forum, consisting of Member States and the EU (the European External Action Service attending CBSS meetings).[51]

Once the EU has joined an international organisation, the decisions of that organisation do not only influence the EU, but – when binding – also become an integral part of its legal order. Also legally non-binding decisions can have an effect on EU decision-making, but do not become part of the legal order as such.[52] CBSS Council communiques and Heads of State Summit declarations or statements do not create legal obligations for Member States. Consequently, while the Helsinki Convention and HELCOM binding recommendations (amendments to Annexes) become part of the EU legal order, other HELCOM recommendations as well as CBSS communiques do not consequently assume a formal status in EU law.

[47] TFEU, Arts 264 and 267.

[48] Case C-188/91 *Deutsche Shell AG v Hauptzollamt Hamburg-Harburg* [1993] ECR I-00363, ECLI:EU:C:1993:24; M Eliantonio, 'Soft Law in Environmental Matters and the Role of the European Courts: Too Much or Too Little of it?' (2018) 37 *Yearbook of European Law* 496.

[49] O Ştefan, 'Helping Loose Ends Meet? The Judicial Acknowledgement of Soft Law as a Tool of Multi-Level Governance' (2014) 21 *Maastricht Journal of European and Comparative Law* 359, 367.

[50] See, eg, Case C-461/13 *Bund für Umwelt und Naturschutz Deutschland, Opinion of Advocate General Jääskinen* ECLI:EU:C:2014:2324; M Eliantonio, 'Judicial Review of Soft Law before the European and the National Courts: A Wind of Change Blowing from the Member States?' in M Eliantonio, E Korkea-aho and O Ştefan (eds), *EU Soft Law in the Member States: Theoretical Findings and Empirical Evidence* (Oxford, Hart Publishing, 2021).

[51] Koivurova and Rosas (n 26).

[52] RA Wessel and S Blockmans, 'The Legal Status and Influence of Decisions of International Organisations and Other Bodies in the European Union' in P Eeckhout and M Lopez-Escudero (eds), *The European Union's External Action in Times of Crisis* (Oxford, Hart Publishing, 2016).

It should be noted, however, that the EUSBSR Action Plan confers several tasks to the PA Secure coordinators (Sweden and the CBSS). As part of the strengthening of mechanisms for joint strategic and operational actions in protecting against criminal threats, the Action Plan envisages the development of an agreement on an international coordination platform for law enforcement agencies, as well as the development of a cooperation agreement for cross-border comprehensive assistance and/or transfer of trafficked persons.[53] The adoption of such agreements would have an impact on the current mode of cooperation and trigger the question of treaty-making competence. EU membership in the CBSS could hereby affect the possibility of states to act within the realm of the CBSS.[54]

B. Regulatory Interdependence

Apart from formal treaty relationships, EU interaction with BSR institutions also takes place through implying one another in regulatory acts. Appreciating this as a form of normative interaction builds on a broad conception of law-making, acknowledging that both well-established legal actors as well as less formal institutions produce outcomes, the impact of which can be difficult to square with formal sources of law.[55] In this light, a formal categorisation of acts of BSR institutions as 'soft' can fail to capture the normative outcome of interaction of these institutions with the EU.

The EU's relationship with international organisations is not always easily reducible to an external–internal dichotomy. Instead, these relationships often become ones of mutual influence.[56] From the point of view of BSR interaction, it has been claimed that the HELCOM and EU processes, in particular, are so intertwined that it would be futile to discuss them as separate phenomena.[57] Although the institutions explicitly embed and build upon the normative activities of one another, the Helsinki Convention and the EU Treaties are, strictly speaking, separate as legal regimes, as are HELCOM and the EU as institutions.

The Marine Strategy Framework Directive (MSFD) is the environmental pillar of EU Maritime Policy.[58] Under the MSFD, regional cooperation assumes special

[53] Commission, SWD(2021) 24 final, 54 (n 3).

[54] See ch 6 by Kuisma in this volume.

[55] J Pauwelyn, RA Wessel and J Wouters (eds), *Informal International Lawmaking* (Oxford, Oxford University Press, 2012); JE Alvarez, *The Impact of International Organizations on International Law* (Leiden, Brill/Nijhoff, 2017) 351–52 and fn 19 with examples.

[56] KE Jørgensen (ed), *The European Union and International Organizations* (London, Routledge, 2010) 14–15.

[57] H Bakker, 'The HELCOM Ecosystem Approach: time for quantification, integration, and measures: 2003–2018 implementation of the Ecosystem Approach concept in the regional intergovernmental work of the Baltic Marine Environment Protection Commission (HELCOM)' (PhD thesis, University of Helsinki 2020).

[58] Directive 2008/56/EC of the European Parliament and of the Council establishing a framework for community action in the field of marine environmental policy (Marine Strategy Framework Directive) [2008] OJ L164/19.

importance. The Directive does not provide for a detailed legal framework, nor does it specify particular governance structures. Instead, it establishes an obligation for EU Member States to 'in respect of each marine region or subregion concerned, develop a marine strategy for its marine waters', and 'where practical and appropriate, use existing regional institutional cooperation structures, including those under regional sea conventions, covering that marine region or subregion'.[59] The main goal of the Directive is to reach good environmental status (GES) measured by 11 quality indicators.[60]

For Baltic Sea States, the regional cooperation required in the Directive consists of the implementation of the Helsinki Convention and corresponding HELCOM acts. The HELCOM Moscow Ministerial Meeting held on 20 May 2010 decided 'to establish, for those HELCOM Contracting States being also EU-Member States, the role of HELCOM as the coordinating platform for the regional implementation of the EU Marine Strategy Framework Directive (EU MSFD) in the Baltic Sea'.[61] The MSFD hereby constitutes the backbone of the normative relationship between the EU and HELCOM.

In the updated HELCOM BSAP implementation is monitored through an online tool as well as through regular HELCOM monitoring and assessments.[62] As the updated BSAP addresses biodiversity, eutrophication, hazardous substances and litter, and sea-based activities, it basically covers relevant EU legislation.[63] Although the BSAP was originally adopted by a HELCOM Ministerial Meeting, it is uncertain whether it can be considered a treaty between states.[64] Nevertheless, the language used in the plan is rather strict, for example, stating that Member States 'commit to taking into account priorities of the revised Action Plan'.[65] In some areas the BSAP sets even higher standards than EU law.[66]

For the EUSBSR PA Nutri, which explicitly aims to enhance the implementation of the MSFD (and other directives) as well as the Helsinki Convention, the HELCOM BSAP is identified as a core implementation tool.[67] The EUSBSR Action

[59] ibid, Arts 5 and 6(1).

[60] Marine Strategy Framework Directive.

[61] HELCOM, 'HELCOM Ministerial Declaration on the Implementation of the HELCOM Baltic Sea Action Plan' (Moscow, 20 May 2010). The revised Convention entered into force on 17 January 2000.

[62] HELCOM, 'Baltic Sea Action Plan 2021 Update' (Lübeck, Germany, 20 October 2021), available at: www.helcom.fi/wp-content/uploads/2021/10/Baltic-Sea-Action-Plan-2021-update.pdf.

[63] For a list of 'Policies and legislation of the European Union supporting the implementation of the Baltic Sea Action Plan', see HELCOM, 'Baltic Sea Action Plan' (n 61) 9.

[64] Engström (n 1).

[65] HELCOM, 'Baltic Sea Action Plan 2021 Update' (n 62) 56.

[66] See, eg, E Wojciechowska et al, 'Nutrient Loss from Three Small-size Watersheds in the Southern Baltic Sea in Relation to Agricultural Practices and Policy' (2019) 252 *Journal of Environmental Management* 109637, comparing Polish compliance with the BSAP and the Water Framework Directive.

[67] European Commission, *Study on Macroregional Strategies and Their Link to Cohesion Policy – Data and Analytical Report for the EUSBSR* (November 2017) (Luxembourg, Publications Office of the European Union, 2018).

Plan makes it explicit that 'The EUSBSR PA Nutri, PA Hazards and HELCOM have established functioning cooperation, where HELCOM sets the policy targets in the region and EUSBSR supports Member States in reaching those targets'.[68] Although this does not indicate a formal transfer or delegation of competence, it does expand the function of HELCOM from a treaty-monitoring body of the Helsinki Convention only, into a core actor for reaching the goals of the MSFD (as well as other related directives). The 2021 updated HELCOM BSAP reciprocally encourages regional cooperation in the context of the MSFD in particular (along with a range of other supportive EU legislation).[69]

C. Modalities of Implementation

'Implementation', in the most general sense of the term, is about giving effect to a regulatory act. Implementation is not solely a question of applying or incorporating EU legislation in domestic law, but also concerns questions of monitoring and enforcement. The key actor in this respect is the European Commission as the guardian of the EU Treaties, tasked with ensuring the application of EU law.[70] As the MSFD requires EU Member States to develop strategies for their marine waters and cooperate with states in the same region, it explicitly requires states to report to the Commission on progress in implementation.[71] In addition to this (as noted above) the EUSBSR explicitly grants the Commission a strong role in monitoring and developing the Strategy, as well as in leading the overall coordination of the attached Action Plan.[72]

The most forceful tool in the toolbox of Commission monitoring is to refer failure to implement EU law to the CJEU. Whereas the possibility of instituting infringement procedures based on the Helsinki Convention or HELCOM recommendations has been discussed above, it is interesting to note that the Commission in its monitoring frequently urges Baltic Sea States to implement measures developed by HELCOM as a way of fulfilling their MSFD obligations.[73] The Commission

[68] Commission, SWD(2021) 24 final, 20 (n 3).

[69] HELCOM, 'Baltic Sea Action Plan 2021 Update' (n 62) 9.

[70] TEU, Art 17(1).

[71] Marine Strategy Framework Directive, Art 18. See, eg, Commission, 'Commission Staff Working Document Accompanying the document Report from the Commission to the European Parliament and the Council assessing Member States' programmes of measures under the Marine Strategy Framework Directive' SWD(2018) 393 final.

[72] Commission, COM(2009) 248 final, 10–11 (n 3).

[73] See Commission, 'Commission Staff Working Document Accompanying the document Report from the Commission to the European Parliament and the Council assessing Member States' monitoring programmes under the Marine Strategy Framework Directive' SWD(2017) 1 final; Commission, 'Commission Staff Working Document Background document for the Marine Strategy Framework Directive on the determination of good environmental status and its links to assessments and the setting of environmental targets Accompanying the Report from the Commission to the European

acknowledges the progressive approach of HELCOM in including the whole range of MSFD requirements in its revised Monitoring and Assessment Strategy. The Marine Strategy Coordination Group of the Commission explicitly considers regional seas conventions as crucial for coherent implementation and monitoring of the MSFD around Europe.[74]

The monitoring role of the Commission also invites overlap, as monitoring of the implementation of the Helsinki Convention is one of the main tasks of HELCOM. Article 16 of the Helsinki Convention sets forth an obligation for contracting parties to report to HELCOM at regular intervals on the 'the legal, regulatory, or other measures taken for the implementation of the provisions of this Convention, of its Annexes and of recommendations adopted thereunder', on the effectiveness of the measures taken, as well as on problems encountered.[75]

As a system of compliance review, HELCOM monitoring does not provide means for sanctioning non-compliance. Yet, monitoring can have a regulatory impact, for example, by enacting domestic processes and generating knowledge which can feed into the legislative process.[76] Particular knowledge produced, such as definitions of ecological quality, may even be highly influential, raising an expectation of at least 'managerial compliance' with HELCOM decisions.[77] State reporting can even be regarded as an efficient means in its own right for inducing systemic change, as it allows taking a broad societal approach to the situation of a country.[78] While this managerial perspective is in normative terms a soft approach to implementation, HELCOM monitoring also covers compliance with (non-binding) recommendations, potentially adding to their impact.

The regional seas convention framework, the Commission finds, is of great benefit in the MSFD context, since there are variances in the implementation of the MSFD among the EU Member States. As to the BSR in particular, the Commission concludes that a high level of coherence between monitoring programmes has

Parliament and the Council on the implementation of the Marine Strategy Framework Directive [Directive 2008/56/EC]' SWD(2020) 62 final; Commission, 'Commission Staff Working Document Key stages and progress up to 2019 Accompanying the Report from the Commission to the European Parliament and the Council on the implementation of the Marine Strategy Framework Directive (Directive 2008/56/EC)' SWD(2020) 60 final.

[74] N Zampoukas et al, *Technical Guidance on Monitoring for the Marine Strategy Framework Directive* (Luxembourg, Publications Office of the European Union, 2014).

[75] See 'HELCOM Monitoring and Assessment Strategy' (n 21) para 2.3–2.5.

[76] D Bodansky, 'The Role of Reporting in International Environmental Treaties: Lessons for Human Rights Supervision' in P Alston and J Crawford (eds), *The Future of UN Human Rights Treaty Monitoring* (Cambridge, Cambridge University Press, 2000) 365–66.

[77] B Bohman 'Transboundary Law for Social-Ecological Resilience? A Study on Eutrophication in the Baltic Sea Area' (PhD thesis, Stockholm University 2017). The definitions could also be considered to function as science-based 'ethical imperatives' limiting at least indirectly the freedom that coastal states and the EU have in the implementation of the 1992 Helsinki Convention. See Bakker (n 57) for practical examples.

[78] See, eg, Bodansky (n 76).

been achieved.[79] This, however, should be read against the HELCOM Second Holistic Assessment Report, which finds that the parallel assessment tools could be more integrated, as both the BSAP and the MSFD have the same overarching goal. Whereas in respect of eutrophication, for example, EU assessment of coastal areas relied on indicators mainly derived from the implementation of the Water Framework Directive, HELCOM mostly uses its own indicators.[80] As a consequence, both the parameters as well as the findings of the overlapping HELCOM and EU Commission monitoring may differ from one another.[81]

Another aspect to implementation is its enactment through a broad range of 'compliance-promoting' tools.[82] Mechanisms such as conformity checking studies, scoreboards and barometers, inspections, package meetings, fitness checks, legal reviews, reporting, guidelines, implementation plans, establishment of networks and committees, and even press releases can be thought of as implementation tools.[83] This turns interest to the Common Implementation Strategy (CIS), which is an informal programme of coordination between EU Member States and the European Commission in the implementation of the MSFD. Working groups within the CIS give practical guidance, for example, in technical matters, including interpretation of the Directive.[84] As an expression of 'new governance' in the EU, a lot has been said about its function as an implementation tool, both in terms of risks and benefits.[85] Notably, the CIS builds strongly on regional seas conventions for the reaching of GES as required by the MSFD, and acknowledges a need for aligning CIS and regional seas convention processes. The CIS also explicitly acknowledges HELCOM activities that assist in meeting that objective, including

[79] Commission, 'Report from the Commission to the European Parliament and the Council assessing Member States' monitoring programmes under the Marine Strategy Framework Directive' COM(2017) 3 final.

[80] HELCOM, 'State of the Baltic Sea – Second HELCOM holistic assessment 2011–16' Baltic Sea Environment Proceedings 155 (2018).

[81] As an example: 'The results may differ from those presented here, as the Habitats Directive assessment is bounded by national borders, and the HELCOM assessment is carried out based on populations or sub-populations equivalent to regionally agreed management units. Another difference is that species are evaluated in comparison to a modern or historic baseline under the Habitats Directive, while threshold values in the HELCOM assessment are set in relation to the future viability of the management unit'. A similar discrepancy is noted for assessing waterbird species. HELCOM, 'State of the Baltic Sea' (n 80) 113; For further examples, see M Kahlert et al, 'Knowledge and Monitoring Gap Analysis with Respect to the EU Directives' (Deliverable 1.1 of BONUS FUMARI, 14 June 2019) available at: www.syke.fi.

[82] M Ballesteros, *Monitoring the implementation of EU law: tools and challenges* (European Union, 2017) 38.

[83] Commission, 'Information from European Union Institutions, Bodies, Offices and Agencies European Commission Communication from the Commission EU Law: Better results through better application' C(2016)8600, OJ C 18/10.

[84] See, eg, Marine Strategy Framework Directive (MSFD) Common Implementation Strategy, Guidance on Article 15 of the Marine Strategy Framework Directive (4 May 2015), available at: circabc.europa.eu/.

[85] See, eg, J Scott and J Holder, 'Law and New Environmental Governance in the European Union' in G de Búrca and J Scott (eds), *Law and New Governance in the EU and the US* (Oxford, Hart Publishing, 2016).

assessment of the status of the Baltic Sea, and the development of tools for making that assessment.[86]

Yet another aspect to implementation of EU law is the role of agencies. EU agencies show great variety. They assist in the implementation of EU law and policy, provide scientific advice for both legislation and implementation, collect information, provide specific services and fulfil central roles in the coordination of national authorities.[87] Although most agencies lack formally binding powers, their policy impact is well acknowledged. Interestingly, the CBSS is, through initiatives like the Baltic Sea Region Border Control Cooperation, brought into close cooperation with the EU agency Frontex, which on its part was initially established to improve the implementation of EU instruments for the management of external borders (and has later turned into the European Border and Coast Guard Agency).[88] A similar linkage can be found through the Baltic Sea Task Force against Organized Crime, acting under the auspices of the CBSS, where CBSS Member States and the European Commission, along with EUROPOL, cooperate. While these may be characterised as law enforcement cooperation initiatives, the initiatives are also mentioned in the EUSBSR Action Plan as cooperation structures ideal for addressing security issues in the region more broadly (and hence for reaching EUSBSR goals).[89] This illustrates how institutional interaction also materialises on levels that escape the EU's formal constitutional framework.[90]

Further still, implementation of EU law and policy also takes place through institutional collaboration external to the EU. This is highlighted by institutional interaction in the field of spatial planning. The EU Maritime Spatial Planning Directive (MSPD) states that all EU Member States must have national plans on spatial planning no later than 2021, and that transboundary and especially cross-border cooperation are important parts of such plans. The MSPD also requires states to 'pursue cooperation through existing regional institutional cooperation structures such as regional sea conventions; and/or (b) networks

[86] Marine Strategy Coordination Group, *Marine Strategy Framework Directive (MSFD) Common Implementation Strategy 2016–2019* (15 June 2017), available at: circabc.europa.eu/; Marine Strategy Coordination Group, Marine Strategy Framework Directive (MSFD) Common Implementation Strategy Work programme 2020–2022 (26 November 2020) 45, available at: circabc.europa.eu/.

[87] Commission, 'Communication from the Commission to the European Parliament and the Council European agencies – The way forward' COM(2008) 135 final; E Vos, *EU Agencies, Common Approach and Parliamentary Scrutiny, European Implementation Assessment* (European Parliamentary Research Service, 2018).

[88] See Å Gustafsson, 'The Baltic Sea Region Border Control Cooperation (BSRBCC) and Border Management in the Baltic Sea Region: A Case Study' (2018) 98 *Marine Policy* 309.

[89] Europol and Frontex are even explicitly mentioned in the original Action Plan: Commission, 'Commission Staff Working Document European Union Strategy for the Baltic Sea Region Action Plan [COM(2009) 248]' SWD(2017) 118 final, 129.

[90] Agencies have even been regarded as new sources of authority at the EU level, in between the Member State and the EU; E Guild et al, *Implementation of the EU Charter of Fundamental Rights and its Impact on EU Home Affairs Agencies: Frontex, Europol and the European Asylum Support Office* (Report to the European Parliament's Committee on Civil Liberties, Justice and Home Affairs (LIBE), 2011) 89–91.

or structures of Member States' competent authorities; and/or (c) any other method that meets the requirements of paragraph 1'.[91] The Directive hereby strongly promotes regional initiatives and elevates the role of existing actors and instruments, such as the EUSBSR, the HELCOM BSAP and the VASAB Long-Term Perspective.[92] The EUSBSR has assigned VASAB and HELCOM the role of joint Policy Area Coordinators in maritime spatial planning.

In order to ensure coherence in the development of plans, a HELCOM–VASAB Working Group was established in 2010. As to its formal mandate, the task of the working group is to:

> Promote the development of maritime spatial planning in the region and follow up its implementation as outlined in VASAB Long Term Perspective as well as HELCOM Baltic Sea Action Plan and relevant HELCOM Recommendations, including supporting the setting-up of governing structures, legislative basis, transboundary consultations as well as developing concepts for common Maritime Spatial Planning Principles.[93]

The Working Group comprises representatives from ministries, national agencies and experts from the Baltic Sea countries. The governance tool at their disposal is the offering of forums for transnational deliberation, with the possibility of adopting for example recommendations and guidelines. One of such acts is the Baltic Sea Broad-Scale Maritime Spatial Planning Principles that were endorsed by both HELCOM and VASAB in late 2010. These principles aim to improve the coordination of national planning strategies. According to the principles, maritime spatial planning is also a tool for contributing to the achievement of GES according to the EU MSFD and HELCOM BSAP.[94]

Furthermore, the HELCOM–VASAB Guideline for the Implementation of an Ecosystem-based Approach in Maritime Spatial Planning in the Baltic Sea Area, sets out to present a common understanding on how the ecosystem-based approach can be applied in drawing up spatial plans for sea areas in accordance with spatial planning legislation in force in the Baltic Sea countries.[95] For EU Member States this legislation in force in essence also includes the EU MSPD and the MSFD. Even if the Working Group outcome lacks legal status, it influences

[91] Directive 2014/89/EU of the European Parliament and of the Council of 23 July 2014 establishing a framework for maritime spatial planning [2014] OJ L257/135, Art 11.

[92] VASAB, 'VASAB Long-Term Perspective for the Territorial Development of the Baltic Sea Region' (VASAB Secretariat, 2010), available at: vasab.org/documents/long-term-perspective/.

[93] Mandate for the Joint HELCOM–VASAB Maritime Spatial Planning Working Group (HELCOM HOD 50-2016 and the 72nd VASAB CSPD/BSR Meeting), available at: www.helcom.fi/wp-content/uploads/2019/08/HELCOM-VASAB-MSP-WG-Mandate.pdf.

[94] Baltic Sea broad-scale Maritime Spatial Planning (MSP) principles (HELCOM HOD 34-2010 and the 54th Meeting of VASAB CSPD/BSR), available at: www.helcom.fi/wp-content/uploads/2019/08/HELCOM-VASAB-MSP-Principles.pdf; B Hassler et al, 'Collective Action and Agency in Baltic Sea Marine Spatial Planning: Transnational policy coordination in the promotion of regional coherence' (2018) 98 *Marine Policy* 138.

[95] Guideline for the Implementation of Ecosystem-based Approach in Maritime Spatial Planning in the Baltic Sea Area (adopted by the 72nd meeting of VASAB CSPD/BSR on 8 June 2016 and approved by HELCOM HOD 50-2016, 15–16 June 2016), available at: portal.helcom.fi/default.aspx.

the evolution of spatial planning frameworks.[96] This positions the VASAB at the fringes of the EU regulatory process in spatial planning, and as an actor in the implementation of EU law.

V. Concluding Remarks

As the Baltic Sea has become an almost EU-internal sea, the EU has grown into the core policymaker in the BSR. The region is, however, also dense with other actors performing various functions and displaying a diversity of institutional design. This chapter has explored the interaction of the EU with three such actors – HELCOM, the CBSS and the VASAB – with a particular interest in the regulatory implications of this interaction. The EU has taken a strong interest in BSR cooperation, as witnessed, in particular, by its engagement with the CBSS and the Helsinki Convention, along with HELCOM, as well as by the enthusiasm with which regional cooperation is promoted. EU law (such as the MSFD) and policy instruments (such as the EUSBSR) not only interlink the EU with other BSR actors, but also elevates the role of some institutions and infuses a sense of permanence to the interaction by bringing them into the realm of EU law and policymaking.

This chapter has illustrated multiple ways by which BSR institutions become entangled with the EU legislative process. The most normatively formalised form of interaction arises from EU treaty ratification (Helsinki Convention), and membership (CBSS, HELCOM). BSR institutions are also enacted through various processes of implementation of EU law and policy (and vice versa). Each of these forms of interaction give rise to their own set of concerns, both from the perspective of EU law as well as for the BSR institutions. The multiple forms of interaction identified in this chapter, combined with an institutionalisation of cooperation with these three BSR institutions, express a functional approach to regional governance. Although evidence regarding the impact of the interaction on compliance is somewhat inconclusive,[97] such a functional approach does enhance integration in EU macro-regions. In assessing Member States' programmes of measures under the MSFD in 2020, the European Commission noted that states have inadequately implemented measures to tackle the existing pressures. This led the Commission

[96] B Hassler et al, 'New Generation EU Directives, Sustainability, and the Role of Transnational Coordination in Baltic Sea Maritime Spatial Planning' (2019) 169 *Ocean & Coastal Management* 254.

[97] See, eg, Commission, 'Report from the Commission to the European Parliament, the Council, the European Economic and Social Committee and the Committee of the Regions on the implementation of EU macro-regional strategies' COM(2020) 578 final, which states that macro-regional strategies have 'particularly helped to improve the state of the Baltic Sea environment'. However, HELCOM has repeatedly noted the poor state of implementation. See, eg, HELCOM, 'Implementation of the Baltic Sea Action Plan 2018: Three years left to good environmental status' (Background document to the 2018 HELCOM Ministerial Meeting) 13; HELCOM, 'State of the Baltic Sea' (n 80).

to recommend 'boosting regional cooperation'.[98] This is likely to emphasise the role of macro-regional strategies even further, and in the BSR, entangle the EU with regional institutions ever more.[99]

This enthusiasm should not, however, overlook that the raison d'être of HELCOM, the CBSS and the VASAB transcends the EU integration project. Institutional interaction can come with drawbacks for pan-Baltic cooperation. Such concerns have been raised both in respect of HELCOM,[100] and the CBSS.[101] This is a reminder that EU interaction with institutions in the BSR is not only a question of EU law and governance, but of governance of the Baltic Sea. While the gradual enlargement of EU membership has elevated the role of the EU in the region, the inclusion of Russia in all three BSR institutions has positioned them as important platforms for cooperation in the intersection of EU internal and external policies.[102] At the time of writing, HELCOM has suspended all meetings of its bodies and project groups with Russian involvement and both the CBSS and VASAB have suspended Russian membership, as a reaction to the Russian aggression against Ukraine. This is potentially a defining moment for the three institutions. Only time will show whether this also affects their interaction with the EU.

[98] Commission, 'Report from the Commission to the European Parliament and the Council on the implementation of the Marine Strategy Framework Directive (Directive 2008/56/EC)' COM(2020) 259 final.

[99] Although macro-regionalisation has also raised criticism. See, eg, R Belloni, 'Assessing the Rise of Macro-regionalism in Europe: The EU Strategy for the Adriatic and Ionian Region (EUSAIR)' (2020) 23 *Journal of International Relations and Development* 814.

[100] S Söderström and K Kern, 'The ecosystem approach to management in marine environmental governance: Institutional interplay in the Baltic Sea region' (2017) 27 *Environmental Policy and Governance* 619.

[101] A Sergunin, 'Is Russia a "good CBSS citizen"?' in A Kuczyńska-Zonik and PF Timofejevs (eds), *The Baltic Sea Region: States, Societies, and Future Development* (Lublin, Instytut Europy Środkowej, 2021).

[102] S Ganzle and K Kern, 'Macro-regions, "Macro-regionalization" and Macro Regional Strategies in the European Union: Towards a New Form of European Governance?' in S Ganzle and K Kern (eds), *A 'Macro-regional' Europe in the Making: Theoretical Approaches and Empirical Evidence* (Basingstoke, Palgrave Macmillan, 2016).

8

The EU and the Council of the Baltic Sea States

ALLAN ROSAS AND PETTERI VUORIMÄKI

I. Introduction

That the Baltic Sea Region (BSR) is one of the regions of interest for the EU (European Union), and not only its Member States belonging to the region in question, is demonstrated most conspicuously by the EU Strategy for the Baltic Sea Region (EUSBSR), launched in June 2009 with a Communication from the European Commission.[1] While this was the first macro-regional strategy of the Union,[2] it did not involve the setting up of new financial instruments, formal institutions or legislation (the 'three NOs').[3] That said, the Strategy has a governance structure consisting of certain bodies composed of Member State representatives and the European Commission holding a coordinating and advisory role. The EUSBSR has been characterised by the Commission as providing 'a unique platform for cooperation and coordination between eight EU Member States … including also with the neighbouring non-EU countries in the region where relevant and appropriate (Belarus, Iceland, Norway and Russia)'.[4]

[1] Commission, 'Communication from the Commission to the European Parliament, the Council, the European Economic and Social Committee and the Committee of the Regions concerning the European Union Strategy for the Baltic Sea Region' COM(2009) 248 final. The EUSBSR, which was endorsed by the Council on 28 October 2009 and by the European Council on 30 October 2009, was accompanied by a detailed Action Plan, which has been subsequently revised several times. On the EUSBSR in general, see S Gänzle, 'The European Union's Strategy for the Baltic Sea Region (EUSBSR): Improving Multilevel Governance in Baltic Sea Cooperation' (2017) 48 *Journal of Baltic Studies* 407; S Gänzle, 'EU Governance, "Experimental Union" and Baltic Sea Cooperation: The Case of the European Union's Strategy for the Baltic Sea Region' [2017] *Schuman Papers* 2. See further ch 4 by Helena Tuuri in this volume.

[2] On EU regional policies, see ch 2 by Teija Tiilikainen in this volume.

[3] See, eg, Council of the European Union, 'Council conclusions on the review of the [EUSBSR]' 3125th Council meeting General Affairs Brussels (15 November 2011) para 7.

[4] See, eg, Commission, 'Commission Staff Working Document EU Strategy for the Baltic Sea Region Action Plan [COM(2009) 248 final]' SWD(2021) 24 final, 4.

This was not the first time the EU became involved in BSR cooperation initiatives and arrangements, however. As will be elaborated below, the European Commission, alongside 10 states (two of which at the time were EU Member States), took part in the founding of the Council of the Baltic Sea States (CBSS) in 1992. In 1994, the then European Community concluded the Helsinki Convention on the Protection of the Marine Environment of the Baltic Sea Area, as revised in 1992.[5] In 1994 and 1996, that is well before the launching of the EUSBSR, the Commission issued Communications on orientations for a Union approach towards the BSR and a Baltic Sea Region Initiative, respectively.[6]

In this context, reference should also be made to the Northern Dimension (ND) Policy, which was initiated by the EU in 1999 and renewed in 2006 as a common policy of the EU, Iceland, Norway and Russia.[7] Its geographical area is much broader than the BSR, covering also the Barents and the European Arctic and Sub-Arctic Areas. Apart from the four partners, the four regional councils in the North, including the CBSS, are among the other participants. As a policy framework based on four thematic Partnerships,[8] the ND cannot be characterised as an international organisation, although it does count on certain loose institutional arrangements.[9] These include a secretariat for each Partnership, either embedded in an existing international organisation[10] or having a more autonomous status.[11]

The presence of institutional arrangements is even more obvious with respect to the CBSS and the three other so-called regional councils in the North, ie, the Nordic Council of Ministers, the Barents Euro-Arctic Council and the Arctic Council. The institutional set-up of these entities is not the same, however, and there are also significant differences with regard to EU participation. The Nordic Council of Ministers, together with the Nordic Council, an assembly of representatives of national parliaments, is based on a legally binding international agreement between Denmark, Finland, Iceland and Norway – the Treaty of Helsinki of 1962

[5] Council Decision 94/157/EC [1994] OJ L73/19. The Helsinki Convention was originally concluded in 1974. See further the chapters by Mirka Kuisma (ch 6) and Viljam Engström (ch 7) in this volume.

[6] Commission, 'Communication from the Commission to the Council Orientations for a Union Approach Towards the Baltic Sea Region' SEC (94)1747 final; Commission, 'Communication from the Commission on the Baltic Sea Region Initiative' SEC(96) 0608 final.

[7] Political Declaration on the Northern Dimension Policy and the Northern Dimension Policy Framework Document, endorsed at a Helsinki Summit on 24 November 2006.

[8] See, eg, the Northern Dimension Partnership in Public Health and Social Well-being (NDPHS), established at a ministerial level meeting in Oslo on 27 October 2003.

[9] Ministerial Meetings, Senior Officials Meetings and a Steering Group.

[10] See, eg, Agreement on the Secretariat of the Northern Dimension Partnership for Transport and Logistics (2010). The Support Fund of the Northern Dimension Environmental Partnership (NDEP) is managed by the European Bank for Reconstruction and Development (EBRD).

[11] See Agreement on the Establishment of the Secretariat of the Northern Dimension Partnership in Public Health and Social Well-being, NDPHS (2011), Finnish Treaty Series (Sopimussarja) 99/2012; Agreement between the Government of Sweden and the Secretariat of the Northern Dimension Partnership in Public Health and Social Well-being (NDPHS) concerning the immunity and privileges of the Secretariat and its staff. The Secretariat however is located at the premises of the CBSS in Stockholm.

as amended – and has no direct EU involvement in its work.[12] The three other regional councils were not established by treaty, but by declarations of a more political character,[13] although subsequent developments have led to a certain institutionalisation and even the conclusion of some international agreements.[14] The EU is a Member of the CBSS and the Barents Euro-Arctic Council, whereas it has the status of a de facto observer in the Arctic Council.[15]

The focus of this chapter is on the role of the EU in the work of the CBSS. We will first analyse the Union's membership from an institutional and legal perspective, which will also require a look at the status of the CBSS as a 'soft organisation' established by a political declaration as opposed to a legally binding agreement. Second, we will discuss what role the Union has played in practice and what its participation in the activities of the CBSS may tell us about its role in BSR cooperation in general. It should also be considered that since the EU enlargements in 1995 and 2004, eight out of the 11 CBSS Member States are EU Member States, while two (Iceland and Norway) have a far-reaching institutional and substantive relationship with the Union (the European Economic Area – EEA). Some attention will also be paid to the other policy platforms and entities mentioned above, to the extent that there may be a link between them and the EU's involvement in the CBSS. This is particularly the case with the EUSBSR, which entails certain tasks to be handled by the CBSS, despite the CBSS not being a Union body.

II. The Status, Organisation and Main Tasks of the CBSS

The CBSS was established in March 1992, at the initiative of Denmark and Germany, when the Ministers for Foreign Affairs of 10 Baltic Sea States and a representative of the European Commission met in Copenhagen to strengthen existing cooperation in the BSR. The CBSS was established by a Ministerial Declaration with a view to providing for an 'overall regional forum' for intensified cooperation and coordination.[16] While some common cooperation arrangements

[12] The Nordic Council also has representatives of the parliaments of the autonomous regions of the Faeroe Islands, Greenland and the Åland Islands.

[13] Kirkenes Declaration on cooperation in the Barents Euro-arctic Region, Conference of Foreign Ministers in Kirkenes (11 January 1993), with participation of the five Nordic countries, Russia and the European Commission; Ottawa Declaration on the establishment of the Arctic Council (19 September 1993), made by the six states establishing the Barents Euro-Arctic Council as well as Canada and the United States (but excluding the European Commission).

[14] For a comparison between these three regional councils, see T Koivurova and A Rosas, 'The CBSS as a vehicle for institutionalised governance in the Baltic Sea Area, in comparison with its two sister organisations in the north' (2018) 98 *Marine Policy* 211.

[15] The webpage of the Arctic Council notes that the EU has applied for observer status and that '[u]ntil such time as Ministers of the Arctic States may reach a final decision, the EU may observe Council proceedings', available at: www.arctic-council.org/about/observers/.

[16] CBSS, '1st Ministerial Session – Copenhagen Declaration Conference of Foreign Ministers of the Baltic Sea States' (Copenhagen, 5–6 March 1992).

between the Baltic Sea countries already existed before 1992 (such as the above-mentioned Helsinki Convention initially concluded in 1974), the CBSS was intended to provide an overarching framework for coordination and cooperation in various fields.

The establishment of the CBSS should also be seen against the background of the important changes in the political landscape of Northern Europe that had occurred in the early 1990s, as manifested by the re-emergence of Estonia, Latvia and Lithuania as independent states and the dissolution of the Soviet Union in 1991.[17] According to the Declaration adopted by the Copenhagen Conference, the 'Ministers agreed that the recent dramatic changes in Europe herald a new era of European relations', and an enhanced Baltic cooperation, also encompassing Russia, Estonia, Latvia, Lithuania and Poland, was said to be a 'natural and logical consequence of these events'. Six areas of cooperation were listed, namely: (1) assistance to new democratic institutions; (2) economic and technical assistance and cooperation; (3) humanitarian matters and health; (4) protection of the environment and energy; (5) culture, education, tourism and information; and (6) transport and communication.

The decision to establish the CBSS was expressed in a declaration adopted but not signed by the participants rather than by a treaty (a binding international agreement) as governed by international treaty law.[18] It thus bears the hallmarks of a 'soft law' instrument providing for political commitments rather than legal.[19] The 'Terms of Reference' for the Council attached to the declaration did not change this picture.[20] The participants at the Copenhagen Conference of 1992 clearly did not fathom the establishment of an intergovernmental organisation proper, as also borne out by some of the language used: 'regional forum', 'regional undertaking', 'forum for guidance and overall coordination', and so on.[21]

The Terms of Reference did refer to a Council presidency rotating between the participating states (but excluding the European Commission) and a Committee of Senior Officials (CSO) but provided, on the other hand, that the new Council 'should not be seen as a new formalized institutional framework

[17] S Hollis and M Ekengren, 'Regional Organisation Study: Council of the Baltic Sea States' (ANVIL – Analysis of Civil Security Systems in Europe, July 2013); Koivurova and Rosas (n 14).

[18] On international treaties see, eg, A Aust, *Modern Treaty Law and Practice*, 2nd edn (Cambridge, Cambridge University Press, 2000). It should be noted, however, that the borderline between binding treaties and instruments of a non-binding character is not clear-cut.

[19] Koivurova and Rosas (n 14).

[20] The Terms of Reference of the Council of the Baltic Sea States were revised in 2005, 2009 and 2020. See Terms of Reference adopted by CBSS, '1st Ministerial Session', revised by CBSS, '13th Ministerial Session of the Council of the Baltic Sea States' (Szczecin, 9–10 June 2005), revised by the Council by written procedure (April 2009), revised by the CBSS Ministers at their meeting (19 May 2020).

[21] T Etzold, 'Reorganization Processes in Small International Organizations. The Nordic Council and the Council of the Baltic Sea States' in MW Bauer and C Knill (eds), *Management Reforms in International Organizations* (Baden-Baden, Nomos, 2007); *cf* A Krohn, 'The Council of the Baltic Sea States (CBSS): Fostering Cooperation in the Baltic Sea Region' (2000) 43 *German Yearbook of International Law* 65.

with a permanent secretariat'.[22] This quite modest germ of institutionalisation was later followed by further steps, including the establishment, in 1994, of the post of CBSS Commissioner on Democratic Institutions and Human Rights,[23] revamped in 2000 to the post of Commissioner on Democratic Institutions, and eventually terminated in 2003. Of more lasting importance was the decision, in 1998, to establish a permanent secretariat in Stockholm, headed by a Director General and regulated in Terms of Reference of the Secretariat, as well as a Host Country Agreement concluded in 1998 between Sweden and the Secretariat.[24] Although the establishment of the Secretariat, did not entail the creation of any large bureaucracy, it did constitute a rather modest step in an institutional sense.

Today the CBSS displays an institutional structure which may remind us of that to be found in some intergovernmental organisations of a more formal character. The chairmanship of the Council and the CSO rotate on an annual basis between the by now 11 participating states. Decisions are taken by consensus and, because of the 'soft law' character of the basic instruments, they, legally speaking, seem to constitute recommendations rather than legally binding decisions (although the Terms of Reference of 1992 referred to '"[d]ecisions" of the Council and its subsidiary bodies' while the Revised Terms of Reference of 2009 refer to '[d]ecisions within the CBSS'). According to the revised Terms of Reference, the CBSS 'takes overall political guidance' from the Baltic Sea States Summit, which however has not been convened since 2012.[25]

There are several expert groups and task forces under the guidance of the CSO.[26] The Secretariat constitutes an important hub for the great variety of activities and projects, with specialised units integrated into the Secretariat, but its size remains modest, comprising an overall staff of some 30 people.[27] Since 2012, a Project Support Facility has been in place to co-finance the development and implementation of Baltic Sea Area cooperation projects. Apart from its members (11 states and the EU since Iceland joined in 1995), several non-Baltic Sea States are allowed to participate in its work as observers, while some intergovernmental, quasi-governmental and non-governmental organisations

[22] Terms of Reference (n 20) para 3.

[23] The full title was 'Commissioner of the Baltic Sea States on Democratic Institutions and Human Rights, Including the Rights of Persons Belonging to Minorities'.

[24] Agreement between the Kingdom of Sweden and the Secretariat of the Council of the Baltic Sea States on the Privileges and Immunities of the Secretariat (Sveriges internationella överenskommelser, SÖ, 14/1999).

[25] CBSS, '9th Baltic Sea States Summit Stralsund, Germany 31 May 2012' (Presidential Communiqué). In addition, there was a High-Level Conference on the Protection of the Environment of the Baltic Sea Region in St Petersburg (5–6 April 2013).

[26] eg, Expert Group on Youth Affairs; Expert Group on Maritime Policy; Expert Group on Children at Risk; Expert Group on Nuclear and Radiation Safety; Task Force against Trafficking in Human Beings; Task Force on Organised Crime.

[27] For details, see Koivurova and Rosas (n 14) ch 4. The Terms of Reference of the Secretariat were adopted by the CBSS Ministers' Deputies at their meeting in Laulasmaa, Estonia on 21 June 2004. They were revised by the Council through written procedure in April 2009 and by CBSS Ministers at their meeting of 19 May 2020.

are defined as Strategic Partners. Additionally, third parties without the status of an observer or strategic partner may be invited to participate in CBSS activities, and the Council also organises coordination meetings involving various BSR actors.[28]

As from 2004, CBSS membership came to comprise eight EU Member States and two states closely associated with Union. This development underscored the role of the CBSS as a forum for EU–Russia cooperation. With the deterioration of the relations between the EU and Russia, especially after the Russian occupation and subsequent annexation of the Crimean Peninsula in 2014 and military operations against eastern Ukraine, the CBSS found itself in a new political setting, which affected, above all, Russian involvement at a high political level. Taking also into account the modest resources and powers of the CBSS, combined with the often perceived limited concrete impact of CBSS activities, doubts were expressed as to the continuing relevance and raison d'être of the Council. It should be added that the task of the CBSS was not facilitated by the fact that there was uncertainty among the Members as to whether the CBSS should be a forum for political cooperation or merely constitute a project organisation of a predominantly technical nature.[29]

Yet, the Members chose to reiterate the relevance of the organisation, for instance, at a CBSS meeting of deputy foreign ministers in Warsaw in June 2016, which reaffirmed the 'core role of the CBSS as a forum for all multilateral intergovernmental cooperation and dialogue in the Baltic Sea Region'.[30] And in the Declaration on the Occasion of the Twenty-fifth Anniversary of the CBSS, the Foreign Ministers and high-level representatives 'agreed on the need to maintain and strengthen the role of the CBSS towards 2020 and beyond'.[31]

To meet the challenges, there has been an effort at streamlining activities and a move towards projects of less political sensitivity and of a more practical and technical nature, as compared with the broad range of tasks listed in 1992 and the mandate of the Commissioner on Democratic Institutions and Human Rights, which was abolished in 2003. In 2014, the five priority areas of the CBSS were revised to three, namely Regional Identity, Sustainable and Prosperous Region, and Secure Region.[32] Each of these contains multiple activities. The activities of the CBSS are, thus, still spread across a broad range, from youth and intercultural dialogue to entrepreneurial and creative industry collaborations, creation of labour markets, research and innovation and scientific cooperation, climate change mitigation and adaptation policy coordination, spatial planning, sector-specific collaborations in the maritime and energy sectors, among others, supporting pilot financial initiatives,

[28] Koivurova and Rosas (n 14) ch 3.

[29] Based on co-author Vuorimäki's observations.

[30] CBSS, 'Warsaw Declaration Regional Responses to Global Challenges' (Meeting of Deputy Foreign Ministers, Warsaw, 8 June 2016).

[31] CBSS, 'Declaration on the Occasion of the 25th Anniversary of the CBSS' (Reykjavik, 20 June 2017).

[32] CBSS, 'Decision by the Council of the Baltic Sea States on a review of the CBSS long term priorities' (20 June 2014).

law enforcement cooperation, critical infrastructure protection and emergency preparedness, child protection and prevention of human trafficking.

In the 2017 Reykjavik Declaration, the CBSS was invited to identify and launch new project activities within the following areas: sustainable development, youth, human trafficking, child protection and civil protection.[33] The Declaration also invited the organisation to appoint an independent group of wise persons, including representatives from civil society. The group, called the 'Vision Group', delivered its report on 9 May 2018, containing a critical assessment of the role of the CBSS and a number of recommendations.[34] According to the report, the CBSS 'is only partly able to address the challenges of the new economic, political and societal environment'. It was said to be confronted 'with a lack of clear commitments and interests by Member States, resources, political will and leadership, hampering its effectiveness and efficiency' and with an overall visibility 'perceived as low'.[35] The Group also argued that the CBSS 'would need to undergo a fundamental reform'.[36] Meanwhile, the main recommendations did not provide for a significant substantive streamlining of CBSS activities, but rather focused on working methods and resources, including contacts and cooperation with third parties.

The Stockholm Declaration of June 2018, taking note of the Vision Group report, recognised the need for CBSS reform and identified three main directions to be followed: (1) more focus and flexibility in the work of the CBSS; (2) improving cooperation with other international fora and formats active in the region; and (3) enabling concrete results in areas in which the CBSS is uniquely suited to add value.[37] Further details are provided in a Roadmap of the CBSS reforms 2018–20, endorsed in the Jurmala Declaration adopted in June 2019.[38] With the Bornholm Declaration of May 2020, the CBSS adopted revised Terms of Reference of the CBSS and of the CBSS Secretariat, presented as the implementation of the Roadmap of the CBSS reforms 2018–20.[39] The changes to the Terms of Reference do not entail any radical overhaul, but provide for some minor additions to the objectives of the CBSS and its Secretariat, such as the explicit mention that the CBSS should foster practical cooperation in the region and contribute to reinforcing the effects of regional policies adopted by the Member States in other fora.[40] Yet, the

[33] CBSS, 'Declaration on the Occasion of the 25th Anniversary of the CBBS' (n 31).

[34] CBSS, 'Vision for the Baltic Sea Region beyond 2020: Report by the Council of the Baltic Sea States Vision Group' (2018), available at: www.eeas.org.

[35] ibid, 7.

[36] ibid, 2.

[37] CBSS, 'Stockholm Declaration' (18 June 2018), adopted by the Foreign Ministers and high-level representatives of the Member States and the EU.

[38] CBSS, 'Jurmala Declaration' (3 June 2019), adopted by the Foreign Ministers and high-level representatives of the Member States and the EU.

[39] CBSS, 'Bornhom Declaration' (19 May 2020), adopted by the Foreign Ministers of the Member States and a high-level representative of the EU.

[40] Revised Terms of Reference of 2020 (n 20) para 5. In the revised Terms of Reference of the Secretariat (n 27), the tasks of the Secretariat are specified to include, inter alia, 'to make proposals and present initiatives to the CSO, in order to promote the objectives and implement the priorities decided by the Council', para 2.

Bornholm Declaration states that the CBSS reforms 2018–20, which were initiated through the Vision Group Report and the Stockholm Declaration, 'should increase the relevance, efficiency, transparency and visibility of the organization'. A more substantive and concrete list of activities, also indicating CBSS and other actors and a timeline, is contained in an Action Plan, welcomed by the Vilnius II Declaration of June 2021.[41]

III. Participation and Representation of the EU in the CBSS

As was noted above, the CBSS was established at a conference in Copenhagen in March 1992, assembling not only the Ministers for Foreign Affairs of 10 Baltic Sea States, but also a representative of the European Commission. According to the Copenhagen Declaration,[42] the CBSS 'will serve as an overall regional forum to focus on needs for intensified cooperation and coordination among the Baltic Sea States' while the Terms of Reference of the CBSS adopted at the conference referred to 'a forum for guidance and overall coordination among the participating states'.[43] As already suggested by these references to the Baltic Sea 'States', including in the very name of the entity, the CBSS was envisaged as an intergovernmental forum established and run by the participating states rather than the EU. It seems significant that according to the Terms of Reference, it was the Ministers for Foreign Affairs that 'decided' to establish the CBSS, albeit 'in the presence of the representative from the European Commission'. It should also be noted that in the 1998 decision to establish a secretariat, it is stated that the decision was taken by the 'Governments' of the CBSS States, without mentioning the Commission.[44]

Certainly, the participants of the conference included 'the representative of the European Commission' and the Terms of Reference states unequivocally that 'Members will be those countries invited to the Copenhagen conference and the European Commission'.[45] An overall reading of the Copenhagen Declaration and the Terms of Reference, nevertheless, gives the impression that the Commission was viewed, if not as a mere observer, then as a participant of somewhat secondary importance. Not only do these documents in most cases speak of participating

[41] CBSS, 'Vilnius II Declaration A Vision for the Baltic Sea Region by 2030' (Vilnius, 1 June 2021); CBSS, 'From Policy to Action! CBSS Action Plan 2021–2025' (2021).

[42] See Copenhagen Declaration (n 16).

[43] See Terms of Reference (n 20).

[44] Establishment of the CBSS Secretariat, proposal by the Presidency, 29 January 1997. See also the Preamble of the Agreement between Sweden and the CBSS Secretariat (n 24). Compare an agreement relating to the Secretariat in Copenhagen of the CBSS Commissioner on Democratic Institutions and Human Rights, set up in 1994 but abolished in 2003 (n 23), which counted among its signatories the Commission as well.

[45] Terms of Reference (n 20) para 4.

'states' or 'countries', but the rotating chairmanship of the Council, including the CSO, is reserved for the participating states, the 'host country' of each session, including CSO meetings, assuming the chairmanship. The chairmanship obviously plays a significant role in preparing meetings and draft documents, presenting initiatives, leading the discussion, and so on. What emerged was a situation of 'mixity', meaning the participation of both the then European Community and some of its Member States.[46] At the same time, the situation can be characterised as 'incomplete mixity', as only some (in 1992, in fact, only two) of the Member States became Members of the CBSS,[47] as well as a situation of 'unbalanced mixity', in view of the fact that the Community (represented by the Commission) did not obtain the same membership rights as its Member States (or those of the non-Community Members of the CBSS).

The particularities of the EU's involvement do not stop here, however. The participant in the Copenhagen Conference and the 'member' of the CBSS is referred to as the 'European Commission', not the European Community or the European Union. The Commission is not a subject of international law but one of the organs of the Union.[48] It shall in most cases 'ensure the Union's external representation', including assuming the role of negotiator of international agreements, but the decision to conclude an agreement is normally reserved for the EU Council.[49] The contracting party to an agreement will be the Union itself (before the entry into force of the Treaty of Lisbon in 2009, in most cases the European Community).[50] In the case of the establishment of the CBSS, there was no Council decision authorising the Commission to join the organisation on behalf of the Community.

Apparently the Commission considered that it was entitled to participate in the Copenhagen Conference and become a member of the CBSS because of the political rather than legal nature of the Copenhagen Declaration and the CBSS itself, coupled with the fact that the participant and member was designated as the Commission rather than the Community.[51] Apparently the Commission

[46] On mixed agreements, adhered to by both the EU and its Member States, see, eg, A Rosas, 'Recent Case Law of the European Court of Justice Relating to Article 218 TFEU' in J Czuczai and F Naert (eds), *The EU as a Global Actor – Bridging Legal Theory and Practice: Liber Amicorum in Honour of Ricardo Gosalbo Bono* (Leiden, Brill-Nijhoff, 217) 365.

[47] ibid.

[48] The Commission is defined as one of the seven 'institutions' of the EU, see Treaty on European Union [2012] OJ C326/13, Art 13(1) (TEU).

[49] See TEU, Art 17(1); and Treaty on the Functioning of the European Union [2012] OJ C326/47, Art 218 (TFEU). On TFEU, Art 218, see Rosas (n 46).

[50] According to TFEU, Art 216(1), it is the Union which may conclude an agreement with third countries and international organisations. According to Art 216(2), agreements 'concluded by the Union shall be binding upon the institutions of the Union and on its Member States'.

[51] Inside the Commission, there was a strand of thought that at least under certain conditions, the Commission, as the external representative of the Community, could sign 'soft law' instruments as well as so-called administrative agreements between two administrations rather than States or other subjects of international law; observations of the co-author Rosas, who during the period from 1995 to 2001 was a Director at the Commission Legal Service, in charge of EU external relations.

President, who was Jacques Delors at the time, considered that it was important, after the political upheavals of 1989 to 1992 redrawing the map of north-eastern Europe,[52] for the Commission to get involved in the work of a new regional body for East–West cooperation as well as cooperation between EU Member States (Denmark and Germany) and BSR states that, at that point, could be expected to join the EU in the short (Finland, Norway and Sweden) or long run (Estonia, Latvia, Lithuania and Poland).

How is the Commission participation to be characterised from an institutional-legal point of view? The basic Treaties (now the Treaty on European Union (TEU) and the Treaty on the Functioning of the European Union (TFEU)) did not – and still do not today – contain rules explicitly regulating the status of legally non-binding 'soft law' instruments or the procedures for their approval on behalf of the EU. Two years after the founding of the CBSS, the European Court of Justice declared void an Act whereby the Commission had sought to conclude a competition law agreement with the United States but the judgment was based on the view that the agreement in question was legally binding.[53] In a case decided 10 years later, at issue was an Act (guidelines on regulatory cooperation and transparency agreed between Commission and US services) which the Court considered not to constitute a binding agreement.[54] The French action contesting the legality of the Act was dismissed, but only because it was based on the idea of a binding agreement and a violation of Article 300 of the then EC Treaty (now Article 218 TFEU). The Court was at pains to explain that the judgment could not be construed as upholding the Commission's argument that the non-binding nature of the Act in question was sufficient to confer on the Commission the power to adopt the Act, and that while Article 300 of the EC Treaty was not applicable, the situation should still be judged on the basis of the Treaty rules relating to the division of powers and institutional balance.[55] That also the adoption of non-binding acts may belong to the prerogatives of the Council rather than the Commission has been more recently confirmed in a case concerning a Memorandum of Understanding concluded by the Commission with Switzerland, in which the Commission's decision to sign without the Council's prior approval was annulled as a violation of the distribution of powers in Article 13(2) TEU and the principle of institutional balance.[56]

Taking this subsequent case law into account, it seems obvious that despite the political nature of the Copenhagen Declaration, the initial entry into membership of the CBSS in 1992 should have been construed as the Community rather than the

[52] We are thinking, inter alia, of the fall of the Berlin Wall in November 1989, the reunification of Germany in October 1990, the dissolution of the Treaty of Friendship, Cooperation and Mutual Assistance (Warsaw Pact) in July 1991, the reborn independence of Estonia, Latvia and Lithuania in 1991 and the dissolution of the Soviet Union in December 1991.

[53] Case C-327/91 *France v Commission* [1994] ECR I-03641, ECLI:EU:C:1994:305.

[54] Case C-2233/02 *French Republic v Commission* [2004] ECR I-02759, ECLI:EU:C:2004:173.

[55] ibid, para 40.

[56] Case C-660/13 *Council v Commission* ECLI:EU:C:2016:616.

Commission joining the CBSS as a 'member' based on an authorisation by the EU Council. On the other hand, the Commission did, in different contexts, inform the Council as well as the European Council (the latter consisting of the Heads of State and Government) of its participation in the work of the CBSS and seems to have sought the Council's authorisation in this respect.[57] A reply from the Council in 1995 was not very forthcoming, requesting the Commission to make proposals relative to the role the latter could be called upon to play, within the scope of its competence, in the work of the CBSS.[58]

Nonetheless, the European Council urged the Commission to propose a regional cooperation initiative to be presented to the Heads of State and Government of the CBSS at their Summit in Visby on 3 and 4 May 1996 and subsequently expressed its satisfaction with the initiative presented by the Commission.[59] It is noteworthy that the Visby Summit took place 'in the presence' not only of the President of the Commission but also the President of the European Council,[60] a formula repeated in the Summits of 1998, 2000, 2002 and 2004 (although at the 2002 and 2004 Summits, the Commission was represented by a member, not the President).[61] The role of the Commission in the work of the CBSS may thus be said to have received high-level political backing from the European Council. As from 2006, only the President, alternatively a representative, of the Commission took part in the Summits and, unlike at the previous Summits, no formal difference was made in the list of participants between the representative of the Commission and those of Member States.[62]

The Commission continued to participate in the work of the CBSS in its own name at least until the entry into force of the Treaty of Lisbon on 1 December 2009. Shortly before this event, the Commission transmitted to the CBSS a Note Verbale, from the Council and the Commission, notifying it of the succession of the European Community by the European Union as from 1 December 2009 (entry into force of the Treaty of Lisbon).[63] The Note Verbale states that as from that date, 'the European Union will exercise all rights and assume all obligations of the European Community, including its status in the Organisation', and that the

[57] See, eg, SEC(94) 1747 final (n 6) 9, where the Commission requested the Council to invite the Commission 'to continue to take a full and active part, as a full member, in the work of the CBSS'.

[58] Conclusions of the Presidency from the General Affairs Council of 29 May 1995, Communication à la presse 7481/95 (Presse 152).

[59] European Council, 'Madrid European Council 15 and 16 December 1995 Presidency Conclusions' Ch III:B; European Council, 'Florence European Council 21 and 22 June 1996 Presidency Conclusions' Ch VIII:4. On the initiative, see also above (n 6).

[60] CBSS, '1st Baltic Sea States Summit, Visby, 3–4 May, 1996' (Presidency Declaration).

[61] CBSS, 'Presidency Declaration Baltic Sea States Summit, Riga, 22–23 January 1998'; CBSS, 'Baltic Sea States Summit, Kolding, 12–13 April 2000 Chairman's Conclusions'; CBSS, '4th Baltic Sea States Summit (St Petersburg, 10 June 2002) Chairman's Conclusions'; CBSS, '5th Baltic Sea States Summit Laulasmaa, Estonia, 21 June 2004 Chairman's Conclusions'.

[62] CBSS, '6th Baltic Sea States Summit Reykjavik, Iceland, 8 June 2006 Chairman's Conclusions'. The last Summit was organised by the German CBSS presidency in Stralsund, 31 May 2012, Presidential Communiqué.

[63] Letter from the Commission to the CBSS (30 November 2009).

Union will accede to existing commitments made by the Community or adopted within the organisation 'and binding on the European Community'.[64] This text is thus based on the assumption that it had been the Community, represented by the Commission, that had been a member of the CBSS; it is of a general character, however, and not specifically tailored to fit the particular status of the CBSS or the fact that in CBSS documents, it had always been the Commission rather than the Community that had been referred to as a member.

The Note Verbale notwithstanding, it is stated in the Oslo Declaration, adopted by a Ministerial Session in June 2011, that the CBSS consisted of the Foreign Ministers of 11 states 'and a member of the European Commission'.[65] In a Ministerial Declaration on Energy Security of February 2012, however, reference is made to a 'representative of the European Union'.[66] Most Ministerial Declarations and other documents adopted subsequently refer to the Union as a member or participant. It is, then, remarkable that the Revised Terms of Reference, adopted as late as May 2020 by a ministerial video conference, lists among the members of the CBSS 'the European Commission', which should be represented by a Member of the Commission.[67] On the other hand, the Bornholm Declaration, adopted by the same conference, lists as one of the participants of the conference 'a high-level representative of the European Union'. It seems obvious that the reference to the Commission in the Revised Terms of Reference is a copy from the previous versions of the Terms of Reference and may be considered a mistake.

Apart from the anomaly represented by this reference to the Commission in the Revised Terms of Reference of 2020, it now seems established that it is the EU which is considered as a member of the CBSS. This conclusion is reinforced by the fact that as from 2011, it has no longer been the Commission but the European External Action Service (EEAS), established in 2010, that has ensured EU participation in the work of the CBSS. The EEAS is a functionally autonomous body of the EU, separate from the General Secretariat of the Council and from the Commission, that shall support the High Representative of the Union for Foreign Affairs and Security Policy (High Representative) in conducting the Union's Common Foreign and Security Policy and ensuring the consistency of the Union's external action. The EEAS is under the authority of the High Representative, who is both President of the Foreign Affairs Council (a Council formation consisting of the Ministers of Foreign Affairs of the EU Member States) and Vice-President of the Commission.

[64] Council of Europe, 'Communication contained in a Note Verbale from the Council of the European Union and the Commission of the European Communities, dated 27 November 2009, registered at the Secretariat General on 30 November 2009 – Or. Engl./Fr'.

[65] CBSS, 'Declaration of the 16th Ministerial Session, Oslo, 7 June 2011'.

[66] CBSS, 'Declaration on Energy Security in the Baltic Sea Region Adopted by the 17th Extraordinary CBSS Ministerial Session, Schloss Ploen, 5 February 2012'.

[67] Revised Terms of Reference (n 20) paras 2 and 3.

The shift from the Commission to the EEAS is explained by the fact that the establishment of the EEAS resulted in a number of Commission external relations staff, including external relations directorates with geographical mandates, being transferred to the EEAS.[68] It is interesting to note that the CBSS was included in the list of organisations that in the future should be handled by the EEAS rather than the Commission services. Apparently, this arrangement was considered appropriate in view not only of the political status of the CBSS, but also of its role as a forum for cooperation between EU Member States, EEA countries (Iceland and Norway) and Russia. A different solution has been followed with respect to the EUSBSR, where the Commission, and more specifically DG REGIO,[69] is the lead institution. This can be explained by the EU-internal nature of the Strategy, which is focused on concrete projects obtaining financing from various EU sources, whereas the CBSS, despite the strong EU representation in its membership, offers a forum for broader cooperation, above all with Russia.

IV. The Operational Relations between the EU and the CBSS

As has been explained above, the EU has not been an initiator or a veritable driving force behind the establishment and development of the CBSS, which was conceived primarily as an intergovernmental platform for the participating Baltic Sea States. The situation may be characterised as not only a form of 'incomplete' mixity, but also 'unbalanced' mixity. The Union has nevertheless taken its membership of the organisation seriously and has normally been represented at summits, ministerial sessions, CSO meetings and in other contexts. At the Baltic Sea States Summit of 31 May 2012 (Stralsund), the EU was still represented by the President of the Commission[70] and at a High-Level Conference relating to the environment of 5–6 April 2013, by a Member of the Commission.[71] As was explained above, EU representation shifted from the Commission to the EEAS after the entry into force of the Treaty of Lisbon. Accordingly, at Ministerial Sessions (which during the period from 2014 to 2016 were held at a lower than ministerial level), the EU has since 2012 been represented once by the High Representative of the Union for Foreign Affairs and Security Policy and otherwise by the Secretary-General or Deputy Secretary-General of the EEAS. Officials from the EEAS have covered other CBSS activities, including serving as senior officials representing the Union in the meetings of the CSO. While the EU has participated regularly in meetings

[68] See Section 2 of the Annex to Council Decision 2010/427/EU of 26 July 2010 establishing the organisation and functioning of the European External Action Service [2010] OJ L201/30.

[69] Commission, Directorate-General for Regional and Urban Policy.

[70] CBSS, '9th Baltic Sea States Summit' (n 25).

[71] CBSS, 'Statement of the High Level Conference on the Protection of the Environment of the Baltic Sea Region (St Petersburg, 5–6 April, 2013)'.

and other events and is, thus, in a position to monitor CBSS activities at close range, it has generally not played a leading role, for instance, by taking initiatives.[72] It should be recalled that the Union is not included in the rotating CBSS chairmanship, which is shared between the Member States.

A possible additional institutional and functional link between the EU and the CBSS could be envisaged with respect to the EUSBSR. Indeed, at the initial phases of the Strategy, the CBSS may have nurtured hopes of obtaining a significant role in its implementation.[73] In the Commission Communication of 2009 proposing the setting up of the EUSBSR, it is, however, noted that 'relations with third countries should be conducted primarily through the Northern Dimension with the option to use alternative channels when useful'.[74] The EU Council conclusions endorsing the EUSBSR again reiterates that cooperation with non-EU countries 'could be pursued, notably but not exclusively, in the context of the Northern Dimension which provides a functioning format for an enhanced cooperation in the region'.[75] Apparently this reference to the ND Policy was more palatable to Russia, which, as was noted above, is one of its four partners (the other being the EU, Norway and Iceland), and to those EU Member States that were not members of the CBSS.[76] That the CBSS was not completely forgotten can be seen from the initial EUSBSR Action Plan of 2009, which, after having noted that 'the Northern Dimension, a common policy of the EU, Russia, Norway and Iceland, provides the basis for [the] external aspects of the strategy', refers to 'other fora which will be useful in this regard' and mentions as examples not only the Nordic Council of Ministers and the Helsinki Commission (HELCOM), but also the CBSS, adding that cooperation with them 'will be without prejudice to their respective decision-making mechanisms'.[77]

Looking at the situation today, it can be noted that cooperation between the EUSBSR and non-EU actors has not been channelled principally through the ND,[78] which may be due to the fact that since the accession of Estonia, Latvia, Lithuania and Poland to the EU, the ND has had its focus principally on northwest Russia.[79] Neither has the CBSS become a central player in the ND, despite being listed in the Northern Dimension Policy Framework Document, together with the Nordic Council of Ministers, the Barents Euro-Arctic Council and the Arctic

[72] Observations by co-author Vuorimäki.

[73] Observations by co-author Vuorimäki.

[74] Commission, COM(2009) 248 final (n 1) point 6.2.

[75] EU Council Doc 13744/09.

[76] Observations by co-author Vuorimäki.

[77] Commission, 'Commission Staff Working Document Accompanying the Communication from the Commission to the European Parliament, the Council, the European Economic and Social Committee and the Committee of the Regions concerning the European Union Strategy for the Baltic Sea Region Action Plan' SEC(2009) 712 (fns 1 and 77) 3.

[78] Commission, 'Commission Staff Working Document EU Strategy for the Baltic Sea Region Action Plan [COM(2009) 248 final] Revised Action Plan replacing the Action Plan of 17 March 2017 – SWD(2017) 118 final' SWD(2021) 24 final, 9–16.

[79] See, eg, Northern Dimension: www.eeas.europa.eu.

Council, as 'another participant'.[80] The CBSS Vision Group report recommends that the CBSS Secretariat carry out an audit of existing regional cooperation structures in the BSR, and that, on the basis of such an audit, 'the CBSS could find the most efficient ways of cooperating with the ND Policy including its Partnerships and other initiatives'.[81]

As to the EUSBSR, implementation governance presents a mixed picture. While the European Commission does continue to play a role mainly as a coordinator and adviser, the main emphasis is on the national level, including national authorities and organisations, complemented by, as the case may be, intergovernmental or non-governmental organisations.[82] Most of the Coordinators (PACs) of the 14 EUSBSR Policy Areas (PAs) are EU Member States, including administrative authorities and German federal states. Some regional organisations or fora, including the ND and the CBSS, do play a role, though. The PACs include: HELCOM and Visions and Strategies Around the Baltic Sea for PA Spatial Planning; the Nordic Council of Ministers together with three Member States for PA Bioeconomy; the Nordic Council of Ministers together with two Member States for PA Innovation; the Northern Dimension Partnership in Public Health and Social Well-being (NDPHS)[83] for PA Health; and the CBSS Secretariat together with Sweden, as represented by the Swedish Civil Contingencies Agency, for PA Secure.

The PA Secure Steering Group also includes representatives of the CBSS Task Force against Trafficking in Human Beings and the Children at Risk Unit at the CBSS Secretariat. Apart from this role as a PAC and involvement in the Steering Group of PA Secure (which relates to the CBSS long-term priority Safe & Secure Region), the CBSS also plays a role in other activities of the EUSBSR, inter alia, by being involved in projects and taking part in the EUSBSR Annual Forum.[84] The CBSS Vision Group report states that the CBSS 'should continue to contribute pro-actively to the implementation of the EU Strategy for the Baltic Sea Region (EUSBSR) and retain responsibility in a number of policy areas/actions and projects'.[85] While the European Commission plays a backstage role in the day-to-day workings of the EUSBSR, CBSS involvement in the Strategy implies cooperation with national governments, authorities, academia and civil society, ie, largely the same actors that are involved in the CBSS' own activities, rather than with the Union as such.

While the Union, if seen as distinct from its Member States, does not generally assume a leading role in the context of the CBSS, its membership of the organisation and regular participation in the organisation's meetings and events carry the potential of a more active role with a view, for instance, of reminding CBSS

[80] See Commission, 'Revised Action Plan' (n 78).
[81] See CBSS, Vision Group Report (n 34) 13–14.
[82] See Commission, 'Revised Action Plan' (n 78) 9–17.
[83] On NDPHS see above (nn 8, 10 and 11).
[84] See CBSS, 'CBSS in EUSBSR Annual Forum 2021' (5 October 2021), available at: www.cbss.org.
[85] CBSS, Vision Group Report (n 34) 14.

decision-makers of the EUSBSR, ND Policy or other relevant plans, resources or activities. Occasionally, some of the CBSS government representatives or other actors may expect the EU to provide funding or take a more active role by presenting new ideas or initiatives. A conspicuous example is provided by the chairmanship of the CBSS Vision Group, which as was noted above, presented the report 'Vision for the Baltic Sea Region beyond 2020' in 2018. The Group, composed of independent experts appointed by the 11 governments and the EU, elected as chair the expert appointed by the Union and as vice-chair an expert appointed by Russia.[86] That said, the role of the chair was clearly that of an honest broker rather than arguing in favour of an overall change in the status and role of the EU in the CBSS. The Vision Group report, while containing some recommendations for the strengthening of the role of the CBSS in BSR cooperation in general, and while referring to the need to liaise with other structures and networks, including the EUSBSR and the EUSBSR Annual Forum, does not advocate any change in the Union's participation in the CBSS as such.[87]

Finally, some factors will be listed which may explain why the EU generally does not assume a leading role in the work of the CBSS and why it even could be said that the Union punches below its weight in this regard. First, it should be recalled that the initial involvement of the Commission in the setting up of the CBSS and entering into its membership in 1992 does not seem to have been based on a carefully worked-out strategy in cooperation with the other institutions of the European Community and the decision to take part in the Copenhagen Conference may have been taken on the spur of the moment. Since the beginning, the EU's inferior status of not being eligible for the overall chairmanship of the CBSS has been an important factor, as the chair inevitably plays a significant role in setting the agenda of the organisation.

Moreover, especially during the first 20 years of the CBSS, EU involvement seems to have been affected by the confusion surrounding the question of 'who am I, the Commission, the European Community or the EU?' And it should also be recalled that the EU is a global actor that is a member of or participates in a great number of universal and regional organisations and networks, while at the same time having relatively limited resources and staff, considering the broad range of internal and external commitments.[88] EU involvement in the work of the CBSS has accordingly been handled by very few people and the possibilities to develop a strategy with an action plan with a view to taking a leading role in the organisation have simply been missing.[89]

[86] Petteri Vuorimäki, co-author of the present chapter, was at the time of the Vision Group a Senior Expert in the EEAS.

[87] See the Recommendations of the Vision Group Report (n 34) 8–14.

[88] See A Rosas and L Armati, *EU Constitutional Law: An Introduction*, 3rd rev edn (Oxford, Hart Publishing, 2018).

[89] Observations by co-author Vuorimäki.

EU participation in the work of the CBSS has nevertheless continued arguably as the BSR has more generally been considered a region of special interest for the EU, which has also manifested in the EUSBSR and the participation of the Union in the ND Policy and the work of HELCOM. Membership of the CBSS has enabled the EU to keep an eye on the overall functioning of these different fora and to ensure sufficient coordination with the EUSBSR. That the CBSS, the ND and HELCOM all involve Russia as well has increased their attractiveness for the EU. The Union's continuing involvement may also be seen as a recognition of the fact that while there have at times been doubts about the usefulness of the CBSS, and while there have also been contradictory signals from the CBSS Member States as to the direction and ultimate fate of the organisation, it can nevertheless be concluded that the CBSS has been reasonably successful in promoting concrete BSR cooperation in the form of projects and networks, involving not only governments but also other actors, such as public bodies and civil society. There is every reason to believe that the CBSS has a future and, if so, the EU will most probably continue its participation as well. Who knows, maybe the future will even hold an intensification of EU involvement in this respect?

9

The Baltic Sea: The Law of the Sea and EU Law Perspectives

ESA PAASIVIRTA

I. Introduction

As the political geography of the Baltic Sea region (BSR) has changed over the last three decades, the role of the European Union (EU) has become increasingly important in the region. Today, eight out of nine Baltic Sea coastal states belong to the EU. Only Russia, which has coastlines in the Gulf of Finland and the Kaliningrad area, remains outside. Almost the entire Baltic Sea is now under the umbrella of EU legislation, policies and activities that impact the maritime environment. Yet, the EU institutions as well as the EU Member States have to respect their broader international obligations, in particular those laid down in the UN Convention on the Law of the Sea (UNCLOS),[1] when legislating, applying or interpreting domestic legal acts.

All Baltic Sea coastal states, as well as the EU,[2] are parties to UNCLOS. The Convention regulates the use of the Baltic Sea and maritime resources, providing for freedoms, obligations and constraints. The states are also members of the International Maritime Organization (IMO) and of the related legal instruments regulating emissions from merchant vessels.

This chapter first reviews the relevant UNCLOS rules and how they frame, enable and constrain the EU's legislative action, and provides examples from the EU's judicial practice and legislation. It then briefly recalls the EU's role as a global actor in maritime affairs and the EU's institutional framework that directs its conduct. Finally, some examples are given to illustrate the multi-level dimensions and issues in the context of Baltic Sea governance. This chapter focuses on matters of general international law and hence avoids specific sectoral developments and issues that are covered in other chapters in this volume.

[1] The United Nations Convention on the Law of the Sea, Montego Bay, 10 December 1982.

[2] Approved on behalf of the European Community by Council Decision 98/392/EC of 23 March 1998 [1998] OJ L179/1, 1.

II. EU Legislation Extended, but Constrained: The Law of the Sea Framework for the EU Action in the Baltic Sea

A. Geography and Competence

Strictly speaking, there is no definition of 'EU territory', even less 'EU maritime areas', though those terms are commonly used. The geographic scope of the EU Treaties and legislation is defined indirectly, by a simple reference to the Member States in its Treaty. Article 52(1) of the Treaty on European Union (TEU)[3] just provides that '[t]he Treaties shall apply *to* the Kingdom of Belgium' (emphasis added), followed by an enumeration of the other EU Member States therein, while Article 355 of the Treaty on the Functioning of the European Union (TFEU)[4] refers to certain areas which are excluded or have a special status. The EU Treaties simply assume a certain geographic scope for the application of EU law as given and settled. Unsettled national borders would disturb effective application of EU law and for this reason, too, be essential for peace and order in the region. The geographic application of EU law is, thus, entirely dependent on the borders of the EU Member States.

The EU Treaties also do not confer legal competence to the EU organisation regarding the delimitation of borders, including delimitation of maritime borders. They are essentially to be defined among the states themselves in accordance with international law.

For example in *Slovenia v Croatia*[5] the EU Court of Justice ruled that it lacked jurisdiction regarding the border dispute between those two EU Member States. Slovenia had brought the action on the basis of Article 259 of the TFEU, contending that Croatia had failed to fulfil its obligations under EU law. Slovenia asserted that Croatia did not comply with the obligations of an international arbitration award, based on an agreement of 2009 between the two states involving Croatia's accession to the EU, in order to settle their sea and land borders. Croatia did not execute that arbitration award given in 2018, invoking irregularities during the arbitral proceedings. However, Slovenia argued that Croatia had infringed a number of obligations under the EU Treaties relating to the Union's fundamental values and the principle of sincere cooperation (Articles 2 and 4(3) of the TEU), and EU secondary legislation, including provisions of its common fisheries policy.[6]

[3] Consolidated version of the Treaty on European Union [2012] OJ C326/13.

[4] Consolidated version of the Treaty on the Functioning of the European Union [2012] OJ C326/47.

[5] Case C-457/18 *Slovenia v Croatia* ECLI:EU:C2020:65.

[6] Regulation (EU) No 1380/2013 of the European Parliament and of the Council of 11 December 2013 on the Common Fisheries Policy [2013] OJ L354/22, Art 5(2) as amended.

The Court concluded that it lacked jurisdiction because the arbitration award was made by an international tribunal established under a bilateral arbitration agreement governed by international law: '[T]he subject matter of which does not fall within the areas of EU competence referred to in Articles 3 to 6 TFEU and to which the European Union is not a party'.[7] That conclusion was reached in spite of the good offices that the EU had rendered to the parties during the border dispute and the fact that the President of the Council had signed the arbitration agreement on behalf of the European Union, as a witness.[8]

That said, the Court stressed that its conclusion was

> without prejudice to any obligation arising – for both of the Member States concerned, in their reciprocal relations but also vis-à-vis the European Union and the other Member States – from Article 4(3) TEU to strive sincerely to bring about a definitive legal solution consistent with international law … that ensures the effective and unhindered application of EU law in the areas concerned, and to bring their dispute to an end.

The practical outcome is that, for the time being, such unsettled situations leave effective application of EU rules in disarray about mutual access for fishing and possibly the functioning of other relevant EU instruments regarding certain segments of the sea.

Fortunately, the maritime borders in the Baltic Sea have been largely settled by a number of bilateral treaties that were concluded in the 1980s with adjustments for the post-Soviet era.[9] Outside the territorial seas, the Baltic Sea is covered by the exclusive economic zones established by the respective coastal states, leaving no high sea areas beyond these zones. These characteristics bear important implications on the reach of EU legislation.

B. How Far Does EU Legislation Go in Coastal Maritime Areas?

i. The Reach of Coastal State Jurisdiction under UNCLOS

Generally, Article 52 of the TEU is understood to cover all the areas within the sovereignty or jurisdiction of the Member States, including maritime zones where they exercise sovereign rights and where they have conferred competence

[7] Case C-457/18 (n 5) point 102.

[8] ibid.

[9] E Franckx, 'Maritime Boundary delimitation in the Baltic Sea' in R Platzöder and P Verlaan (eds), *The Baltic Sea: New Developments in National Policies and International Cooperation* (The Hague, Martinus Nijhoff Publishers, 1996); H Ringbom (ed), *Regulatory Gaps in Baltic Sea Governance: Selected Issues* (Berlin, Springer, 2018).

to the EU.[10] The exercise of such rights and competences in maritime areas is, however, subject to the provisions of UNCLOS and other relevant international instruments.

To a large extent, UNCLOS takes a zonal approach to the sea and lays down the rules on rights and obligations which depend on which activity is concerned and where the activity takes place. The Convention contains rules on internal waters, territorial seas (Articles 2–32), contiguous zones (Article 33), the continental shelf (Articles 76–85), the exclusive economic zone (Articles 55–75), the high seas (Articles 86–120), the area of deep sea bed (Articles 133–91), international straits (Articles 34–45), and archipelagic waters (Article 46–54).[11] The jurisdiction and powers of a coastal state are widest closest to its territory and gradually decrease the further out from shore one goes. Accordingly, the coastal states may exercise 'sovereignty' (internal waters, ports, territorial sea) or 'sovereign rights' (continental shelf, exclusive economic zone, EEZ) in the zones connected to their coastal areas, but they must reserve certain freedoms to others, pursuant to the relevant provisions of UNCLOS (Articles 2, 56–58, 77). As parties to UNCLOS, the Baltic Sea States, as well as the EU, are subject to such provisions.

However, Part XI of UNCLOS, concerning the protection and preservation of the marine environment, applies to the entirety of the marine environment. While Part XI concerns primarily issues of pollution, Articles 192 and 193 set out general obligations to protect and preserve the maritime environment. The Preamble to the Convention also states that the problems of ocean space are 'inter-related' and need to be considered as a whole.

'Internal waters' cover the waters on landward of the baseline from which the 'territorial sea' and other maritime zones are measured. In this area the coastal state enjoys full territorial sovereignty over its internal waters just as it does over land territory.[12]

Ports are part of the land territory of a state and thus subject to its full sovereignty. Though ports are generally kept open for economic reasons, the port state can restrict access to its ports, as there is no general access to ports rights under international law except in emergency situations.[13] As part of the land territory of

[10] Case C-347/10 *Salemink* ECLI:EU:C:2011:562, point 54. The Opinion of Advocate General Villalón expressed this as follows: 'As stated in Art 1 TEU, the European Union is the result of the desire of the States establishing it to attain their common objectives by conferring on it certain competences. Whether such competences belong to the Member States by virtue of their sovereignty or were originally the result of international law conferring a sovereign right is immaterial for the purposes of defining the limits of Union competences, as the Union will exercise precisely those competences conferred on it (Art 5 TEU), on the terms agreed in the Treaties, having regard to the content and extent of such competences when exercised by the States themselves prior to entering into the Union'.

[11] Generally, see, JE Hickey Jr, 'The 1982 United Nations Convention on the Law of the Sea' in DC Baur, T Eichenberg and M Sutton (eds), *Ocean and Coastal Law and Policy*, 2nd edn (American Bar Association, 2015).

[12] The United Nations Convention on the Law of the Sea (UNCLOS) Art 8.

[13] P Badura, 'Ports' in R Wolfrum (ed), *The Max Planck Encyclopedia of Public International Law*, e-resource (Oxford University Press, updated April 2011) para 9. On the debate concerning the access to ports generally, see H Ringbom, *The EU Maritime Safety and International Law* (Leiden, Martinus Nijhoff Publishers, 2008) 204–10, 380–81.

its Member States, EU law generally covers ports and there is specific ports-related EU legislation concerning, for example, port security.[14] Given the absence of the right to access to ports, the EU has imposed restrictive measures on Russia following its invasion of Ukraine with a ban on Russian flagged vessels' access the ports.[15]

The sovereignty of the coastal state extends to its territorial sea, which is the adjacent seaward belt next to the internal waters, and includes the air space above the sea, the seabed and subsoil. Every state is entitled to a territorial sea, up to a limit not exceeding 12 nautical miles measured from the baselines.[16] Yet, ships of all states enjoy the right of 'innocent passage' in the territorial sea.[17]

In a zone contiguous to the territorial sea ('contiguous zone'), the coastal state may exercise limited enforcement powers to 'prevent and punish' infringement of its laws and regulations applying within its territory or territorial sea. However, the enforcement powers are limited to customs, fiscal, immigration or sanitary laws. The contiguous zone may not extend beyond 24 nautical miles from the baselines from which the breadth of the territorial sea is measured.[18]

Large portions of the world's oceans are today covered by Exclusive Economic Zones (EEZs) of the coastal states, including all of the Baltic Sea except for territorial sea and internal waters. The concept of the EEZ is included in UNCLOS with provisions concerning its establishment, extent and coastal states' rights.[19] The EEZ and continental shelf beyond the territorial sea are not part of the territorial sovereignty of the coastal state. In the EEZ the coastal state can exercise its sovereign right for particular purposes, primarily relating to the use and preservation of fisheries and other maritime resources.

Under Article 56(1)(a) of UNCLOS, the coastal state can exercise sovereign resources rights over its EEZ for exploring and exploiting natural resources of the waters super-jacent to the seabed and of the seabed and its subsoil, and with regard to other activities relating to economic exploitation and exploration of the zone, such as the production energy from the water, currents and winds.[20]

[14] Directive 2005/65/EC of the European Parliament and of the Council of 26 October 2005 on enhancing port security [2005] OJ L310/28. On the EU rules relating ports, see also Ringbom, *The EU Maritime Safety and International Law* (n 13) 91–106.

[15] Council Regulation (EU) 2022/576 of 8 April 2022 amending Regulation No 833/2014 concerning restrictive measures in view of Russia's actions destabilising the situation in Ukraine [2022] OJ L111/1, Art 1(11), adding Art 3ea providing: 'It shall be prohibited to provide access after 16 April 2022 to ports in the territory of the Union to any vessel registered under the flag of Russia.'

[16] UNCLOS, Arts 2–4. Arts 5–16 contain detailed guidance concerning different methodologies for measuring baselines.

[17] UNCLOS, Art 17.

[18] UNCLOS, Art 33. Pursuant to Art 111 enforcement measures in hot pursuit situations may be extended even beyond the territorial sea or the contiguous zone under certain conditions concerning violations of local laws and regulations, commencement and continuity of hot pursuit measures. See the Arctic Sunrise Arbitration (*Netherlands v Russia*), Award on the Merits, 14 August 2015, PCA Case No 2014-02, paras 242–75, available at: pca-cpa.org/en/cases/.

[19] Of the vast literature, see eg, G Andreone, 'The Exclusive Economic Zone' in DR Rothwell et al (eds), *The Oxford Handbook of the Law of the Sea* (Oxford, Oxford University Press, 2017).

[20] UNCLOS, Art 56(1)(a), under which the coastal state has in particular sovereign rights for the purpose of exploring and exploiting, managing and conserving the natural resources, whether living or

Under Article 56(1) (b) and (c), the coastal state has jurisdiction with regard to: (i) the establishment and use of artificial islands, installations and structures; (ii) marine scientific research; (iii) the protection and preservation of the marine environment; and other rights and duties provided for in the Convention. The coastal state's rights to establish installations and structures in its EEZ are relevant for instance to renewable energy production in the Baltic Sea.[21]

In the exercise of its sovereign rights, coastal states may also take enforcement measures as necessary, such as boarding, inspection, arrest and judicial proceedings, to ensure compliance with national and EU laws and regulations, subject to relevant notification and other conditions provided in Article 73 of UNCLOS. For example, in *Kvitsjoen v Commission*,[22] a Norwegian vessel fishing in the waters an EU Member State had its licence withdrawn as result of the Commission decision for non-compliance with an EU fisheries regulation, and sanctions were imposed. The vessel owner complained and the annulment action in the EU Court of First Instance was dismissed, including in respect of the pleas relating to the general principles of proportionality and misuse of power.

Freedom of navigation and the freedom to lay submarine pipelines apply nevertheless in the EEZ. Their relation to the Baltic Sea coastal states rights is further explored through the case studies in section V.

ii. Implications for EU Legislation

Under Article 2(1) of UNCLOS the coastal state enjoys full sovereignty in internal, archipelagic and territorial waters. These waters can be regulated by the coastal state and are subject to full enforcement by the coastal state.

The extension of EU law has not raised particular problems in the territorial sea. The Court of Justice has confirmed the applicability of EU law in this sea area, for instance, in several Sixth VAT Directives related cases brought to it relating to the supply of goods and services.[23] While, nonetheless, it is for the coastal state to establish its maritime boundaries, EU law is extended accordingly, thus preserving the rights and obligations stemming from the EU Treaties.[24]

non-living, of the waters superjacent to the seabed and of the seabed and its subsoil. It also has, under Art 56(1)(b)(iii), jurisdiction with regard to the protection and preservation of the marine environment as provided for in the relevant provisions of UNCLOS.

[21] A Proelss, 'Exclusive Economic Zone' in A Proelss (ed), *United Nations Convention on the Law of the Sea: A Commentary* (Munich, CH Beck, 2017) 428.

[22] Case T-46/00 *Kvitsjoen v Commission* [2001] ECR II-3713, ECLI:EU:T:2001:285.

[23] Accordingly, a Member State is required to subject to VAT a supply of goods and services which takes place in its territorial sea, on the bed thereof and in its subsoil. See: Case C-111/05 *Aktiebolaget NN v Skatteverket* [2007] ECR I-02697, ECLI:EU:C:2007:195, point 58; with regard to the supply of transport services, see Case C-331/94 *Commission* v *Greece* [1996] ECR I-02675, ECLI:EU:C:1996:211, point 10; see also Case C-30/89 *Commission v France* [1990] ECR I-00691, ECLI:EU:C:1990:114, point 15.

[24] See: Case C-61/77 *Commission v Ireland* [1978] ECR-00417, ECLI:EU:C:1978:29, point 50, noting that 'any extension of the maritime zones in question automatically means precisely the same extension of the area to which the regulation applies'.

Any EU legislation has to observe international law rights of third states. In *Paulsen/Diva Navigation*,[25] the Court considered the scope of EU legislation in different maritime zones in the context of a criminal law in a fisheries case. It confirmed that the EU rules laying down certain technical measures for the conservation of fish resources caught in the high seas do not apply to a third-country vessels exercising either innocent passage through territorial waters or freedom of navigation in the EEZ of a Member State. On the other hand, EU rules would apply in a situation when the vessel is temporarily in the internal waters or in the port of a Member State.[26]

Coastal states rights under EU law in the EEZ and continental shelf remained unsettled for some time. However, several rulings by the Court of Justice have brought further clarification for purposes of EU legislation.

In *Commission v UK*,[27] concerning the Habitats Directive, the EU framework and strategy for biodiversity conservation,[28] the Court accepted the Commission's claim that the UK had failed in its duties to designate special areas of conservation and to fully implement in a sufficiently precise manner its obligations under the Directive. The Court extended this obligation, not only to the territorial sea, but beyond it to the EEZ where the UK exercised sovereign rights.[29]

Along the same lines, in *Salemink*,[30] involving a preliminary ruling from a Dutch court, the Court of Justice confirmed that the gas work carried out on fixed or floating installations on the Netherlands' continental shelf for prospecting and/or the exploitation of natural resources should be regarded as work carried out in the territory of the state for the purposes of applying EU law. The issue concerned EU free movement of persons and related coverage by the Dutch social security scheme of an employee resident in another EU Member State. The Court referred to the nature of the continental shelf as the natural prolongation of the land territory, as ruled by the International Court of Justice (ICJ) in the *North Sea Continental Shelf* cases,[31] and to UNCLOS Article 77 (rights of the coastal state over the continental shelf) in conjunction with Article 80 (installations) and concluded:

> A member State which takes advantage of the economic rights to prospect and/or exploit natural resources on that part of the continental shelf which is adjacent to it

[25] Case C-286/90 *Anklagemindigheden v Paulsen and Diva Navigation* [1992] ECR I-06019, ECLI:EU:C:1992:453.

[26] ibid, paras 25–29, 33–34.

[27] Case C-6/04 *Commission v UK* [2005] ECR I-09017, ECLI:EU:C:2005:626.

[28] Directive 92/43/EEC on the conservation of natural habitats and of wild fauna and flora [1992] OJ L206/7.

[29] Case C-6/04 (n 27) para 117.

[30] Case C-347/10 *Salemink* ECLI:EU:C:2012:17.

[31] ICJ, 'Reports of Judgments, Advisory Opinions and Orders North Sea Continental Shelf Cases (Federal Republic of Germany/Denmark; Federal Republic of Germany/Netherlands) Judgment of 20 February 1969' [1969] ICJ Rep 3, para 19.

> cannot avoid the application of the EU law provisions designed to ensure the freedom of movement of persons working on such installations.[32]

The Advocate General explained further:

> The determining factor in defining the scope of EU law is, therefore, the extent of the competences lawfully exercised by the Member States within the framework of international law. EU law will apply to whatever extent the Member States exercise official authority in the areas of competence conferred on the Union, subject to conditions established by EU law and irrespective of the source of the entitlement to the State competence transferred to the EU; in other words, irrespective of whether the source of the entitlement was State sovereignty itself (as recognised and protected by international law) or the conferral by the international community of a sovereign right.
>
> In order to reply to the question referred in these proceedings, we must therefore look to the specific collection of competences actually conferred on the Union in the substantive area at issue, and the question of whether they are exercised over the territory of the Netherlands in the strict sense or in a different geographical area and in the guise of sovereign rights is immaterial for these purposes. In other words, for EU purposes, the 'territory' of the Member States is the area (not necessarily territorial, in the spatial or geographical sense) of exercise of the competences of the Union.[33]

In *Aktiebolaget NN v Skatterverket*, involving the application of the Sixth VAT Directive to the laying and supply of submarine cables, the Court stressed that the sovereignty of the coastal state over the continental shelf and the EEZ was merely 'functional and limited' to the right to exercise the activities of exploration laid down in Articles 56 and 77 of UNCLOS.[34] Accordingly, to the extent that the supply and laying down of undersea cable was not included in the activities listed in those Articles, the part of the operation carried out in the EEZ and the continental shelf is not within the sovereignty of the coastal state. Thus, those activities were not subject to VAT for the part of the transaction carried out in those two maritime zones.[35]

The practice of the EU legislature falls both within the above case law and may also provide for further specification as appears from the examples of EU legislation below.

The Marine Strategy Framework Directive,[36] which establishes a framework for Union action in the field of marine environmental policy, defines 'marine waters' as 'waters, the seabed and subsoil on the seaward side of the baseline from

[32] Case C-347/10 (n 30) point 36; also earlier in Case 37/2000 *Weber* [2002] ECR I-02013, ECLI:EU:C:2002:122, point 36, concerning place of work carried out by an employee on fixed or floating installations on or above the part of the continental shelf, for the purposes of the 1968 of Art 5(1) of the Convention of 27 September 1968 on Jurisdiction and the Enforcement of Judgments in Civil and Commercial Matters, in the context of the prospecting and/or exploitation of its natural resources.

[33] Case C-347/10 (n 10) Opinion of Advocate General Cruz Villalón, points 55–56.

[34] Case C-111/05 (n 23) point 59.

[35] ibid, point 60; similarly with regard to transport services, Case C-30/89 (n 23) point 17.

[36] Directive 2008/56/EC establishing a framework for community action in the field of marine environmental policy [2008] OJ L164/19, Art 3(1) (Marine Strategy Framework Directive).

which the extent of territorial waters is measure extending to … the area where the Member State has/or exercises jurisdiction in accordance with the UNCLOS' with certain exceptions.

The Maritime Spatial Planning Directive shall apply to 'marine waters of Member States', without prejudice to other Union legislation and with certain exceptions. It is specified that the Directive

> shall not affect the sovereign rights and jurisdiction of Member States over marine waters which derive from relevant international law, particularly UNCLOS. In particular, the application of this Directive shall not influence the delineation and delimitation of maritime boundaries by the Member States in accordance with the relevant provisions of UNCLOS.[37]

Directive (EU) 2016/802[38] relating to a reduction in the sulphur content of certain liquid fuels, and incorporating rules of Annex VI to the Protocol of 1997 the Marpol Convention for the Prevention of Pollution from Ships, applies within Member States' 'territory, territorial seas and exclusive economic zones or pollution control zones'.

The Impact Assessment Directive 2011/92/EU[39] concerning the effects of certain public and private projects on the environment covers a range of defined public and private projects. It does not contain a provision of its scope of application. However, the environmental impact assessment should identify factors such as 'land, soil, water, air and climate'.

The Waste Directive 2009/98/EC[40] sets measures for prevention of waste in 'marine environments' and aims to halt marine litter.

The EU's common fisheries policy covers fishing activities on the 'territory … to which the Treaty applies'; in Union waters including by fishing vessels flying the flag of third countries; by Union fishing vessels outside Union waters; by nationals of the EU Member States without prejudice to the primary responsibility of the flag State.[41]

Sometimes legislation that could be potentially relevant to marine areas does not contain further precision or indication, as seen, for instance, in the EU Chemical legislation (REACH).[42] Insofar as there is no limitation of the scope, it must be assumed that the act applies in the territorial sea and other maritime

[37] Directive 2014/89/EU establishing a framework for maritime spatial planning [2014] OJ L257/135, Art 2(1) and 2(4).

[38] Directive (EU) 2016/802 of 11 May 2016 relating to a reduction in the sulphur content of certain liquid fuels [2016] OJ L132/58.

[39] Directive 2011/92/EU on the assessment of the effects of certain public and private projects on the environment [2012] OJ L026/1, Art 4(1), as amended by Directive 2014/52 OJ L124/1.

[40] Directive 2008/98/EC of the European Parliament and of the Council of 19 November 2008 on waste and repealing certain Directives, as amended [2008] OJ L312/3, Art 9(1) (k) and (l).

[41] Regulation (EU) No 1380/2013 (n 6) Art 1(2). Certain restrictions to access to waters are allowed pursuant to Art 5(2) and Annex I.

[42] Regulation (EC) No 1907/2006 establishing a European Chemicals Agency (REACH Regulation) [2006] OJ L396/1.

zones within the limits of UNCLOS, unless the legislator has intended to restrict the scope in some respect.[43]

The practical impact of the extension of the EU Treaty rules to the above maritime zones is that it brings these areas under a common policy framework and enforceable rules. Among other things, this promotes coordinated, integrated and transboundary approaches as well as the application of an ecosystem-based approach. It contributes to sustainable development of the coastal economies and sustainable resources.

III. The Baltic Sea is a Regional Sea: Duty of Cooperation – Maritime Environment

The Baltic Sea is a semi-closed sea area. It is connected to the North Sea through the Danish Straits (the Sound, the Little and the Great Belt) as well as the Kiel Canal.[44] The Great Belt is the main entrance/exit and, while part of Danish territorial waters, ships from all states traditionally enjoy free passage as provided in the 1857 Copenhagen Treaty for the Redemption of the Sound Dues and maintained even under UNCLOS.[45] The whole Baltic Sea seabed constitutes a continental shelf and beyond the territorial sea it is covered by the EEZs of the coastal states.

The BSR has a long tradition of effective close cooperation.[46] Such cooperation in closed or semi-closed seas is also foreseen in Article 122 of UNCLOS, which provides that the bordering coastal states in closed or semi-closed seas 'should cooperate' with each other, directly or through regional organisations. This somewhat lightly formulated provision contemplates primarily coordination of the management of living resources, the protection and preservation of

[43] See, eg, Case C-6/04 *Commission v UK*, Opinion of AG Kokott [2005] ECR I-09017, ECLI:EU:C:2005:372, point 132: 'While the Habitats Directive admittedly contains no express rule concerning its territorial scope, it is consonant with its objectives to apply it beyond coastal waters. In accordance with Article 2(1), the directive is meant to contribute towards ensuring bio-diversity through the conservation of natural habitats and of wild fauna and flora in the European territory of the Member States to which the Treaty applies. This objective supports the conclusion that the area within which the directive applies coincides with that of the Treaty'.

[44] For a comprehensive review, see P Ehlers, 'Baltic Sea' in R Wolfrum (ed), *The Max Planck Encyclopedia of Public International Law*, e-resource (Oxford University Press, updated February 2014).

[45] UNCLOS, Art 35(c). In the *Great Belt* case (*Finland v Denmark*), Finland made an application to the ICJ in 1991 concerning right of passage through the Great Belt alleging that the construction of the bridge would prevent passage for oil rigs and other special ships to the North Sea. The ICJ rejected the Finnish request for interim measures. Finland later withdrew its application and the dispute settled against payment of ex gratia compensation. See ICJ, 'Reports of Judgments, Advisory Opinions and Orders Case Concerning Passage through the Great Belt (Finland v Denmark) Request for the Indication of Provisional Measures Order of 29 July 1991' [1991] ICJ Rep 12. For an analysis, see M Koskenniemi 'Case concerning Passage through the Great Belt' (1996) 27 *Ocean Development & International Law* 255.

[46] Ehlers (n 44) para. 15.

the marine environment and the coordination of scientific research. It does not mention, for instance, security-related or other matters of cooperation. The cooperation is effected in regional frameworks, such as the Helsinki Convention,[47] governed by the Baltic Marine Environment Protection Commission (Helsinki Commission, HELCOM), and the Council of the Baltic Sea States (CBSS).[48] The Helsinki Convention is one of the four regional seas conventions and covers the whole of the Baltic Sea area, including internal waters as well as the Baltic Sea waters and the seabed. The Convention applies measures taken in the entire catchment area of the Baltic Sea to reduce land-based pollution. It also obliges the parties to cooperate with the IMO and apply Marpol 73/78 concerning prevention of pollution from ships. The IMO has designated the Baltic Sea as a special area under Annexes I, II, IV and V of Marpol 73/78 and a sulphur emission control area under its Annex VI. In addition, the IMO has designated the Baltic Sea as a particularly sensitive sea area, with the exception of the Russian sector.[49] All Baltic Sea States are parties to these international agreements and bodies.

Generally, much of the Baltic Sea cooperation has now shifted to the EU level. The EU is party to the Helsinki Convention. However, the EU's relationship with the IMO is institutionally rather complex. The EU is not a member of the IMO. Despite its many legislative and other activities in the maritime field, it is indeed quite surprising that the EU has no formal status in that organisation. This means in particular that it cannot participate in its own name and its own representatives in the work of the IMO committees and institutions.[50] On the other hand, all EU Member States are IMO members and therefore in reality the EU acts through them at IMO meetings, normally along internally coordinated positions. For the EU, significant parts of certain IMO conventions have been implemented separately through internal EU legislation, including Marpol 73/78 and its Annexes[51] as well relevant provisions in conventions such as the International Convention for the Safety of Life at Sea (SOLAS Convention, 1974)[52] and the International Convention on Standards of Training, Certification and Watchkeeping for Seafarers (1978).[53]

Baltic fisheries-related activities are regulated in the framework of the EU's common fisheries policy, in particular Regulation (EU) 1380/2013[54] and Regulation

[47] HELCOM, 'The Convention on the Protection of the Marine Environment of the Baltic Sea Area (Helsinki Convention)' (Helsinki, 22 March 1974), later amended.

[48] The CBSS was established as an overall regional political forum at a meeting of the region's Ministers of Foreign Affairs in Copenhagen on 6 March, 1992: cbss.org.

[49] See MJ Kachel,' Particularly Sensitive Sea Area, 229s. The IMO's Role in Protecting Vulnerable Marine Areas', 13 *Hamburg Studies on Maritime Affairs* (Springer, 2008) 222, 229, 246.

[50] Case C-161/20 *Commission v Council* ECLI:EU:C:2022:260, paras 60, 70.

[51] Directive 2005/35/EC on ship-source pollution and on the introduction of penalties for infringements [2005] OJ L255/11.

[52] Directive 2002/59/EC establishing a Community vessel traffic monitoring and information system [2002] OJ L208/10, as amended.

[53] Directive 2008/106/EC of the European Parliament and of the Council of 19 November 2008 on the minimum level of training of seafarers [2008] OJ L323/33, as amended.

[54] Regulation (EU) No 1380/2013 (n 6).

(EU) 2019/1241 on the conservation of fisheries resources and the protection of marine ecosystems through technical measures[55] and annual Council regulations on tariffs and quotas.

Russia is a party to UNCLOS and the Helsinki Convention and a member of the IMO. However, due to the Russian invasion of Ukraine in February 2022, cooperation under the Helsinki Convention has been suspended.[56]

IV. The EU Empowers Concerted International Action and Enhances Legal Compliance Locally

The EU Treaties empower internationally concerted action for the benefit of its members. Certain multilateral agreements play an important role in the Baltic Sea. In addition to UNCLOS, the EU is a contracting party to a number of multilateral environmental agreements. For the Baltic Sea, the Convention on Biological Diversity[57] and the Convention on the Protection of the Marine Environment of the Baltic Sea Area (Helsinki Convention)[58] are particularly important. The role of bilateral agreements in the Baltic Sea, on the other hand, has become marginal after the EU enlargements in 1995 (Finland and Sweden) and 2004 (the Baltic States and Poland). They are now replaced by EU legislation.

The joint European action is empowered internationally by the internal 'conferral of competences' or public powers from the Member States at the Union level, as established in the EU's founding Treaties.[59] The EU's international action is made possible externally, because the EU's political and legal role has been recognised by third states and the wider international community, especially through their engagement in negotiations, treaty-making and other action with the Union. It is apparent in the large number of international agreements to which the EU is a contracting party alongside third states.

In pursuing its action at the international level, the EU acts either in lieu of its Member States or, as is more common, jointly with them (mixed agreements), as in the case of UNCLOS and environmental agreements. In the first case, it

[55] Regulation (EU) No 2019/1241 on the conservation of fisheries resources and the protection of marine ecosystems through technical measures [2019] OJ L198105, as amended.

[56] Statement by the German chairmanship of HELCOM on behalf of the European Union and the Contracting Parties to HELCOM that are Member States of the European Union, 4 March 2022, available at: helcom.fi/helcom-meetings-suspended-through-1-april-2022/.

[57] The Convention on Biological Diversity (Rio de Janeiro, 5 June 1992); concluded by the EU: Council Decision 93/626/EEC [1993] OJ L309/1. Pursuant to its Art 22(2) of the Convention the Parties 'shall implement this Convention with respect to the marine environment consistently with the rights and obligations of States under the law of the sea'. In respect of the Baltic Sea, see eg, H Ringbom, B Bohman and S Ilvessalo, *Combatting Eutrophication in the Baltic Sea: Legal Aspects of Sea-Based Engineering Measures* (Leiden, Brill, 2018) 16–17.

[58] Concluded by the EU: Council Decision 94/157/EC [1994] OJ L73/19.

[59] TEU, Art 5(2). As the Court of Justice of the EU has stated: '[T]he EU has only conferred powers'. Opinion 1/13, ECLI:EU:C:2014:2303, pursuant to Art 218(11) TFEU (14 October 2014) para 74.

is a question of one legal person performing the action, while in the second case the action is performed by one group. In this latter case, both the organisation and its Member States act together on the international plane, since the legal competences are shared in a number of areas. These different configurations of EU action raise a number of issues, such as those relating to allocation of responsibilities, which are not addressed here,[60] except to mention that, when acting as a group in international treaty relations, the EU has often been required to give a declaration concerning the respective competences of the organisation and its Member States.[61]

It follows from its treaty-making competences that the Union has also been a party to international dispute settlement, including in the fisheries field[62] and, as noted further below, in the pending Nord Stream 2 arbitration concerning Russian gas pipelines in the Baltic Sea.

The EU Treaty framework also enhances the implementation of international obligations at national levels. It brings an additional layer of legal obligations and related institutional supervision to oversee the implementation in the territories of the Member States. The founding EU Treaties commit the EU to 'strict observance and development of international law'.[63] All international agreements to which the Union is a party are made a part of the EU legal system and are binding on both the institutions and the Member States.[64] These basic constitutional rules add guarantees and establish a basis for implementation of international commitments at the national and EU level. International compliance is also facilitated by specific provisions on international commitments or by enabling access to EU courts.

In addition, the EU legislature especially in maritime and environmental areas often refers to the relevant international agreements. This further consolidates them as an integral part of EU law. For example, the Maritime Strategy Framework Directive (MSFD)[65] sets out a common approach and objectives for the prevention, protection and conservation of the marine environment to encounter the pressures and impacts of damaging human activities. It makes direct references to UNCLOS and the Convention on Biological Diversity and

[60] On issue of responsibility see, eg, PJ Kuijper and E Paasivirta, 'EU International Responsibility and its Attribution: From the Inside Looking Out' in M Evans and P Koutrakos (eds), *The International Responsibility of the European Union* (Oxford, Hart Publishing, 2013).

[61] The first multilateral agreement where such a declaration of competences was given was UNCLOS. See Council Decision 98/392 [1998] OJ L179/129; also available at the United Nations Treaty Collection, Multilateral Treaties Deposited with the Secretary General, Chapter XXI Law of the Sea: treaties.un.org. For further discussion on the modalities of EU participation see, eg, E Paasivirta, 'The European Union and the United Nations Convention on the Law of the Sea' (2015) 38 *Fordham International Law Journal* 1045, 1047–51.

[62] See, eg, E Paasivirta and A Bouquet, 'Resolution of International Fisheries Disputes and Regional Experiences: The Case of the European Union' in *ITLOS at 20: Looking into the Future Symposium, 18 March 2017* (International Tribunal for the Law of the Sea, 2018).

[63] TEU, Art 3(5).

[64] TFEU, Art 216(2).

[65] Marine Strategy Framework Directive (n 36).

thus aims to ensure their relevance at all stages of the development of marine strategies. The Directive also requires Member States to cooperate with their neighbours in the Baltic, North-East Atlantic, Mediterranean and Black Sea regions in developing their marine strategies. The EU Member States are required to use existing regional cooperation structures, like the Helsinki Convention, which is one of the four European Regional Sea Conventions,[66] to coordinate among themselves and with third countries. On the one hand, the Regional Sea Conventions are used to implement progressive action compatible with the Directive. On the other hand, the Directive contains a number of provisions to ensure that implementation builds upon the experiences under the Regional Sea Conventions. For instance, Article 6 of the MSFD requires Member States to use the institutional structures and activities of the Regional Sea Conventions to support the implementation of the Directive especially in relation to third countries. This helps to bring further coherence and effectiveness to national implementation and provides for opportunities to coordinate relevant third-country activities. Similarly, in the EU's Spatial Planning Directive,[67] the legislature's approach incorporates international obligations and relies on the use of structures in the existing Regional Sea Conventions and has provisions on cooperation duties with third countries.

EU courts are frequently faced with issues concerning international obligations, especially in preliminary ruling proceedings originating from the national courts. It is an established practice for EU courts to follow consistent interpretation of EU secondary legislation, which takes into account the relevant international obligations. The Commission has a central role in monitoring, facilitating and coordinating national implementation and, if necessary, to initiate infringement proceedings to bring a Member State to the EU Court of Justice.

The possibility for individuals and economic operators to challenge the legality of EU rules on the basis of the 'direct effect' of an international agreement has strict conditions relating to the nature, precision and unconditionality of the provisions at stake. For instance, UNCLOS does not qualify for a direct effect status as ruled in the well-known *Intertanko* case.[68] Nor does the direct effect doctrine easily apply in respect of customary international law rules or in the area environmental agreements, which usually require further implementing measures.[69]

[66] The other three conventions are: the Convention for the Protection of the Marine Environment in the North-East Atlantic (OSPAR Convention, Paris, 22 September 1992); the Convention for the Protection of Marine Environment and the Coastal Region of the Mediterranean (Barcelona, 16 February 1976, amended and renamed 1995); and the Convention for the Protection of the Black Sea (Bucharest Convention, Bucharest, 21 April 1992).

[67] Directive 2014/89/EU (n 37) Arts 11(2) and 12.

[68] Case C-308/06 *Intertanko* [2008] ECR I-04057, ECLI:EU:C:2008:312, para 64, which confirmed that UNCLOS is not intended to be invoked directly by individuals.

[69] Case C-366/10 *Air Transport Association of America and Others* [2011] ECR I-13755, EU:C:2011:864, paras 110–11, which addressed the status of customary international law of the sea under the EU law, and applied the demanding 'manifest error' test to assess whether customary rules can be invoked against the validity of EU secondary legislation. This was refused in this case, which involved the extension of the EU Emission Trading Scheme (ETS) to aviation activities. For discussion of related case law,

Thus, the constitutional framework established in the EU Treaties has far-reaching implications for concerted EU international action, including in the BSR. The principal features of this legal framework – conferral of public power, own legal system and common institutions – are also important for the processes of preparation, coordination and external representation. All internal preparation for international meetings or treaty negotiations with third countries takes place within the framework of common institutions with established practices and work habits. This involves interaction between the independent institutions (Council and Commission) and close cooperation with the representatives of the Member States.

The outcomes of these internal EU meetings are expressed at international fora by a representative of the Commission (or the High Representative in matters of security policy) regarding the EU competences[70] or by the Member States on issues relating to the national competences. In practice, interventions by the EU and its Member States are often conducted in the name of both as shared competences. This mixed mode of action is guided, and kept together, by respecting the EU Treaty principle of the duty of loyal cooperation.[71]

V. Three Case Studies Over the Maritime Freedoms and Coastal State Jurisdiction in the Baltic Sea

A. Freedom of Navigation Prevails over the Powers of the Coastal State in a Vessel-Source Pollution Incident: *Bosphorus Queen Shipping* as followed by the Judgment of the Finnish Supreme Court

The freedom of navigation in the EEZ, on the one hand, and the powers of the coastal state in the EEZ, on the other, are often in a tenuous relationship with each other. This is due to the hybrid nature of the EEZ: the high sea navigation freedoms apply, but at the same time extended jurisdictional rights have been granted to the coastal state. Article 58 of UNCLOS provides that vessels of all states benefit from the freedom of navigation in the EEZ. However, Article 220,

see I Hadjiyianni, *The EU as a Global Regulator for Environmental Protection* (Oxford, Hart Publishing, 2021) 197–209.

[70] Case C-161/20 (n 50) paras 69, 71. In cases where the EU is not a member of an international organisation, like the IMO, the EU positions can be represented by the Member States acting jointly, under the duty of sincere cooperation referred to in Art 4(3) TEU, in the interests of the EU.

[71] Generally, on development of the duty of loyal cooperation and the related principle of unity of external representation, see P Eeckhout, *EU External Relations Law*, 2nd edn (Oxford, Oxford University Press, 2012) 241–55

furthermore, provides that the coastal state can take enforcement measures under certain conditions in different coastal areas and maritime zones (ports, territorial sea, EEZ) where a foreign ship has violated or is suspected of violating international rules on pollution. The powers of the coastal state and the nature of the measures and procedures vary in these different zones depending on several conditions, such as the location of the vessel and the violation. There are also different standards of evidence depending on the violation. Generally, the further the vessel is from the coast, the more difficult it is to exercise the coastal state powers. For example, Article 220(6) of UNCLOS provides that proceedings, including detention, can be instituted under certain conditions where there is clear 'objective evidence' that a vessel navigating in the EEZ (or the territorial sea) has violated certain pollution-related rules or standards resulting in a discharge causing 'major damage or threat of major damage' to the 'coastline and related interests' or to 'any resources' of its territorial sea or the EEZ. The judgment of the EU Court of Justice in *Bosphorus Queen Shipping*[72] and the related judgment by the Finnish Supreme Court[73] interpreted and applied Article 220 of UNCLOS in a multilayered interface between the European and national judiciary in international circumstance. The dispute in these cases involved an oil discharge from a Panama flagged vessel, the Bosphorus Queen, in transit in the Finnish EEZ in the Gulf of Finland in 2011. The discharge took place on the outer edge of the Finnish EEZ, approximately 25–30 km from the coast. The oil spread over about 37 kilometres in a strip 10 metres wide. When the vessel returned from St Petersburg and again passed through the Finnish EEZ, the Border Protection Agency took an interim measure ordering a financial security of €17,112 to cover any oil spill fine imposed and detained the ship. After the financial security was deposited, the ship resumed its journey. A fine was imposed on the ground that the oil spill had caused major damage or a threat of major damage to Finland's coastline or to resources of its territorial sea or EEZ. The owners of the Bosphorus Queen sought to annul the decision. The Helsinki District Court and the Court of Appeal rejected that Panama had jurisdiction and maintained the decision.[74]

The Supreme Court referred the case to the EU Court of Justice for interpretation of Article 220(6) of UNCLOS and similar terms of Article 7 of EU Directive 2005/35/EC on ship-source pollution which incorporates those provisions into EU law. The latter, in turn, has been transposed into Finnish law by the 'merenkulun ympäristönsuojelulaki' No 1672/2009 (Law relating to the protection of the environment in relation to maritime transport).[75]

The Court of Justice noted that UNCLOS is binding on the EU and is an integral part of EU law. In interpreting UNCLOS, the Court also 'took account'

[72] Case C-15/17 *Bosphorus Queen Shipping* ECLI:EU:C:2018:557.
[73] Diary number: S2015/71, date of issue: 25 June 2019, ECLI:FI:KKO:2019:61.
[74] Case C-15/17 (n 72) paras 30–40.
[75] ibid, paras 27–29.

of the Marpol 73/78 Convention, to which the EU Member States (but not the Union) are parties, since it falls within the application of Directive 2005/35.[76]

The Court concluded that the 'clear objective evidence' standard covers not only the commission of the violation, but also the consequences of that violation.[77] The Court noted that Article 220 sets out 'graduated' measures that the coastal state can take, which are subject to different conditions depending on the circumstances.[78] It stated that Article 220(6) is comparable to the slightly different provision in Article 220(5) relating to physical inspection, as both refer to serious consequences. The violation must have 'resulted' in a discharge causing major damage or threat of major damage to the coastline or related interests or to any resources of its territorial sea or EEZ. However, the two provisions differ in that Article 220(6) makes the power of the coastal state subject to the requirement of 'clear objective evidence' that a violation having serious consequences has actually been committed, and not only 'clear grounds for believing' that a violation has been committed. Article 220(6) allows a particularly robust measure of the detention of the vessel, not limited to a physical inspection or request for information only. It considered that this is also supported by the objective of UNCLOS to strike a 'fair balance' between the interests of the coastal states and flag states.[79]

The Court clarified that the damage to the 'coastline or related interests' under Article 220(6) extends to non-living resources of the territorial sea and to any resources in the EEZ, living or non-living,[80] and applies to both harvested species and species associated and dependent on harvested species, such as animal and plant species.[81] The cumulative nature damage needs to be identified and the differences in sensitivity of the coastal state must be taken into account. Account should be taken of the foreseeable harmful consequences based on the available scientific data, and the nature of the substances discharged and the volume, direction, speed and the period of time over which the oil spill spreads.[82]

Interestingly, the Court noted that the Baltic Sea is an internationally recognised special area with a particularly sensitive ecosystem. It took into account the Marpol 73/78 Convention, which defines the Baltic Sea as a sensitive sea area. However, the Court clarified that such ecological characteristics of the area should not 'automatically' lead to conclusion of major damage or threat of major damage. The Finnish Supreme Court considered this damage aspect in subsequent proceedings.

[76] Similarly, it took account of the Convention Relating to Intervention on the High Seas (1969), though not binding on the Union and to which only some of the Member States are parties, as the latter Convention is 'part of the relevant rules' for the interpretation of UNCLOS, see: ibid, paras 44–47. Similar 'take account' – formula has been followed already in earlier interpretations. See Case C-308/06 (n 68) para 52.

[77] Case C-15/17 (n 79) para 65.

[78] ibid, paras 52–54.

[79] ibid, paras 59–63.

[80] ibid, paras 77–79.

[81] ibid, para 84.

[82] ibid, para 102.

Hence, when the case was litigated at national level, it turned on the question of proof. The Supreme Court considered proof relating to the quantity and quality of oil, the geographic location of the incident and the spread of the leak.

It was established that the discharge of approximately 900 litres of so-called persistent oils was harmful to various marine organisms and that the oil had partly evaporated, partly mixed with water and partly sunk to the bottom. The Court noted that no further explanation or even an estimate had been given of the proportions or the rate at which the oil has spread.[83] Likewise, no explanation had been provided as to the magnitude and duration of the expected effects that would indicate that the discharge would have caused major damage or threat to the natural resources of the EEZ.[84] Neither had it been sufficiently clarified how likely it would be for the oil to reach the Finnish coast and natural resources sites to such an extent that it could have caused significant adverse effects on coastal seabirds or other marine environments or to coastal recreational use.[85]

The Supreme Court set aside the lower courts' judgments and concluded that the oil spill had 'not been shown' to have caused major damage to the Finnish coastline, or related benefits, or to the natural resources of the Finnish territorial sea or economic zone.

The freedom of navigation prevailed due to insufficient evidence by the coastal state administrative authorities. There was no place for 'automatic' assumptions about the damage even if it was a sensitive sea area. The Finnish Supreme Court took the no-automatic assumptions approach and focused on the objective evidence, while putting the burden of proof squarely on the Finnish authorities.

The two judgments, taken together, illustrate the multilayered nature of EU law and the judicial enforcement system. The case demonstrates how international agreements, even mixed agreements, increasingly come before EU Court of Justice, instead of being decided by the national court. The Finnish Supreme Court gave no explanation for its preliminary ruling request. On reflection, it must have been for the reason of the impact of the ship-source pollution Directive 2005/35 transposing provisions of Marpol 73/78 into EU law. Since that Directive also refers to UNCLOS and international law, as defining the scope and compliance of the Directive,[86] the interpretation of UNCLOS provisions impacts that Directive. The issue had in fact become a matter of exclusive jurisdiction for the EU Court.[87]

[83] ECLI:FI:KKO:2019:61 (n 73) para 47.
[84] ibid, para 48.
[85] ibid, para 49.
[86] Directive 2005/35 on the ship-source pollution (n 51) Arts 3 and 9.
[87] In the sense of Art 19 TEU and Art 344 TFEU. Note that the 'declaration of competences', made by the EU and the Member States at the time of adhering to the Convention, states: 'With regard to the provisions on maritime transport, safety of shipping and the prevention of marine pollution contained inter alia in Parts II, III, V, VII and XII of the Convention, the Community has exclusive competence only to the extent that such provisions of the Convention or legal instruments adopted in implementation thereof affect common rules established by the Community. When Community rules exist but are not affected, in particular in cases of Community provisions establishing only minimum standards, the Member States have competence, without prejudice to the competence of the Community to act in this field' [1998] OJ L179/129; also available at the United Nations Treaty Collection, Multilateral Treaties Deposited with the Secretary General, Chapter XXI Law of the Sea: treaties.un.org.

As a general issue, there are good reasons to obtain a common interpretation from the EU Court of Justice, as the issue of coastal state powers is a horizontal question that is central to the zonal approach of UNCLOS provisions, and their interpretation generally bears on the scope of the EU's maritime related legislation.

B. The Nord Stream 2 Saga

The Nord Stream 2 saga highlights the EU's wavering between its search for energy autonomy and the dependency on external energy supplies. The Nord Stream 2 has been a continuing bone of contention within the EU and in transatlantic relations. Following the Russian invasion of Ukraine in February 2022 the quest for energy autonomy has found new force and accelerated the plans to make Europe independent of Russian fossil fuels.[88] This has left entirely open not only the use of the Nord Stream 2, but energy cooperation with Russia in general.

The Nord Stream 2 gas pipeline – already constructed, but now suspended – between Vyborg (Russia) and Lubmin (Germany) illustrates forcefully the multilayered legal governance, involving aspects of the law of the sea, EU energy law, the Energy Charter Treaty and national law.

The law of the sea allows all states to enjoy the freedom to lay underwater pipelines in the high seas areas.[89] This freedom and 'other internationally lawful uses of the sea related to these freedoms' also applies to the EEZ.[90] There are limitations relating to the right of the coastal state over its natural resources, fishing activities and pollution control, but the coastal state may not impede the laying and maintenance of the pipelines.[91]

However, where a pipeline is not just crossing the EEZ or territorial sea of a coastal state, but enters the territorial sea of the coastal state and its land territory, the coastal state may establish conditions for the entry for the landing pipeline.[92] The status of the pipeline ceases to be a matter of the law of the sea alone, since certain parts of the pipeline, its construction and operation become subject to the territorial sovereignty of the coastal state. This requires coastal state authorisation under domestic law, in addition to EU law and relevant legislation. Consequently,

[88] The EU Commission has proposed an outline of a plan to make Europe independent from Russian fossil fuels well before 2030, starting with gas, in light of Russia's invasion of Ukraine. Commission, 'Communication from the Commission to the European Parliament, the European Council, the Council, the European Economic and Social Committee and the Committee of the Regions REPowerEU: Joint European Action for more affordable, secure and sustainable energy' COM(2022) 108 final, 5; Commission, 'Communication from the Commission to the European Parliament, the European Council, the Council, the European Economic and Social Committee and the Committee of the Regions REPowerEU Plan' COM (2022) 230 final, putting forward a broad agenda for a large number of measures to accelerate clean energy transition, diversify energy sources and save energy.

[89] UNCLOS, Art 87(1)(c).

[90] UNCLOS, Art 58(1).

[91] UNCLOS, Art 79((2) and (3).

[92] UNCLOS, Art 79(4); see also R Lagoni, 'Pipelines' in R Wolfrum (ed), *The Max Planck Encyclopedia of Public International Law*, e-resource (Oxford University Press, updated April 2011) para 13.

the pipeline and its operation are exposed to those rules, including possible amendments to the rules, unless there is an international agreement that provides otherwise. The Nord Stream 2 pipeline project has run into legal trouble stemming from the application of the EU's Gas Directive and its later amendment and shift in relation to German territorial sea.

The aim of the EU Gas Directive is to address conflicts of interest between producers, suppliers and transmission system operators, and to guarantee the access of new market entrants. The Directive separates networks from the activities of physical production and supply. It lays down an obligation to unbundle transmission systems and transmission system operators (Article 9) and introduces a system of non-discriminatory third-party access to gas on the basis of published tariffs (Article 32). Under Article 36 of the Gas Directive, major new gas infrastructure, including interconnectors, may, upon request and under certain conditions, be exempted for a defined period of time from some of the obligations.

The legal issues of the Nord Stream 2 pipeline concern the adoption of Directive (EU) 2019/692 which amends the existing Gas Directive.[93] The Amendment Directive, pursuant to its recital 3, addresses obstacles to competition in the internal market for natural gas, which have resulted in not applying the EU market rules to gas transmission lines to and from third countries. The Amendment Directive now extends the scope to transmission lines between a Member State and third countries.[94]

This has significant implications for the Nord Stream 2 pipeline. It would need to get a derogation from the Directive's unbundling and other obligations when entering Germany. In principle, such derogation may be granted, under certain conditions, by the national authorities.[95]

The Gas Directive's amendment has given rise to litigation at both EU and international level. First, Nord Stream 2 AG, a Swiss subsidiary of Russian company

[93] Directive 2009/73/EC of the European Parliament and of the Council of 13 July 2009 concerning common rules for the internal market in natural gas and repealing Directive 2003/55/EC [2009] OJ L211/94. Pursuant to its Art 1, the Gas Directive establishes common rules for the transmission, distribution, supply and storage of natural gas. It lays down the rules relating to the organisation and functioning of the natural gas sector, access to the market, the criteria and procedures applicable to the granting of authorisations for transmission, distribution, supply and storage of natural gas and the operation of systems.

[94] Directive (EU) 2019/692 of the European Parliament and of the Council of 17 April 2019 amending Directive 2009/73/EC concerning common rules for the internal market in natural gas [2019] OJ L117/1. This is technically accomplished by modifying the definition of an 'interconnector' in Art 2(17), to the effect that it covers not only '[any] transmission line which crosses or spans a border between Member States for the purpose of connecting the national transmission system of those Member States', but now also '[any] transmission line between a Member State and a third country up to the territory of the Member States or the territorial sea of that Member State'.

[95] This includes, however, the criterion requiring gas transmission lines in respect of which certain derogations have been requested to have been completed before 23 May 2019 (the date on which the amending Directive entered into force). The decisions of the national authorities can in turn be challenged in national courts, where invalidity of the Directive or its amendment could be invoked.

Gazprom, has brought a legal challenge to the EU courts seeking annulment of the Directive under Article 263(4) of the TFEU. The EU's General Court dismissed the challenge on the ground that the applicant was not directly and individually concerned.[96] On appeal, the Court of Justice declared the action admissible, considering that direct effect on the applicant could not be excluded, in particular since the appellant had already made significant investments in the construction of the interconnection pipeline. For the rest, the case was returned to the General Court for determination of merits.[97]

In parallel to the litigation before the EU courts, Nord Stream 2 AG has begun arbitration proceedings against the EU in the Permanent Court of Arbitration under Article 26 of the Energy Charter Treaty (ECT).[98] The EU is a party to the ECT,[99] along with its Member States, and thus bound by its rules in respect of EU legislation and other decisions. Russia is not a party, as it never ratified the ECT, but the Russian gas company Gazprom can benefit from the Treaty's investment protection provisions through its Swiss subsidiary, Nord Stream 2 AG, which is the owner and intended operator of the pipeline. As a non-EU company from a state (Switzerland) which is a party to the ECT, it can bring claims against the EU under the ECT's investor–state arbitration provisions.[100] It argues that the amended Gas Directive constitutes a breach of the ECT provisions, in particular, Article 10(1), which lays down fair and equitable treatment standard for investments, and Article 13, which provides for safeguards for expropriation.[101] The EU has denied the alleged breaches and asked the Tribunal to dismiss the claim, stating, inter alia, that the Amendment Directive is consistent with long-standing trends in EU gas and related competition policy and practice, and the Gas Directive could even be interpreted so as to apply to offshore import gas pipelines. For now, the arbitral proceedings have been suspended following the Russian invasion of Ukraine in and the related sanctions.[102]

C. Use of the Baltic Sea for Peaceful Purposes

The peace and security of the Baltic Sea underpins all cooperation obligations in the region. However, so far there has been very little specific security-related work

[96] Case T-526/19 *Nord Stream 2 v Parliament and Council* ECLI:EU:T:2020:210; Case T-530/19 *Nord Stream AG v Parliament and Council* ECLI:EU:T:2020:213.

[97] Case C348/20 P *Nord Stream 2 v Parliament and Council* ECLI:EU:C:2022:548, para 80.

[98] PCA Case *Nord Stream 2 AG v The European Union*, No 2020-07, available at: pca-cpa.org/en/cases/239/.

[99] Energy Charter Treaty, Lisbon [1994] OJ L380/24; approved on behalf of the Communities by Council and Commission Decision 98/181/EC, ECSC, Euratom [1998] OJ L69/1.

[100] On the other hand, it has been confirmed in Case C-741/19 *Komstroy*, ECLI:EU:C:2021:655, para 66, that the ECT arbitral procedures are not applicable to disputes between a Member State and an investor of another Member State concerning an investment made by the latter in the first Member State. The same principle should apply to arbitral proceedings against the EU itself.

[101] PCA Case No 2020-07, Claimants to arbitration, 26 September 2019, paras 49 and 52.

[102] PCA Case No 2020-07, Tribunal's Procedural Order No 8 of 30 June 2022.

or arrangements in the framework of the BSR. One commentator has astutely noted that '[t]here is, still, no close relationship between the existing restrictions on military activities, on the one hand, and the new spirit of Baltic regionalism, on the other'.[103] This remains true today. In stark contrast to successful cooperation in environmental matters, especially in HELCOM, security issues have played a marginal role within the Baltic Sea institutions, especially the Baltic Sea Council which, in principle, is the forum best able to deal with them.

Of course, there have not been actual naval conflicts in the Baltic Sea since the Second World War. However, the security concerns in Europe have suffered greatly following the recent Russian invasion of Ukraine. There are now movements of warships, naval exercises, troop deployments in the close-by coastal areas, an increase in overflights by military aircrafts and violations of national airspaces. These security-related activities increased with the 2014 annexation of Crimea by Russia and the full Russian invasion in 2022. The 2020 Finnish Government Report on Foreign and Security Policy described the situation in relation to the Baltic Sea as follows:

> From the great power perspective, Finland is located in a strategically important area, on which changes in the international security situation are directly reflected. The security in Northern Europe is increasingly interlinked and any shifts in the security situation in the Baltic Sea region, the Arctic neighbourhood of Finland and on the North Atlantic are closely connected. The development in Europe's neighbourhood also remains unstable.[104]

The respective 2022 Finnish Government Report described the shifts in the security in the BSR and the evolution of new security cooperation in the following terms:

> In the changed security environment, the strategic importance of Northern Europe has increased, which is why NATO has opened new avenues for cooperation for Finland and Sweden. Dialogue and practical military cooperation on the security situation in the Baltic Sea region increase Finland's opportunities to influence its security environment and improve predictability and stability in the region. After Russia's invasion of Ukraine, Finland and Sweden have deepened their bilateral cooperation and enhanced their contacts with NATO to improve their shared situation awareness.[105]

Following the 2022 Russian invasion of Ukraine, all meetings of HELCOM bodies have been suspended, since the EU and its Member States declared that they were not in a position to attend as a consequence of the Russian Federation being a party to HELCOM.[106] It is unclear when the work of these regional bodies can resume.

[103] M Lehto, 'Restrictions on Military Activities in the Baltic Sea – A Basis for a Regional Regime?' (1991) 2 *Finnish Yearbook of International Law* 38, 61.

[104] Finnish Government, 'Government Report on Finnish Foreign and Security Policy' (Publications of the Finnish Government, 2020:32, 29 October 2020) 19.

[105] Finnish Government, 'Government Report on changes in the security environment' (Publications of the Finnish Government, 2022:20, 13.April 2022) 25.

[106] Statement by the German Chairmanship of HELCOM (n 56).

The sea routes in the Baltic Sea are located between the North Atlantic, Russian heartlands and the Arctic. These sea routes are strategically and commercially important. Militarily, Russia has a naval and missile base in Kaliningrad with capacity to deny access to the Baltic Sea. Unhindered sea routes are vital to all states, but especially to the Baltic States to whom unfettered sea and air access by NATO is indispensable for military defence purposes.[107] The varied interests for free communication are in any event self-evident and shared by all the coastal states.

In international armed conflict situations, there is a separate body of rules, *jus in bello*, which apply from the moment armed force is used. These includes the UN Charter rules, in particular relevant Security Council Resolutions and Article 51's self-defence provisions, as well as rules contained in a number of international conventions. The 1907 Hague Conventions complemented by rules of customary international law contain rules on warfare at sea.[108] These rules apply both to belligerent states and may significantly affect neutral states where seas are involved in blockades, denials of port access and the like.[109]

In peacetime, the normal rules of law of the sea, especially those contained in UNCLOS, apply in full. They regulate the use of seas for 'peaceful purposes' – a fundamental principle of UNCLOS. However, unlike the Antarctic Treaty of 1959,[110] UNCLOS does not de-militarise the areas of seas and oceans.[111] That said, there are constraints and restrictions concerning military activities in the territorial sea of the coastal states.

Under UNCLOS, all ships, including warships, have the right to 'innocent' passage through the territorial sea of coastal states.[112] Passage is innocent if it, inter alia, is not prejudicial to the 'peace, good order or security' of the coastal state.[113] This includes any exercise and practices with weapons of any kind; any act aimed at collecting information to prejudice the defence or security of the coastal

[107] On the strategic aspects see, eg, the contributions in A-S Dahl (ed), *Strategic Challenges in the Baltic Sea Region* (Washington, DC, Georgetown University Press, 2018).

[108] The customary rules are restated with some progressive elements in the San Remo Manual on International Law Applicable to Armed Conflicts at Sea, 12 June 1994, available at: ihl-databases.icrc.org/ihl/INTRO/560.

[109] See generally, WH von Heinegg, 'Blockades and Interdictions' in M Weller (ed), *The Oxford Handbook of the Use of Force in International Law* (Oxford, Oxford University Press, 2015); RR Churchill and AV Lowe, *The Law of the Sea*, 3rd edn (Manchester, Manchester University Press, 1999) 421–32.

[110] Antarctic Treaty (Washington, DC, 4 December 1959) Art 1(1) prohibits 'any measures of military nature'.

[111] The Treaty on the Prohibition of the Emplacement of Nuclear Weapons and Other Weapons of Mass Destruction on the Seabed and the Ocean Floor and in the Subsoil Thereof (Seabed Treaty, 11 February 1971), Art 1 prohibits the emplacement of nuclear and other weapons of mass destruction to the seabed beyond a 12-mile coastal zone. There have also been efforts, especially by the UN General Assembly, to demilitarise certain sea areas such as the Indian Ocean and the South Atlantic. See SP Subedi, *Land and Maritime Zones of Peace in International Law* (Oxford, Clarendon Press, 1996) 1–40.

[112] UNCLOS, Art 18.

[113] UNCLOS, Art 19(1).

state; or any activity not having a direct bearing on passage. In the territorial sea, submarines are required to navigate on the surface and to show their flag.[114] There are particular requirements for nuclear powered ships and ships carrying nuclear or other dangerous substances.[115] The coastal state may prevent the passage which is not innocent and suspend temporarily innocent passage in specified parts of its territorial sea if the suspension is essential to protect security or necessary because of weapons exercises.[116]

In addition, special rules apply to warships and other government ships operated for non-commercial purposes.[117] For example, a coastal state may order a warship to immediately leave its maritime zones if it does not comply with the laws and regulations of the coastal state.[118] However, prior notification is not foreseen in UNCLOS for warships traversing territorial sea.[119]

In international straits, the transit passage regime requires ships and aircraft to pass expeditiously in their normal modes.[120] However, there are exceptions to the general transit passage rules. This general rule does not apply where passage is regulated 'in whole or in part by long-standing international conventions in force'.[121] This applies to the Danish Straits (the Little Belt, the Great Belt and the Sound), the only outlet to the world's oceans for many Baltic Sea States. This is regulated in the 1857 Treaty of Copenhagen with several European states, and a similar Treaty with the United States, under which no ship in passage through the Sound or Belts shall be subjected to any detention or hindrance. The 1857 Treaties do not apply to warships and, according to Danish and Swedish views, the regime of innocent passage through applies.[122] The exception to UNCLOS transit rules on straits also applies to the Aland Islands Strait, between Finland and Sweden.[123] The removal from the general regime of transit passage to the innocent

[114] UNCLOS, Art 20.

[115] UNCLOS, Art 23.

[116] UNCLOS, Art 25.

[117] UNCLOS, Arts 29–32.

[118] UNCLOS, Art 30.

[119] For instance, Finland has abolished its earlier prior notice procedure following the enlargement of the territorial sea and its adherence to UNCLOS. See M Lehto and M Koskenniemi, 'Finland and the Law of the Sea' in L Pineschi and T Treves (eds), *The Law of the Sea: The European Union and its Member States* (The Hague, Martinus Nijhoff Publishers, 1997) 131. During the negotiations at the UNCLOS III Conference the prior notification requirement concerning warships, unlike authorisation, was argued not to be incompatible with the coastal state's regulatory powers under Art 21 of Convention· See RA Barnes, 'Articles 21 and 23' in A Proelss (ed), *United Nations Convention on the Law of the Sea: A Commentary* (Munich, CH Beck, 2017) 203, 247.

[120] UNCLOS Art 38(2).

[121] UNCLOS, Art 35(c). Denmark, Sweden and Finland made their respective declarations at the time of their ratification of UNCLOS. See Declarations or Statements upon UNCLOS at: www.un.org/depts/los.

[122] There are differing views on the status of the Danish Straits and the interactions of the treaty regime with customary international law. See AGO Elferink, 'The Regime of Passage Through the Danish Straits' (2000) 15 *International Journal of Marine and Costal Law* 555.

[123] Lehto and Koskenniemi (n 119) 133. Here, the 1921 Convention on the Non-Fortification and Neutrality of the Aland Islands (LNTS 1922, 213, FTS 1922, 1–8) Arts 3–6, provide for innocent passage, and introduce certain prohibitions and restrictions on warships and military aircraft, and neutrality in time of war. The other 'long-standing international conventions' relevant to Finland were

passage implies that submarines cannot traverse submerged, military aircraft does not benefit from freedom of overflight and innocent passage can be suspended in certain circumstances.[124]

In the narrow heavily trafficked passage in the Gulf of Finland, between Finland and Estonia, neither innocent passage nor transit passage rules apply. Instead, the two states have limited the width of their respective territorial seas to extend no closer than three nautical miles from the centre line in the Gulf of Finland,[125] effectively leaving at least a six-mile wide freedom of navigation 'EEZ corridor' between them.[126]

The EEZ is *sui generis* in nature and has a mixed regime which incorporates high seas freedom of navigation and certain exclusive rights of the coastal state regarding the exploitation and preservation of natural resources. The UNCLOS provisions are the outcome of compromises and seek to maintain a balance between the interests of the coastal states and those of other states. In particular, the freedom of navigation applies to all ships, including warships. However, the relevant provisions are open-ended as to the activities of the ships. There are no express limitations concerning the activities of warships in the EEZ.[127]

The freedom of navigation ensures the mobility of warships, which may nevertheless be a source of concern to coastal states. The presence of foreign warships and naval exercises in the EEZ of coastal states was contested during the UNCLOS negotiations,[128] and it still is.[129] The presence of foreign warships,

the 1856 Convention relating to the Non-Fortification and Neutralisation of the Aland Islands (annexed to the 1856 Paris Peace Treaty (FTS 1922, 9–10) and the 1940 Treaty between Finland and the Soviet Union regarding the Aland Islands (FTS 1940, No 24, 120–25). P Klemola-Juntunen, 'Passage Rights in International Law. A Case Study of the Territorial Waters of the Aland Islands' (2014) 284 *Acta Universitatis Lapponiensis* 329. On the demilitarised status, see also, L Hannikainen, 'The Continued Validity of the Demilitarised and Neutralised Status of the Åland Islands' (1994) 54 *ZaöRV* 614.

[124] For further discussion, see Klemola-Juntunen (n 123); see also, Churchill and Lowe (n 109) 208.

[125] 1994 Exchange of Notes Constituting an 'Agreement on the Procedure to be followed in the Modification of the Limits of the Territorial Waters in the Gulf of Finland' (40/1995); 1996 Agreement between Finland and Estonia in the 'Agreement on the boundary of the maritime zones in the Gulf of Finland and the Northern Baltic Sea' (99/1996).

[126] For a detailed account, see A Lott, 'The Estonian Straits: Exceptions to the Strait Regime of Innocent or Transit Passage' [2017] *University of Tartu Press* 99.

[127] UNCLOS, Art 58(1), which provides that in the EEZ all states enjoy 'the freedoms referred to in Article 87 of navigation and overflight and of the laying of submarine cable and pipelines' as well as 'other internationally lawful uses' of the sea related to these freedoms. Pursuant to Art 58(2), the high sea freedoms apply to the EEZ 'in so far as they are not incompatible' with the Convention's provisions on the EEZ. In the same vein, the list of high sea freedoms in Art 87, which is also relevant to the EEZ, is not exhaustive. Generally, see D Andersson, 'Freedoms of the High Seas in the Modern Law of the Sea' in D Freestone, R Barnes and DM Ong (eds), *The Law of the Sea: Progress and Prospects* (Oxford, Oxford University Press, 2006) 332.

[128] S Bateman, 'Security and the Law of the Sea in East Asia: Navigational Regimes and Exclusive Economic Zones' in D Freestone, R Barnes and DM Ong (eds), *The Law of the Sea: Progress and Prospects* (Oxford, Oxford University Press, 2006) 381.

[129] eg, when ratifying the Convention Germany stated that the rights of the coastal state in the EEZ do not include the rights to obtain notification of military exercises or manoeuvres or to authorise them. On the contrary, India stated its understanding that the Convention does not authorise other

especially when conducting naval and weapon exercises, may appear as preparedness to use armed force.[130]

There are nevertheless some constraints in Article 301 of UNCLOS relating to 'peaceful uses of the seas'. These constraints oblige states to refrain from the threat and use of force in a manner inconsistent with the UN Charter. Article 141 reserves the high seas for 'peaceful purposes', which at the minimum prohibits acts of aggression.[131] Article 2(4) of the UN Charter of course prohibits the 'threat' of use of force.[132]

It seems difficult to argue, on the basis of UNCLOS alone, that naval and weapons exercises in the EEZ are excluded, in spite of the general tendency of favouring the coastal states in that zone. The following considerations may be relevant with regard to any military manoeuvres in the Baltic Sea EEZs.

First, the 'due regard' principle may apply in certain circumstances. UNCLOS Article 53(3) requires states to have 'due regard to the rights and duties of the coastal State' and to comply with its laws and regulation. In essence, this is a case-by-case assessment to determine what is reasonable conduct.[133] Here, certain sorts of military exercises, disturbances of 'safety zones' and environmental impacts may all come into play.

In January 2022, during the Ukraine conflict, Ireland opposed Russia's intention to hold navy military exercises in international waters off the western coast of Ireland within its EEZ. The Irish Foreign Minister told the Russian Ambassador that such exercises are 'not welcome' and explained that 'Russia, under international law, can take military exercises in international waters, but the fact they are choosing to do it on the western borders of the EU, off the Irish coast, is in our view not welcome and not wanted right now'.[134] The Russian Ambassador to Ireland replied that Russia decided 'as a gesture of goodwill, to relocate the

states to carry out in the EEZ and on the continental shelf military exercises or manoeuvres, in particular those involving weapons or explosives without the consent of the coastal state. See The United Nations Treaty Collection, Multilateral Treaties Deposited with the Secretary General, Chapter XXI Law of the Sea, available at: treaties.un.org. The aspect of military survey activities has been a matter of controversy regarding the EEZ claimed by China and the surveys conducted by the United States. The issue has been whether non-resource related activities are subject to the coastal state's regulation. It has been suggested that such military related data collection activities are lawful, provided they fall beyond Art 246 of UNCLOS and do not pose a direct threat to the coastal state permitting self-defence. See DR Rothwell and T Stephens, *The International Law of the Sea* (Oxford, Hart Publishing, 2010) 276.

[130] There are still diverging practices restricting naval manoeuvres and weapon exercises by other states. For example, in South-East Asia, consider that military exercises in or over their EEZ cannot be carried out without their consent. See Bateman (n 128) 381.

[131] Churchill and Lowe (n 109) 208.

[132] It is admitted that there is a high bar requiring that it must be a question of use of armed force directed towards a specific behaviour of another state to be unlawful. See B Simma (ed), *The Charter of the United Nations: A Commentary*, Vol I, 2nd edn (Oxford, Oxford University Press, 2002) 124; F Dubuisson and A Lagerwall, 'The Threat of the Use of Force and Ultimata' in M Weller (ed), *The Oxford Handbook of the Use of Force in International Law* (Oxford, Oxford University Press, 2015).

[133] Churchill and Lowe (n 109) 206.

[134] Cormac Mcquinn, 'Russian drills off Irish coast "not welcome", says Simon Coveney' *Irish Times* (24 January 2022), available at: www.irishtimes.com.

exercises by the Russian Navy, planned for February 3–8, outside the Irish exclusive economic zone (EEZ), with the aim not to hinder fishing activities by the Irish vessels in the traditional fishing areas'.[135] Such situations arguably are all about 'due regard'.

Second, UNCLOS resolution of Article 59 'due regard' issues on the basis of 'equity and in the light of relevant circumstances' takes account of individual factors such as those relating to the distance from the territorial sea, length of the operations and impact on the freedom of navigation.[136] The scope of 'due regard' often remains necessarily uncertain and controversial in particular situations. For example, the United States considers military activities as part of its freedom of navigation, overflight or related uses of sea.[137]

The Ukraine war raises the question whether Russian belligerency would have made its naval military exercises illegitimate in the EEZs of the other Baltic Sea States as *ipso facto* threatening the peace and security in the region. It could be credibly argued even more forcefully, with regard to the Baltic Sea, that Russian belligerency has foreclosed any legitimate naval exercises in this region.

There is no overall regional Baltic Sea legal arrangement beyond those contained in UNCLOS. The Baltic Sea has successfully addressed regional cooperation on the protection of the maritime environment, especially in the context of HELCOM. It has not produced any noteworthy regional arrangement for security matters. Its sister organisation, the CBBS, originally established in 1994, does have aims for broader regional cooperation which could embrace military matters.[138] As a 'forum for political dialogue' it could, in principle, address Baltic Sea security issues, but it has no track record in this regard.[139] The Russian invasion of Ukraine leaves no reason to think of any security initiatives at a regional level for the time being. This leaves NATO as the only viable security framework for most Baltic Sea coastal states. With NATO enlargement in sight, this would also include Finland and Sweden. In that event, NATO and EU membership would overlap fully in the

[135] Sarah Burns and Simon Carswell, 'Russia moves naval exercises outside Ireland's Exclusive Economic Zone' *Irish Times* (29 January 2022), available at: www.irishtimes.com.

[136] Rothwell and Stephens (n 129) 280.

[137] A Proelss, 'Article 59' in A Proelss (ed), *United Nations Convention on the Law of the Sea. A Commentary* (Munich, CH Beck, 2017) 460.

[138] CBSS, 'The Council of the Baltic Sea States Terms of Reference' (adopted by the 1st CBSS Ministerial Session in Copenhagen in March 1992, revised several times, most recently at the CBSS Ministers' meeting on 19 May 2020) provide in point 5: 'The CBSS encompasses all multilateral intergovernmental regional cooperation in areas agreed by its Members and serves as a forum for political dialogue'; and in point 6: 'The CBSS will initiate and implement regionally important, strategic projects and explore their financing with a view to focusing work in areas where it creates most added value, in line with CBSS long-term priorities', available at: cbss.org/about-us/strategic-documents/.

[139] The CBSS has had activities for instance relating to human trafficking and civil protection. See, CBSS, 'Terms of Reference of the CBSS Task Force against Trafficking in Human Beings' (Copenhagen, 9 June 2020), available at: cbss.org/about-us/strategic-documents/; CBSS, 'Joint Position on Enhancing Cooperation in Civil Protection Area 15th Meeting of Directors General for the Civil Protection in BSR' (Keflavik, 12 May 2017, and amended, Copenhagen, 8 June 2020), available at: cbss.org/about-us/strategic-documents/.

Baltic Sea. The two organisations are already cooperating and coordinating their activities in a wide variety of security-related fields and are like to do so increasingly in the future.[140]

In the future, there may come a time for revised security arrangements, either at a general European security level and/or in respect of the Baltic Sea specifically. One could anticipate some sort of confidence building measures in this region. Above all, there is a common interest in keeping sea lanes open and undisturbed. If nothing else, such confidence building measures could contribute towards peaceful atmospherics in the future.

VI. Concluding Remarks

This chapter has viewed the Baltic Sea from the twin perspectives of the law of the sea and EU law. It describes the rules of the law of the sea and its relation to EU legislation and its constraints. It has set out certain aspects, with examples, of the EU framework for concerted European action internationally and enhanced implementation of international obligations. In addition, some examples have been given of current issues relating to the Baltic Sea.

EU legislation has come to play a dominant legal role in the Baltic Sea. This is probably the single most important thing that the EU has brought about. This ensures uniform rules, and the common institutional framework adds to their efficient application and enforcement. The Baltic Sea environment itself is probably the greatest beneficiary; otherwise, there would have to be alternative legal arrangements, and more treaty-making, which are likely to result in less coherence and differences in local application and enforcement.

The EU does have a role in the making of security policy, but not regarding operational defence action. In the future, the role of NATO will increase in safeguarding peace and security in the Baltic Sea, especially following the NATO membership of Finland and Sweden. It is also to be expected that the coordination and exchange of information between the EU and NATO will increase in the BSR.

What is missing is a common peace and security perspective applicable to the BSR that would involve Russia. Until its belligerence no longer inherently threatens the peace and security of the Baltic Sea, the legitimate maritime uses of the Baltic Sea are not fully resolved.

[140] The Warsaw NATO–EU Joint Declaration of 2016 would like, inter alia, to 'Broaden and adapt our operational cooperation including at sea, and on migration, through increased sharing of maritime situational awareness as well as better coordination and mutual reinforcement of our activities in the Mediterranean and elsewhere'. NATO, 'Joint Declaration by the President of the European Council, the President of the European Commission, and the Secretary General of the North Atlantic Treaty Organization' (Warsaw, 8 July 2016), available at: www.consilium.europa.eu/media/21481/nato-eu-declaration-8-july-en-final.pdf. The NATO–EU cooperation has advanced in a number of security related areas, including the maritime field. See NATO, 'Seventh progress report on the implementation of the common set of proposals endorsed by EU and NATO Councils on 6 December 2016 and 5 December 2017' (20 June 2022), available at: www.consilium.europa.eu/media/57184/eu-nato-progress-report.pdf.

10

Influence of the EU on Regional Environmental Governance: Application of the Marine Directives in the Baltic Sea

SUVI-TUULI PUHARINEN AND ANTTI BELINSKIJ

I. Introduction

Environmental governance in the Baltic Sea Region is regulated by the Convention on the Protection of the Marine Environment of the Baltic Sea Area (Helsinki Convention).[1] The Convention's purpose is that parties take action to protect the Baltic Sea environment from all sources of pollution in order to promote the ecological restoration and the preservation of the ecological balance of the Baltic Sea Area.[2] The main environmental problem in the Baltic Sea is eutrophication due to excess nutrient inputs, which makes the reduction of nutrient pollution a priority action under the Convention.[3] The Convention also establishes the Baltic Marine Environment Protection Commission (HELCOM), which is tasked with continuous monitoring of the implementation of the Convention and making recommendations on measures relating to its purposes.[4]

In addition to the Helsinki Convention's regime, the environmental governance of the Baltic Sea is widely influenced and regulated by the EU (European Union), for, with the exception of Russia, all Baltic Sea riparian countries are EU Member States. The EU is also a signatory to the Helsinki Convention. According to the Treaty of the Functioning of the European Union, the EU and its Member States have shared competence in environmental policy, whereas the EU has exclusive competence in the conservation of marine biological resources, granted to it

[1] Convention on the Protection of the Marine Environment of the Baltic Sea Area (Helsinki, 6 October 1992) (Helsinki Convention).

[2] Helsinki Convention, Art 3.

[3] See HELCOM, 'Baltic Sea Action Plan 2021 Update' (Lübeck, Germany, 20 October 2021) 20, available at: www.helcom.fi/wp-content/uploads/2021/10/Baltic-Sea-Action-Plan-2021-update.pdf.

[4] Helsinki Convention, Arts 19 and 20.

under the common fisheries policy.[5] Legislative action by the EU has the potential to enhance environmental protection in the Baltic Sea, as it can impose stricter pollution standards than those set under regional sea conventions or those that Member States would individually adopt.[6] In practice, the EU has developed an increasingly active, dominant regulatory role in governance of the Baltic Sea and even replaced HELCOM as the most important actor in the region.[7] This notwithstanding, for a long time the EU regulation on protection of the marine environment has proceeded in a piecemeal fashion, focusing on sectors such as transport and fisheries, without protecting and preserving the marine environment in a holistic manner.[8]

In 2008, the EU adopted the Marine Strategy Framework Directive (MSFD),[9] addressing the need for measures designed to reduce impacts on the marine environment and to coordinate different EU legal acts with the aim of reducing pollution and protecting marine waters.[10] The principle aim of the MSFD is to achieve and maintain good environmental status (GES) in the marine environment through an integrated marine management process, ie, the development of marine strategies. The MSFD has close linkages to the EU Water Framework Directive (WFD),[11] which addresses the management of coastal waters. The WFD requires Member States to prevent deterioration of coastal waters and originally obliged states to ensure that GES and good chemical status would be reached in those waters by 2015. To facilitate the achievement of these aims, the WFD sets out a process for planning river basin management.[12] In this chapter, the MSFD and WFD are referred to collectively as 'the Marine Directives'.[13]

[5] Consolidated version of the Treaty of the Functioning of the European Union [2012] OJ C 326/47, Arts 3–4 (TFEU).

[6] R Churchill, 'The European Union and the Challenges of Marine Governance: From Sectoral Response to Integrated Policy?' in P Schei and D Vidas (eds), *The World Ocean in Globalization: Climate Change, Sustainable Fisheries*, Biodiversity, Shipping, Regional Issues 412 (Leiden, Brill, 2011).

[7] N Tynkkynen et al, 'The Governance of the Mitigation of the Baltic Sea Eutrophication: Exploring the Challenges of the Formal Governing System' (2014) 43 *AMBIO* 105; H Ringbom and M Joas, 'Concluding article: The changing regulatory landscape of the Baltic Sea – An analysis' (2018) 38 *Marine Policy* 317, 320 and 322.

[8] R Long, 'The Marine Strategy Framework Directive: A New European Approach to the Regulation of the Marine Environment, Marine Natural Resources and Marine Ecological Services' (2011) 29 *Journal of Energy & Natural Resources Law* 1, 5–7.

[9] Directive 2008/56/EC of the European Parliament and of the Council of 17 June 2008 establishing a framework for community action in the field of marine environmental policy (Marine Strategy Framework Directive) [2008] OJ L164/19 (MSFD).

[10] MSFD Preamble, para (2); Long, 'Marine Strategy Framework Directive' (n 8) 5–7.

[11] Directive 2000/60/EC of the European Parliament and of the Council establishing a framework for Community action in the field of water policy [2000] OJ L327/1 (Water Framework Directive, WFD).

[12] WFD, Art 4(1), para (a).

[13] In addition to the MSFD and WFD, the establishment of marine protected areas under Council Directive 92/43/EEC on the conservation of natural habitats and of wild fauna and flora [1998] OJ L206/7 (Habitats Directive); and Directive 2009/147/EC of the European Parliament and of the Council of 30 November 2009 on the conservation of wild birds [2010] OJ L20/7 (Birds Directive) are important contributions to the good status of the marine environment; MSFD Preamble, para (6).

The environmental governance of the Baltic Sea has been substantively shaped by the adoption of the ecosystem approach in the Helsinki Convention's regime and the Marine Directives.[14] The approach is often defined as an integrated, adaptive approach that takes a holistic perspective on the ecosystem and makes its environmental status and ecological prerequisites the basis for regulation.[15] In keeping with the ecosystem approach, the Helsinki Convention regime and the Marine Directives base their aims on the environmental quality of the marine waters to which they apply; the regulatory structure builds on assessing and including the status of the marine ecosystem in the legal measures.[16]

The ecosystem approach was integrated in the regime of the Helsinki Convention with the adoption of the Baltic Sea Action Plan (BSAP) in 2007, which set the aim of reaching good environmental status of the Baltic Sea by 2021.[17] For its part, in the MSFD, the EU requires Member States to apply the ecosystem approach in developing the marine strategies for reaching or maintaining GES by 2020.[18] While the WFD makes no direct references to the ecosystem approach, its ecosystem-focused, goal-oriented regulatory structure, designed to achieve good water status by 2015, is generally considered to represent that approach.[19] Nevertheless, combating eutrophication continues to be a major challenge in the Baltic Sea,[20] and GES was not reached in the time frames set out in the Marine Directives or the BSAP. Consequently, the BSAP was updated in 2021 with a new aim of ensuring its successful implementation by 2030.

The Helsinki Convention and the EU legislation form a multi-level legal structure for marine environmental governance in the Baltic Sea on international, EU,

[14] S Söderström and K Kern, 'The ecosystem approach to management in marine environmental governance: Institutional interplay in the Baltic Sea region' (2017) 27 *Environmental Policy and Governance* 619.

[15] See UN, 'Convention on Biological Diversity' (Fifth Ordinary Meeting, Rio de Janeiro 5 June 1992, CBD); UN, 'Decision no V/6 Ecosystem approach' (1760 UNTS 79, Rio de Janeiro, 22 May 1992); and the subsequent UN, 'Malawi Principles for the Ecosystem Approach' (Lilongwe, Malawi, 26–28 January 1998). See also, B Bohman, 'Transboundary Law for Social-Ecological Resilience? A Study on Eutrophication in the Baltic Sea Area' (PhD thesis, Stockholm University, 2017) 6; N Soininen and F Platjouw, 'Resilience and Adaptive Capacity of Aquatic Environmental Law in the EU: An Evaluation and Comparison of the WFD, MSFD, and MSPD' in D Langlet and R Rayfuse (eds), *Ecosystem Approach in Ocean Governance and Planning: Perspectives from Europe and Beyond*, Publications on Ocean Development, Vol 87 (Leiden, Brill, 2019) 17–18.

[16] Bohman, 'Transboundary Law' (n 15) 96.

[17] HELCOM, 'HELCOM Baltic Sea Action Plan' (HELCOM Ministerial Meeting, Krakow, Poland, 15 November 2007) Preamble and the Eutrophication Segment, 7.

[18] MSFD, Art 1(3).

[19] B Bohman, 'The Ecosystem Approach as a Basis for Managerial Compliance: An Example from the Regulatory Development in the Baltic Sea Region' in D Langlet and R Rayfuse (eds), *The Ecosystem Approach in Ocean Planning and Governance: Perspectives from Europe and Beyond*, Publications on Ocean Development, Vol 87 (Leiden, Brill, 2019) 89.

[20] European Court of Auditors, 'Combating eutrophication in the Baltic Sea: further and more effective action needed' (Special report no 03/2016, Luxembourg, Publications Office of the European Union, 2016), available at: www.eca.europa.eu/Lists/ECADocuments/SR16_03/SR_BALTIC_EN.pdf.

regional and sub-regional scales.[21] Effective ecosystem management requires dynamic legal interactions if it is to accommodate the different scales and elements of the ecosystem.[22]

In this chapter, we discuss the EU's influence on regional environmental governance of the Baltic Sea, with a focus on the relationship between the environmental requirements of the Helsinki Convention and the Marine Directives. We approach the question in three sections that together seek to paint a comprehensive picture of the interactions between the different regimes. Section II analyses the regulatory structure and geographical and legal scales of the three focal instruments, outlining the basis for interaction and interlinkages of the regimes. Section III focuses on the legal implications and interaction of the objectives of GES in the Helsinki Convention and the Marine Directives; it takes up the particular case of eutrophication as the main environmental pressure. Section IV goes on to discuss legal measures to prevent eutrophication in the Baltic Sea in more detail. Finally, in section V, we draw conclusions on the added regulatory value of the Marine Directives and their interaction with the Helsinki Convention in the environmental governance of the Baltic Sea.

II. Regulatory Interaction between the Helsinki Convention and the Marine Directives

A. Overview of the Regulatory Strategies

The Helsinki Convention requires the parties to put forward policies to prevent pollution, conserve natural habitats and biological diversity, and protect the ecological processes of the Baltic Sea.[23] The Convention highlights the operationalisation of general environmental law principles, such as the precautionary principle, the principle of best available technique and best environmental practice, as well as the requirement to apply a priori environmental impact assessments.[24] Further, the Convention imposes specific requirements, including prohibitions of incineration and dumping, and prevention of pollution from ships.[25] As it stands, the Convention can be said to illustrate a traditional, command-and-control approach to environmental regulation.[26]

Traditional approaches are challenged, however, by increased environmental complexity; a multifaceted environmental problem, such as eutrophication in the

[21] Bohman, 'The Ecosystem Approach as a Basis for Managerial Compliance' (n 19) 93–94.
[22] ibid, 92.
[23] Helsinki Convention, Arts 3 and 15.
[24] ibid, Arts 3 and 7. See J Ebbesson, 'A Critical Assessment of the 1992 Baltic Sea Convention' (2000) 43 *German Yearbook of International Law* 38, 39–40.
[25] Helsinki Convention, Arts 8, 10 and 11.
[26] Bohman, 'Transboundary Law' (n 15) 74.

Baltic Sea, and the complex environmental responses required are hard to pin down with prescriptive regulation.[27] This being the case, the BSAP was adopted to steer the regulatory approach of the Convention towards integrated and adaptive ecosystem-based management. The BSAP stipulates that the objectives of GES are to be the basis for work under the Convention and lays down the overall framework for the parties' actions to achieve these objectives. In relation to eutrophication, GES has been translated into nutrient reduction targets for each state party, with the states urged to implement national programmes of measures and actions commensurate with these targets.[28] The Convention requires that progress towards the targets be measured and that adjustments to national programmes be considered where necessary.[29]

In EU law, the MSFD requires that the Member States develop and implement marine strategies for their national marine waters, enabling them to manage the marine environment and human activities affecting it and thereby to achieve GES.[30] Marine strategies are developed in a marine management process laid down in the Directive and following a six-year cycle.[31] The process includes an initial assessment of the state of the marine waters and human activities[32] and a determination of GES for the Member States' marine waters and marine regions based on the 11 qualitative descriptors listed in Annex I.[33] Following this assessment, Member States are to establish environmental targets and associated indicators and compile and implement programmes of measures to guide progress towards achieving GES.[34] In addition, Member States are required to establish coordinated monitoring programmes that will facilitate updating the marine strategies.[35]

The WFD employs a regulatory strategy similar to that of the MSFD. It requires Member States to implement a process of river basin management planning in order to prevent the deterioration of surface waters and groundwater bodies and to achieve good status in them. Like marine management, river basin management is planned following a six-year cycle. River basin management includes gathering knowledge on water bodies and water uses,[36] defining good status and applying exemptions[37] and compiling programmes of measures to achieve the environmental objectives.[38] Furthermore, Member States are required to establish constant monitoring,[39] which should feed into updating assessments[40]

[27] ibid.
[28] ibid, 141.
[29] HELCOM, 'Baltic Sea Action Plan' (2007) (n 17) 4; Bohman, 'Transboundary Law' (n 15) 141.
[30] MSFD, Art 1(1)–(3).
[31] MSFD, Art 17.
[32] MSFD, Art 8.
[33] MSFD, Art 9.
[34] MSFD, Arts 10 and 13.
[35] MSFD, Art 11.
[36] WFD, Art 5.
[37] WFD, Art 4 and Annex V.
[38] WFD, Art 11.
[39] WFD, Art 9.
[40] WFD, Art 5(2).

and modifying environmental objectives, exemptions and overall policy, as new knowledge is gained.[41]

The MSFD and WFD are based on what is known in EU law as the programmatic approach, which aims to account for complexity. On the one hand, Member States are to ensure that their marine and water policies adhere to the common objectives and the procedural framework laid down in the Marine Directives; on the other, they are left with considerable discretion as to the policy instruments, measures and exact means by which the objectives are pursued.[42]

B. Geographical Scales of the Regulatory Instruments

An ecosystem approach seeks to take into account the integrity of the focal ecosystem in the design of the management. In the case of the Baltic Sea, this means the integrity of the entire sea, thus comprising ecosystem components at different scales and with different functions ranging from the local to the biosphere level.[43] Indeed, it is widely recognised that ecosystem management should be implemented at appropriate spatial and temporal scales with due consideration for the multi-level dynamics of the ecological systems concerned.[44]

Legal systems, too, are bound to different scales, spanning the international, national and local levels.[45] Legal geography theories note that legal systems, when paired with the geographic context in which they are applied, create 'administrative ecosystems' in which management takes place.[46] The choice of legal scale has an impact on the regulatory outcomes: a local scale has a higher resolution, as it were, and is better equipped to produce detailed rules, whereas national or even international scales, which have a lower resolution, produce general frameworks and guidance.[47] Effective ecosystem management requires interaction and implementation of management across legal jurisdictions and scales.[48]

[41] WFD, Arts 1(8), 4(4)–(7).

[42] See F Groothuijse and R Uylenburg, 'Everything according to plan? Achieving environmental quality standards by a programmatic approach' in M Peeters and R Uylenburg (eds), *EU Environmental Legislation: Legal Perspectives on Regulatory Strategies* (Northampton, Edward Elgar Publishing, 2014).

[43] B De Sousa Santos, 'Law: A Map of Misreading – Toward a Postmodern Conception of Law' (1987) 14 *Journal of Law and Society* 279, 283–84.

[44] UN, 'Malawi Principle' No 7; R Long, 'Legal Aspects of Ecosystem-Based Marine Management in Europe' in A Chircop, ML McConnell and S Coffen-Smout (eds), *26 Ocean Yearbook* (Leiden, Brill Nijhoff, 2012).

[45] See De Sousa Santos (n 43) 287–89.

[46] D Langlet, 'Scale, space and delimitation in marine legal governance – Perspectives from the Baltic Sea' (2018) 38 *Marine Policy* 278; A Westholm, 'Delimiting Marine Areas: Ecosystem Approach(es?) in EU Marine Management' in D Langlet and R Rayfuse (eds), *Ecosystem Approach in Ocean Governance and Planning: Perspectives from Europe and Beyond*, Publications on Ocean Development, Vol 87 (Leiden, Brill, 2019) 119.

[47] De Sousa Santos (n 43); Westholm (n 46) 119–20.

[48] Long, 'Legal Aspects' (n 44) 92.

The Helsinki Convention constitutes an international-scale instrument focusing on the entire Baltic Sea ecosystem.[49] The Convention and the BSAP set out general aims and objectives that are to be reached through joint efforts of the parties but lack specific rules on what each party is obliged to do in its respective territory and jurisdiction.[50] The scope of application of the Convention encompasses the parties' marine waters, but it also contains provisions on preventing and eliminating land-based pollution.[51]

For its part, the MSFD establishes a national legal scale for marine ecosystem management. The Directive's obligations apply to Member State marine waters that extend from the baseline[52] to the outer limit of their exclusive economic zones (EEZ), ie, the areas where they exercise jurisdictional rights.[53] Member States can make further subdivisions of their marine waters at appropriate levels in implementing the MSFD.[54] The EU Member States' EEZ encompass almost the entire Baltic Sea, excluding the area of Russia's EEZ of course. Accordingly, the Directive essentially applies to the area covered by the Helsinki Convention.

The WFD's scope of application covers the Member State coastal waters, to which the MSFD also applies in a supplementary manner.[55] Under the WFD, coastal waters encompass the waters from the coastline up to a distance of one nautical mile on the seaward side of the baseline.[56] Depending on the shape of the coastline, the baseline – and thus the scope of the WFD – may vary from only a narrow strip of marine waters[57] to a substantially wider area. For example,

[49] The Convention defines its area of application as the Baltic Sea Area, encompassing the Baltic Sea and its entrance as well as the parties' internal, ie, territorial waters. See: Helsinki Convention, Arts 1(1) and 4(1) and (2). Although perhaps most relevant to and specifically geared towards the environmental aspects of the Baltic Sea, the Helsinki Convention is of course not the only international legal instrument on Baltic Sea maritime governance. The backbone of the international regulatory setting for marine governance is the United Nations Convention on the Law of the Sea (Montego Bay 10 December 1982, UNCLOS), to which all Baltic Sea riparian states and the EU are parties. UNCLOS contains significant requirements on States to protect and preserve the marine environment (Arts 192–95). Further, many fields of marine governance, such as fisheries, biodiversity and maritime traffic, are regulated to a varied degree at the international level. Consequently, the international law regimes form a multilayered framework with various legal interactions. See V Engström, 'Complexities of the Baltic Sea Regulatory Framework' (2018) 98 *Marine Policy* 191, 191–92.

[50] See Ebbesson (n 24) 39–40; Bohman, 'Transboundary Law' (n 15) 121.

[51] Helsinki Convention, Arts 6 and 2(2).

[52] The baseline refers to the line from which the breadth of territorial waters is measured in accordance with UNCLOS.

[53] MSFD, Art 3(1) para (a). In accordance with Art 56(1) of UNCLOS, the coastal state has sovereign rights for conserving and managing the natural resources and jurisdiction with regard to the protection and preservation of the marine environment in the EEZ. On the legal and geographical scaling of the MSFD, see Langlet (n 46) 282–84.

[54] For instance, in the Baltic Sea context, Finland has divided its marine waters into six subdivisions, whereas Sweden, among other countries, has chosen to keep its entire marine waters area as the scale of implementation of the MSFD. On Finland, see S Korpinen et al (eds), *Suomen meriympäristön tila 2018* (SYKEn julkaisuja, 4/2018) 64; On Sweden, see Westholm (n 46) 129.

[55] MSFD, Art 3(1) para (b).

[56] WFD, Arts 1(1) and 2(7).

[57] As stated by S Boyes and M Elliot, 'Marine legislation – The ultimate "horrendogram": International law, European directives & national implementation' (2014) 86 *Marine Pollution Bulletin* 39, 41.

Figure 1 Baltic Sea EEZ and Territorial Seas

Note: H Ringbom, B Bohman and S Ilvessalo, 'Combatting Eutrophication in the Baltic Sea: Legal Aspects of Sea-Based Engineering Measures' (2008) 2 Brill Research Perspectives Law of the Sea 1, available at: doi.org/10.1163/24519359-12340007.

Finland has shallow archipelago areas reaching far out to sea from the mainland coast. The WFD also applies to inland surface waters, ie, rivers and lakes,[58] through which the land-based pressures on the Baltic Sea pass. As most of the Baltic Sea riparian and basin area states are members of the EU, the WFD strongly supports the Helsinki Convention's provisions on controlling land-based pollution and other pressures.

In terms of legal scaling, the WFD's management approach falls on the level of river basin districts and units for which river basin management plans and

[58] WFD, Art 1(1).

programmes of measures are established.[59] Coastal water bodies are assigned to the district that is most likely to influence their quality.[60] The WFD further divides waters into smaller units, ie, water bodies, such as stretches of coastal waters.[61] The WFD's objectives apply to the ecological status of each individual water body.[62] Operating at this resolution – regional river basins and local water bodies – the WFD represents the most detailed scale of the Baltic Sea marine environmental governance.[63]

Table 1 The scales, regulatory orientation and interactions of the Baltic Sea environmental governance instruments

Regulatory instrument	**Legal and geographical scale**	**Regulatory orientation and supporting interactions**
Helsinki Convention + BSAP	international entire Baltic Sea Area + drainage area in the Convention parties	overview, principles and general types of actions, direction and schemes requires implementation mechanisms at national and regional scales
Marine Strategy Framework Directive	national EU Member States' marine waters (territorial waters + EEZs)	medium scale, provides legal and policy instruments national scale needs to be supported by transboundary/ecosystem-scale arrangements, and regional and local implementation
Water Framework Directive	regional (river basin districts) and local (water bodies) EU Member States coastal waters (territorial waters) and inland waters	use of legal and policy instruments in a delimited context, regulation of legal relations and obligations of individuals detailed regional and local focus needs to be supported by wider ecosystem-scale arrangements legal and policy instruments needed for implementation provided on national scale

Note: De Sousa Santos (n 43) 287–89; Westholm (n 46) 121.

[59] WFD, Arts 2(15), 3(1), 11(1) and 13(1).

[60] Common Implementation Strategy for the Water Framework Directive (2000/60/EC) Guidance Document No 5, 23–24, available at: www.ec.europa.eu/environment/water/water-framework/objectives/pdf/strategy2.pdf; Westholm (n 46) 124.

[61] WFD, Arts 3(1) and 2(10).

[62] WFD, Art 4(1).

[63] See also, on the geographical and legal scales of the WFD, Langlet (n 46) 281–82.

C. Interactions and Cross-References between the Regulatory Instruments

In terms of formal hierarchy, the MSFD and the WFD are means for implementing the EU's obligations under the Helsinki Convention.[64] In addition to citing the Marine Directives, the BSAP lists a number of pieces of EU environmental legislation as important tools for its implementation.[65] Regarding nutrient pollution, the list includes the Nitrates Directive (ND),[66] the Urban Wastewater Treatment Directive (UWWTD)[67] and the Industrial Emissions Directive (IED),[68] as well as EU policies such as the Action Plan of the EU Strategy for the Baltic Sea Region and the common agricultural policy (CAP). In practice, the implementation of the obligations of parties to the Helsinki Convention occurs within the framework of EU law.[69]

The interaction of the Baltic Sea legal instruments is not, however, strictly hierarchical but can be characterised as a complex mix of multiple regulatory layers.[70] The MSFD recognises that coordinated effort at the marine region or sub-region level is essential for its implementation. Consequently, the Directive requires Member States to cooperate among themselves in each region or sub-region to ensure that their marine strategies are coherent and coordinated and, whenever possible, to work with third countries.[71] Accordingly, while the focus of the Directive's obligations is national marine areas, it requires coordination at the ecosystem level, the synergies of which should then be reflected in the national marine strategies.[72] Furthermore, Member States bordering the same region or sub-region need to devise specific plans of action where the status of the sea is so critical that urgent action is needed.[73] In coordinating their work, Member States must use established regional frameworks, such as regional sea conventions.[74]

[64] The MSFD was adopted partly because of the EU accession to an increasing number of regional marine conventions, including the Helsinki Convention; and the Directive declares itself to be a contribution to the fulfilment of the obligations and commitments of the EU and the Member States under those conventions. See MSFD Preamble, para (19).

[65] HELCOM, 'Baltic Sea Action Plan' (2021) 9.

[66] Council Directive 91/676/EEC concerning the protection of waters against pollution caused by nitrates from agricultural sources (Nitrates Directive, ND) [1991] OJ L375/1.

[67] Council Directive 91/271/EEC concerning urban waste-water treatment (Urban Wastewater Treatment Directive, UWWTD) [1991] OJ L135/40.

[68] Directive 2010/75/EU of the European Parliament and of the Council on industrial emissions (integrated pollution prevention and control) (Industrial Emissions Directive, IED) [2010] OJ L334/17.

[69] See also N Giannopoulos, 'The Interplay Between EU Law and Regional Sea Conventions: Shaping Environmental Protection in Relation to Offshore Energy Production Across Europe?' (2022) 31 *European Energy and Environmental Law Review* 2, 11.

[70] See Ringbom and Joas (n 7) 320.

[71] MSFD, Arts 5(2) and 6(2).

[72] MSFD Preamble, para (11).

[73] MSFD, Art 5(3).

[74] MSFD, Art 6(1) and (2).

In the Baltic Sea Region, the Baltic Marine Environment Protection Commission (HELCOM) structure serves as a platform for implementation of the MSFD's obligations on marine regional or sub-regional cooperation. For its part, the BSAP constitutes a plan of action, adopted to promote urgent actions to address the critical state of the sea.[75]

The WFD's water management is strongly integrated with the national marine strategies and transboundary water cooperation. The MSFD makes several references to the WFD urging Member States to integrate water and marine management. The MSFD prescribes that water management must be integrated in the assessment of marine waters, that the environmental targets for marine strategies need to be compatible with the WFD's water management objectives, and that the programmes of measures under the MSFD must be integrated with the WFD's water management measures.[76]

The WFD also requires Member States to ensure coordinated implementation of the Directive in river basins extending over the territory of more than one Member State and to engage with third countries in these efforts.[77] The MSFD requires Member States to use the WFD's coordination structures for transboundary river basins to support the MSFD's own aims; those structures make it possible to extend the coordination of marine strategies to the catchment area of a marine region or sub-region, including land-locked countries.[78]

III. GES Objectives

A. Legal Objectives for the Baltic Sea Region

i. HELCOM: Good Environmental Status of the Baltic Sea

While the Helsinki Convention requires parties to promote the ecological restoration of the Baltic Sea and the preservation of its ecological balance, it does not set any specific criteria that would characterise that balance.[79] The objective of GES comes from the 2004 HELCOM vision that entails a 'healthy Baltic Sea environment, with diverse biological components functioning in balance, resulting in a good environmental/ecological status and supporting a wide range of sustainable human economic and social activities'.[80] The vision has been elaborated to

[75] The BSAP was initially drafted at the same time as the MSFD and thus the Action Plan and its objectives were considerably affected by the EU legislative work and partly adopted to support the implementation of the MSFD. See Bohman, 'Transboundary Law' (n 15) 20, 142.

[76] MSFD, Arts 8(2), 10(1) and 13(2).

[77] WFD, Art 3(3) and (4).

[78] MSFD, Art 6(2).

[79] Helsinki Convention, Art 6(1).

[80] HELCOM, 'Baltic Marine Environment Protection Commission Minutes of the 25th Meeting' (Annex 14, Helsinki, 2–3 March 2004), available at: www.portal.helcom.fi/Archive/archive2/HELCOM%2025_2004_Minutes%20of%20the%20Meeting.pdf.

incorporate strategic goals and specific ecological objectives for thematic areas that represent the major human activities threatening the Baltic Sea ecosystem: (1) eutrophication caused by excessive inputs of nutrients; (2) inputs of hazardous substances; (3) pollution by maritime activities; and (4) loss of biodiversity.[81] The 2007 BSAP constituted HELCOM's strategic programme of measures and actions for achieving GES by 2021.

The BSAP affirmed the determination of GES and the general objectives for the four thematic areas. These goals include ecological objectives, which reflect the desired state of the environment, and management objectives, which describe the desired change in pressures or conservation status as a result of the actions and measures planned.[82] For example, the general objective for eutrophication is a 'Baltic Sea unaffected by eutrophication', which translates into ecological objectives for nutrient concentrations, water clarity, algae blooms, oxygen levels, as well as the distribution and occurrence of plants and animals. In turn, the management objective for eutrophication is simply to minimise inputs of nutrients from human activities. However, the BSAP has translated this objective into more specific reduction targets for nutrients for each Baltic Sea basin and each signatory state.

GES was not achieved by 2021 in any of the four thematic areas.[83] In 2021, HELCOM adopted a new BSAP, which re-establishes the aim of achieving GES but does not set a specific deadline for doing so. Rather, the new instrument sets deadlines for the actions and commitments specified in the plan and an overall goal of its full implementation by 2030 at the latest. As regards actions to tackle eutrophication, the updated BSAP states that measures to reduce nutrient inputs should be fully implemented by 2027.[84] It retains the actions agreed in the original plan but includes new ones that are to be undertaken as a joint effort by the parties.[85]

ii. The MSFD: GES of Marine Waters

The main aim of the MSFD was to ensure that the Member States take the necessary action to achieve or maintain GES in the marine environment by the year 2020 at the latest.[86] Notably, GES was not reached by 2020 in any of the marine regions

[81] HELCOM, 'HELCOM Ecological Objectives for an Ecosystem Approach' (Stakeholder Conference on the Baltic Sea Action Plan, Helsinki, 7 March 2006) 2, available at: www.portal.helcom.fi/Archive/Shared%20Documents/HABITAT%208-2006-7-3%20EcoO.pdf.

[82] HELCOM, 'Baltic Sea Action Plan 2021 Update' (n 3) 8.

[83] In addition to the four previously addressed major concerns, impacts of pressures such as introduction of invasive species, marine litter and underwater noise as well as the effects of climate change are already evident and will continue to have an increasingly significant impact on the Baltic Sea ecosystem. HELCOM, 'State of the Baltic Sea – Second HELCOM holistic assessment 2011–2016' (2018) 155 *Baltic Sea Environment Proceedings*; HELCOM, 'Baltic Sea Action Plan 2021 Update' (n 3) Preamble.

[84] HELCOM, 'Baltic Sea Action Plan 2021 Update' (n 3) 22.

[85] ibid, 6.

[86] MSFD, Art 2(1).

or sub-regions covered by the Directive.[87] GES is defined in Article 3(5) of the MSFD as 'the environmental status of marine waters where these provide ecologically diverse and dynamic oceans and seas which are clean, healthy and productive within their intrinsic conditions, and the use of the marine environment is at a level that is sustainable, thus safeguarding the potential for uses and activities by current and future generations'.[88]

Each Member State must determine more specifically what GES entails in its own marine waters. The determination is based on the 11 descriptors provided in Annex I of the Directive, which indicate the state of different elements of, as well as pressures and impacts on, marine ecosystems. For example, descriptor number 5 applies to eutrophication, with the general quality objective requiring that human-induced eutrophication be minimised and adverse effects thereof be reduced, these being losses of biodiversity, ecosystem degradation, harmful algae blooms and oxygen deficiency in bottom waters.

Member States must revise their definitions of GES every six years, guided by the European Commission's Decision on its characterisation.[89] The Decision provides specific criteria for defining GES; for example, in the case of eutrophication these include nutrient concentration levels, occurrence of harmful algae blooms and oxygen conditions. The characterisations of GES need to fit the most suitable geographical scale, covering concerns ranging from the state of national marine waters (eg, marine litter) to regional populations of species (eg, biodiversity). Moreover, Member States are required to ensure the uniformity of the definition of GES throughout a given marine region.[90]

The MSFD requires Member States to establish specific environmental targets to guide the progress towards achieving GES.[91] These targets can specify either desired conditions in the marine environment or reduction targets for pressures and impacts affecting the state of the descriptors.[92] The targets should specify the level of reduction in each anthropogenic pressure needed to achieve GES, for example, the maximum allowable input of nutrients.[93] The programmes of

[87] The European Commission estimated in 2018 that GES was unlikely to be achieved by 2020 in the EU marine waters. Commission, 'Report from the Commission to the European Parliament and the Council assessing Member States' programmes of measures under the Marine Strategy Framework Directive' COM(2018) 562 final.

[88] MSFD, Art 3(5) para (a).

[89] Commission Decision (EU) 2017/848 laying down criteria and methodological standards on good environmental status of marine waters and specifications and standardised methods for monitoring and assessment, and repealing Decision 2010/477/EU.

[90] MSFD, Art 5(2).

[91] MSFD, Art 10.

[92] MSFD, Art 3(7).

[93] Commission, 'Commission Staff Working Document Background document for the Marine Strategy Framework Directive on the determination of good environmental status and its links to assessments and the setting of environmental targets Accompanying the Report from the Commission to the European Parliament and the Council on the implementation of the Marine Strategy Framework Directive (Directive 2008/56/EC)' SWD(2020) 62 final, 21–22, 61.

measures for marine strategies must include the necessary measures to comply with the environmental targets.[94]

The Directive also provides a derogation regime that establishes the grounds on which Member States may be exempted from the attainment of GES or the environmental targets. The regime allows states to identify instances in which GES or environmental targets cannot be achieved due to measures taken or not taken by another state, natural causes or conditions, force majeure or physical modifications or alterations undertaken for reasons of overriding public interest.[95]

Overall, GES, as elaborated in the MSFD, translates into far more exact and geographically specific standards compared with the ecological objectives of the BSAP, which apply to the marine area in its entirety. Instrumentally, the environmental targets of the MSFD are operational tools similar to the management objectives of the BSAP. However, while the BSAP's management objectives are general commitments of the Helsinki Convention parties, the environmental targets under the MSFD are more specific and measurable, and must be operationalised by each Member State in the marine strategy, for the Member State's obligations under the Directive to be fulfilled.

iii. The WFD: Good Status of Coastal Waters

The WFD establishes two main objectives for coastal water bodies: (1) non-deterioration; and (2) the achievement of 'good surface water status' by 2015.[96] Good surface water status comprises good ecological status, which indicates a healthy and functioning ecosystem, and good chemical status, which is determined based on the concentrations of certain harmful chemical compounds in the water.[97] The Directive also allows Member States to designate artificial or heavily modified water bodies for which the applicable ecological objective is good ecological potential.[98]

Ecological status is assessed according to a five-level classification system that uses biological, physio-chemical and morphological quality elements.[99] For coastal waters, the biological elements include the composition and abundance

[94] Commission, 'Marine Strategy Framework Directive Common (MSFD) Implementation Strategy Programs of Measures under the Marine Strategy Framework Directive Recommendations for implementation and reporting' (Final version, 25 November 2014) 5, available at: www.circabc.europa.eu/sd/d/0ee797dd-d92c-4d7c-a9f9-5dffb36d2065/GD10%20-%20MSFD%20recommendations%20on%20measures%20and%20exceptions_25-11-2014.pdf.

[95] MSFD, Art 14(1) paras (a)–(e).

[96] WFD, Art 4(1) para (a).

[97] The environmental quality standards for surface water chemical status are imposed in Directive 2008/105/EC of the European Parliament and of the Council of 16 December 2008 on environmental quality standards in the field of water policy, amending and subsequently repealing Council Directive 82/176/EEC, 83/513/EEC, 84/491/EEC, 86280/EEC and amending Directive 2000/60/EC of the European Parliament and of the Council [2008] OJ L348/84.

[98] WFD, Art 4(3) and Annex V, section 1.2.5.

[99] Further, each water body category includes different water body types that Member States have determined in accordance with WFD, Annex II, section 1.2 and 1.3.

of phytoplankton, aquatic flora and benthic fauna, while the physio-chemical elements encompass measures such as transparency, oxygenation, nutrient conditions and specific pollutants.[100] Taken together, the indicators in the classification system reveal the level of eutrophication in the coastal water bodies. In good ecological status, the result for each factor considered will deviate only slightly from what it would be in waters virtually unimpacted by human activity.[101]

Like the MSFD, the WFD provides an exemption regime that allows Member States to justify their failing to meet the Directive's objectives in the water bodies. Failures to prevent deterioration of water status may stem from accidents or other unforeseen events (force majeure)[102] or result from undertaking new, sustainable human development activities.[103] The WFD includes two possibilities for Member States to deviate from the obligations to achieve good water status by 2015: extending the deadline for achieving good status[104] or setting less stringent environmental objectives for individual water bodies in which good status cannot be achieved.[105]

GES as characterised in the WFD is much more precise and geographically specific than it is in the MSFD. The WFD sets water body-specific environmental objectives supported by a detailed classification system. The environmental objectives linked to GES are specific and measurable and, by 2015, good status should have been achieved in coastal waters, except where exemptions were applied.

B. Legal Status of the GES Objectives

i. The Helsinki Convention and the BSAP

The obligations of the Helsinki Convention, including the prevention and elimination of pollution and preservation of the ecological balance of the Baltic Sea, are legally binding commitments on the Convention parties. However, the Convention's provisions are loosely worded and, thus, the states have considerable latitude in deciding what actions are appropriate to meet their commitments.[106] In addition, the Convention does not put forward a mechanism whereby parties could be sanctioned for non-compliance.[107] Indeed, the entire regulatory regime has often been considered weak – a shortcoming suggested by the rather high level of alleged non-compliance by the parties.[108]

[100] WFD, Annex V, section 1.1.4 and 1.2.4.
[101] WFD, Annex V, section 1.2.
[102] WFD, Art 4(6).
[103] WFD, Art 4(7).
[104] WFD, Art 4(4).
[105] WFD, Art 4(5).
[106] Ebbesson (n 24) 39–40; Bohman, 'Transboundary Law' (n 15) 121.
[107] Helsinki Convention, Art 16.
[108] B Bohman, 'Lessons from the regulatory approaches to combat eutrophication in the Baltic Sea region' (2018) 38 *Marine Policy* 227, 230–32; Bohman, 'The Ecosystem Approach as a Basis for Managerial Compliance' (n 19) 80–81.

The BSAP provides more concrete ecological and management objectives, which can be seen as benchmarks for states' action under the Helsinki Convention. However, many of these objectives constitute commitments common to all parties rather than specific obligations for individual states; the BSAP describes the desired state of the entire Baltic Sea and the pressures impacting it and relies upon joint efforts to achieve it. Yet, the BSAP also aims to translate some of its objectives into actions for individual states. For instance, GES in relation to eutrophication is translated into nutrient reduction targets for each state, the intention being to prompt states to implement national programmes commensurate with the targets.[109]

The BSAP is an action plan, not a legal instrument binding on its own merits.[110] While the objectives and actions of the BSAP have been adopted by HELCOM with the approval of the Convention parties, the Convention does no more than grant HELCOM the competence to make recommendations on measures.[111] Consequently, the legal status of the BSAP objectives is debated.[112] On the one hand, it has been suggested that the desired legal force for the BSAP could be derived from the Convention's provisions that are binding on the states.[113] On the other hand, this would not solve the problems relating to the Convention not being legally enforceable in general.[114]

ii. Legal Status of the MSFD Objectives

The MSFD provides clearer obligations for Member States with regard to their marine waters than the Helsinki Convention regime. In the case of GES, the MSFD states that 'Member States shall take the necessary measures to achieve or maintain good environmental status in the marine environment by the year 2020 at the latest'. Moreover, EU environmental law includes formal compliance control by the Commission and the Court of Justice of the European Union (CJEU), which, although focused on overseeing the implementation of EU acts, can also address Member State compliance with international conventions, such as the Helsinki Convention, particularly if both the Member State in question and the EU are parties to that Convention.[115] However, the legal status of the MSFD's objectives has remained unclear in the absence of CJEU case law. The Commission has merely recommended that Member States consider laying down their definitions of GES and related environmental targets in legislation to improve their enforceability.[116]

[109] Bohman, 'Transboundary Law' (n 15) 141.

[110] ibid, 20, 141, 148.

[111] Helsinki Convention, Art 20.

[112] Bohman, 'Transboundary Law' (n 15) 126, 148; Engström (n 49) 192–93.

[113] Bohman, 'Transboundary Law' (n 15) 122–23, 149.

[114] Bohman, 'The Ecosystem Approach as a Basis for Managerial Compliance' (n 19) 80–81.

[115] See E Morgera, 'European Environmental Law' in S Alamn et al (eds), *Routledge Handbook of International Environmental Law 428* (New York, Routledge, 2012); Engström (n 49) 198.

[116] Commission, 'Commission Staff Working Document Annex Accompanying the document Commission Report to the Council and the European Parliament. The first phase of implementation of the Marine Strategy Framework Directive (2008/56/EC) – The European Commission's assessment and guidance' SWD(2014) 49 final, 73–74.

Generally speaking, provisions in EU law that establish objectives or targets can entail either obligations of result or obligations of best effort for Member States.[117] The two types of legal obligation differ in the scope of the actions required and the basis for assessment of potential breaches of EU law. In the case of obligations of result, Member States are required to ensure by any means necessary that the focal objectives are achieved. Failure to do so constitutes a breach of EU law, unless a duly granted exemption applies.[118] In the context of the MSFD, an obligation of result would mean that Member States should have achieved GES in their marine waters by 2020, unless they were able to invoke an exemption as provided in Article 14. In turn, obligation of best effort requires that a Member State implements reasonable measures constituting its best efforts towards achieving the focal objectives. Failure to attain an objective does not automatically constitute a breach of EU law even if potential exemptions have not been invoked.[119] Accordingly, with obligations of result, Member States are required to apply exemptions in every case where the Directive's objectives are not met, whereas with obligations of best effort, the Directive may provide for exemptions but does not strictly require they be applied as a justification for failing to achieve a given objective.[120]

It seems that the MSFD's GES obligations are obligations of best effort. While Article 1(1) of the MSFD might be construed as an obligation of result, as it stipulates that Member States are to take necessary measures to achieve or maintain GES, the exemptions in Article 14 are options rather than requirements, in that they may – but need not – be applied where GES is not met. The Commission appears to share this interpretation, as it has not started infringement proceedings against Member States for not meeting the GES objectives, even though many Member States – including the Baltic Sea States – have not applied the Directive's exemptions to their full potential.[121]

An obligation of best effort under the MSFD still requires that Member States take all reasonable measures to achieve the relevant objectives and do not overuse exemptions. For example, Member States need to enhance regional cooperation[122] to achieve the GES objectives and not just claim that actions or inactions of other states provide grounds for an exemption.[123,124] In the Baltic Sea Region, Member

[117] See, on the distinction, J van Kempen, 'Countering the Obscurity of Obligations in European Environmental Law: An Analysis of Article 4 of the European Water Framework Directive' (2012) 24 *Journal of Environmental Law* 499.

[118] ibid, 513–14.

[119] ibid.

[120] ibid.

[121] See Commission, 'Commission Staff Working Document Accompanying the document Report from the Commission to the European Parliament and the Council assessing Member States' programmes of measures under the Marine Strategy Framework Directive' SWD(2018) 393 final.

[122] MSFD, Art 6.

[123] MSFD, Art 14(1)(a).

[124] MSFD, Art 15; Commission, 'Marine Strategy Framework Directive Common (MSFD) Implementation', 11, available at: www.circabc.europa.eu/sd/d/0ee797dd-d92c-4d7c-a9f9-5dffb36d2065/GD10%20-%20MSFD%20recommendations%20on%20measures%20and%20exceptions_25-11-2014.pdf.

States need to initiate and implement actions under the Helsinki Convention to tackle transboundary environmental problems such as eutrophication. However, subject to application of an exemption,[125] Member States will not be held liable for how failures of other states to act affect the state of the marine region.

A relevant question for the implementation of the MSFD is the legal impact of the Directive's objectives in relation to the authorisation and revision of activities and projects affecting the marine environment. In practice, GES cannot be achieved unless it is translated into operative norms and standards for actions combating pressures on the marine environment. The Directive also recognises a possibility to derogate from the GES objectives and environmental targets due to new projects.[126]

An individual project is unlikely to produce adverse environmental effects so massive that it would have an impact on the possibilities for reaching the GES objective of the MSFD. Nevertheless, an obligation of best effort may require measures to minimise these effects, for example through permit conditions. Significantly, the WFD supports the MSFD objectives in coastal waters and sets more concrete legal requirements for different activities. These WFD requirements are discussed next.

iii. Legal Status of the WFD Objectives

The WFD's obligations on preventing deterioration of water status and achieving good ecological and chemical status have increasingly been regarded as constituting obligations of result for Member States, as opposed to obligations of best effort.[127] This means that Member States are required to ensure, by any means necessary, that the objectives are achieved in all water bodies, unless they apply appropriate exemptions.[128] A large number of Member States failed to achieve GES in their coastal water bodies by 2015, most having applied the WFD's exemptions extensively.[129]

The WFD does not prescribe specific, substantive rules on the rights or obligations applicable to individual activities affecting the status of water bodies. However, the Directive requires Member States to enact the necessary implementation mechanisms, including enforceable substantive rules, in their national water laws to achieve the environmental objectives. Moreover, it requires the prior

[125] MSFD, Art 14(1)(a).

[126] MSFD, Art 14(1)(d).

[127] van Kempen (n 117) 524–26.

[128] In turn, obligations of best effort require implementing all reasonable measures towards achieving the Directive's objectives, but the mere fact that the objectives are not reached does not automatically constitute a breach of EU law, for Member States are allowed to include considerations of reasonableness, feasibility and cost-effectiveness in the implementation. See van Kempen (n 117) 513–14.

[129] eg, Finland where good ecological status has not been reached in a most of the coastal water bodies. See Finnish Environment Institute, 'State of surface waters' (2020), available at: www.ymparisto.fi/en-US/Waters/State_of_the_surface_waters.

authorisation or other controls of many activities and the periodical and needs-based review of these controls. All in all, the WFD provides a range of means to control land-based and coastal-based activities affecting the marine environment of the Baltic Sea.

In 2015, the CJEU's *Weser* ruling[130] confirmed that the environmental objectives for surface waters constitute binding substantive rules on the permitting of new water use activities. Unless an exemption applies, Member States cannot grant a permit for projects that would cause deterioration[131] of water status or that would jeopardise the achievement of good ecological status.[132] The judgment has had a profound impact on the implementation of the Directive in the Baltic Sea States.[133]

IV. Measures for Nutrient Reduction

Eutrophication is the major threat to the Baltic Sea and has caused significant changes in its ecosystem; over the last hundred years, the Baltic has changed from an oligotrophic clear-water sea into a eutrophic marine environment.[134] While there has been progress under the Helsinki Convention in decreasing nutrient inputs from point sources, no significant reduction of input from diffuse sources has been observed. Currently, agriculture is the main contributor to the diffuse load of nutrients.[135]

Achieving the GES objectives for eutrophication in the Baltic Sea Region would necessitate tackling diffuse pollution and further reducing inputs from point sources both in marine areas and on land. Efforts to remove nutrient through algae cultivation should also be made, as should measures to reduce the internal nutrient reserves in sediments.[136]

As discussed above, the Baltic Sea regulatory instruments adhere to the ecosystem approach. This is built on a goal-oriented regulatory strategy in which the state of the ecosystem is put at the centre of regulation. With regard to eutrophication, the three focal legal instruments discussed in the chapter set similar ecological objectives that apply in a spectrum of geographical scales.

[130] Case C-461/13 *Bund für Umwelt und Naturschutz Deutschland* ECLI:EU:C:2015:433 (*Weser* ruling).

[131] Deterioration concerns even individual quality elements used in the ecological status assessment. *Weser* ruling (n 130) para 70.

[132] *Weser* ruling (n 130) paras 50–51.

[133] See S Kymenvaara et al, 'Variations on the same theme: Environmental objectives of the Water Framework Directive in environmental permitting in the Nordic countries' (2019) 28 *Review of European, Comparative & International Environmental Law* 197.

[134] HELCOM, 'Baltic Sea Action Plan' (2007) (n 17) 7; HELCOM, 'Baltic Sea Action Plan 2021 Update' (n 3) 20.

[135] HELCOM, 'Baltic Sea Action Plan 2021 Update' (n 3) 20.

[136] ibid, 20 and 22; Ringbom et al, 'Combatting Eutrophication'.

Table 2 Objectives, legal obligations and implementation mechanism on eutrophication in the Baltic Sea environmental governance instruments

Regulatory instrument	Principle objective for eutrophication	Legal obligations	Management objective / targets	Implementation mechanism
Helsinki Convention + BSAP	GES for the Baltic Sea basins; Baltic Sea unaffected by eutrophication	ambiguous legal obligations	minimise inputs of nutrients from human activities; maximum allowable inputs for each basin	state-specific nutrient reduction targets = nutrient input ceilings national implementation programmes + sectoral measures required by the Convention and the BSAP
MSFD	GES for national marine waters; human-induced eutrophication is minimised, especially adverse effects thereof	obligation of best effort	environmental targets set by the MS; can include nutrient input reduction targets	programme of measures; indicative list of measures in Annex VI of the MSFD
WFD	good ecological status of coastal water bodies; quality elements deviate only slightly from unimpacted conditions	obligation of result	–	programme of measures; implementation of EU legislation and all necessary supplementary measures

Goal-oriented regulatory approaches do not dictate specific measures and rules that would attempt to manage a complex system such as the Baltic Sea. Instead, they allow the states to have considerable flexibility to assemble a set of different policy instruments and measures suitable for addressing the main pressures in their respective national context.[137] However, the shift towards ecological goals has replaced neither the validity of nor the need for specific sector-based regulation that controls sectors and individual activities contributing to the eutrophication problem.[138] HELCOM and EU regulation do lay down principles and frameworks for formulating management policies and measures on eutrophication.

[137] See Groothuijse and Uylenburg (n 42); Bohman, 'Transboundary Law' (n 15) 108–09; Ringbom and Joas (n 7) 321–22.

[138] Ringbom and Joas (n 7) 322.

The BSAP translates ecological objectives into more specific targets that constitute maximum allowable inputs of particular nutrients for each Baltic Sea basin as well as nutrient input ceilings for the states in the catchment area.[139] Each state has its own set of targets that forms the basis for implementing nutrient reduction measures.[140] While the reduction targets are not legally binding, they serve to concretise the level of ambition a state must aspire to in taking measures.[141] The BSAP underscores that the reduction targets are based on current scientific knowledge, which is subject to uncertainties and, as such, requires periodic review and revision.[142]

The BSAP does not prescribe in detail how the reduction targets are to be reached by each party, but requires states to develop national programmes of implementation measures to reduce inputs in different sectors.[143] States have discretion to choose how the reduction burden is allocated between sectors and regions. Progress towards the targets is to be evaluated and the programmes adjusted whenever necessary.[144] The BSAP also stipulates specific actions for agriculture, atmospheric nitrogen emissions, the wastewater sector and nutrient recycling.[145] These requirements are primarily imposed through the HELCOM recommendations listed in the BSAP as well as more general policy documents with suggested measures.[146] However, assessments show that the parties to the Convention comply with the BSAP's recommendations very poorly, which undermines the effectiveness of its aim of reducing nutrients entering the Baltic Sea.[147] In practice, the BSAP's national implementation programmes are in the EU Member States combined with the programmes for the implementation of the Marine Directives.[148]

According to the MSFD, Member States must set environmental targets with due regard for pressures stemming from nutrients. These targets form the basis for programmes of measures. The targets may set out either general overall reductions in nutrients or more detailed, sector-specific or region-specific objectives. In the first marine strategies adopted in 2015, only one of the coastal Member States (Finland) established quantified targets for nutrient loads.[149]

Member States also have the freedom to compile programmes of measures for marine strategies from any measures they deem most suitable for reaching the

[139] HELCOM, 'Baltic Sea Action Plan 2021 Update' (n 3) 22–23.
[140] ibid.
[141] Bohman, 'The Ecosystem Approach as a Basis for Managerial Compliance' (n 19) 98.
[142] HELCOM, 'Baltic Sea Action Plan 2021 Update' (n 3) 22.
[143] ibid, 24.
[144] ibid; Bohman, 'Transboundary Law' (n 15) 141.
[145] The adoption of the 2007 BSAP prompted several HELCOM Recommendations with stricter requirements on wastewater treatment, phosphorus in detergents, and further criteria on prevention of pollution from agriculture. See HELCOM Recommendations 28E/4, 28E/5, 28E/6, 28E/7.
[146] Helsinki Convention, Art 20(1); HELCOM, 'Baltic Sea Action Plan 2021 Update' (n 3) 24–25; See also Bohman, 'Lessons from the regulatory approaches' (n 108) 229.
[147] European Court of Auditors, 'Combating eutrophication in the Baltic Sea' (n 20) 19–21.
[148] Bohman, 'Transboundary Law' (n 15) 148.
[149] Commission, SWD(2014) 49 final 'The first phase' (n 116).

environmental targets; Annex VI of the MSFD lists the types of measures that can be included in the programmes, including input controls, economic incentives, mitigation and remediation, but does not require Member States to employ specific measures in response to any given pressure. The MSFD requires the measures to be integrated with the relevant measures required under EU law, most notably the WFD's programmes of measures, wastewater treatment measures under the UWWTD and bathing water management measures under the Bathing Water Directive.[150]

The WFD provides the most detailed framework on the management policies and measures for reducing nutrient inputs. The Directive's objectives are to be reached through compilation and implementation of programmes of measures for water management, including what are designated as mandatory basic measures as well as supplementary measures for addressing the key environmental pressures.[151] Basic measures include implementing other water-related EU legislation, such as the ND, the UWWTD and the IED, as well as a requirement set in the WFD for prior authorisation or registration of all point source discharges and measures to control the inputs of pollutants from discharge sources.[152] Further, the CJEU has ruled that Member States may not grant authorisation for projects that will cause deterioration of water status or jeopardise the achievement of good status.[153] In contrast to the more general frameworks of the BSAP and the MSFD, the WFD sets out specific measures and also substantive rules governing activities that cause pressures on the aquatic environment.

The WFD requires Member States to operationalise a combined approach for point- and diffuse-source pollution. Member States must ensure that the control of point sources is based on best available techniques or emission limit values, and that the control of diffuse impacts employs best environmental practices, which are set out in other EU legislation, such as the ND, the UWWTD and the IED. In turn, in cases where achieving the WFD's objectives necessitates stricter conditions than are prescribed in other EU Directives, the WFD requires Member States to set more stringent emission controls in implementing those Directives.[154]

All in all, the progress in reducing the nutrient inputs from the biggest diffuse-source sector, agriculture, has remained limited under EU law. The WFD requires that diffuse impacts be controlled but does not provide concrete means for doing so. The ND, in turn, requires Member States to designate 'nitrate vulnerable zones' in areas draining into waters that are polluted or at risk of pollution. In these zones, Member States are required to implement nitrate action programmes comprising measures to reduce the nutrient run-off from agricultural land. However, the

[150] MSFD, Art 13(2).
[151] WFD, Art 11(1) and (2).
[152] WFD, Art 11(3) para (g) and (h).
[153] *Weser* ruling (n 130) paras 50–51.
[154] WFD, Art 10.

implementation of the ND lacks effectiveness as the action programmes have thus far contained only few mandatory measures for farmers.[155]

In the agricultural sector, the national state aid schemes and the EU CAP constitute the main policy instruments influencing agricultural practices. Even with the increasing legal weight of the WFD's objectives, these schemes make few references to the WFD and do not sufficiently address the salient environmental concerns, such as nutrient run-off and eutrophication, in their payments to producers.[156]

V. Conclusions

This chapter has analysed how the legal regimes of the Helsinki Convention and the EU Marine Directives (MSFD and WFD) interact in seeking to achieve and maintain GES for the Baltic Sea marine environment. Drawing on this analysis, the chapter then sought to identify concrete mechanisms by which regimes could support each other in pursuing the GES objective. Of particular interest is the prospect of successfully tackling the problem of eutrophication.

The Helsinki Convention provides an overview on and regulates the entire Baltic Sea ecosystem. Its regime brings together all Baltic Sea riparian states – EU Member States and Russia – in a joint effort to manage and conserve the marine environment. In addition to creating a platform for international cooperation, the Convention provides concrete support for the implementation of the EU Marine Directives. The Convention regime produces assessments and sets ecological objectives for the Baltic Sea ecosystem that can be readily applied in the implementation of the Directives at the EU and Member State levels. Moreover, the BSAP's nutrient reduction targets form an important basis for nutrient load reduction in the implementation of the Marine Directives.

In turn, the Marine Directives add value to the regional environmental governance of the Baltic Sea. They do so in three ways. First, the Directives create – in addition to the overall scale of the Helsinki Convention regime – two legal scales for ecosystem management towards good status in the Baltic Sea.[157] The Helsinki Convention and BSAP are based on joint commitments of the parties and only operate at the transboundary scale. The MSFD stipulates obligations for Member States regarding GES for their national marine waters. It provides a concrete view of the level of ambition for each state and a legal standard for assessing and implementing national legislative, administrative and other types of measures.

[155] European Court of Auditors, 'Combating eutrophication in the Baltic Sea' (n 20) 32–34.

[156] European Court of Auditors, 'Opinion No 7/2018 (pursuant to Article 322(1)(a) TFEU) concerning Commission proposals for regulations relating to the common agricultural policy for the post-2020 period (COM(2018) 392, 393 and 394 final)' [2019] OJ C 41/1.

[157] See also Langlet (n 46) 284.

To be effective, law needs large-scale objectives but also a narrow enough spatial scale if, for example, it is to control problems, such as nutrient loads, from individual activities. If the impacts of individual activities were only assessed at the level of the Baltic Sea (Helsinki Convention) or national marine areas (MSFD), they would appear marginal. In comparison, the WFD's GES objective for each coastal water body is a far more concrete basis for legal obligations designed to prevent and minimise different impacts.[158] As can be seen from the CJEU's *Weser* ruling, water body-specific objectives make it possible to assess the impacts of activities at a local and environmentally relevant scale. In this light, the WFD's scale can provide concrete rules deriving from the objectives, thus supporting the goals of general frameworks and sectoral policies established by the Convention and the MSFD.

In a second enhancement that EU law brings to the regional governance of the Baltic Sea, the Marine Directives lay down more specific, clear and enforceable legal obligations for states with regard to the marine environment than do the Helsinki Convention and the BSAP. The Marine Directives can be seen to translate the Convention's general objectives into legally binding and enforceable obligations on Member States, ie, to increase the normative authority of the rules and bring more rigorous implementation and enforcement tools.[159] This, in turn, supports efforts to achieve GES throughout the Baltic Sea.[160] Moreover, since the EU Member States are required under the MSFD to cooperate through regional sea conventions, the Marine Directives' obligations regarding GES may well prompt higher degrees of compliance and ambition among the states in HELCOM work.[161] In practice, the EU's participation in the regional sea conventions has prompted significant legal development and implementation of those conventions.[162]

As regards eutrophication, the MSFD and the WFD create strong incentives for the EU Member States to implement nutrient input reductions in their national policies that extend to individual activities.[163] Here the regimes create a scale of binding effects in the objectives: while the Helsinki Convention and the BSAP put forward merely general principles, the MSFD stipulates clear obligations for Member States to achieve the objectives set for their marine waters. However, these are obligations of best effort, which allow Member States more latitude in level of ambition and compliance, contrasting sharply with the obligations imposed by the WFD, which are obligations of result.

[158] De Sousa Santos (n 43) 287–89.

[159] See also Engström (n 49) 198; Bohman, 'Lessons from the regulatory approaches' (n 108) 230–31; Ringbom and Joas (n 7) 320.

[160] See also Giannopoulus (n 69) 12.

[161] The MSFD explicitly states that it aims to enhance the coherence of the contribution of the EU and its Member States under international agreements. See: MSFD Preamble, para (16).

[162] Giannopoulus (n 69) 11–12.

[163] Bohman, 'Transboundary Law' (n 15) 148–49.

Third, the Marine Directives, together with the sectoral EU legislation, put forward a more concrete framework for formulating and implementing measures to tackle pressures such as nutrient inputs. In particular, the WFD makes explicit references to sectoral legislation regulating activities causing nutrient pollution, and demonstrates clearly how water management objectives impact the implementation of the legislation. For instance, all EU Member States on the Baltic Sea coast rely on the programme of measures under the WFD as their main planning instrument to achieve the HELCOM nutrient reduction targets.[164] Here it merits mention that the actions specified in the BSAP regarding agriculture and other sources of nutrient emissions, as well as the HELCOM recommendations issued pursuant to implementing the BSAP, in many ways complement and support the EU legislation.[165]

On balance, the interplay between the Helsinki Convention regime and the EU Marine Directives is not strictly hierarchical, with superior international norms dictating the content and implementation of EU legislation. Rather, the regimes interact in multiple ways, constituting an integrated, pluralistic legal structure capable of capturing the different scales and dynamics of ecosystem components as well as legal systems. The added value of this legal pluralism is best realised when Member States integrate the three instruments seamlessly in protecting their waters.

In general, the EU has provided a fresh impetus and concrete legal measures for the protection of the Baltic Sea marine environment. The Marine Directives complement long-term international cooperation under the Helsinki Convention by providing national and water body-specific scales for the GES objectives and measures needed to achieve them. The EU has made a positive contribution to the protection of the Baltic Sea, but many challenges remain – such as eutrophication – and require more concrete legal responses.

[164] European Court of Auditors, 'Combating eutrophication in the Baltic Sea' (n 20) 17.
[165] See also Engström (n 49) 193.

11

The EU and Baltic Shipping: With a Particular Focus on Greenhouse Gas Reductions

HENRIK RINGBOM

I. Introduction

The title of this chapter implies a double regional perspective in a matter which is mainly governed by global, rather than regional rules. Both the European Union's (EU) and the Baltic Sea Region's (BSR) shipping regulations are closely based on – and intertwined with – existing global rules and standards, as developed and adopted by the International Maritime Organization (IMO). The overwhelming majority of requirements that apply to shipping in the Baltic Sea are thus global in origin and scope, albeit that some regional particularities have occasionally been accepted in the global rules. In addition, there is considerable – and increasing – interaction between the rules of two regional regulatory bodies discussed here.

The purpose of the chapter is to highlight the interaction and complexities involved in multiple layers of rule-making for the same matter. Following a brief 'layer-by-layer' overview of the respective roles of the three main regulatory layers in section II (global), section III (BSR) and section IV (EU), a more detailed review of the regulation of greenhouse gases from ships is made in section V. This field represents one of the key regulatory challenges for shipping for the moment and one on which the policy is still being formed, at global as well as EU level. Some concluding thoughts on the role of the EU in shaping maritime regulation in the Baltic Sea are offered in section VI. The substantive scope of the chapter is limited to rules aimed at environmental protection or promoting maritime safety.

II. Global Shipping Rules

There are two kinds of global rules that are relevant to the subject matter. First, the jurisdictional rules on what actions states can and cannot take to protect the marine environment from ships are set out in considerable detail in the 1982

UN Convention on the Law of the Sea (UNCLOS). These rules lay down the general framework for what rules and measures both the EU and the Baltic Sea States may and may not adopt to address foreign ships. UNCLOS, frequently referred to as the 'Constitution for the Oceans', is today widely ratified worldwide and, as far as its provisions on vessel-source jurisdiction are concerned, generally considered to represent customary international law.[1]

The rights and duties in this regard are differentiated separately for each maritime zone and depending on whether the state acts in the capacity as a flag state, coastal state or port state. Very briefly put, the law of the sea places important constraints on the extent to which a coastal state may regulate foreign ships that only pass through their waters, but includes many fewer limitations with respect to ships entering their ports or internal waters.[2] The position of a regional body, be it the EU or a traditional intergovernmental organisation like HELCOM,[3] is essentially the same; no additional jurisdictional rights are granted to such organisations.[4] However, there are other advantages with regional rule-making in this field. If more states collaborate in implementing the requirements, for example, in the form of common port access conditions, there is a higher chance that passing ships will be covered by the rule, too, as they will normally be heading for some port in the region. This is particularly the case in the Baltic Sea, where there is, for geographical reasons, no through traffic. On the other hand, the fact that the Russian Federation is not a member of the EU means that there are always limits on how effective port state-based requirements at EU level will be in the BSR.

The second category of global rules is the technical rules that lay down the more detailed standards for ships and their operators, on a variety of matters that affect safety and environmental performance, such as ships' equipment and construction requirements and conditions for discharging substances into the sea. These technical rules are predominantly developed by the IMO and form a dynamic relationship with the rules of UNCLOS through a complex web of references and cross-references.[5] The main conventions of relevance include the International

[1] By September 2021, UNCLOS had 168 contracting parties, including the European Union.

[2] For a fuller review, see eg, EJ Molenaar, *Coastal State Jurisdiction over Vessel-Source Pollution* (The Hague, Kluwer Law International, 1998).

[3] HELCOM is the common abbreviation for the Helsinki Commission for the Protection of the Marine Environment of the Baltic Sea, established by the 1974/1992 Helsinki Convention the Protection of the Marine Environment of the Baltic Sea (Helsinki Convention).

[4] The regime applying to international organisations that are parties to UNCLOS, such as the EU, is detailed in Annex IX to the Convention. For sea areas like the Baltic Sea, Part IX of UNCLOS, entitled 'Enclosed and semi-enclosed seas' was of significant interest during the negotiation of UNCLOS, but in the end, no special jurisdictional arrangements were accepted for such sea areas.

[5] See, eg, W van Reenen 'Rules of Reference in the New Convention on the Law of the Sea, in Particular in Connection with the Pollution of the Sea by Oil from Tankers' (1981) 12 *Netherlands Yearbook of International Law* 3; International Law Association London Conference (2000), 'Committee on Coastal State Jurisdiction Relating to Marine Pollution' (Final Report, 2000) 443–500, available at: ila.vettoreweb.com/Storage/Download.aspx?DbStorageId=1075&StorageFileGuid=ef7face7-57f7-462c-b4c2-8b48d9bd6380; LN Nguyen, 'Expanding the Environmental Regulatory Scope of UNCLOS Through the Rule of Reference: Potentials and Limits' (2021) 52 *Ocean Development & International Law* 419.

Convention on the Safety of Life at Sea and the International Convention on the Prevention of Pollution from Ships (MARPOL). The key IMO rules are generally widely ratified worldwide[6] and moreover include innovative mechanisms to ensure that their standards apply to the entire global commercial fleet, irrespective of whether they have or not been formally approval by flag states.[7]

The general regulatory situation for maritime safety and ship-source pollution is, in other words, both relatively clear and settled. As a rule, there is little uncertainty about what standards apply for which ships or where to look for the limits of applicability of national requirements to foreign ships, in the BSR or beyond. In terms of substantive content, it is probably fair to conclude that most aspects of maritime safety and environmental protection matters are already covered by existing IMO rules. Clearly, there are still some gaps to be filled,[8] but the key issues are being covered by (reasonably stringent) rules at global level that apply to all ships, following decades of active regulatory work by the IMO. The main exception to this generally satisfactory regulatory picture is the regulation of greenhouse gases from ships, which has so far resulted in rather limited requirements at IMO level. This matter is discussed in section V below.

III. The Regulatory Tradition in the Baltic Sea

The Baltic Sea environment is heavily impacted by shipping.[9] One feature that distinguished the original 1974 Helsinki Convention from other (subsequent)

[6] The precise number of parties to MARPOL Annexes and the percentage of the world fleet that these states represent were as follows by the end of 2021: Annexes I (oil) and II (noxious liquid substances in bulk), 160 states representing 99% of the world's tonnage; Annex III (harmful substances in packaged form), 150 states, 98%; Annex IV (sewage), 146 states, 96%, Annex V (garbage), 155 states, 99%; and Annex VI (air pollution), 101 states, 97%. Two more key environmental IMO conventions adopted in early 2000 have the corresponding figures: IMO, 'International Convention on the Control of Harmful Anti-fouling Systems on Ships, 2001' (AFS/CONF/26, IMO 18 October 2001), available at: www.schonescheepvaart.nl/downloads/regelgeving/doc_1362145555.pdf, with 91 states, representing 96% of the world tonnage; and IMO, 'International Convention for the Control and Management of Ships' Ballast Water and Sediments, 2004' (BWM/CONF/36, IMO, 16 February 2004), available at: www.fdfa.be/sites/default/files/atoms/files/1125_Ondertekende%20akte%20in%20het%20Engels.pdf, with 88 states, representing 91% of the tonnage.

[7] eg, by implicitly relying on port state jurisdiction, many key IMO conventions establish that there shall be no difference in treatment between ships flying the flag of parties and non-parties to the conventions when visiting ports of states parties. See, eg, MARPOL, Art 5(4). Moreover, in order to ensure a broad participation in the numerous amendments to the conventions, a specific amendment procedure has been introduced to many conventions, which makes the amendments automatically binding on all parties unless they specifically object to them (the so-called 'tacit acceptance'-procedure). See eg, MARPOL, Art 16.

[8] eg, with respect to ships' noise, given that shipping is the largest anthropogenic source of low-frequency sound, creating a variety of forms of disturbance for marine life. See eg, GESAMP, 'Pollution in the Open Oceans 2009–2013 – A Report by a GESAMP Task Team, Reports and Studies 91' (IMO FAO UNESCO-IOC WMO UNIDO IAEA UN UNEP UNDP, 2015), available at: wedocs.unep.org/bitstream/handle/20.500.11822/32907/POO.pdf?sequence=1&isAllowed=y; and (n 90) below.

[9] See, eg, helcom.fi/action-areas/shipping/; and J-P Jalkanen et al, 'Modelling of discharges from Baltic Sea shipping' (2021) 17 *Ocean Science* 699.

regional seas conventions is the attention given to shipping and ship-source pollution.[10] However, the quite detailed provisions of the Convention's Annex IV (dealing with prevention of pollution from ships) were in reality mainly reproducing the (special area) provisions of MARPOL's Annexes, which at the time were not in force and hence not generally applicable. Once the MARPOL annexes entered into force, the Convention was progressively amended to include mere references to the global rules (Annex IV, Regulation 4). The new 1992 Helsinki Convention accordingly included detailed provisions only for Marpol Annex IV on sewage, which had not entered into force at that time.

Despite this overall preference given to global (IMO) rules, the Helsinki Convention does include certain specific rules addressing ship-source pollution. For example, Article 8(2) requires the parties to develop and apply uniform requirements for the reception of ship-generated waste and Article 9 calls for special measures relating to pleasure craft.

Additional requirements on ship-source pollution are found in Annex IV to the Helsinki Convention, which under Article 28 represent an integral part of the Convention and are hence binding on the states parties. The Annex includes, inter alia: a prohibition of incineration of ship-generated waste (Regulation 7); an AIS-based traffic monitoring system (Regulation 9); requirements on port state control (Regulation 10); marine casualty investigations (Regulation 11); and places of refuge for ships in distress (Regulation 12). The majority of these requirements have a basis in either IMO requirements or EU legislation, but that was not always the case at the time of their adoption. Some of the Helsinki Convention's requirements still include independent elements, for example, in relation to the details of the application of mandatory waste delivery at ports in the BSR.[11]

Apart from this 'hard law' legal framework, some 80 recommendations have been adopted for preventing pollution from ships, roughly half of which are currently valid.[12] Generally, the HELCOM recommendations are uncontroversial

[10] The original Helsinki Convention from 1974 included an annex with detailed rules on ship source pollution. These rules were by and large identical to the MARPOL rules, having the effect to bring the latter in force earlier among the Baltic Sea states. Once the MARPOL Annexes entered into force globally, the rules of Annex IV were gradually amended to mere MARPOL references. Treaties for other regional sea areas usually emphasise other sources of marine pollution, but in some cases subsequent protocols have been adopted to address particular shipping-related matters of concern. See, eg, the UNEPMAP, '2002 Malta Protocol Concerning Cooperation in Preventing Pollution from Ships and, in Cases of Emergency, Combating Pollution of the Mediterranean Sea' (2002), available at: wedocs.unep.org/rest/bitstreams/2190/retrieve; and UNEPMAP, 'Convention for the Protection of the Marine Environment and the Coastal Region of the Mediterranean' (Barcelona, 10 June 1995), available at: wedocs.unep.org/bitstream/handle/20.500.11822/7096/BarcelonaConvention_Consolidated_eng.pdf.

[11] See, eg, HELCOM, 'Annex IV Prevention of Pollution from Ships Reg 6: Mandatory Discharge of all Waste to a Port Reception Facility', available at: helcom.fi/about-us/convention/annexes-to-the-convention-2/annex-iv/.

[12] HELCOM website, 'HELCOM at work, Recommendations', available at: www.helcom.fi/helcom-at-work/recommendations.

from an international law point of view. Apart from their limited legal status, they normally do not challenge existing global rules in substantive terms either. Typically, the recommendations confirm the international standards and specify elements relating to their *implementation* within the BSR in greater detail.

Shipping also features prominently in the Baltic Sea Action Plan (BSAP, adopted in 2007 and last updated in October 2021), which is the main document guiding the policy actions of HELCOM.[13] The principal objective of the actions relating to shipping is that maritime activities are 'carried out in an environmentally friendly way'. More detailed management objectives are listed to achieve this, prioritising illegal discharges and accidental pollution. Among the actions listed to address pollution from ships, the majority relate to implementing existing IMO (but not EU) policies in shipping, the focus being on undertaking studies on selected issues of relevance to the BSR, to developing roadmaps for future policies in the fields.

In summary, the approach adopted by the BSR has focused on collaboration and has not sought to pre-empt international negotiations. That said, the Baltic Sea States have sometimes agreed to coordinate their position to make their collective voice heard at the IMO.[14] Apart from the occasional academic complaint,[15] it seems that this rather cautious policy approach by the Baltic Sea States with respect to international shipping has been widely endorsed.

IV. The EU: The Bull in the China Shop?

The EU's involvement in matters relating to maritime safety and ship-source pollution began in the early 1990s and has continuously expanded since. Today, EU legislation in the field comprises some 40 directives and regulations, around half of which have an explicit environmental purpose.

In view of the policy risks involved with imposing additional requirements on EU flagged ships alone, such as flagging out, the EU rules generally apply to all ships, irrespective of their flag. Jurisdiction-wise this can be done by limiting the applicability of the requirements to ships that voluntarily enter EU ports. When 27 states act in concert, however, the effects of such regional requirements are significant. Most ships in the region will be heading for some port in the EU, but even for ships trading elsewhere, it is normally significant to be capable of making a voyage to an EU port, should the need for it arise. At least insofar as the requirements concern static conditions, such as equipment or construction requirements, unilateral EU requirements will therefore – despite their regional origin and scope – in reality have worldwide implications.

[13] See: helcom.fi/media/publications/BSAP-full-publication-v21-220405.pdf.

[14] For a series of successful examples, see H Backer, 'Regional work on prevention of pollution from ships in the Baltic Sea – A paradox or a global forerunner?' (2018) 98 *Marine Policy* 255.

[15] See, eg, H Ringbom, 'Why are we so timid on ship-source pollution?' (Expert Article 2880, Baltic Rim Economies 2021), available at: sites.utu.fi/bre/why-are-we-so-timid-on-ship-source-pollution/.

In substantive terms, however, the EU shipping rules are normally quite closely related to the IMO standards. Essentially, the 40 or so directives and regulations referred to above even duplicate IMO rules. Merely copying IMO rules into EU legislation is not as pointless as it may sound, for many reasons. First, EU rules ensure that all Member States are bound by the same rules, irrespective of their formal participation in the international convention in question. Second, it follows from the constitutional nature of EU law that the EU rules thus adopted will take hierarchical precedence over any conflicting national law. An EU rule that copies the material standards IMO rules ensures that the said international rules have direct applicability or effect in the entire EU and that Member States cannot set aside their implementation by referring to conflicting national rules. Third, by bringing the rules into the realm of EU law, the legal machinery of the EU can be invoked against Member States that fail to implement the standards. This includes the European Commission's role as a regulatory watchdog and potential court proceedings against non-complying Member States, which may result in the imposition of monetary penalties in cases of continuous infringement.[16] Fourth, as EU law – in contrast to public international law – in many cases applies directly to individuals, it is often used to translate the international obligations of states into obligations of the individual concerned, be it classification societies, port authorities, ship operators or masters. In this way, the rules often tend to get another type of dynamism when imposed at EU level. Finally, the adoption of rules at EU level affects the EU's external competence over the subject in question, on the basis of the so-called AETR principle.[17]

Yet, even if the majority of EU rules on ship-source pollution implement international rules, they often include some elements that go beyond the IMO requirements, providing for a regional 'added value'. The flag state approach to regulation has generally been avoided by the EU, not to place its Member States' fleet in a disadvantageous position in relation to other ships.[18] Instead, mainly through the exercise of port state jurisdiction, the EU requirements have covered all ships and have tended to gain gradual independence from the international rules over time.[19]

In the beginning, starting from the late 1990s, the differences were smaller. The EU, for example, sought to implement international rules that were not yet in force

[16] Consolidated version of the Treaty on the Functioning of the European Union [2012] OJ C326/47, Arts 258, 269.

[17] Case 22/70 *AETR* [1971] ECR 263. See also the contributions by Viljam Engström (ch 7) and Mirka Kuisma (ch 6) in this volume.

[18] Measures adopted from the perspective of the flag state refer to EU legislation that only covers ships flying the flag of EU Member States or standards for EU flag state administrations. A port state perspective signifies that the target of regulation is ships of all flags to the extent they call at ports of EU Member States, while coastal state measures cover ships of all flags which transit the coastal waters of Member States without calling at an EU port.

[19] For a more detailed review, see H Ringbom, *The EU Maritime Safety Policy and International Law* (Leiden, Martinus Nijhoff Publishers, 2008).

internationally (like the early application of the international safety management code for passenger ships)[20] or international rules that had been adopted in the form of recommendations only (such as the standards for loading and unloading of bulk carriers) on ships visiting its ports.[21] Gradually, independence increased and EU requirements relating to issues that had not been specifically agreed by the IMO (like certain equipment requirements for cargo ships)[22] or that even caused tensions with the international rules (double hull oil tanker construction requirements of 2003).[23]

A similar development is noted with respect to the enforcement of the rules. Whereas non-compliance with the early rules normally resulted in the detention of the ship in the port (through port state control)[24] or other types of pre-departure obligations (eg, the prohibition to leave the port if the ship has not delivered its waste in accordance with EU requirements),[25] the measures were subsequently expanded. Measures now include conditions for accessing EU ports or even the complete banning of individual ships from all ports in the region – temporarily, or even on a permanent basis.[26] Expulsion from EU ports forms an integral enforcement mechanism in the most recent EU proposals in the field of greenhouse gases.[27] With respect to pollution, there is also a directive specifically calling for criminal sanctions to be imposed on parties found to have contributed to MARPOL violations intentionally or by serious negligence.[28]

Since around 2005, the EU has generally adopted a less confrontational stance in relation to global shipping rules. However, as the ongoing discussions on the EU's role in the regulation of greenhouse gas (GHG) emissions from ships demonstrate, the tension between regional and global rules has not gone away and the EU has not given up its preparedness to make use of its territorial jurisdiction to adopt regional measures in matters of global scope (see section V below).

[20] Regulation (EC) No 3051/95 on the safety management of roll-on/roll-off passenger ferries (ro-ro ferries) [1995] OJ L320/14.

[21] Directive 2001/96/EC establishing harmonised requirements and procedures for the safe loading and unloading of bulk carriers [2002] OJ L13/9.

[22] Directive 2002/59/EC establishing a Community vessel traffic monitoring and information system and repealing Council Directive 93/75/EEC [2002] OJ L208/10, notably as regards the scope of its Art 10 on voyage data recorder systems.

[23] Regulation (EC) No 417/2002 on the accelerated phasing-in of double hull or equivalent design requirements for single hull oil tankers and repealing Council Regulation (EC) No 2978/94 [2002] OJ L64/1, including subsequent amendments.

[24] Directive 95/21/EC concerning the enforcement, in respect of shipping using Community ports and sailing in the waters under the jurisdiction of the Member States, of international standards for ship safety, pollution prevention and shipboard living and working conditions (port State control) [1995] OJ L157/1.

[25] Directive 2000/59/EC on port reception facilities for ship-generated waste and cargo residues [2000] OJ L332/81.

[26] Directive 2009/16/EC on port State control (Recast) [2009] OJ L131/57, Art 16.

[27] See, eg, Regulation (EU) 2015/757 on the monitoring, reporting and verification of carbon dioxide emissions from maritime transport, and amending Directive 2009/16/EC [2015] OJ L123/55 and the 'Fit for 55' – proposals discussed in section V.C below.

[28] Directive 2005/35/EC on ship-source pollution and on the introduction of penalties for infringements [2005] OJ L255/11.

Merely reviewing EU rules on shipping fails to give a full picture of the role of the Union in the maritime regulatory framework. On the one hand, its impact in initiating new global rules at the IMO has been very significant. A considerable share of the past decade's new global environmental standards for shipping (including oil tanker construction, fuel quality requirements and liability and compensation rules) have emanated from the EU, or have been adopted as a response to ongoing discussions on unilateral European regulation. On the other hand, and less controversially, the EU has played an important role in coordinating Member State policy positions at the IMO to ensure a successful adoption of the global rules that it prefers. Confronted with the prospect of regional rules, the international maritime community is faced with the dilemma that unless the IMO agrees to certain rules, those same rules might nevertheless be implemented on a port state basis at national or regional level, which in turn would undermine the IMO's authority and its claim to be the sole maritime regulator.

A more recent development is the 'agencification' of the EU in this particular field, through the establishment and growth of the European Maritime Safety Agency (EMSA). The number of EU officials dealing with maritime safety and environmental matters have grown more than tenfold in two decades due to the creation and growth of EMSA.[29] Interestingly, the increased resources and expertise that this process has entailed appears to have reduced the EU's appetite for challenging IMO rules. Rather, EMSA has placed emphasis on collecting and managing information on ships and maritime traffic in Europe and related operational tasks, which in itself makes it well placed to collaborate with other regional and global organisations when the need arises. EMSA has also made an impact in monitoring oil pollution through satellites and through the inter-agency collaboration maintaining 'coast guard functions' in selected sea areas, notably the Mediterranean Sea. More recently, EMSA's elaborate data system on port state control, THETIS, has been extended for implementation of the sulphur in fuel requirements and monitoring and verification of GHG emissions under Regulation (EU) 2015/757 on the monitoring, reporting and verification of carbon dioxide emissions from maritime transport (MRV Regulation),[30] while EMSA-funded remotely piloted aircraft systems have been developed, inter alia, for maritime emissions monitoring.[31]

The hypothesis that the EU in pursuing its maritime safety policy consciously flouts international law finds very little support in the brief review undertaken above. The opposite seems like a more correct contention, ie, that international law considerations closely underlie the EU's policy in this field and that both the substance of the rules and the methods chosen for their regulation are normally based on careful consideration of what can and what cannot be done within the

[29] For details, see P Langlais, *Sécurité maritime et integration européenne* (Brussels, Bruylant, 2018).
[30] See above (n 27).
[31] See, eg: www.emsa.europa.eu/rpas-operations.html.

jurisdictional limits of international law. While question marks might well be raised as to whether the EU has always landed on the right side of the borderline between legality and illegality,[32] it is nevertheless submitted that no piece of EU maritime legislation represents a clear and direct violation of international law of a kind to justify the suspicion that disregard of international law forms part of the EU's maritime safety policy.

V. Interaction between Multiple Regulatory Levels: The Case of GHG Emissions

A. General

One of the key contemporary regulatory challenges for the IMO relates to climate change and the reduction of GHG emissions from ships. This matter is the main environmental issue currently on the IMO's agenda and presents an unusually complex mix of regulatory, policy and technical challenges. It also aptly illustrates the dynamism between UNCLOS, the IMO and general international law, as well as the various pressures that underlie the work of the IMO, including pressure from the EU.

Shipping contributes, mainly through burning fossil fuels, to some 2–3 per cent of anthropogenic emissions and the share is widely expected to grow, due to predicted growth in world trade.[33] Therefore, even dramatic improvements of fuel efficiency in individual ships would not achieve overall reductions in the sector as a whole. Indeed, total emissions have been projected to rise by 50 per cent to 250 per cent of 2012 levels by 2050.[34] The dominant role of the increase in world trade in the projected increase of emissions raises two issues. First, is it fair to demand that shipping reduce its total emissions when the cause of the

[32] The question was brought to the Court of Justice of the European Union (CJEU) in the *Intertanko* case in 2010 (Case C-308/06) [2008] ECR I-04057, ECLI:EU:C:2008:312, but the Court did not conclude on the substantive question. More generally on the legal relationship between EU's shipping policy and international law, see eg, V Frank, *The European Community and Marine Environmental Protection in the International Law of the Sea* (Leiden, Martinus Nijhoff Publishers, 2007); Ringbom, *The EU Maritime Safety Policy and International Law* (n 19); I Christodoulou-Varotsi, *Maritime Safety Law and Policies of the European Union and the United States of America: Antagonism or Synergy?* (Heidelberg, Springer, 2009); and L Tsaroucha and J Terling, 'EU Maritime Safety Rules: Raising the Bar within Europe and Beyond' in J Nawrot and Z Peplowska-Dabrowska (eds), *Maritime Safety in Europe: A Comparative Perspective* (London, Informa Law from Routledge, 2021).

[33] IMO, 'Reduction of GHG Emissions from Ships Fourth IMO GHG Study 2020 – Final report Note by the Secretariat' (MEPC 75/7/15, 29 July 2020), available at: imoarcticsummit.org/wp-content/uploads/2020/09/MEPC-75-7-15-Fourth-IMO-GHG-Study-2020-Final-report-Secretariat.pdf.

[34] ibid. See also IMO, 'Reduction of GHG Emissions from Ships Third IMO GHG Study 2020 – Final report Note by the Secretariat' (MEPC 67/INF.3, 25 July 2014), available at: www.verifavia-shipping.com/bases/resource_pdf/17/MEPC-67-6-INF3-2014-Final-Report-complete.pdf; and the somewhat moderated predictions made in Fourth IMO study referred to in n 33 above.

increase lies in factors beyond shipping? While ship-based reduction targets may be easier to justify, it is more difficult to establish a 'fair share' of the total emissions reduction by the sector as a whole, as the growth in trade is neither known nor controllable by the industry itself. Second, how is the balance to be struck between technical feasibility and promotion of innovation? On the one hand, it appears widely accepted that technological solutions and fuels that are currently in use will not be able to achieve reductions of the magnitude required,[35] which make very ambitious reduction requirements seem unrealistic. On the other hand, it is equally well understood that stringent forward-looking requirements with a clear goal are needed to foster technological change and promote investments and research and development into new technologies, in this case notably regarding alternative fuels for ships.

B. The Global Level

i. General

For the moment, it seems well accepted that the global institution in charge of regulating GHG emissions from shipping is the IMO. The significant increase in the pace of activities since 2015 has further cemented the IMO's position in this respect. It is important to bear in mind, however, that the IMO does not have a regulatory monopoly on the subject and that maritime transport could be included within the scope of the more general climate regime, under the UN Framework Convention on Climate Change (UNFCCC), without any change of the latter's instruments or mandate.[36]

Climate change is by no means new to the IMO which, along with the International Civil Aviation Organization (ICAO), had already been given a particular responsibility to regulate the matter in the 1997 Kyoto Protocol.[37] Yet, despite decades of work aimed at reducing GHG emissions from ships, the IMO's progress is so far modest in terms of emission reduction requirements. Work on this subject has been hampered by uncharacteristically difficult political divisions among the IMO's membership, but also by pressures from other regulatory

[35] See, eg, the presentations, available at: www.imo.org/en/About/Events/Pages/Symposium-alternative-low-carbon-and-zero-carbon-fuels.aspx.

[36] UNFCCC refers to contributions by 'all economic sectors', and even includes certain references to transport in some of the key provisions (Arts 3 and 4(1)(c)). In Art 2(2) of the 1997 Kyoto Protocol to the UNFCCC matters relating to bunker fuel from shipping and aviation was specifically left for the IMO and the International Civil Aviation Organization (ICAO) to regulate, but such a provision no longer features in the 2015 Paris Agreement. See also, B Martinez Romera, 'The Paris Agreement and the regulation of international bunker fuels' (2016) 25 *Review of European Community & International Environmental Law* 215, 221; and A O'Leary and J Brown, 'Legal bases for IMO Climate Change Measures' (Report by Environmental Defense Fund, Columbia Law School, 2018), available at: columbiaclimatelaw.com/files/2018/06/OLeary-and-Brown-2018-06-IMO-Climate-Measures.pdf.

[37] Art 2(2) of the Kyoto Protocol called for states to 'pursue limitation or reduction of emissions of greenhouse gases … from … marine bunker fuels, working through … the International Maritime Organization'.

authorities at global and regional level, as well as other non-governmental stakeholders. While it is still far too early to claim success, several recent developments in this field indicate a shift towards a better regulatory environment, allowing the IMO to focus on meeting the aims of its 'Initial Strategy' adopted in 2018.[38]

Broadly speaking, the discussions at the IMO to date have centred on three types of measures to reduce GHG emissions from ships: technical measures (ship design and equipment); operational measures; and market-based measures. In view of the difficulty in agreeing on market-based measures, the discussions have mainly focused on the first two categories to date. To support these tools, a global data collection system for maritime transport was adopted in 2016 to address the absence of reliable ship emissions data and to facilitate the development of further regulatory measures.[39]

ii. Technical and Operational Measures

The first regulatory progress was achieved in 2011, when new design requirements for the energy efficiency of new ships were introduced as Chapter 4 to MARPOL Annex VI, which entered into force on 1 January 2013.[40] These rules make mandatory the 'Energy Efficiency Design Index' (EEDI) for new ships. The index is based

[38] Following the adoption of the Paris Agreement in 2015, the IMO adopted a 'Roadmap for developing a comprehensive IMO strategy on reduction of GHG emissions from ships' (MEPC 70/18/Add.1, Annex 11, 2016, available at: www.mardep.gov.hk/en/msnote/pdf/msin1707anx3.pdf). In line with the Roadmap, IMO, 'Resolution MEPC.304(72) Initial IMO Strategy on Reduction of GHG Emissions from Ships' (MEPC 72/17/Add.1 Annex 11, adopted on 13 April 2018, available at: wwwcdn.imo.org/localresources/en/KnowledgeCentre/IndexofIMOResolutions/MEPCDocuments/MEPC.304(72).pdf) for dealing with the matter was agreed to be replaced with a comprehensive strategy in 2023. The Initial Strategy envisages a reduction in carbon intensity of international shipping (to reduce CO_2 emissions per transport work, as an average across international shipping, by at least 40% by 2030, pursuing efforts towards 70% by 2050, compared with 2008), and that total annual GHG emissions from international shipping should be reduced by at least 50% by 2050 compared with 2008. It includes a list of possible short-term, mid-term and long-term further measures for the purpose, with timelines, to be revised as appropriate as additional information becomes available.

[39] Starting from 2020, IMO's data collection system requires all ships above 5,000 gross tonnage to collect consumption data for each type of fuel oil they use, as well as other, additional, specified data including proxies for transport work. The data is reported by owners to the flag State on a yearly basis. See IMO, Resolution MEPC.278(70) introducing a new Reg 22A to Marpol Annex VI, including two new appendices. See also IMO, 'Amendments to the Annex of the Protocol of 1997 to Amend the International Convention for the Prevention of Pollution from Ships, 1973, as Modified by the Protocol of 1978 Relating Thereto' (MEPC 293(71), adopted on 28 October 2016), available at: wwwcdn.imo.org/localresources/en/KnowledgeCentre/IndexofIMOResolutions/MEPCDocuments/MEPC.278(70).pdf, containing the 2017 Guidelines for the development and management of the IMO Ship Fuel Oil Consumption Database; and IMO, '2017 Guidelines for Administration verification of ship fuel oil consumption data' (MEPC.292(71), adopted on 7 July 2017), available at: wwwcdn.imo.org/localresources/en/KnowledgeCentre/IndexofIMOResolutions/MEPCDocuments/MEPC.292(71).pdf, including guidance for shipowners. See also: www.imo.org/en/MediaCentre/PressBriefings/Pages/04MARPOLamendments.aspx.

[40] IMO, 'Amendments to the Annex of the Protocol of 1997 to Amend the International Convention for the Prevention of Pollution from Ships, 1973, as Modified by the Protocol of 1978 Relating Thereto' (MEPC 62/24/Add.1, adopted on 15 July 2011), available at: wwwcdn.imo.org/localresources/en/OurWork/Environment/Documents/Technical%20and%20Operational%20Measures/Resolution%20MEPC.203%2062%29.pdf.

on a formula dividing the emissions (from main and auxiliary engines, subject to various correction factors) by the benefits for society (capacity and speed of the ship), and establishes index levels that new-built ships (differentiating between different categories of ships) have to comply with before they are entitled to operate. The index requirements will be gradually strengthened, so as to require higher energy efficiency by ships built in the future than by those built today.[41] The reduction factors and reference line values, which form the basis of the energy efficiency requirements, are to be reviewed subject to technical developments and the first adjustments have already been made.[42] However, since the measure only covers new ships (or major conversions), a significant time lag for its impact on global emissions is inevitable. Ships normally have a commercial life of some 30 years, and it will therefore take several decades until all ships have been built to EEDI standards.

The addition of the new Chapter 4 to MARPOL Annex VI in 2011 also included a provision aimed at reducing GHG emissions from ships by means of operational measures.[43] However, the normative effect of the requirement is limited, as it only represents a requirement that a Ship Energy Efficiency Management Plan (SEEMP) exists. It does not include any standards on the content of the plan, nor any reduction targets that ships must meet.[44]

Further developments to both requirements were agreed in June 2021.[45] The Energy Efficiency Existing Ship Index (EEXI) will extend the principles of the

[41] IMO, 'Amendments to the Annex of the Protocol of 1997 to Amend the International Convention for the Prevention of Pollution from Ships, 1973, as Modified by the Protocol of 1978 Relating Thereto 2021 Revised MARPOL Annex VI' (Resolution MEPC.328(76), Reg 21, 2021), available at: wwwcdn.imo.org/localresources/en/OurWork/Environment/Documents/Air%20pollution/Certified%20copy%20of%20MEPC.328(76).pdf.

[42] The EEDI originally covered only the largest and most energy intensive segments of the world merchant fleet, ie, tankers, bulk carriers, gas carriers, general cargo ships, container ships, refrigerated cargo carriers and combination carriers. In 2014, Marpol Annex VI was amended to extend the scope of EEDI to: LNG carriers, ro-ro cargo ships (vehicle carriers), ro-ro cargo ships; ro-ro passenger ships and cruise passenger ships having non-conventional propulsion. For certain ship types the implementation dates were strengthened in May 2019. See IMO, 'Report of the Marine Environment Protection Committee on its Seventy-Fourth Session' (MEPC 74/18, 9 June 2019), available at: www.iadc.org/wp-content/uploads/2019/08/MEPC-74-18-Report-Of-The-Marine-Environment-Protection-CommitteeOn-Its-Seventy-Fourth-Session-Secretariat.pdf.

[43] All ships above 400gt are, based on Reg 22, required to have a Ship Energy Efficiency Management Plan (SEEMP). The plan seeks to help ship operators to improve the energy efficiency of a ship by means of operational measures (eg, through improved voyage planning or more frequent hull cleaning, or introduction of technical measures such as waste heat recovery systems or a new propeller).

[44] IMO (n 41) Reg 22. See also IMO, 'Guidelines for Voluntary Use of the Ship Energy Efficiency Operational Indicator (EEOI)' (MEPC.1/Circ.684, 17 August 2009), available at: gmn.imo.org/wp-content/uploads/2017/05/Circ-684-EEOI-Guidelines.pdf; for new and existing ships.

[45] IMO, 'Annex 1 Resolution MEPC.324(75) (adopted on 20 November 2020) Amendments to the Annex of the Protocol of 1997 to Amend the International Convention for the Prevention of Pollution from Ships, 1973, as Modified by the Protocol of 1978 Relating Thereto 2021 Revised MARPOL Annex VI' (MEPC 75/18/Add. 1, adopted on 20 November 2020), available at: wwwcdn.imo.org/localresources/en/OurWork/Environment/Documents/Air%20pollution/MEPC.324%2875%29.pdf; IMO Docs. MEPC 76/3 and MEPC 76/WP.1/Rev.1, para 3.32.

EEDI to existing ships,[46] while the 'Annual operational carbon intensity indicator' (CII) requires ships to determine the annual reduction factor needed to ensure continuous improvement in a ship's operational carbon intensity and to document the achieved annual operational CII in the SEEMP.[47] Failure to attain CII targets will not, under the current rules, automatically result in operational limitations or other forms of sanctions.[48] However, many details about the practical application of these measures remain to be settled through further guidelines on, inter alia, exemptions, corrections, methods for setting the targets and on the enforcement of the rules.[49]

iii. Market-Based Measures

Of the measures discussed to date, market-based measures (MBMs) have proven by far the most controversial. MBMs refer to a broad range of measures that provide for economic incentives for ship operators to reduce their bunker fuel consumption.[50] They range from various forms of 'levies' or 'carbon taxes' on bunker fuel to efficiency credit trading programmes and fully-fledged 'cap and trade' emissions trading schemes where emission rights could be sold and purchased on a market. These types of measures have the potential to generate significant funds, which could be used for emission reduction measures where they can be most cost-effectively implemented (including emission reductions outside the realm of shipping, if so decided). Work on MBMs has only recently resumed, and choices between the measures will have to be made soon, based on demanding criteria set out earlier (in 2008), under which any market-based measure adopted should be 'effective in contributing to the reduction of total global greenhouse gas emissions' as well as 'cost-effective, binding and equally applicable to all flag states in order to avoid evasion' and able to minimise competitive distortion and without penalising world trade and growth. In addition, the measures should be goal-based, not

[46] IMO, 'Resolution MEPC.328(76) Amendments to the Annex of the Protocol of 1997 to Amend the International Convention for the Prevention of Pollution from Ships, 1973, as Modified by the Protocol of 1978 Relating Thereto 2021 Revised MARPOL Annex VI' (MEPC 328(76), Regs 23 and 25, 17 July 2021), available at: wwwcdn.imo.org/localresources/en/OurWork/Environment/Documents/Air%20pollution/Certified%20copy%20of%20MEPC.328(76).pdf.

[47] ibid, Reg 24.

[48] ibid, Reg 28.

[49] IMO Doc MEPC 76/WP.1/Rev.1, paras 7.44–7.105, 49–73.

[50] The OECD has defined market-based measures more narrowly by stating that they 'seek to address the market failure of "environmental externalities" either by incorporating the external cost of production or consumption activities through taxes or charges on processes or products, or by creating property rights and facilitating the establishment of a proxy market for the use of environmental services'. See: stats.oecd.org/glossary/detail.asp?ID=7214. See also, HN Psaraftis, 'Market-Based Measures for Greenhouse Gas Emissions from Ships: A Review (2012) 11 *WMU Journal of Maritime Affairs* 211.

prescriptive, promote innovation and research and leading technologies while also being 'practical, transparent, fraud free and easy to administer'.[51]

iv. Assessment

The IMO has a broad legal discretion to choose the measures it wished to regulate GHG emissions from ships. Law neither provides an obstacle for the development of further measures in this regard nor a tool for deciding on what measure should be chosen. The question is rather what can be achieved politically within the organisation.

The adoption of the Paris Agreement and the subsequent developments at the IMO have removed some of the long-standing difficulties that have beset the regulation of GHG emissions from international shipping. This may give reason for some optimism with respect to regulatory progress in the future. A key milestone for measuring the IMO's success in the field will be in 2023.[52] Much of the result will depend on how the organisation manages to face the challenge of MBMs and, in the longer term, on the pace of the industry's shift towards alternative zero-carbon fuels.

It is too early to speculate on what the outcome of the MBM negotiations might be, but the most realistic scenario for now appears to be the least complex one, based on a fuel levy collected for a fund to stimulate sustainable climate solutions for shipping.[53] This would make fossil fuel somewhat more expensive, but would include no overall reduction target or trading facilities.

In the long term, work also needs to focus on new types of fuels to make possible the shift to carbon neutral shipping. Without clear rules on how new fuel types are to be used, handled and stored on board ships and beyond, the necessary shift towards sustainable low-carbon fuels will not take place. An important task will accordingly be to prepare the ground for new types of marine fuels by adopting the necessary technical standards. The first proposals for a low GHG fuel standard that would prescribe a decreasing limit value for the average GHG emissions intensity

[51] IMO, 'Annex 1 Resolution MEPC.169(57) Adopted on 4 April 2008 Procedure for Approval of Ballast Water Management Systems that Make Use of Active Substances (G9)' (MEPC 57/21, para 4.73–4.77, adopted on 4 April 2008), available at: www.liscr.com/sites/default/files/liscr_imo_resolutions/Res%20MEPC.169%2857%29%20-%20%28G9%29%20-%20Procedures%20for%20approval%20of%20Ballast%20Water%20Management%20Systems%20that%20make%20use%20of%20active%20Substances.pdf.

[52] The year 2023 is not only the time for the review of the IMO's GHG Strategy, but also the year for the first global stocktake of the Paris Agreement and the deadline set by the EU for IMO measures that 'duly contribute' to achieving the climate goals of the Paris Agreement under recital No 4 of Directive 2018/410.

[53] The EU proposal to include shipping in the regional ETS (section V.C below) has probably further increased the prospect of a levy-based fund at the IMO, given that most states supporting a global cap and trade system will be covered by a future EU ETS.

of fuels used by ships and thus promote a quicker use of renewable and low-carbon fuels in shipping have already been made.[54]

C. The EU's Response

i. General

For more than a decade, the EU, and in particular the European Commission, has been critical of the format and pace of the development of GHG reduction measures at the IMO. The EU has taken a broad interest in climate policy more generally and has had relatively little understanding for the needs for special solutions, delays or exemptions for shipping. The absence of emission reduction rules for shipping has repeatedly been indicated as a concern for the Union, more recently coupled with the observation that shipping is the only sector which is not expressly addressed by an EU emissions reduction objective or legislation to contribute to the EU general CO_2 reduction targets.[55] Policy warnings have at times been issued that EU rules targeting shipping may be introduced in this area if satisfactory global rules cannot be agreed at the IMO.[56]

ii. 'Fit for 55'

After decades of expressing concern and threatening regional action in this field, the Commission came forward with concrete proposals in the so-called 'Fit for 55'

[54] ISWG-GHG 10/5/6 and ISWG-GHG 10/5/3, based on IMO Doc MEPC 76/7/15, supported by the European Commission. See also, pending Case C-161/20 *Commission v Council* [2020] at the CJEU, where the competence for making submissions in this field (by Member States or the EU as a whole) is under dispute.

[55] See, eg, Commission, 'Communication from the Commission to the European Parliament, the Council, the European Economic and Social Committee and the Committee of the Regions Integrating maritime transport emissions in the EU's greenhouse gas reduction policies' COM (2013) 479 final, 7; Commission, 'Proposal for a Regulation of the European Parliament and of the Council amending Regulation (EU) 2015/757 in order to take appropriate account of the global data collection system for ship fuel oil consumption data' COM (2019) 38 final, 1.

[56] See, eg, third recital of Directive 2009/29/EC of the European Parliament and of the Council of 23 April 2009 amending Directive 2003/87/EC so as to improve and extend the greenhouse gas emission allowance trading scheme of the Community (Text with EEA relevance) [2009] OJ L140/63: 'All sectors of the economy should contribute to achieving these emission reductions, including international maritime shipping and aviation … In the event that no international agreement which includes international maritime emissions in its reduction targets through the International Maritime Organization has been approved by the Member States or no such agreement through the UNFCCC has been approved by the Community by 31 December 2011, the Commission should make a proposal to include international maritime emissions according to harmonised modalities in the Community reduction commitment, with the aim of the proposed act entering into force by 2013. Such a proposal should minimise any negative impact on the Community's competitiveness while taking into account the potential environmental benefits'.

package in July 2021.[57] Three of the 13 legislative proposals included in the package specifically target the shipping sector: the inclusion of shipping into the EU emissions trading scheme (EU ETS Directive);[58] the 'FuelEU Maritime' initiative aiming to increase demand and deployment of renewable alternative transport fuels;[59] and removing the current taxation exemption regarding fuel used by ships (Energy Taxation Directive).[60]

iii. Inclusion of Shipping in the ETS

Including shipping in the European ETS has been the preferred way of addressing GHG reductions from shipping by both the Commission and the European Parliament. It also follows the steps, that were only partially successful to do the same with aviation as from 2012.[61] Generally speaking, the measure proposes that shipping should be included in the ETS in the same manner as other industry sectors. Under the proposal, shipping is to be phased in gradually, from 2023 to 2025.[62] Therefore, 2026 is accordingly the first year in which the shipping companies have to surrender 100 per cent of their emissions.

In terms of verification and reporting, the proposal builds closely on the existing EU data system, established through the so-called MRV Regulation,[63] and

[57] Through the 'Fit for 55' package the Commission concretised its policy and ambitions significantly across a range of policy areas and economic sectors: climate, energy and fuels, transport, buildings land use and forestry. The package includes five entirely new measures, and eight substantial amendments to existing ones. See Commission, 'Communication from the Commission to the European Parliament, the Council, the European Economic and Social Committee and the Committee of the Regions "Fit for 55": delivering the EU's 2030 Climate Target on the way to climate neutrality' COM(2021) 550 final.

[58] Commission, 'Proposal for a Directive of the European Parliament and of the Council amending Directive 2003/87/EC establishing a system for greenhouse gas emission allowance trading within the Union, Decision (EU) 2015/1814 concerning the establishment and operation of a market stability reserve for the Union greenhouse gas emission trading scheme and Regulation (EU) 2015/757' COM(2021) 551 final.

[59] Commission, 'Proposal for a Regulation of the European Parliament and of the Council on the use of renewable and low-carbon fuels in maritime transport and amending Directive 2009/16/EC' COM(2021) 562 final.

[60] Commission, 'Proposal for a Council Directive restructuring the Union framework for the taxation of energy products and electricity (recast)' COM(2021) 563 final, 3.

[61] The EU's legislation on the regional emissions trading system was amended by Directive 2008/101 to include aviation within the scope of the EU ETS as from 2012. However, due to strong protests from third countries, it was decided to postpone application of this amendment for flights between the EU and third countries. Intra-EU flights remain included in the ETS, while the future inclusion of flights to and from third countries will depend on regulatory progress made at ICAO. See: ec.europa.eu/clima/policies/transport/aviation_en. The application of EU rules to non-EU flights raised legal concerns, too, but in Case C-366/10 *Air Transport Association of America and Others v Secretary of State for Energy and Climate Change* [2011] ECR I-13755, the CJEU considered that the extension did not amount to a breach of international law. The judgment has been criticised in legal literature for being too superficial on the question of extraterritorial jurisdiction. See, eg, G De Baere and C Ryngaert, 'The ECJ's Judgment in Air Transport Association of America and the International Legal Context of the EU's Climate Change Policy' (2013) 18 *European Foreign Affairs Review* 389, 402.

[62] For 2023, 20% of verified emissions must be reported; for 2024, 45%; and for 2025, 70%. COM(2021) 551 final (n 58) 16.

[63] See above (n 27).

proposes a number of amendments to the latter to secure that the two systems function together. As under the MRV Regulation, reporting is to be done on an annual basis to an accredited verifier that confirms the emissions of all ships trading in EU ports, and reports the data to the Member State in charge.

The measure thus covers ships of any flag trading to or from EU ports. While all emissions within or between Member States shall be accounted for, only half of the emissions to and from non-EU ports will be included. The stated reason for this is to allow space for other MBMs to supplement the regime, including presumably a future IMO regime.[64] The revenues from the EU ETS are allocated to the Union budget and Member States and used for various purposes in the realm of tackling climate change.[65]

As regards the link between the EU measure and potential future IMO measures, the proposal provides that in the event that the IMO adopts a global market-based measure to reduce GHG emissions from maritime transport, and in any case before 2028, the Commission will present a report to the European Parliament and to the Council to assess such measure.[66]

iv. *FuelEU Maritime*

The purpose of the FuelEU Maritime proposal is to 'increase the share of renewable and low-carbon fuels in the fuel mix of international maritime transport without creating barriers to the single market' and to establish a clear and predictable long-term regulatory framework for the shift to new fuels and energy solutions that facilitates planning and investment regarding all stakeholders.[67]

A key aspect of the proposal is that it sets a limit on the GHG intensity of energy used on board by a ship arriving at, staying within or departing from EU ports. The limit, which shall not be exceeded, concerns the yearly average GHG intensity of the energy used on board during a reporting period.[68] Annex I of the Regulation provides a more detailed methodology to calculate the amount of GHG emissions per unit of energy to determine GHG intensity.[69] The GHG intensity limit will become stricter every five years from 2025 until 2050 according to the formula set out in Article 4(2).

If the ship does not meet the required energy intensity reductions, the company must pay a penalty for each non-compliant port-call, the amount of which is to be

[64] Art 3g(1). Recital 17 explains that 'it is appropriate that the EU ETS covers a share of the emissions from voyages between a port under the jurisdiction of a Member State and a port under the jurisdiction of a third country, with the third country being able to decide on appropriate action in respect of the other share of emissions'. See also, Commission, COM(2021) 551 final (n 58) 155, on the coverage options considered by the Commission in this respect.

[65] For details, see: ec.europa.eu/clima/eu-action/eu-emissions-trading-system-eu-ets_en.

[66] Commission, COM(2021) 551 final (n 58) Art 3ge.

[67] Commission, COM(2021) 562 final (n 59) 2.

[68] ibid, Art 4.

[69] ibid, Art 4(3).

calculated by the verifier according to a specific formula.[70] Once the penalties are paid, the verifier will issue a FuelEU certificate of compliance. The funds from the penalties will be allocated to support common projects aimed at the rapid deployment of renewable and low-carbon fuels in the maritime sector by stimulating production of greater quantities of renewable and low-carbon fuels, facilitating the construction of appropriate bunkering facilities or electric connection ports, and supporting the development, testing and deployment of the most innovative European technologies in the fleet to achieve significant emission reductions.[71]

In this case, too, only half the journeys to or from EU ports are to be accounted for. Recital 4 clarifies that the main reason for the limitation is indeed policy based, as it 'limits the risk of evasive port calls and the risk of delocalisation of transhipment activities outside the Union'.

In order to overcome the enforcement challenges linked to monitoring fuel purchases and quality worldwide, the FuelEU Maritime proposal requires ships to hold a Certificate of Compliance issued by an accredited verifier. It is then the on-board presence and validity of this certificate which, in Article 22, is made a condition for entry into an EU port.

v. Assessment

The EU proposals raise many difficult issues, including legal ones. As has already been seen when a similar proposal was approved in respect of aviation in 2008,[72] the inclusion of international shipping in the EU ETS gives rise to a number of intricate questions of policy and international law.[73] In particular, the inclusion of foreign entities in the regional ETS, for emissions emitted worldwide, raises legal concerns relating to extraterritorial jurisdiction that are closely linked to the law of the sea and general principles of international law.[74]

In brief, international law does not prevent a port state, or the EU, from implementing requirements affecting international shipping, even if they have implications beyond its territorial jurisdiction. It does, however, qualify that jurisdiction in several important ways. In particular, the jurisdiction depends on the nature of the requirement, on the measures chosen to enforce them and on the respect of the criteria of reasonableness that follow from general international law

[70] ibid, Art 20.

[71] ibid, Art 21.

[72] See above (n 61).

[73] The international law concerns centre around the extent to which a state (or region) may require foreign ships to comply with unilateral requirements that extend beyond its territorial jurisdiction, on the basis of its temporary presence in the port. It is, in other words closely related to the discussion on port state jurisdiction in section II.B above. See also H Ringbom, 'Global Problem – Regional Solution? – International Law Reflections on an EU CO_2 Emissions Trading Scheme for Ships' (2011) 26 *International Journal for Marine and Coastal Law* 613.

[74] See, eg, De Baere and Ryngaert (n 61).

and potential treaties which may limit the EU's or port state's jurisdiction in this regard.[75]

Both EU proposals discussed above, however, seek to distance themselves from classical law of the sea issues such as the freedom of navigation and passage rights, by focusing on the long-term combined emissions accumulated over a year rather than on individual voyages, and by imposing financial obligations on the operator of the ship rather than navigational restraints on the ship as such. Nor is the subject of regulation a classical matter of 'pollution' or 'air emission' as regulated in UNCLOS, but rather a set of policy obligations targeting the actions and choices of the ship operator without direct implications for the hands-on operation of the ship itself. The proposed scheme, in other words, does not limit navigation as such, but only makes the voyage somewhat more expensive, presumably in a non-discriminatory manner. The concerns of ship owners, flag states or the maritime community as a whole might therefore not be given the same prominence in this case as in a more clear-cut case of extraterritorial jurisdiction *versus* navigational rights.

The EU proposals also seek to temper the extraterritorial effects by covering only half of the emissions/energy generated between routes where one of the ports is outside the EU. This limitation is not based in law of the sea considerations but represents a more diffuse sign of flexibility towards third parties, presumably to avoid policy opposition. While the 50 per cent limitation may be justified in the ETS proposal as a mechanism to avoid multiple counting for the same transport legs by competing MBMs, presumably including the one to be adopted by the IMO, the corresponding limitation of Article 2(c) of the FuelEU Maritime proposal is more difficult to understand, as it targets the quality of fuel as much as the quantity consumed, and as there are no competing proposals targeting the shift towards low-carbon fuels. Whether such legal mitigating mechanisms suffice for sparing the EU measures from legal challenge remains to be seen, but to this author at least it seems that the EU proposals appear to handle the international law restraints carefully and do not raise immediate concerns of legality from this perspective.[76]

In the end, the legal assessment will eventually boil down to a generic reasonableness requirement to be concretised by balancing the different interests at stake. In such a balancing of interests, important elements favouring the EU's actions in the field relate to the growing climate crisis and the fact that the IMO has failed to adopt measures that would significantly reduce GHG emissions from ships despite discussing the matter for almost 25 years. The EU may, under this view, be seen as acting regionally on behalf of the world community as a whole, and with no

[75] Ringbom, 'Global Problem' (n 73).

[76] See also, L Finska and H Ringbom, 'GHG Study Regulation of GHGs from Ships – On the available discretion for regulatory solutions in a European and Finnish perspective' (Final report, 2022), available at: www.centrumbalticum.org/files/5185/Regulation_of_GHGs_from_ships_final.pdf.

particular benefit to the region (depending on how potential funds are distributed). If anything, the UNFCCC and the Paris Agreement specifically accept the principle that industrialised countries have a greater responsibility than other states to take measures to prevent global warming, on behalf of the world as a whole. However, in view of the significance of what starting point is chosen for analysing this matter (law of the sea, climate change, the EU perspective or general international law), it is quite possible that the choice of forum will influence the outcome if or when a ruling on the legality of the EU's action were to be sought in the future.

D. Baltic Sea Perspectives

The ongoing initiatives in the field of GHG reductions from ships have not generated major policy initiatives at regional level in the BSR.[77] There is, for example, no specific HELCOM position on the matter and the revised BSAP from 2021 does not identify ships' energy efficiency or GHG reduction among the management objectives for sea-based activities. The plan itself includes a few actions aimed at enhancing energy efficiency in shipping and the promotion of clean technologies and low-carbon fuels, but the actions do not specify particular policy priorities in this regard. The one exception is Action S25, which specifically calls upon states to actively follow and contribute to IMO discussions, including ensuring that 'ice navigation and its special requirements are duly taken into account'.[78] A 'Baltic Sea Platform for Green Technology and Alternative Fuels in Shipping' (HELCOM Green Team) has been established to ensure that shipping in the Baltic Sea meets the targets of the IMO's GHG Strategy by 2030. EU measures in this field, including the MRV Regulation, are not referred to at all in the BSAP.[79]

Winter navigation poses a particular challenge for the efforts to reduce GHG from ships. For a vessel to pass through a layer of thick ice, there is a need not just for special structures and extra engine power but also more fuel (some 20–60 per cent increase), which translates into additional costs for ships operating in icy

[77] On the impact of climate change on the Baltic Sea environment generally, see eg, M Viitasalo and E Bonsdorff, 'Global climate change and the Baltic Sea ecosystem: Direct and indirect effects on species, communities and ecosystem functioning' (2022) 13 *Earth System Dynamics* 711.

[78] The safety of winter navigation has been subject to two earlier HELCOM recommendations: HELCOM, 'Safety of Winter Navigation in the Baltic Sea Area' (Revised HELCOM RECOMMENDATION 25/7, 2004), available at: www.helcom.fi/wp-content/uploads/2019/06/Rec-25-7.pdf; and HELCOM, 'Further Measures to Improve the Safety of Navigation in Ice Conditions in the Baltic Sea' (HELCOM RECOMMENDATION 28E/11, 2007), available at: www.helcom.fi/wp-content/uploads/2019/06/Rec-28E-11.pdf, but while highlighting the need for ice-strengthened ships, they do not include a specific GHG or energy efficiency angle to them.

[79] More generally, a certain reluctance to refer to EU measures is evident throughout the revised BSAP, where references to EU legislation are few and far between and, where such references exist, they are often followed by an identical reference to legislation by the Russian Federation.

conditions. The cost increase is not limited to operations in ice, however, as ice-strengthened vessels consume (some 2–5 per cent) more fuel in open waters too, compared with a similar vessel without ice capacity.[80]

Exceptions to rules in this field will always be difficult to promote, as they work against the main purpose of the rules (which is to encourage energy efficiency by targeting GHG emissions from ships), but also since exceptions risk generating complexities and raising issues of fairness in relation to other sectors or regions in the system.

To some extent this disadvantage compared with ships in other areas has already been recognised in the IMO rules. A correction factor based on ice performance had already been accepted in the first EEDI version in 2011. Regulations that take into account the special design features of ships having an ice class and ice-class correction factors for capacity and power have since been adopted in the 2014 Guidelines on the method of calculation of the attained EEDI for new ships.[81] The EEXI Regulations, too, incorporate ice-class correction factors to correct the installed power, for example, for ice-class ships, as well as to correct capacity, for example, to consider structural enhancement.[82]

Whether the same will apply for operational measures is still open. A proposal to this effect was made by four Baltic Sea States in 2021,[83] but has not yet been approved.[84] It is therefore not clear if and how there will be a link made between

[80] For a full economic calculation of the costs linked to winter navigation and ice-class ships, see the Finnish Ministry of Transport and Communication of 3 February 2022, available at: www.lvm.fi/-/siirtyma-vahapaastoiseen-meriliikenteeseen-eu-ssa-lisaa-kustannuksia-samalla-ilmastotoimet-luovat-liiketoimintaa-1650474.

[81] IMO, '2014 Guidelines on the method of calculation of the attained Energy Efficiency Design Index (EEDI) for new ships' (Resolution MEPC.245(66), adopted on 4 April 2014), available at: wwwcdn.imo.org/localresources/en/OurWork/Environment/Documents/245(66).pdf, as amended by IMO, 'Amendments to the 2014 Guidelines on the method of calculation of the attained Energy Efficiency Design Index (EEDI) for new ships, as amended' (Resolution MEPC.281(70), adopted on 28 October 2016), available at: wwwcdn.imo.org/localresources/en/KnowledgeCentre/IndexofIMOResolutions/MEPCDocuments/MEPC.281(70).pdf.

[82] IMO, Resolution MEPC 328(76) (2021) Regs 23 and 25.

[83] IMO, 'Consideration and Adoption of Amendments to Mandatory Instruments Proposal for a possible addition to regulation 22B.1 of MARPOL Annex VI concerning voyage exclusions for ice-class ships when sailing in ice conditions Submitted by Estonia, Finland, Russian Federation and Sweden' (MEPC 76/3/5, 7 April 2021), available at: www.eduskunta.fi/FI/vaski/Liiteasiakirja/Documents/EDK-2021-AK-369758.pdf maintaining, inter alia, that in addition to correction factors for design, also voyage exclusions, when sailing in ice conditions, are required. The longer the distance the ship sails in ice conditions, the more challenging it is for the ship to comply with the CII regulations without applying voyage exclusions when sailing in ice conditions. For a proposed definition of the term 'sailing in ice conditions', see also the submission by the same states in IMO Doc MEPC 76/7/21.

[84] The MEPC Committee did not agree to the proposal for an exclusion for ice-class ships in the MARPOL and decided that the matter should be considered as part of the ongoing discussion with regard to correction factors/voyage exclusions taking place in the Intersessional Working Group, through the guidelines on the application of the CII under development. See IMO, 'Amendments to the Annex of the Protocol of 1997 to Amend the International Convention for the Prevention of Pollution from Ships, 1973, as Modified by the Protocol of 1978 Relating Thereto' (MEPC 76/15, 2021) 8, available at: wwwcdn.imo.org/localresources/en/OurWork/Environment/Documents/Air%20pollution/MEPC.328(76).pdf.

the CII and CII ratings and ice-class correction factors of ships. Currently the relevant guidelines only provide that the MEPC 'AGREES to consider substantiated proposals for CII correction factors for certain ship types, operational profiles and/or voyages with a view to enhance the annexed Guidelines before entry into force of the aforementioned amendments to MARPOL Annex VI'.[85]

A similar discussion at EU level has not yet resulted in any proposal to take the concerns of the northernmost Member States into account. If exceptions for winter navigation are to be made at EU level, it would seem that the most natural directive to include them in is the ETS Directive, which is the proposal that most directly targets the amount of fuel consumed by ships. On the other hand, accepting amendments to this instrument is probably more difficult than in the FuelEU Maritime Regulation, in view of the multi-sector nature of the ETS and the fact that exemptions and special arrangements for one sector could trigger questions and similar requests from other sectors.

Apart from the concern with ice navigation, there is another concern linked to fuel consumption that is relevant for the northern areas of the Baltic Sea in particular. The peripheral geographical position of the BSR in the EU raises, on the one hand, concerns about the general dependency of maritime transport and the expenses that follow from long marine distances. On the other hand, the geographical position of the most peripheral states, raises risks linked to carbon leakage and other rule evasion, in view of its proximity to areas where the EU rules do not apply, in the present case, Russia. These concerns are by their nature unlikely to be met with understanding at the global scale, but the latter concern (risk of leakage close to the EU's outer borders) may well be a matter that the EU needs to study more closely.

E. Conclusions on GHG Emissions

The regulation of GHG emissions has been the key environmental challenge for shipping for decades and nothing suggests that that will change in the decades to come. From a multi-level regulation point of view, the topic is also interesting as the variety of regulatory authorities and types of measures involved provide an unusually good opportunity to study the interaction and relationships between regulatory layers in shipping and the role assumed by different actors in the BSR and beyond.

In view of today's very incomplete regulatory situation, where most pieces of the regulatory jigsaw puzzle only exist in the form of proposals or strategies, it is

[85] IMO Doc ISWG-GHG 8/J/7, IMO, '2021 Guidelines on operational carbon intensity indicators and the calculation methods (CII Guidelines, G1)' (MEPC 76/15/Add.2, 17 June 2021) 1, available at: wwwcdn.imo.org/localresources/en/OurWork/Environment/Documents/Air%20pollution/MEPC.336(76).pdf.

too early to undertake a detailed legal analysis of this relationship, for example, in the form of assessing compatibilities or conflicts between rules or regulatory layers. Yet, even in the absence of the key regulatory building blocks at IMO and EU level, it is possible to provide some general conclusions.

The IMO is under significant pressure to deliver tangible results in this field within a few years. It has been noted above that failure to deliver concrete reduction requirements for the shipping sector would fit very uneasily with the aims and targets of the UNFCCC framework in general, and with the commitments of the Paris Agreement in particular. Policy pressure to include MBMs among the measures imposed has further increased significantly following the adoption in 2016 by the ICAO of a market-based global emissions reduction scheme for the aviation sector.[86]

However, at least from a European perspective, the main tension clearly lies between the IMO and the EU for the moment. Both institutions find themselves at a critical stage of regulating the matter; both institutions are in the middle of negotiating multiple legal rules targeting different aspects of the shift towards greener maritime transport. The rules under negotiation target somewhat different aspects of the challenge and use different tools for reaching their aims. They are not incompatible, although some overlaps exist. From a legal perspective, it has been concluded that there is scope for the EU to complement the international rules in this field and that the EU proposals adopted in July 2021 probably qualify under the reasonableness criteria that apply to port state-based requirements of this kind, but the eventual assessment of this matter must be made once the more detailed content of the rules is known. If the IMO decides to opt for a full-scale cap-and-trade system, there may be significant overlaps and even legal tensions in relation to the EU ETS regime, if ships were to be included in that as proposed.

This multitude of regulatory initiatives involves practical aspects as well, which is illustrated by the – already existing – complexities of having two parallel reporting systems in place for implementing the system. EU efforts to reduce the differences indicate that while some of the most important differences could be removed, there will still be differences between the European and the global data systems to support the implementation of GHG emission reduction measures.[87]

For the BSR, focus has not been on developing separate rules for green shipping, but on ensuring that the relevant policy concerns of the region are taken into consideration at the negotiations at the IMO in particular. The initiative has not been regionally coordinated but has been undertaken individually by the states most concerned with the development. Interestingly, so far it appears that the IMO has been more attentive to Baltic Sea States' concerns than the EU and hence more

[86] ICAO Assembly Resolution 39-3 setting up the 'Carbon Offsetting and Reduction Scheme for International Aviation' (CORSIA).

[87] See, eg, H Ringbom, 'Regulating Greenhouse Gases from Ships – Some Light at the End of the Funnel?' in E Johansen, S Veierud Busch and IU Jakobsen (eds), *The Law of the Sea and Climate Change: Solutions and Constraints* (Cambridge, Cambridge University Press 2021) 152–53.

willing to accept deviations in relation to winter navigation concerns. However, this is probably a function of the nature of the rules as much as a question of policy flexibility. Whether the IMO is prepared to accept 'discounts' for emissions linked to ice navigation in its operational or market-based measures is not yet settled. As to the EU, it remains to be seen how much of the Baltic Sea States' concerns will be accommodated in the final legal texts if and when adopted. On the basis of the proposals alone, there does not seem to be much reason to expect great concessions from fellow EU States. The prospect for exceptions will probably improve, though, if similar exceptions or arrangements have already been agreed at IMO level.

VI. Concluding Thoughts

The role and functions of the EU in the regulation of shipping are not easily summarised. The Union is a regional player in a decidedly global policy environment where regional solutions are usually met with significant suspicion and unease. The Union often acts and argues like a single state, but does not have its own fleet, ports or maritime zones, which would serve as an easy justification for such an approach. Moreover, in contrast to many of its Member States' national shipping policies, the EU has generally sided with the interests of coastal states, the environment and passengers, at the expense of the concerns of flag states and shipowners, often as a consequence of specific shipping accidents occurring in European waters.

The founding Treaties of the EU included almost nothing on a common maritime policy. From almost no activity in the field during the first decades of European integration, significant regulatory activity followed from the mid-1990s and has continued to date. Somewhat confusingly, perhaps, the EU assumes a very active role in certain policy fields, while for others there might be no common European interest at all. For an outsider it may be difficult to predict what to expect in advance and there is no single easily identifiable institution in charge of the EU's shipping policy. Moreover, the EU has changed its role significantly during its first decades of being active in the regulation of ship-source pollution. Following a period of ever-increasing independent activity in relation to global (IMO) rules, that lasted from the mid-1990s to around 2005, it has since focused more on implementation and institutional capacity building, notably through the European Maritime Safety Agency. However, the 'Fit for 55' proposals of July 2021 indicate that at least the European Commission is again prepared to challenge the international consensus in shipping regulation. For the foreseeable future, the regulation of GHG emissions and other measures aimed at mitigating climate change will clearly represent the main focus of the Union's prescriptive ambitions in shipping.

From a BSR perspective, the EU's increasing regulatory activity in shipping over the past few decades has probably mostly been a positive development for the states in the region that are also members of the Union. Despite general downsides, such as the additional complexity added by the introduction of another (notoriously complex) regulatory layer into the picture, or the limitation of national discretion that EU rules necessarily entail, the EU has largely served the interests of the BSR from a policy point of view. The port and coastal state approach of the EU, and its preoccupation with safety, environment and passenger rights, fits well with the interests and priorities of the Baltic Sea States. The EU's favoured method of regulating shipping, through standards imposed on all ships entering ports of its Member States are particularly effective in a region such as the BSR, given the absence of through-traffic in the region. The absence of one key Baltic Sea State from the scope of EU regulation is compensated by the presence of 18 other states, providing EU legislation with the economic and policy muscle needed to exercise an independent regional environmental policy for shipping, which the Baltic Sea States have chosen not to make use of themselves.

The Baltic Sea States have not therefore traditionally objected to the EU's increased role in shipping regulation.[88] Earlier, when fewer Baltic Sea States were members of the EU, HELCOM recommendations and policies were sometimes even adopted to facilitate the implementation of EU policies in the entire BSR.[89] On the other hand, the states surrounding the Baltic Sea have not particularly called for EU regulatory action either. The general focus of the BSR in shipping matters has always been, and still is, directed towards the global regulatory framework, that is, the IMO. If a regulatory gap of importance to the region is identified, it will typically be the IMO, rather than the EU, that will be the focus of HELCOM's policy efforts.[90] This approach is less confrontational than regional action, both internally within the BSR and in relation to the outside world and has obvious advantages in terms of global outreach of the measure. In pursuing such policies, the Baltic Sea States have been remarkably successful in having their regional concerns acknowledged and translated into IMO conventions. That same pattern appears at least in part to continue in the context of GHG reductions from ships.

Whether the Baltic Sea States have managed to shape the EU's shipping policy is another matter. To some extent this has certainly been the case. In particular where rules are already in place in the HELCOM framework, the EU, not least due

[88] See, eg, H Ringbom 'Regulation of Ship-Source Pollution in the Baltic Sea' (2018) 98 *Marine Policy* 246.

[89] A notable example is the 2001 revision of Annex IV of the Helsinki Convention which is closely related to various post-Erika EU rules. It included requirements on double-hulled tankers, automatic identification systems, port state control, safety management and places of refuge, sometimes with express reference to the relevant EU legislation. See HELCOM, 'Amendments to the Convention On The Protection Of The Marine Environment Of The Baltic Sea Area (Annex IV; Regulations 4 and 9–12)' (Helsinki 2001), available at: iea.uoregon.edu/treaty-text/4290.

[90] Backer (n 14). Another example is the regulation of ships' noise for which the BSAP calls for a number of concerted actions to be presented at the IMO, without any references to the EU. See, in particular, HELCOM, 'Additional information on the actions in the updated Baltic Sea Action Plan' (Actions S55–S57, Helsinki 2021), available at: helcom.fi/wp-content/uploads/2021/10/Additional-information-on-the-actions-in-the-updated-Baltic-Sea-Action-Plan.pdf.

to its formal acceptance of the 1992 Helsinki Convention, has tended to follow such measures, at times even by extending BSR policies to the entire Union.[91] In the absence of such regulatory 'advantages' for the BSR, the situation is less clear. EU negotiations in Council are not very transparent.

All in all, however, the general picture is that both regional regulatory layers discussed in this chapter represent useful contributions to the overall governance scheme of shipping in the Baltic Sea, despite the decidedly global character of the activity they seek to govern. It would, in other words, be a mistake to reduce the current collaborative structure for shipping in the BSR into an EU–Russia dialogue, as has happened in certain other fields.[92] Rather, both the recent history and ongoing developments suggest that the EU and the governance framework around HELCOM collaborate and interact well and complement each other. Regulatory activities in the BSR tend to be inherently multilayered, and shipping constitutes no exception. The EU's entry onto the regulatory scene in the past decades has caused a number of changes and broadened the available tools and options for the Baltic Sea States, but has not done away with the need for a body that specifically looks after the specific interests of the BSR and its often unique environmental concerns.

[91] A good example of this is the work on port waste reception facilities referred to in Directive 2000/59/EC on port reception facilities for ship-generated waste and cargo residues [2000] OJ L332/81. A less obvious example is penal sanction for pollution violations, which has been subject to a HELCOM recommendation since 1998. See HELCOM, 'HELCOM Recommendation 19/14 A Harmonized System of Fines in Case a Ship Violates Anti-Pollution Regulations' (Helsinki 1998), available at: helcom.fi/wp-content/uploads/2019/06/Rec-19-14.pdf.

[92] See ch 12 by David Langlet in this volume on the management of fisheries resources.

12

The Role of the EU in the Regulation of Baltic Sea Fisheries

DAVID LANGLET

I. Introduction

Hardly anyone can be surprised to hear that all is not well with the Baltic Sea. Alarm bells have been ringing for decades concerning different aspects of the environmental state of the Sea. High levels of toxic substances, such as PCB and DDT, drew much attention in the 1980s. Later the focus has been more on dioxin, which for a long period has made fat fish from the sea very problematic as food. Eutrophication is a recurring theme in any discussion about the state of the Baltic Sea, which is considered to hold the largest human-induced hypoxic area in the world.[1]

As for fish, the sea still supports commercial fishing fleets from nine countries,[2] but important stocks are in strong decline. Most famously, the Baltic Sea cod is in a particularly bad state and there have been repeated reports of cod stocks on the verge of collapse or already having collapsed. In the early 1980s, cod represented almost 50 per cent of the total landings. In the early 2010s, that had dropped to around 10 per cent. During the same period, the share of sprat in the total landings increased about tenfold.[3] Following emergency measures in 2019, fishing for the eastern Baltic cod was effectively banned in 2020 due to the poor state of the stock. Fishing opportunities were reduced by 92 per cent compared with the previous year and the remaining catch was only to be taken as bycatch when fishing for other species. Also other quotas were drastically reduced, including a 60 per cent

[1] EEA, 'The European environment – state and outlook 2015' (Copenhagen, 2015).

[2] For more information, see ICES, 'ICES Fisheries Overviews, Baltic Sea ecoregion' (Version 2: 3 December 2020, 30 November 2020), available at: www.ices.dk/sites/pub/Publication%20Reports/Advice/2020/2020/FisheriesOverviews_BalticSea_2020.pdf.

[3] T Raid et al, 'Dynamics of the commercial fishery in the Baltic Sea: What are the driving forces?' in C Guedes Soares, R Dejhalla and D Pavletic (eds), *Towards Green Marine Technology and Transport* (London, CRC Press, 2015).

reduction of western Baltic cod and large reductions for herring.[4] For 2022, the advice from the International Council for the Exploration of the Sea (ICES), a scientific organisation that provides fisheries advice to the European Union (EU), was no catch at all of the eastern Baltic stock,[5] and a mere 698 tonnes of western Baltic cod.[6]

The reasons for the problematic situation for Baltic Sea fisheries are multifaceted and subject to much scientific discussion.[7] Doubtless, however, fishing pressure and the way fishing has been conducted in recent decades have played a significant part in this development.[8]

What makes this particularly interesting from a regulatory perspective is that the decline of Baltic Sea fisheries, and in particular cod fisheries, largely coincides with quite significant changes in the overall conditions for fisheries management in the Baltic Sea. From the late 1970s to the early 2000s, the Baltic Sea has gone from being a sea where fishing was governed by individual states engaged in traditional international cooperation, based on international law and effectively requiring the consent of all concerned parties, to a situation where the vast majority of all fishing activities are regulated by a supranational institution, ie, the EU, through its common fisheries policy (CFP). Since 2004, all Baltic Sea coastal states except Russia are EU members. This means that apart from the fairly small Russian section, the whole Baltic Sea is subject to only one fisheries governance regime.

The conservation of fish stocks that are shared between several states is the classic example of a (large-scale) collective action problem, with such stocks likely to suffer the tragedy of the commons.[9] Drastically reducing the number of decision-makers for Baltic Sea fisheries management would hence have been expected to generate a better state of the fish stocks, or at least better preconditions for sustainable management.[10]

This chapter does not attempt to provide any definitive answer as to why that has not happened. That is far too complex a question to be addressed through the

[4] Council Regulation (EU) 2019/1838 of 30 October 2019 fixing for 2020 the fishing opportunities for certain fish stocks and groups of fish stocks applicable in the Baltic Sea and amending Regulation (EU) 2019/124 as regards certain fishing opportunities in other waters [2019] OJ L281/1.

[5] ICES, 'ICES Advice on fishing opportunities, catch, and effort Baltic Sea ecoregion, Cod (Gadus morhua) in subdivisions 24–32, eastern Baltic stock (eastern Baltic Sea)' (28 May 2021), available at: www.ices.dk/sites/pub/Publication%20Reports/Advice/2021/2021/cod.27.24-32.pdf.

[6] ICES, 'ICES Advice on fishing opportunities, catch, and effort Baltic Sea ecoregion, Cod (Gadus morhua) in subdivisions 22–24, western Baltic stock (western Baltic Sea)' (10 September 2021), available at: www.ices.dk/sites/pub/Publication%20Reports/Advice/2021/2021/cod.27.22-24.pdf.

[7] M Eero, M Cardinale and M Storr-Paulsen, 'Emerging challenges for resource management under ecosystem change: Example of cod in the Baltic Sea' (2020) 198 *Ocean & Coastal Management* 105314.

[8] S Opitz and R Froese, 'Ecosystem Based Fisheries Management for the Western Baltic Sea' (Geomar, 2019), available at: oceanrep.geomar.de/id/eprint/51946/1/WBS_ComFish_Report_Final.pdf.

[9] G Hardin, 'The tragedy of the commons' (1968) 162 *Science* 1243.

[10] A large number of actors has been identified as perhaps the most important obstacle for achieving collective action at large scales. See SC Jagers et al, 'On the preconditions for large-scale collective action' (2020) 49 *AMBIO* 1282, 1285.

study of regulatory structures, not to mention the study of one specific such structure, namely that pertaining to fisheries. What is attempted here is instead to chart how the regulation of fisheries management has changed in the Baltic Sea over the last few decades and to have a closer look at some of the regulatory challenges encountered as well as how they have been dealt with. It will also be inquired what has generally been found to be important strengths and shortcomings of the EU's CFP with relevance for Baltic Sea fisheries management. Before engaging with the regulatory regime for fisheries, a brief introduction is given to the Baltic Sea. That is followed by a general discussion on the origins, nature and development of the CFP. Against that background, the specific developments concerning Baltic Sea fisheries regulation is then discussed and some attempts at conclusions as to what has gone wrong with Baltic Sea fisheries management are made.

II. A Short Characterisation of the Baltic Sea

The Baltic Sea has been characterised as 'an extreme marine environment', connected as it is to the North Sea only by narrow and shallow sills in the Öresund and Danish Belts.[11] The limited inflow of water from the North Sea makes water renewal (turnover time) slow.[12] With an area of approximately 415,000 km^2,[13] the Baltic Sea is small compared with other seas and its average depth of little more than 50 metres also makes it quite shallow. These characteristics contribute to making the Sea sensitive to run-off from the surrounding landmasses and to various other anthropogenic pressures. Large parts of the deeper areas of the Baltic proper are hypoxic or anoxic, ie, suffering from a dearth or complete lack of oxygen.[14]

The extreme conditions of the Baltic Sea result in a generally low species diversity with about a tenth or less of the species richness found in the North East Atlantic.[15] However, species variety and composition differ strongly between different parts of the Baltic Sea, with the southern and western parts being significantly more diverse and harbouring more marine species, including a number that have developed specific traits allowing them to tolerate the still relatively low salinity. This is also where the traditionally large cod stocks are found. The same species often occur in separate populations in different areas and these populations can

[11] K Johannesson and C Andre, 'INVITED REVIEW: Life on the margin: genetic isolation and diversity loss in a peripheral marine ecosystem, the Baltic Sea' (2006) 15 *Molecular Ecology* 2013, 2014.

[12] It takes around 30 years for the water to be renewed in the southernmost part of the sea and around 40 years in the north. See P Snoeijs-Leijonmalm and E Andrén, 'Why is the Baltic Sea so special to live in?' in P Snoeijs-Leijonmalm et al (eds), *Biological Oceanography of the Baltic Sea* (Dordrecht, Springer, 2017) 29, 47.

[13] Snoeijs-Leijonmalm and Andrén (n 12) 29.

[14] EEA, 'The European environment' (n 1).

[15] Johannesson and Andre (n 11).

have different abundance dynamics, ie, can vary significantly in relative abundance in the same year.[16]

Over timescales of hundreds and thousands of years, the Baltic Sea has seen major fluctuations in its environmental conditions driven by non-anthropogenic factors, primarily climate variations. Today, large-scale changes caused by human activities occur at dramatically higher speed.[17] Among other things, the Baltic Sea has seen one of the highest recorded temperature increases among large marine ecosystems.[18]

The insight that human activities can strongly affect and even fundamentally change the marine environment has emerged since the 1960s.[19] However, from the early twentieth century human activities, such as extensive draining of wetlands, growing use of fertilisers and intense seal hunting, are likely to have contributed to fundamental changes in the Baltic Sea ecosystem(s), including a likely irreversible shift from an oligotrophic clear-water sea to a eutrophic sea, and a linked shift from cod as the dominating fish species to a system dominated by sprat and herring.[20]

In conclusion, the Baltic Sea is evidently a complex ecosystem, or rather a set of interacting ecosystems, that is heavily influenced by human activities and has been so for some time. Managing the environment and the natural resources of the Baltic Sea is clearly a challenge; both since it is scientifically challenging to understand the many interlinked ecosystem processes and how these respond to various human pressures, and since the natural processes cannot be separated and governed in isolation from the social systems comprising the people and the societies whose activities affect the Baltic Sea and whose lives are in one way or another affected by the sea.[21]

III. The EU CFP

A. General

Although the regulation of fishing, or 'the conservation of marine biological resources under the common fisheries policy' as it is formally termed, is now one of

[16] E Ojaveer, *Ecosystems and Living Resources of the Baltic Sea: Their Assessment and Management* (Cham, Springer, 2017) 52.

[17] Snoeijs-Leijonmalm and Andrén (n 12) 64.

[18] ibid, 74.

[19] R Elmgren, 'Understanding human impact on the Baltic ecosystem: changing views in recent decades' (2001) 30 *AMBIO* 222, 223.

[20] H Österblom and others, 'Human-induced trophic cascades and ecological regime shifts in the Baltic Sea' (2007) 10 *Ecosystems* 877, 879.

[21] D Langlet and A Westholm, 'Realizing the Social Dimension of EU Coastal Water Management' (2021) 13 *Sustainability* 2261.

the few policy areas subject to exclusive EU competence,[22] it took some time before the then European Economic Community (EEC)[23] developed a common regulatory framework for fisheries. During the 1950s and 1960s, fisheries management was not perceived as an important common issue. Most commercially interesting fish stocks were, or were perceived to be, in good condition and did not require extensive regulations for their conservation. Much of the fishing in the Atlantic and the North Sea was also conducted in international waters.[24] Largely for tactical reasons, the EEC Member States had contented themselves with claiming a three-nautical-mile territorial sea. They did not want to legitimise the expanding claims of countries like Iceland and Norway, since they threatened to exclude Member State fleets from important fishing grounds. When, in the mid-1970s, it became evident that the international trend towards much larger exclusive fishing zones could not be stopped, the Member States changed tactics and jointly declared exclusive fishing zones of 200 nautical miles to apply from 1977. Most fishing was subsequently conducted within EU waters, ie, marine areas under the exclusive control of the Member States. The international developments also created political pressure to compensate those Member States that had suffered significant losses of traditional fishing ground as a consequence of non-Member States claiming a 200 nautical miles exclusive fishing zone.[25]

Although the first steps towards a common fisheries policy were taken in the 1970s,[26] it was in 1983, through the adoption of Regulation (EEC) No 170/83 establishing a Community system for the conservation and management of fishery resources,[27] that a comprehensive legal framework for common fisheries management was put in place. This was the first in a series of basic regulations, setting out the core rules and principles of the CFP. It has subsequently been supplemented by numerous other regulations with specific rules on, inter alia, allowable

[22] Consolidated version of the Treaty on the Functioning of the European Union [2007] OJ C115/1, Art 3 (TFEU). Other areas subject to exclusive EU competence are the customs union, competition rules necessary for the functioning of the internal market, monetary policy for the Member States using the euro, and the common commercial policy, ie, rules on trade with third countries.

[23] In the following, 'the EU' is used to also refer to the previous incarnations of what is today the European Union.

[24] E Penas Lado, *The Common Fisheries Policy: The Quest for Sustainability* (Hoboken, Wiley-Blackwell, 2016) 38.

[25] ibid, 46–47.

[26] See Regulation (EEC) 2141/70 of the Council of 20 October 1970 laying down a common structural policy for the fishing industry [1970] EGT L236/1; Regulation (EEC) 2142/70 of the Council of 20 October 1970 on the common organisation of the market in fishery products [1970] OJ L236/5; Joined Cases 3, 4 and 6-76 *Kramer* ECR-01279, ECLI:EU:C:1976:114. On developments during the 1970s, see also, TJ Hegland and J Raakjær, 'Recovery Plans and the Balancing of Fishing Capacity and Fishing Possibilities: Path Dependence in the Common Fisheries Policy' in SS Gezelius and J Raakjær (eds), *Making Fisheries Management Work. Reviews: Methods and Technologies in Fish Biology and Fisheries* (Dordrecht, Springer, 2008).

[27] Council Regulation (EEC) 170/83 of 25 January 1983 establishing a Community system for the conservation and management of fishery resources [1983] OJ L24/1.

gear in different fisheries, the allocation of fishing quotas between EU Member States and the control of fishing activities. In addition to this so-called resource policy, ie, the regulation of fishing activities, EU Fisheries Policy has comprised a structural policy that aimed to modernise and develop the fisheries sector, and a market policy that primarily aimed to ensure the existence of a stable market for fish products.

To understand the CFP, it is important to know that it was originally developed not so much to ensure the long-term sustainable management of fish stocks and the ecosystems of which they are part, but primarily to promote market stability and ensure the allocation of a limited resource, ie, fish, in a politically acceptable way between the Member States. The 1957 Treaty of Rome, originally setting up what is today the EU, did not contain any specific provisions on fisheries, which was instead treated as a dimension of agricultural policy. Still today the objectives of the EU Fisheries Policy, as set out in the Union's foundational documents, are the same as those for the agricultural policy. In the current Treaty on the Functioning of the European Union (TFEU) 'agricultural products' include 'the products of the soil, of stockfarming and of fisheries'.[28] The objectives of the policy for such products are, slightly simplified, to increase productivity, ensure a fair standard of living for the agricultural community, to stabilise markets, to assure the availability of supplies, and to ensure that supplies reach consumers at reasonable prices.[29]

A core element of the CFP is that it has enabled the EU Member States to essentially pool their respective fisheries resources and fishing waters,[30] and subject them to joint management. In principle, any fishing vessel flying the flag of a Member State and being registered in the Union has, with few exceptions, equal access to waters and resources in all Union waters.[31] Rather than each Member State having access to fishing grounds in their respective maritime zones, which fleet gets to catch what fish and where is decided through negotiations between the Member States. At the core of the system is the notion of total allowable catch (TAC), ie, catch limits – expressed in tonnes or numbers – that are set for most commercial fish stocks. With respect to the Baltic Sea, TACs are set for cod, herring, sprat, salmon and plaice.[32] Under the CFP, the fixing and allocation of fishing opportunities between Member States, including the setting of TACs, is the prerogative of the Council, ie, the representatives of the Member State governments.[33]

[28] TFEU, Art 38.

[29] ibid.

[30] Except for waters within 12 nautical miles from the baseline of any Member State where such State may restrict fishing. See further Regulation (EU) No 1380/2013 of the European Parliament and of the Council of 11 December 2013 on the Common Fisheries Policy, amending Council Regulations (EC) No 1954/2003 and (EC) No 1224/2009 and repealing Council Regulations (EC) No 2371/2002 and (EC) No 639/2004 and Council Decision 2004/585/EC [2013] OJ L354/22, Art 5(2).

[31] ibid, Art 5(1).

[32] ICES, 'Baltic Sea ecoregion' (n 2) 11.

[33] TFEU, Art 43(2).

While the TAC limits the fishing pressure on a specific stock, which fleet gets to fish is regulated based on so-called relative stability. This essentially means that each year the TAC for a specific stock, for example, eastern Baltic cod, is divided between the same Member States so that each State gets the same share of the TAC. Since the TAC varies (primarily) depending on the availability of fish, the actual volume of fish available to any Member State's fleet may vary significantly between years while remaining the same as a proportion of the TAC. The main benefit of the relative stability principle is that it does away with the need for repeatedly conducting politically contentious negotiations about how to divide the resource. The size of the shares in the relative stability system is based on considerations such as historical catches, dependence on fisheries and previous losses of fishing grounds due to the expansion of exclusive economic zones by non-Member States.[34]

In addition to TACs, the resource policy of the CFP has two more distinct but related components: the regulation of fishing capacity, ie, limiting the number and size or capacity of fishing vessels; and so-called technical regulation, ie, rules on the way in which fishing is conducted, including provisions on permitted gears, mesh sizes and areas where certain fishing activities are prohibited or restricted. In principle, TACs and technical regulations would suffice to ensure sustainable fishing practices, at least to the extent that science is able to provide sufficient guidance. However, it has been deemed necessary to also have a specific policy for adjusting the capacity of the fleets to the desired fishing pressure. TACs are not effective in handling problems associated with, for example, bycatch, discards and illegal landings of fish caught by a fleet capable of catching much more than is legally available.[35] If the capacity is bigger than the available resource (as defined by the TAC), which has persistently been the case in the EU, that also creates incentives for lobbying to set the TAC above what fisheries science deems to be appropriate levels. The capacity policy has also had social dimensions, compensating fishers economically for scaling down the fleet. In practice, however, is has been hard to decrease the effective capacity of many fleets. Reductions in the fishing capacity measured in tonnage of the fleet has in many cases been more than outweighed by technological developments enabling the same or a smaller fleet to catch as much or more fish.[36]

B. The Allocation of Fish to Fishers

Despite the exclusive EU competence and high level of centralisation that characterise the CFP, one of the core issues of fisheries management, namely how fishing

[34] Penas Lado (n 24) 49–50.

[35] Hegland and Raakjær (n 26) 133.

[36] S Villasante and UR Sumaila, 'Estimating the effects of technological efficiency on the European fishing fleet' (2010) 34 *Marine Policy* 720, 720

opportunities are allocated to individual boats or fishers, has always been left to the Member States to decide.[37] There is broad scientific support for the lack of ownership of the resource being a main problem with fisheries management.[38] If ownership of fish, and the associated value, can only be claimed once the fish has been caught, fishers will have an incentive to catch as much as possible as quickly as possible in order to secure the largest possible share of the joint resource, in this case represented by the national quota of the TAC. This has made many states set up rights-based systems, such as individual transferable fishing quotas (also known as catch shares) that entail a right to a certain volume of the resource, thereby doing away with the incentive to catch the fish as fast as possible. Forerunners in this regard have been, for example, New Zealand and Iceland. A comparison between the EU and these countries, which have had rights-based fisheries management schemes for decades, indicates that the EU has overall been less successful, both in terms of conserving fish stocks and managing resources effectively from a socio-economic perspective.[39]

However, rights-based systems are associated with their own challenges, not least that transferable quotas can, if not diligently designed, lead to a concentration of fishing rights to a few efficient and resourceful actors and overall create winners and losers among groups of fishers.[40] From a purely economic, and sometimes also environmental perspective, that may not be negative. However, when fisheries policy also contains a social dimension, which comprises values like promoting small-scale fisheries, preserving cultural values in coastal communities and protecting employment, a concentration of fishing to fewer actors with larger boats may not be a welcome development. This has made rights-based systems controversial in many quarters.

In its initial proposal for what became the 2013 basic regulation of the CFP, the European Commission had included provisions on transferable quotas, but they failed to gain sufficient support from the Member States. The regulation as finally adopted contains a mere recognition that EU Member States 'may establish' systems of so-called transferable fishing concessions.[41] Since Member States had essentially been free to do that before, this did not imply any actual change. Member States are, however, required to use transparent and objective criteria for the allocation of fishing opportunities. The criteria may be of an environmental,

[37] Regulation (EU) No 1380/2013 (n 30) Art 16(6).

[38] See, eg, HS Gordon, 'The economic theory of a common-property resource: the fishery' (1954) 62 *Journal of Political Economy* 124; E Ostrom, *Governing the Commons: The Evolution of Institutions for Collective Action* (Cambridge, Cambridge University Press, 1990).

[39] P Marchal et al, 'A comparative review of fisheries management experiences in the European Union and in other countries worldwide: Iceland, Australia, and New Zealand' (2016) 17 *Fish and Fisheries* 803.

[40] OR Young et al, 'Moving beyond panaceas in fisheries governance' (2018) 115 *Proceedings of the National Academy of Sciences* 9065.

[41] Regulation (EU) No 1380/2013 (n 30) Art 21.

social or economic nature and include the impact of fishing on the environment, the history of compliance and historic catch levels.[42] Several Member States around the Baltic Sea have introduced rights-based fisheries management for at least some of their fisheries.[43]

IV. Reforming the CFP

A. General

Over the years, the CFP and its implementation have been subject to extensive criticism,[44] including from the EU's own institutions.[45] It has, inter alia, been found to be ineffective, wasteful and poorly implemented. An assessment of the CFP against 17 criteria for effective resource policy finds the CFP to not fully meet any of the criteria and to perform badly on five, namely those concerning simplicity of rules, the user-pays principle, resource efficiency, accountability and compliance mechanisms.[46] Some of these are, however, linked to decisions or practices at Member State level rather than the CFP as such.

At the same time, the CFP has been a dynamic policy with its basic regulation being reformed about every 10 years since 1983. The first revision, in 1992, was fairly modest, but set in motion development towards multi-species management and multi-year plans to tackle the prevailing short-sightedness of EU fisheries management. In contrast, the 2002 reform was more far-reaching. The crisis for important cod stocks created support for the introduction of multi-year recovery plans that limit fishing effort for stocks outside safe biological limits, and also provided an opportunity to decide on less intrusive multi-year management plans for other stocks.[47] The involvement of stakeholders was strengthened through the

[42] ibid, Art 17.

[43] See, eg, E Merayo and others, 'Are individual transferable quotas an adequate solution to overfishing and overcapacity? Evidence from Danish fisheries' (2018) 87 *Marine Policy* 167; M Bonow, 'Swedish Fishing in the Wake of ITQ' in G Winder (ed), *Fisheries, Quota Management and Quota Transfer* (Cham, Springer, 2018); M Hanstén, P Haapasaari and S Kuikka, 'A realist evaluation of the individual transferable quota system used in Finnish herring fisheries' (2021) 78 *ICES Journal of Marine Science* 3603.

[44] See, eg, S Khalilian et al, 'Designed for failure: a critique of the Common Fisheries Policy of the European Union' (2010) 34 *Marine Policy* 1178; BC O'Leary et al, 'Fisheries mismanagement' (2011) 62 *Marine Pollution Bulletin* 2642.

[45] Commission, 'Proposal for a Council Regulation establishing a Community control system for ensuring compliance with the rules of the Common Fisheries Policy' (Communication) COM(2008) 718 final; SPECIAL REPORT No 7/2007 on the control, inspection and sanction systems relating to the rules on conservation of Community fisheries resources together with the Commission's replies [2007] OJ C317/01.

[46] T Belschner et al, 'Evaluating fisheries systems: A comprehensive analytical framework and its application to the EU's Common Fisheries Policy' (2019) 20 *Fish and Fisheries* 97, 104.

[47] Penas Lado (n 24) 431.

establishment of Regional Advisory Councils (RACs; now Advisory Councils, ACs) to create a better knowledge base for fisheries management and to counter conflicts.[48]

Although keeping stocks within safe biological limits was an aim of the management plans, it had not been made clear what that meant in terms of long-term objectives for management. The concept of Maximum Sustainable Yield (MSY) gradually began to be applied as a non-binding principle for EU fisheries management, although MSY appeared as a distant target for many EU stocks.[49] When the CFP was again revised in 2013, it became an explicit objective of the policy to maintain populations of harvested species above levels which can produce MSY. More specifically, the MSY exploitation rate was to be achieved by 2015 where possible and, on a progressive, incremental basis at the latest by 2020 for all stocks.[50] A definition of MSY was also introduced, according to which it is 'the highest theoretical equilibrium yield that can be continuously taken on average from a stock under existing average environmental conditions without significantly affecting the reproduction process'.[51]

Since 2013, the CFP shall also explicitly implement 'the ecosystem-based approach to fisheries management' with the aim to ensure that negative impacts of fishing activities on the marine ecosystem are minimised, and also to endeavour to ensure that such activities avoid the degradation of the marine environment.[52] It is rather striking that the CFP talks about *the* ecosystem-based approach to fisheries, since in practice this is quite a broad and rather contentious concept. The use of an ecosystem approach has been discussed for a long time in fisheries management,[53] and the more precise definition and meaning of this has varied over time and depending on local conditions.[54] Several different, but similar concepts have also been used.[55]

However, unlike several other EU acts, which provide for the use of an ecosystem approach, the CFP now contains a fairly comprehensive definition of what is meant by an ecosystem approach to fisheries management, namely:

> [An] integrated approach to managing fisheries within ecologically meaningful boundaries which seeks to manage the use of natural resources, taking account of fishing and

[48] S Linke, M Dreyer and P Sellke, 'The Regional Advisory Councils: What is Their Potential to Incorporate Stakeholder Knowledge into Fisheries Governance?' (2011) 40 *AMBIO* 133.

[49] Penas Lado (n 24) 436.

[50] Regulation (EU) No 1380/2013 (n 30) Art 2(2).

[51] ibid, Art 4.1(7).

[52] ibid, Art 2(3).

[53] S Garcia et al, 'The ecosystem approach to fisheries. Issues, terminology, principles, institutional foundations, implementation and outlook' (FAO fisheries technical paper, No.443, Rome, 2003).

[54] R Long, 'Legal Aspects of Ecosystem-Based Marine Management in Europe' in A Chircop, ML McConnell and S Coffen-Smout (eds), 26 *Ocean Yearbook* (Leiden, Brill Nijhoff, 2012); JT Trochta, 'Ecosystem-based fisheries management: Perception on definitions, implementations, and aspirations' (2018) 13 *PLoS ONE* e0190467, available at: doi.org/10.1371/journal.pone.0190467.

[55] KA Waylen, 'The Need to Disentangle Key Concepts from Ecosystem-Approach Jargon' (2014) 28 *Conservation Biology* 1215, 1216; T Skovgaard Kirkfeldt, 'An ocean of concepts: Why choosing between ecosystem-based management, ecosystem-based approach and ecosystem approach makes a difference' (2019) 106 *Marine Policy* 103541.

> other human activities, while preserving both the biological wealth and the biological processes necessary to safeguard the composition, structure and functioning of the habitats of the ecosystem affected, by taking into account the knowledge and uncertainties regarding biotic, abiotic and human components of ecosystems.[56]

Even with this definition, however, many questions remain about what an ecosystem approach means in concrete terms and how different types of objectives should be weighed against each other.[57] Although progress is being made, the effective incorporation of ecosystem data into fisheries management is challenging, and there are huge complexities that need to be handled.[58] There is also a lack of clear legal requirements that can ensure the proper application of the approach.[59]

A key element of ecosystem-based fisheries management (EBFM) is a shift from the management of individual species to a model that takes into account the effects of fishing on several target species together and also on other species with which these interact in the ecosystem.[60] However, the number of factors that must be considered in order to talk about EBFM and, essentially, whether models comprising interactions between several target species without also aiming to describe many other ecosystem dynamics qualify as EBFM, remains contentious.[61] Developments towards EBFM have been slower in the EU than in several other places. This has at least partly been ascribed to the fact that short-term interests have often dominated the decision-making within the CFP.[62]

The application of MSY as an objective can be difficult to reconcile with EBFM, in particular, as is often the case, when the maximum sustainable yield is set separately for individual species. The fishing activity required to achieve MSY for one species is not necessarily compatible with the MSY for another species in the same ecosystem. A strong focus on MSY, as well as species management in general, also comes with the risk of placing other environmental considerations in the background.[63]

A core feature of the 2013 CFP reform was a decision on the gradual phasing in of a landing obligation. This was in response, inter alia, to the long-criticised practice of so-called high grading, which refers to fishers discarding less valuable

[56] Regulation (EU) No 1380/2013 (n 30) Art 4.1(9).

[57] R Prellezo and R Curtin, 'Confronting the implementation of marine ecosystem-based management within the Common Fisheries Policy reform' (2015) 117 *Ocean & Coastal Management* 43.

[58] JW Bentley et al, 'Refining Fisheries Advice With Stock-Specific Ecosystem Information' (2021) 8 *Frontiers in Marine Science*, available at: doi.org/10.3389/fmars.2021.602072.

[59] G Michanek and A Christiernsson, 'Adaptive Management of EU Marine Ecosystems – About Time to Include Fishery' (2014) 59 *Scandinavian Studies in Law* 228.

[60] C Möllmann et al, 'Implementing ecosystem-based fisheries management: from single-species to integrated ecosystem assessment and advice for Baltic Sea fish stocks' (2014) 71 *ICES Journal of Marine Science* 1187.

[61] P Sellke, M Dreyer and S Linke, 'Fisheries: A Case Study of Baltic Sea Environmental Governance' in M Gilek et al (eds), *Environmental Governance of the Baltic Sea* (Heidelberg, Springer, 2016).

[62] S Jennings and J Rice, 'Towards an ecosystem approach to fisheries in Europe: a perspective on existing progress and future directions' (2011) 12 *Fish and Fisheries* 125.

[63] Prellezo and Curtin (n 57); Trochta (n 54).

fish in order to make as much money as possible from the volume of fish that is permissible to land. In mixed fisheries, ie, when the same fishing activity is likely to catch significant numbers of fish from more than one species, discarding is also often incentivised as a way to prevent having to stop fishing when the TAC of one species has been fully used. With limited exceptions, it is now no longer permitted to discard fish covered by a TAC, for example, because it is considered too small or does not belong to the target species that is being fished for. However, this landing obligation is associated with considerable challenges relating, inter alia, to control and the creation of markets for fish that would not have been landed had it not been for the landing obligation.[64]

One important change to the CFP, that is of a formal rather than substantive nature, but may still have significant implications, is the shift through the Treaty of Lisbon (in effect 2009) from decisions within the CFP being made only by the Council, ie, the representatives of the EU Member State governments, to so-called co-decision between the Council and the European Parliament.[65] While co-decision can make decision-making more cumbersome and time-consuming, it adds to the democratic legitimacy of the decisions. The European Parliament also has a tradition of placing more weight on environmental and sustainability perspectives compared with the Council. However, one important kind of fisheries management decision remains under the control of the Council, namely decisions on the fixing and allocation of fishing opportunities, including the setting of TACs.[66] What is often the most contentious issue thus remains with the ministers. When deciding on TACs, the Council has access to scientific advice from the ICES, as well as from the EU's own Scientific, Technical and Economic Committee for Fisheries. However, the Council has a long track record of setting a significant share of the TACs well above what has been recommended by its scientific advisers.[67] Encouragingly, there seems to be a positive trend in this regard meaning that scientific advice is being more closely adhered to.[68]

An important exception to the high level of centralisation of the CFP is that authority has been delegated to the individual EU Member States to take non-discriminatory measures for the conservation and management of fish stocks and the maintenance or improvement of the conservation status of marine ecosystems

[64] On the landing obligation see, eg, M Christou et al, 'Monitoring the Environmental, Social and Economic Dimensions of the Landing Obligation Policy' (2019) 6 *Frontiers in Marine Science* 594; B Bohman, 'Regulatory control of adaptive fisheries: Reflections on the implementation of the landing obligation in the EU common fisheries policy' (2019) 110 *Marine Policy* 103557.

[65] The co-decision procedure is now prescribed by TFEU, Art 43(2).

[66] TFEU, Art 43(2).

[67] L Borges, 'Setting of total allowable catches in the 2013 EU common fisheries policy reform: possible impacts' (2018) 91 *Marine Policy* 97; G Carpenter et al, 'Landing the blame: The influence of EU Member States on quota setting' (2016) 64 *Marine Policy* 9.

[68] S Princen, K Siderius and S Villasante, 'Information processing in the European Union's Common Fisheries Policy' (2021) 41 *Journal of Public Policy* 532.

within 12 nautical miles of their baselines. However, this right only applies as long as the EU has not adopted measures addressing conservation and management specifically for that area or specifically addressing the problem identified by the Member State concerned. If a measure is liable to affect fishing vessels of other Member States, the Commission, relevant Member States and ACs must be consulted.[69]

B. Control

Overfishing can occur in different ways. One is when the TACs are set too high, usually because short-sighted economic or social considerations are allowed to trump the available scientific advice. The other major cause of overfishing is that more fish is caught then allowed by the TAC and national quotas. As noted above, major reasons for this tend to be overcapacity in the fleet and incentives to catch as much as possible as quickly as possible. Discarding of fish that is of low value or does not fit within the applicable TAC can also contribute. Not surprisingly, the European Commission has found the success of the CFP to be highly dependent on the implementation of an effective control system.[70] Despite there having been a common, and in many respects complex, control system ever since 1982, the CFP has always been associated with extensive compliance problems and inadequate control.[71] The rules of the control system are decided at the Union level, but, with few exceptions, it is national authorities and inspectors from the individual Member States who apply them.

Problems with non-compliance have contributed to the overexploitation of fish resources and justified the introduction of further and stricter regulations, thereby adding to the regulatory burden and complexity. At the same time, the complexity has often been identified as a factor contributing to low compliance. There are also many indications that individual Member States have been reluctant to take effective control measures because that was seen as constituting a competitive disadvantage for their own fishing fleet compared with those of other Member States, which are assumed to be subject to less compliance control.[72]

[69] Regulation (EU) No 1380/2013 (n 30) Art 20.

[70] Commission, 'Report from the Commission to the European Parliament and the Council Implementation and evaluation of Regulation (EC) 1224/2009 establishing a Union control system for ensuring compliance with the rules of the common fisheries policy as required under Article 118 REFIT Evaluation of the impact of the fisheries regulation' COM(2017) 192 final, 2.

[71] Commission, 'Communication from the Commission to the European Parliament and the Council on the proposal for a Council Regulation establishing a Community control system for ensuring compliance with the rules of the Common Fisheries Policy' COM(2008) 718 final; J Hentati-Sundberg, J Hjelm and H Österblom, 'Does fisheries management incentivize non-compliance? Estimated misreporting in the Swedish Baltic Sea pelagic fishery based on commercial fishing effort' (2014) 71 *ICES Journal of Marine Science* 1846.

[72] Penas Lado (n 24) 288.

A reform in 2009 introduced a number of changes to the control system. The rules were simplified and most of the provisions were gathered in one regulation.[73] The sanction mechanisms were strengthened, including the introduction of a system of penalty points for infringements. Harmonised inspection routines, requirements for electronic logbooks, special control measures for multi-year plans and discards, as well as requirements for certain measures to control recreational fishing have been introduced. The Commission was also given more power to act against Member States that do not fulfil their fisheries control obligations.[74]

Following a 2017 evaluation of the effects of the control regulation, the European Commission found many positive developments. Overall, the EU Member States have implemented the main obligations of the regulation. They have set up the necessary instruments, procedures and standards for monitoring and inspection of fishing activities.[75] Vessel Monitoring Systems and Electronic Reporting Systems are used throughout the fishing fleets for vessels above 12 metres, thereby increasing control and reliability of catch data. The overall fishing capacity was also found to have decreased according to set objectives. The Commission also found a 'general recognised better compliance with CFP rules, both from operators and Member States'.[76] However, several remaining deficiencies were identified, among them insufficient follow-up of infringements, and problems with data exchange and sharing between Member States as well as monitoring and catch reporting tools for smaller fishing vessels (<12 metres).[77]

V. The Development of Fisheries Regulation for the Baltic Sea

Before Baltic Sea fishing became a predominantly internal EU affair, the coastal states concerned collaborated on its management through the International Baltic Sea Fishery Commission (IBSFC), set up in 1974. The legal basis was provided by the Convention on Fishing and Conservation of the Living Resources in the Baltic Sea and the Belts,[78] signed in 1973 in Gdansk by the governments of seven Baltic Sea States.[79] Through this so-called Gdansk Convention, the parties committed to

[73] Council Regulation (EC) 1224/2009 of 20 November 2009 establishing a Community control system for ensuring compliance with the rules of the common fisheries policy amending Regulations (EC) No 847/96, (EC) No 2371/2002, (EC) No 811/2004, (EC) No 676/2007, (EC) No 1098/2007, (EC) No 1300/2008, (EC) No 1342/2008 and repealing Regulations (EEC) No 2847/93, (EC) 1627/94 and (EC) No 1966/2006 [2009] OJ L343/1.

[74] Penas Lado (n 24) 294–95.

[75] Commission, COM(2017) 192 final (n 70) 3.

[76] ibid, 4.

[77] ibid.

[78] Convention on Fishing and Conservation of the Living Resources in the Baltic Sea and the Belts (Gdansk, 13 September 1973) (Gdansk Convention).

[79] The Convention's original seven parties were: Denmark, the Federal Republic of Germany, Finland, the German Democratic Republic, Poland, Sweden and the Soviet Union. After the dissolution of the Soviet Union, Estonia, Latvia, Lithuania and Russia became members in their own right.

'co-operate closely with a view to preserving and increasing the living resources of the Baltic Sea and the Belts and obtaining the optimum yield, and, in particular to expanding and co-ordinating studies towards these ends'.[80] Within its geographical area of applicability, the Convention applied to all fish species and other living marine resources.[81]

When the Gdansk Convention was adopted, national fisheries zones did not exceed 12 nautical miles and the quotas allocated to the parties could be fished out anywhere in the Baltic high seas. However, starting in 1976 the coastal states extended their fishing zones, placing by 1978 all fishing in the Baltic Sea under national jurisdiction.[82] After that, the quotas were related to the national zones of the respective party, with the exception of the Member States of the EU, who reallocated the quotas for their zones according to the CFP system for TAC allocation.[83] However, national fleets continued to fish in areas beyond their own national waters, but could now do so only subject to an agreement with the concerned coastal state.

The tasks of the IBSFC were essentially of two kinds. One related to the review of the living resources and the fisheries in the Convention area, primarily by collecting, analysing and disseminating statistical data on things such as catch and fishing effort and to make proposals for the coordination of scientific research in the Convention area. The other task was to make recommendations for the regulation of fishing. This included recommendations on fishing gear and catch methods, size limits for different species, areas and seasons closed to fishing, measures relating to the allocation of total catch or fishing effort between the parties, as well as control measures.[84] While the parties undertook to give effect to recommendations made by the IBSFC, there was also a mechanism allowing any party to object, within 90 days, to any recommendation and thereby be relieved of the obligation to give effect to it.[85] As for scientific advice, in addition to drawing on data submitted by the parties, the IBSFC requested advice from the ICES, which submitted recommendations for TACs for relevant species annually.[86]

Even long before the signing of the Gdansk Convention, a series of agreements concerning different aspects of fishing, including some conservation measures, had been concluded between Baltic Sea coastal states. But most of them were bilateral treaties and their substantive scope was limited, for example, by focusing on the fisheries of only one or a few species.[87] When more comprehensive regional fisheries agreements were developed for the North Sea, the Baltic Sea coastal states

[80] Gdansk Convention, Art I.
[81] Gdansk Convention, Art II.
[82] M Fitzmaurice-Lachs, 'The Legal Regime of the Baltic Sea Fisheries' (1982) 29 *Netherlands International Law Review* 174, 234.
[83] ibid, 213–14.
[84] Gdansk Convention, Arts IX and X.
[85] Gdansk Convention, Art XI.
[86] Fitzmaurice-Lachs (n 82) 210.
[87] ibid, 193.

failed to make similar agreements.[88] In the 1950s, the overexploitation of some Baltic Sea fish stocks, not least cod and salmon, attracted much scientific and also political attention.[89] In the early 1970s, some improvement in the generally tense political relations between eastern and western European countries provided an opportunity for an expanded cooperation on fisheries, which led to the signing of the Gdansk Convention in 1973 and its entry into force the following year.

With the establishment of the CFP, the Gdansk Convention started to change character from a traditional international agreement to one structuring the cooperation between an international organisation, what is now the EU, comprising a growing number of Baltic coastal states, and a decreasing number of other parties. In 1984, the EU became a party to the Convention and accepted all the Convention-related rights and obligations of the then two Member States that were parties to the Convention, ie, Denmark and the Federal Republic of Germany.[90] With the eventual accession to the EU of all Baltic Sea coastal states except Russia, the Gdansk Convention was in 2009 replaced by a bilateral agreement on cooperation in fisheries and the conservation of the living marine resources in the Baltic Sea between the EU and Russia.[91]

Throughout the 1980s and 1990s the IBSFC continued to be the main mechanism for regulating fishing and promoting conservation of fish stocks in the Baltic Sea. When, in the early 1990s, it was recognised that important stocks were in a poor state, the IBSFC adopted several resolutions with the intention to reduce fishing mortality and improve selectivity, in particular for cod. The actions of the IBSFC resulted in a number of instruments, including the 1997 Baltic Salmon Action Plan, the 1999 Long-Term Management Strategy for Cod Stocks in the Baltic Sea, and a 2001 Recovery Plan for Baltic Sea Cod.[92] However, insufficient efforts were made for the proper implementation of these measures and for the general curbing of the overexploitation of stocks.[93]

VI. The Baltic Sea Region (BSR) within the CFP

There have long since been calls for the strengthening of regional influence over fisheries management in the EU, but this has been legally challenging since EU

[88] ibid, 196.

[89] ibid, 198.

[90] Council Decision 83/414/EEC of 25 July 1983 on the accession of the Community to the Convention on fishing and conservation of the living resources in the Baltic Sea and the Belts, as amended by the Protocol to the Conference of the representatives of the States Parties to the Convention signed in Warsaw on 11 November 1982 [1983] OJ L237/4.

[91] Council Regulation (EC) 439/2009 of 23 March 2009 concerning the conclusion of the Agreement between the European Community and the Government of the Russian Federation on cooperation in fisheries and the conservation of the living marine resources in the Baltic Sea [2009] OJ L129/1.

[92] R Aps and H Lassen, 'Recovery of depleted Baltic Sea fish stocks: a review' (2010) 67 *ICES Journal of Marine Science* 1856, 1856.

[93] ibid.

law largely lacks provisions enabling the delegation of decision-making to regional bodies.[94] However, there have been different ways in which the regional level, and in the present context specifically the BSR, has been given more prominence in fisheries management. Also without regionalisation of the decision-making, specific measures have been adopted for regional areas such as the Baltic Sea.

Starting in 1986, the EU has adopted several regulations giving effect to recommendations made by the IBSFC.[95] These have included provisions relating to the use of specific gear and mesh sizes. Also since the termination of the Gdansk Convention, specific rules for fishing activities in the Baltic Sea have continuously been adopted.

In 2007, the EU reacted to advice from the ICES indicating that some cod stocks in the Baltic Sea had declined to levels where they suffered from reduced reproductive capacity and were being harvested unsustainably.[96] This prompted the adoption of a multi-annual plan for fisheries management of the cod stocks in the Baltic Sea with the aim of gradually reducing the fishing effort in fisheries catching cod to levels enabling cod stocks to be rebuilt to safe biological limits, maintain their full reproductive capacity and ensuring that the highest long-term yields are reached.[97] In 2016, a new multi-annual plan was adopted, including not only the Baltic Sea cod stocks, but also stocks of herring and sprat, the reason being the strong biological interactions between the cod and pelagic stocks and the need to consider the dynamics between them.[98] The 2013 basic regulation of the CFP requires fishing opportunities to be fixed in accordance with the targets set out in the multi-annual plans.[99] This should at least partly tackle the persistent problem of TACs being set above the scientifically recommended levels for short-term economic and political reasons. However, multi-annual plans have been criticised, inter alia, for not sufficiently considering the actual behaviours of fishers or dealing properly with the economic dimensions of the plans' implementation.[100] In 2020,

[94] R Long, 'The Role of Regional Advisory Councils in the European Common Fisheries Policy: Legal Constraints and Future Options' (2010) 25 *International Journal of Marine and Coastal Law* 289.

[95] Council Regulation (EEC) 1866/86 of 12 June 1986 laying down certain technical measures for the conservation of fishery resources in the waters of the Baltic Sea, the Belts and the Sound [1986] OJ L162/1; Council Regulation (EC) 88/98 of 18 December 1997 laying down certain technical measures for the conservation of fishery resources in the waters of the Baltic Sea, the Belts and the Sound [1998] OJ L9/1; Council Regulation (EC) 2187/2005 of 21 December 2005 for the conservation of fishery resources through technical measures in the Baltic Sea, the Belts and the Sound, amending Regulation (EC) 1434/98 and repealing Regulation (EC) 88/98 [2005] OJ L349/1.

[96] Council Regulation (EC) 1098/2007 of 18 September 2007 establishing a multiannual plan for the cod stocks in the Baltic Sea and the fisheries exploiting those stocks, amending Regulation (EEC) 2847/93 and repealing Regulation (EC) 779/97 [2007] OJ L248/1, preambular paras 1 and 2.

[97] ibid, preambular paras 6 and 7 and Art 6.

[98] Regulation (EU) 2016/1139 of the European Parliament and of the Council of 6 July 2016 establishing a multiannual plan for the stocks of cod, herring and sprat in the Baltic Sea and the fisheries exploiting those stocks, amending Council Regulation (EC) 2187/2005 and repealing Council Regulation (EC) 1098/2007 [2016] OJ L191/1, preambular paras 6 and 8.

[99] Regulation (EU) No 1380/2013 (n 30) Art 16(4).

[100] SBM Kraak et al, 'Lessons for fisheries management from the EU cod recovery plan' (2013) 37 *Marine Policy* 200, 210.

the ICES found that fishing mortality of western Baltic cod had remained much too high, despite the management plan.[101]

As for the regional influence of the Baltic Sea fisheries management, there have been several measures involving some level of regionalisation. Building on the experience of regional stakeholder workshops organised in the late 1990s,[102] RACs composed of representatives from the fisheries sector and other interest groups affected by the CFP were created after the 2002 reform of the CFP.[103] The decision provided for seven RACs, including one for the Baltic Sea that was set up in 2006. With the 2013 CFP reform the original decision on the RACs was replaced by provisions in the new basic regulation.[104] The RACs, now included in the broader concept of ACs, have no decision-making authority. They do have a mandate to submit recommendations regarding the management of fisheries and the socio-economic and conservation aspects of fisheries to the European Commission and the EU Member State concerned, as well as to inform the Commission and Member States of problems relating to the management and the socio-economic and conservation aspects of fisheries in their geographical area and propose solutions to overcome such problems.[105] The ACs also have a right to be consulted in some other circumstances, such as when a Member State intends to, within its 12 nautical mile zone, take conservation measures that are liable to affect fishing vessels of other Member States.[106] When the ACs have been consulted and the final measures that are adopted diverge from the opinions, recommendations and suggestions of an AC, the Commission or the Member State concerned are required to provide detailed reasons for the divergence.[107]

Due to the lack of formal decision-making power, the RACs have been described as a weak form of regionalisation. They have also, however, been deemed an important and overall successful step towards a more inclusive and regionally grounded fisheries management.[108] Still, it is hard to determine to what extent the RACs have had any significant impact on fisheries management.[109]

Another form of regionalisation is regional councils for cooperation among Member States in a particular region. In 2009, a regional council, the Baltic Sea Fisheries Forum (BALTFISH), was formed among the BSR's EU Member States and subsequently formalised in 2013 through a Memorandum of Understanding

[101] ICES, 'Baltic Sea ecoregion' (n 2).

[102] Penas Lado (n 24) 253.

[103] Council Decision 2004/585/EC of 19 July 2004 establishing Regional Advisory Councils under the Common Fisheries Policy [2004] OJ L256/17.

[104] Regulation (EU) No 1380/2013 (n 30).

[105] ibid, Art 44(2).

[106] ibid, Art 20(2).

[107] ibid, Art 44(4).

[108] Jennings and Rice (n 162).

[109] P Andersen and VB Larsen, 'From open access to rights-based management fisheries' in P Nedergaard and A Wivel (eds), *The Routledge Handbook of Scandinavian Politics* (Abingdon, Routledge, 2017).

between eight EU Member States.[110] BALTFISH, which became an inspiration for regionalisation in the 2013 CFP reform,[111] functions as a forum for EU Member States in the BSR to discuss fisheries management issues of regional relevance. Simultaneously, the forum has been criticised for not being sufficiently transparent or open to stakeholder involvement in decision-making.[112] Since 2013, BALTFISH has also been used to discuss and submit joint recommendations to the European Commission in accordance with the new structure for regionalisation. The current basic regulation namely provides regional groups of Member States with certain powers to initiate formal decision-making processes.

When the Commission has been granted powers, including in multi-annual plans or temporary discard plans, to adopt measures by means of delegated or implementing acts in respect of a conservation measure applying to a relevant geographical area, Member States that have a direct management interest affected by such measures are authorised to submit joint recommendations for achieving the relevant objectives. If compatible with the relevant conservation measure and/or multi-annual plan, the Commission can adopt such joint recommendation by means of delegated or implementing acts. The Member States concerned may instead choose to adopt, within a set deadline, measures further specifying an EU conservation measure, such as a multi-annual plan, that applies to a relevant geographical area. The content of the respective national measures must be subject to agreement by all the Member States concerned. Member States with a direct management interest in a fishery in a defined geographical area can also in other cases make joint recommendations on measures to be proposed or adopted by the Commission.[113] However, since the Member States are not required to submit proposals nor the Commission to act in accordance with any such proposals, this, as well, has been deemed a rather weak form of regionalisation.[114]

VII. Concluding Reflections

The regulation of fisheries in the Baltic Sea has suffered from the general problems of the CFP, including short-sightedness, regulatory complexity and insufficient controls. In some respects, the Baltic Sea has developed to be seen as a role model for more proactive and regionally grounded fisheries management. Despite this,

[110] Sellke, Dreyer and Linke (n 61) 53.

[111] TJ Hegland, J Raakjær and J van Tatenhove, 'Implementing ecosystem-based marine management as a process of regionalisation: Some lessons from the Baltic Sea' (2015) 117 *Ocean & Coastal Management* 14, 16.

[112] P Ramírez-Monsalve et al, 'Ecosystem Approach to Fisheries Management (EAFM) in the EU – Current science–policy–society interfaces and emerging requirements' (2016) 66 *Marine Policy* 83, 90.

[113] Regulation (EU) No 1380/2013 (n 30) Art 18.

[114] Hegland, Raakjær and Tatenhove (n 111)

some of the traditionally most important stocks in the Baltic Sea are in a very poor state, prompting drastic measures, such as complete closures of fisheries, in recent years. Claiming that this crisis would be due only to flawed fisheries management is too simplistic. The Baltic Sea is a complex natural system experiencing, in many respects, extreme conditions, both due to natural characteristics, such as its small size, shallowness and brackish water, and because of the high level of anthropogenic impacts that have had profound effects on the sea over a long period of time. Fisheries management alone cannot change the fate of the Baltic Sea. But continued improvement of the CFP, including strict application of multi-annual plans based on best scientific understanding, can be part of a solution. Combining measures within the CFP with further development of rights-based systems for allocating fishing opportunities within Member States, which give individual fishers better incentives for long-term planning, could further improve management. However, such systems are no panacea and need to be designed in a way that takes into consideration social and behavioural dimensions of fisheries.

As for the general impact of the EU and the CFP on Baltic Sea fisheries, it is important to note that heavy anthropogenic pressures and unsustainable fishing predates the time when EU law became applicable to most of the BSR. Whether fisheries management would have been more successful without the involvement of the EU is obviously hard to know. There are countries, such as Norway, that have been significantly more successful in achieving sustainable fisheries. However, the challenges in the Baltic Sea are rather unique, both in terms of the characteristics of the ecosystem(s) and the profound anthropogenic impacts and due to it being such a small sea divided between many coastal states. It is hard to see how rational or sustainable fisheries can be achieved under such conditions without far-reaching cooperation and coordination among the states concerned.

With the extension of maritime zones in the late 1970s, high seas areas disappeared from the Baltic and all fishing became subject to coastal state control, at least in a formal sense. With the CFP, however, fish was again essentially made into a common resource, but now allocated between states through decisions within the EU. The small size of the sea and the movement of the fish across jurisdictional boundaries make it rational to manage the fish as a common resource, rather than as a number of distinct national resources that cannot in fact, in many cases, be separated.

Given the multiple challenges facing the Baltic Sea, there is also a clear need to coordinate measures across policy areas. Even if there are problems with effectively coordinating the CFP with EU environmental law and policy,[115] at least the EU offers a platform where policies for tackling the various challenges confronting the Baltic Sea can be developed and their coordination gradually improved. Before most Baltic Sea coastal states joined the EU, fisheries issues were addressed within the IBSFC while marine environmental protection, excluding the effects of fishing,

[115] Ramírez-Monsalve et al (n 112) 87.

was coordinated within the Baltic Marine Environment Protection Commission. There are good reasons to believe that better coordination can be achieved within the EU, as can better enforcement, since the traditional platforms for regional cooperation lack teeth in those regards. But this is not to say that individual states could not have been more successful in managing specific stocks had they been able to do so without the involvement of the CFP.

Finally, it is important to remember that the Baltic Sea has undergone profound changes in the last century or so and will not return to any pristine state, whatever that would mean. But it can still be, in many respects, a functioning and productive ecosystem, or assemblage of ecosystems, if the many good intentions set out in the CFP and other pieces of law are made fully operational.

INDEX

www.ingramcontent.com/pod-product-compliance
Ingram Content Group UK Ltd.
Pitfield, Milton Keynes, MK11 3LW, UK
UKHW020247290926
15470UKWH00002B/781

9 781509 956241